RITE FOR THE TIMES

2nd Edition

Rite for the Times

2nd Edition

Plus Additional Cogent Observations

Daniel D. Lelong

Scripture quotations marked KJV are from the Holy Bible, King James Version (Authorized Version). First published in 1611. Quoted from the KJV Hebrew-Greek Key Word Study Bible, copyright (c) 1991 by AMG International, Inc.

Scripture quotations marked NASB are taken from the *New American Standard Bible®*, Copyright © 1960, 1962, 1963, 1968, 1971, 1972, 1973, 1975, 1977, 1995 by The Lockman Foundation. Used by permission.

Scripture quotations marked NLT are taken from the *Holy Bible, New Living Translation*, copyright © 1996, 2004, 2007. Used by permission of Tyndale House Publishers, Inc. Carol Stream, Illinois 60188. All rights reserved.

Scripture quotations marked NIV are taken from the *Holy Bible, New International Version®. NIV®.* Copyright © 1973, 1978, 1984 by International Bible Society. Used by permission of Zondervan. All rights reserved.

For more information and additional copies: www.DanielDLelong.com

Rev. date: 06/03/2015

To order additional copies of this book, contact:
Xlibris
1-888-795-4274
www.Xlibris.com
Orders@Xlibris.com
543877

Contents

Rite for the Times, 2nd Edition is written in appreciation of the Father in heaven, who chooses to be a Father, not a *Fuhrer*.

God the Father could have chosen to be an Emperor over a King with a throng of princes, powers and peasants; a company President over a Chief Executive Officer with a staff of vice-presidents, managers and employees; or, a Commander-in-Chief over a General with an army of colonels, sergeants and privates.

Instead, He chooses to be our set-apart, earnest heavenly Father above a family of sons and daughters, through our narrowly-true big Brother and Savior, the LORD Jesus Christ!

RT2 is dedicated to each student whose bright-faced, lies-defiant, headstrong distrust of herdlike self-satiety propels him to build his conscience, intellect, and personality upon hard-won narrow truths.

Each successive generation must love the truth enough, at odds over it with their torpid fellows, to be permitted to enter the Promised Land and avoid being sent back with them, out into the desert.

Preface

Rite for the Times, 2ⁿᵈ Edition, is written to Christian and Messianic congregational leaders, to apt students of reality, and to the brighter fraction of society. In the words of Oswald Chambers, "Jesus Christ demands of the man who trusts Him the same reckless sporting spirit that the natural man exhibits. If a man is going to do anything worthwhile, there are times when he has to risk everything on his leap, and in the spiritual domain Jesus Christ demands that you risk everything you hold by common sense and leap into what He says . . . We act like pagans in a crisis, only one out of a crowd is daring enough to bank his faith in the character of God."[1]

God may use the Messianic congregational movement to raise up some of the hundred forty-four thousand firstfruits, the Born Again Hebrew missionary evangelists who will minister in the Trinity to the nations during the time in history of the United Nation's one world government. Many of the ideas discussed in *RT2* will remain relevant for the remainder of civilization.

This book started as a Web page written for seminary academic credit. The ideas in *Rite for the Times* have been the subject of much zeal tempered by Bible study, fasting, prayer, and contemplation. Any criticism of Messianic congregationalism contained herein is expressly intended to be constructive criticism, offered in the Spirit of God the Father's *agape* love. Any *pilpul* (Heb., peppery speech) toward my Messianic friends is from love of truth, in a spirit of charity and brotherhood. Not all of your critics intend to make soap of you.

The *minchaw* grain offering is a voluntary bloodless offering made by fire unto the LORD that can be helpful and ennobling to those in need of comfort. The *minchaw* is exegeted in chapter one of *Rite for the Times* from Leviticus 2, 6, and 23, and Deuteronomy 12. This *minchaw* grain offering is the rite for the times addressed in the title of this book. The other chapters address various other aspects of these trying times.

Given that tens of millions of men have studied the Bible, *Rite for the Times* is the first known published connection between the feasts of the LORD and the *minchaw* grain offering.

Of the five offerings made by fire unto the LORD, only the blood-free *minchaw* grain offering fulfills both a half-dozen Toraic commandments (to observe the feasts of Christ the LORD with an offering made by fire) and the New Covenant (to not ritually replicate Messiah Jesus' atonement). This new theology of the *minchaw* is truly historic! The *minchaw* grain offering is a theological loophole left in place by God so that we may continue to observe Leviticus 23: 8, 14, 18, 25, 27, and 36, pertaining to the Feasts of the LORD, under His New Covenant. The *minchaw* is a doctrinal footnote that can impart to us days of ennobling sanctity.

Via the theology of the *minchaw*, Messianic Jews (and also Christians) may optimally observe the feasts of the LORD, may temporarily sanctify and ennoble themselves and others, and may do both of these without offense to the New Covenant. As a theological loophole, the non-atoning *minchaw* does not require an Aaronic bloodline, a bricks-and-mortar Temple, or the locale of Mount Moriah in order to temporarily sanctify men, women and children via an offering made by fire unto the LORD God of Israel, who is Jesus Christ.

The indwelling Holy Ghost imparts enough of God's name, a Believer's faith-sanctified body constitutes enough of His temple, and this *minchaw* theology presents enough of sound doctrine, for *minchot* to be acceptable by God under the New Covenant. God the Father imparts the Melchisedecian priesthood, His Spirit, and His holy, covenant, personal name (*Y'howah!*) to each Believer in Jesus, at the instant of his or her true saving faith. Faith in Christ imparts to Believers authority to burn-offer this Levitical *minchaw* and reap its many benefits. In the Hebrew language, the word *minchot* is plural for *minchaw*.

The meaning of this is that Jews are free to offer this type of 'burnt offering.' Modern Believing Jews and Christians, their bodies made temples of God's name-bearing Spirit by faith in the Messiahship of Jesus of Nazareth, may offer this 'burnt offering' to fulfill the feasts of the LORD and for temporary ennobling sanctification of themselves and others, even in the Diaspora, without any offense against either the Old or New Covenant. In the course of researching and writing this book, by grace I offered God approximately five-hundred *minchot* over sixteen years, with good effects and zero bad consequences whatsoever.

The math-like internal consistency of this Old-with-New Covenant theology regarding the *minchaw* grain offering is equal to that of any root-affirming, this-worldly ritual within unbelieving Judaism. And, it proceeds from canon, not from tradition.

Only the *minchaw* grain offering can satisfy both six Toraic commandments (to observe the feasts of the LORD with an offering made by fire unto Him) and the New Covenant (to not ritually replicate Christ Jesus' blood atonement for sin).

Rite for the Times is an excellent witnessing tool to serious Torah scholars, because identification of the spiritual limitations of the *minchaw* grain offering emphasizes (by contrast) the perfect completeness of Christ Jesus' atoning death and resurrection. *The minchaw doctrinal loophole uniquely fulfills six commandments in the Torah without infringement upon the New Covenant, and simultaneously imparts ennobling holiness for each day of offering.*

This lapidary book of theology, psychology, prophecy, apologetics, and philosophy of religion is notable for chapter one's exegesis of the *minchaw* grain offering, for chapter two's identification of Judaism's LORD God of Israel as Christianity's glorified Christ Jesus, and for chapter ten's exposition of an identity management system's significance to global governance. These and other chapters' treatments of the grain offering, Toraic earned righteousness, countercult ministry, logic, holistic health, chastity, meta-politics, psychology, and prophecy are highly germane to modern readers. The term "Toraic earned righteousness" as used here is meant as neutral, non-pejorative, and to merely connote earned righteousness (as distinct from righteousness-by-faith).

Pivotal theology explained in chapter five includes *Eloheynu ha Shiloosh haKodesh* (idiomatic Hebrew for "our God the Holy Trinity"); Adonai the Christ; and, Jesus of Nazareth's higher standard of conduct than that required by the Torah. These crucial doctrinal concepts are scarce as yet in some Messianic congregations, because theological liberals contest the telling of them.

Civilization is the set of societal forms that reassure mankind that trust in Elohim the Father, the Abba of the *Logos* His Son, is authentic and safe. This is the Christian aspect of patriotism (Gr., *pater* (father) + *osis* (infusion)). Antitheses to it are New Age globalism and jingoism. Advocates of global governance strive to eliminate Christian patriotic societal forms, because religion drives politics, not vice versa.

From the theology in *Rite for the Times*, I foresee potentially thousands of congregations offering the *minchaw* for the feasts of the LORD, and for counseling to sanctify attendees in need of grace.

Persons named in this book do not necessarily endorse the views stated herein. My thanks to Matthew and Jennifer Taylor for first demonstrating a *minchaw* to me on a sanguine Friday afternoon in summer, 1997, thereby stirring my curiosity about *minchaw* theology. Thanks to Bob Kelso, Chuck Reynolds, Mike Price, Fran Kuhlman, and David Burdick for accountability toward faith in God by Christ Jesus. Thanks to Dave and Norma Clemons. Thanks to Steve Reynolds, Bob Eagy, Gary Moritz, Les Howell, Donnie Reynolds, Dirk Lieb, Ben and Jess Kellerman, Tony and Jennifer Ma, Jon and Cindy Burgess, Jeff Frazier, Tony Pyle, Chip Walton, Melissa Jerota, Billy Penny, Eric Larsen, Michelle Barb, Pete Frenquelle, Julie Van Brunt, Stephanie Antone, Jim Glassford, John Antone and Robert Fisher, of Capital Baptist Church in Annandale, Virginia, for constructive criticism of various chapters of this manuscript, for encouragement in writing it, and for intercessory prayer. I especially thank Marion Pasteur Lelong and Louise P. Lelong for their steadfast examples of personal maturity and Christian love. Thanks to Lawrence E. Kennedy, Jr. Thanks to Chester Rockwell, my high school geometry teacher; Ann Wiles, my undergraduate logic professor; and Wayne Engel, my undergraduate psychology professor. Thanks to Stephen and Reid Lowe. Thanks to Jim and Claire Taylor. Thanks to Stan and Piper Ivins. Thanks to Ed and Ann Burdick. Thanks to Doug Stearman and Bruce Bakaysa. Thanks to Stephen and Laura Katz, for his keen Biblical research into the word *minchaw*. Thanks to Larry and Deb Dubin, Lynn and Wayman McCoy, and Peter and Marcia Rice. Thanks, too, to Scott Brown, Peter Gorog, Dennis Karp, Bob Ramskill, Scott Moore, Marty Peltz, Dan Juster, and Sandra Sheskin Brotman. Finally, thanks to Daniel Prabhakar, James Saul, Vince Houslin, Brian Rhoades, Vince MacIsaacs, and Michael Oxentenko.

Preface note:

[1]   Oswald Chambers. *My Utmost for His Highest: May 30*. Grand Rapids: Discovery House, 1963, 151.

Introduction

My name is Daniel D. Lelong. I am a firstborn son in my parents' family, with two younger sisters. My paternal grandfather had the alcohol gene and was a very-marginal Catholic. My Dad is a high school valedictorian turned chemical engineer then patent attorney, and my faithful mother, a college English major. By my seventh summer, my beloved mother tenderly led me to faith—to believe and profess that Jesus is the Christ, and to invite God the Father's Holy Spirit to live in my heart.

The LORD Jesus became my boyhood spiritual playmate. From about age six, He was to me like an older brother, constantly two years ahead of me in school, who helped me understand and evaluate my teachers. As a boy, I silently promised Jesus I'd help those smaller than myself. I was raised with faith, prayer, Bible study and memorization, regular Bible church attendance, and Protestant Christian elementary and junior high school as prominent parts of my childhood. As a preteen, I had the Comforter in my heart, and knew eruditely and conscientiously much about God. As a youth, I yearned to become a geologist and admired the Mennonites. But, I was not cognitively instructed in the moral orthodoxy of personally why to keep the vessel of my body. Sorrowfully, in my late teens, I rebelled against benign neglect. I needed dialogic definition and debriefing of temptations, to prevent double mindedness. Such conversation's awkwardness and scarcity intimidated me into silence on the topic.

As a sophomore in public high school, I took a proctored I.Q. test and was admitted to the school's gifted and talented program. "For unto whomsoever much is given, of him shall much be required." (Luke 12:48) Unfortunately, in my teens and away at college, in a vacuum of informed accountability and in denial about conscientious absolutes, I backslid and became prodigal. Due to my subliminal syncretism, I became a double-minded pre-adolescent and a confused youth, lapses for which I heartily repent. I matured in denial that the Creator's grace to me depended upon my meeting His terms of endearment: all of His moral law and none of my "flesh." Eventually, He brought me to repentance, instead of letting me become a hopeless casualty in the culture war between Jesus Christ and Satan.

As an undergraduate at James Madison University, I became interested in psychology, and decided to major in that subject. During the course of my undergraduate education, I read articles and books on human potential. I met New Agers who had jumped on the Age of Aquarius bandwagon, teaching that soul evolution is in full swing and that yoga represents a valid alternative path to salvation. Alienated from my godly parents, I was introduced to street drugs in my dorm room by Steve, my nominally-Catholic, attestedly-nonsmoking, freshman college roommate. Although I never abused drugs in high school, as an undergraduate I tried to medicate turmoil with altered states of consciousness. I was similarly enticed into and practiced yogic stretches (Skt., *asanas*), eye exercises (*tratakam*), and meditation (*samyama*). It wasn't until later that I identified in yoga the theological errors of pantheism, monism, and interfaithism, which displease Christ Jesus and obscure God the Father. Books I read in the course of my psychology studies, such as Andrew Weil's *The Natural Mind*, Kenneth Pelletier's *Mind as Healer, Mind as Slayer*, and Carlos Castenada's various tomes, wrongly lauded altered states of consciousness (ASC's) as valid to psychology and to grace. As an undergraduate, I'm ashamed to say, I lived like a pagan. If God sanctified me, He can sanctify almost anybody.

From the mid-1980's, the holy Trinitarian God of my boyhood began to call me urgently out of the occultism and promiscuity I had strayed into, before Christ Jesus' *bima* judgment seat. I was then perplexed as to why it was such an issue with Him. Then, in 1986 I chanced across the book *Peace, Prosperity and the Coming Holocaust* by Dave Hunt, and the tumblers of my mind started to click. The New Age movement and its occult spirituality, which had seemed like valid alternative religion, were revealed to have devious utility to Satan. Around that time Jim, a New Age leader, rebuked me, "Daniel, your problem is you love Jesus too much." He hoped meditation and attunement (i.e., vibrational centering), would make him a Christ in his own right.

Around 1990, I qualified to join Mensa, the high-IQ society. In the course of my higher education, I memorized chemistry's periodic table of the elements. "Who hath measured the waters in the hollow of his hand, and meted out heaven with the span, *and comprehended the dust of the earth in a measure* . . ." (Isaiah 40:12, emphasis added) The word *mathematics* derives from the

Greek word *mathematikos* meaning 'learning, mental discipline.' Math is the language and science of measurement. Math's rules measure objects. Pachelbel's baroque *Canon in D* can make me weep. My main spiritual gifts are teaching, evangelism, prophecy and miracles. Genius is recognition of the orderly pre-existent mind of God the Father within literature, relationships, children, society, nature, theology, law and materials.

The jubilee revival of the mid- to late-1990's ensued. During it, I worked as a computer programmer, attended Messianic congregations, observed Toraic righteousness, Davidic-danced during Saturday worship services, and distributed Gospel tracts in street-evangelistic sorties with Jews for Jesus. The Toraic earned righteousness instilled emboldening radical godliness. I carefully tithed to the coffers of Messianic ministries. During one counseling session, Scott, a Messianic-congregational elder, said to me, "I think I discern a calling. Do you mind if we lay hands on you?" Then, he and another elder ordained me to countercult ministry, although my personal interest lay more in the realm of languages. They ordained temperament more than calling, but I bore that yoke. I also taught the Bible to school children, and conducted archery shoots for boys, girls and adults at congregational retreats. God showed me in ways that I could understand to evangelize by other methods, also. I commenced putting gospel tracts in public places, and giving them away boldly to perfect strangers I met in the course of a day. In a church-league softball game, playing for a Messianic congregation, I broke my collarbone from a fall while sprinting around the bases, in the process of hitting a homerun. Those Messianics lost that game, despite my tagging home plate ahead of the throw, with a fractured clavicle.

On a sanguine Friday afternoon in early summer, 1997, a friend named Matt invited me to his rural home to attend a Bible study. I arrived well before sunset. To my surprise, he was preparing to offer God a *minchaw* grain offering on a stone barbeque grill in the back yard. He let me handle the dough, then smoldered it upward to God. The fragrant *minchaw* smoke ascended, lit by the late-afternoon sunlight. I quickly felt brighter, holier and more hopeful within myself, and resolved to search the Bible for the theology of what I had just seen and handled. The doctrine of the *minchaw* grain offering is described in chapter one of this book.

While researching and writing *Rite for the Times*, between 1997 and 2013, by grace I offered God approximately five-hundred *minchot* (Heb., plural for *minchaw*), with many wonderful pinnacles of holiness and grace.

Although I am not well qualified after the flesh (genetically and by weight of transgression) to be a priest of God, I have had zero adverse reactions from the hundreds of *minchot* I've offered. On the contrary, the *minchaw* grain offerings are blessings to my household, during seasons of spiritual drought and siege warfare.

During the jubilee revival of the mid- and late-1990's, I read more about neopagan globalism, and felt increasing concern. I authored the countercult tract *New Age Trojan Horse*. True to my ordination and reasoning that such knowledge would do the most good to hungry students, between 1996 and 2003, I inserted 14,000 gospel tracts addressing New Age religion and the occult into publicly-accessible self-improvement books, between Charleston, South Carolina and Manhattan Island, New York, to lead some souls to salvation. "It is good for a man that he bear the yoke in his youth." (Lamentations 3:27) However, the occult is dangerous and vengeful. Being an enemy of God's enemies is not the same as being God's friend. Hudson Taylor said, "God's will, done God's way, will not fail of God's supply."

That bookmarking, admittedly a type of guerilla evangelism and less than truly ethical, was neither destructive of property nor vandalism. Those messages of God's salvation remained latent, like life preservers hung on a cliffside path above a stormy ocean, waiting for hungry seekers to happen along. However, God is an ethical Person, and requires a higher standard of ethics than I displayed by my guerilla tract evangelism, although the end of saving souls seemed to justify those means.

During those same years, occultism proliferated within American society, with the increase of TV shows, movies and books glorifying mysticism and the occult. I read the books and newsletters of Gary H. Kah and his ministry, *Hope for the World*, and studied global governance, the political arm of New Age religion. In the Messianic segment of my walk with Christ, I developed the fundamentally good habits of resting on the Saturday sabbath, wearing *tzit-tzit* (blue tassels), avoiding dietary pork and shellfish, observing the feasts of the LORD, and reading and applying the Bible to my conversation and decisions. I yet observe due righteousness. "For whatsoever a man soweth, that shall he also reap." (Galatians 6:7)

Around the turn of the new millennium, I took a couple of seminary classes at a theologically conservative Protestant Christian seminary. For one of them, I accepted the assignment to write a missions website. I addressed it to youth, to intelligentsia and to Hebrews, and called it *The Chesed Outreach*

Website. I stamped the Internet address of the website on gospel tracts, and slipped them into accessibly-shelved books on New Age-ism and psychology. That website became this manuscript, integrating theology, psychology, prophecy, apologetics, and philosophy of religion. The original Chesed Outreach website began the manuscript that became this book.

Why Chesed Outreach? *Chesed* is the Hebrew word for mercy or graciousness. Chesed Outreach is the name I coined for my nascent countercult ministry, between 1999 and 2003, which led to the writing of this book. My original website by that name was *www.chesedoutreach.org*. In it, I tried to integrate theology and apologetics with the psychology and politics of liberty. But, God's dispensation, historically supportive of liberty, changed for the worse with the early 3rd millennium and its New Age.

In my tenth year of walking with Christ in the Messianic way, God authorized Satan to scourge me, mostly for long-past prodigality but for minimal new sin, with trials that included construction-job-derived lead toxicosis. The lead affected my cognitive processes. Over a period of months, the collective unconscious infused my intellect. Combined with spiritual warfare in retaliation to my countercult ministry, that lead-related infusion amounted to cognitive and spiritual death, and was a "sift" experience. (Luke 22:31) Multiple-intelligences metatheory (tetrapartite psychology) resulted from my analyzing, synthesizing, and evaluating that ordeal.

I had long since thoroughly confessed to God. By confession, I indicated my willingness to be chastened, and God acted to scourge me. I thank God the Father for scourging me like a son. (Hebrews 12:8) My suffering commendably had dignifying effects upon me. I anticipate more hope from being scourged like a son than had I been ignored like a spiritual bastard, given that I first chose to sin.

During the trials that accompanied lead toxicosis, I let the Internet domain name for Chesed Outreach expire. It was subsequently purchased by someone else, who put a different website by that same name, out on the Internet. The trauma of the trials swayed my opposition to valid criticism of Judaizing. I perused Hank Hanegraaff's impartial views on the Messianic congregational movement.

Despite a total absence of oral or documented Hebraic family history, a saliva-swab DNA test indicates that I probably have a fraction of Hebrew blood. I am more-immediately descended from at least three Huguenot families (the DuBoses (DuBoscs), the Pasteurs, and the LeGares), and tend to be rigorous and a whistleblower. Pursuing the truth of God, I don't want to be a wannabe. I admit to being more of an observant God-fearer and theologian than a Jew, and find the Talmud antithetical to evangelism and prophecy, and unwise for Messianic congregations. In any large demographic group, there are some good, some bad, and some indifferent. This is true of both Christians and Jews.

I retain an academic interest in Messianic congregations and continue to observe due righteousness, but as a Protestant Christian I fellowship, usher, and teach a small group at a local Baptist church on Sundays. I worship Triune Yahweh at a nearby Seventh-day Adventist church on blessed Saturday sabbaths, and serve there as a deacon at that sabbatarian congregation.

While serving as an Adventist deacon, I watch for larger Messianic congregationalism's sound-doctrinal repentance of deeply-entrenched rabbinic forms, unto the revealing of the "one new man" in Christ Jesus, uniting Jews and Christians. (Ephesians 4:24) Stan Telchin writes presciently about this spiritual controversy, in his book *Messianic Judaism Is Not Christianity*, which aptly describes the epic struggle going on for the soul of Jewish evangelism. By saying 'No' to what is good (rabbinic forms in Messianic congregationalism), perhaps someday I may say 'Yes' to what is great ("one new man" in Christ Yeshua). Some Messianics cruelly vilified Stan Telchin, for his breaking ranks with them to reason about their ethnic theology. Biblically, "Rebuke a wise man and he will love thee." (Proverbs 9:8)

Writing *RT2* involved much fasting on my part, due to my calling to write God's narrow truths with authenticity and excellence. The following pages contain provocative views of a Mensan and pedagogue, from the commencement of the 3rd millennium *anno domini*.

Chapter 1

The Rite for these Times

The Levitical *minchaw* grain offering imparts ennobling holiness to its modern-day offerers. Why? How can this be? The *minchaw* grain offering comprises part of the ceremonial Torah. The ceremonial Torah is completely fulfilled in Christ Jesus, but "Whatsoever a man soweth, that shall he also reap." (Galatians 6:7)

The five books of the Torah may be classified into the civil law, the moral law, and the ceremonial law. The civil law does not apply to the church, since she is not a nation but exists within sovereign national societies. The moral law is the Ten Commandments plus those reiterated or first given in the New Testament, and is yet binding upon all mankind. The moral law includes God's laws about the sabbath day. The ceremonial law was technically fulfilled in Christ Jesus and His atoning death and resurrection. Executions for sabbath-breaking don't occur in modern times, but God may apply Jesus' perfect righteousness to whomever He wills. Although the ceremonial Torah is already fulfilled, observance of it is not sin. Man's Toraic righteousness is his earned righteousness, as distinct from righteousness-by-faith. It evokes primitive godliness oriented toward Elohim, and emboldens evangelism. As used here, Toraic self-earned righteousness is not identical with self-justification, but may be a temptation to it.

The Torah lists five types of 'offerings made by fire' [Heb., *ishaw*] unto the LORD. They are: the grain offering [*minchaw*, Lev. 2 and 6]; the burnt offering [*olaw*, Lev. 1]; the peace offering [*shelem*, Lev. 3]; the sin offering [*chattawth*, Lev. 4]; and, the trespass offering [*awshawm*, Lev. 5]. Deuteronomy 12 somewhat ambiguously commands that the *olaw* (Heb., burnt offering or ascent) be done only in Jerusalem (where the LORD God of Israel, the preincarnate God the Son, placed His name), with the possible implication that all five types of *ishaw*, as ascents, were to be done only there. Some types of *ishaw* are specifically commanded to be offered at Israelites' homesteads, not only at Jerusalem. In the Hebrew language, *minchot* is the plural word for the *minchaw* grain offering.

Of the five types of *ishaw*, only the *minchaw* grain offering does not include animal flesh and blood. Thus, the *minchaw* alone, of the five offerings by fire unto the LORD, cannot be said to attempt replication of Messiah Jesus' sacrificial blood atonement. The meaning of this is that only bloodless *minchot* will be accepted by God, post-Calvary, for the feasts of the LORD or for therapy. The *minchaw* grain offering is the only offering made by fire unto the LORD that He will accept in the context of the New Covenant, because it alone offers no blood to remediate sins. "And their sins and iniquities I will remember no more. Now *where remission of these is, there is no more offering for sin.*" (Hebrews 10:17,18, emphasis added) Blooded sin offerings became obsolete at Calvary, but *minchot* contain no animal products.

Among the five types of offerings of the LORD made by fire, and apart from Yeshua of Nazareth's completely-sufficient blood atonement, the ceremonial *minchaw* is the sole licit priestly instrument still available to fulfill Leviticus 23: 8, 14, 18, 25, 27, and 36, via an offering made by fire unto Triune Elohim, as He commanded in the Torah, upon as many as seventeen feast days each year. Of the five types of offerings (Heb., *ishaw*) made by fire unto the LORD, four utilize sacrificial blood to improve the status of sin, but the *minchaw* does not.

What this means is that, theologically speaking, Jews and Christians may offer a 'burnt offering'! Modern Believing Jews and Christians, their bodies made temples of God's name-bearing Spirit by faith in the Messiahship and resurrection of Jesus of Nazareth, may burn this grain offering, this *minchaw*, for the feasts of the LORD and for temporary sanctification and ennoblement of themselves and others, even in the Diaspora, without any offense against either the Old or New Covenant. Believing Jews today may licitly burn this unique offering to God. They don't need a Temple on Mount Moriah in Jerusalem, Israel, or an Aaronic bloodline. They need only faith in Jesus of Nazareth and His resurrection, their own living bodies, and grace from God to gratefully love Him and observe His ways.

The indwelling Holy Ghost is enough of God's name, a Believer's faith-sanctified body is enough of His temple, and this *minchaw* theology is enough sound doctrine, for *minchot* to be acceptable by God in the 3rd millennium under the New Covenant, but not for covering of men's sins.

Diagram 1.1: Types of Levitical offerings made by fire unto the LORD.

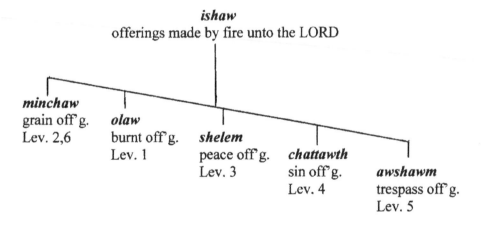

A *minchaw* of fire accepted by God is comparable to a discretionary sabbath-for-the-asking. Like the sabbath, the day following a *minchaw* accepted by God brings an intermission in spiritual strife, with greater-than-usual peace for the heart and soul, and a sense of protectedness. For it, God temporarily blesses the offerer, and all persons who that day touched his *minchaw* loaf, until the next sunset. Retaliatory demonic oppression, such as might adversely affect elderly persons resident near the offering site, may be a possible side effect if scent control is ignored. *Minchot* may become addictive. The pleasant buoyancy and extroversion that the *minchaw*'s sanctity produces may become a positive habit.

By applying this theology of the *minchaw* grain offering, Messianic Hebrews (and Christians who desire to) may observe more of the Torah pertaining to the feasts of the LORD, may sanctify and ennoble themselves and others, and can accomplish both of these without offending either the Old or the crucial New Covenant. Offerers of the *minchaw* don't depend upon prerequisites of an Aaronic priest, a bricks-and-mortar Temple, or the locale of Mount Moriah in order to successfully burn-offer this type of *ishaw*, and thereby ennoblingly sanctify human beings. If there exists even one holy person on the face of the earth, God possibly shows more interest in collective humanity. God the Father imparts the Melchizedekian priesthood, His Spirit, and His Name at the instant of one's true saving faith. Faith in Jesus is what permits to Believers full freedom to offer this Levitical *minchaw*, and enjoy its many benefits.

The *minchaw* grain offering is a doctrinal footnote, a theological loophole that God left in place so that we may yet observe the perpetual commandments of Leviticus 23: 8, 14, 18, 25, 27 and 36 (pertaining to the Feasts of Christ the LORD), even under the New Covenant.

Definition of Terms

God allows this relaxed exegesis of the *minchaw* grain offering in order to propagate the theology and sound doctrine proceeding from it. The ideas of the *minchaw* presented here are true, in action. Done in gratitude more than in ambition, God honors them. They work as described.

The word *meen-chaw* is a Hebrew feminine noun spelled *mem nun chet hay*, in that tongue. It equates to Strong's number 4503. This word is defined as 'bloodless, voluntary offering.' It or its variants occur 72 times in the Old

Testament (the Jewish TaNaK), where it is translated 'offering, present, meal offering, oblation, tribute, or gift.' Although the Hebrew word *minchaw* is translated in the King James Version as meat offering, there is no animal flesh or blood involved in it. There are no theological conflicts or thematic overlaps between *minchot* and Yeshua haMashiach's sacrificial atonement for the sins of mankind, because 'Without the shedding of blood, there is no remission of sin.' (Leviticus 17:11, Hebrews 9:22) *Minchot* are bloodless. Faith in Messiah Jesus, and in His blood and resurrection, ably does for mankind what *minchot* don't and were never intended to do: atone for sin. The King James Version Bible's translation of the word *minchaw* as 'meat offering' means 'meat as the class of edibles, of food in general, not specifically animal flesh.' The New American Standard Bible translates the word *minchaw* as 'grain offering,' which is closer to the reality of it. Offering *minchot* develops the spiritual gift of prophecy, if it pre-exists. Done correctly, imparted holiness from *minchaw* grain offerings may develop all pre-existing spiritual gifts.

The Jewish Book of Why? briefly mentions *mincha* as a mid-day prayer service commemorating afternoon Temple offerings held prior to 70 A.D.[1] Son of David Congregation, in Wheaton, Maryland, planned an afternoon *mincha* prayer service for Yom Teruah, 2009, but they did not then include "an offering made by fire" [*ishaw*] unto the LORD. There may be a Talmudic argument for refraining from obligatory *minchaw* of firstfruits and *minchaw* of fire for the feasts of the Lord, but the Talmud cannot overrule either the Toraic commandment for, or New Covenant freedom to offer, voluntary bloodless *minchot* as offerings made by fire unto the LORD for the Biblical feast days.

A Believer's heart is named of Y'howah, and his body is made the temple of His Spirit, by his decision to believe "Adonai Yeshua haMashiach, resurrected!" Bearing God's name as the bodily temple of His Spirit permits latter-day Diasporic offerings of the *minchaw*.

Context

If Toraic ceremonial offerings are ever again called for, the *minchaw* grain offering exegeted in this chapter will be the only licit offering made by fire unto the LORD that is acceptable to our God for its Toraic purpose, since it uniquely, among the five Levitical offerings made by fire unto Him, does not utilize animal blood to improve the status of human sin. To offer blood, post-Calvary, would be to imply replication of Christ Jesus' once-and-for-all atoning death, and would therefore offend God. The by-definition voluntary nature of the *minchaw* makes special sense, ever since Christ Jesus' New Covenant. He technically fulfilled the Torah, by His life, death and resurrection.

The ceremonial law, although completed in Christ Jesus, is pertinent to certain Jewish missionary outreaches. Done properly, ceremonial-law righteousness is not sin, and may even elicit a type of grace that is perceptible, although much inferior to the grace resulting from obedient, true saving faith. Toraic earned righteousness emboldens and instills an unassuming primitive godliness, which helps with evangelism. Ceremonial law ritual elevates God's expectations for the offerer. While the moral law (Dan Juster calls it 'the universal Torah') is binding upon all mankind, the more-sweeping 'Jewish-calling Torah' attempts to make evangelists of the Gospel authentic to Israeli's, in preparation for the prophesied end-time latter-rain revival.

Geographically, *olaw* (Heb., burnt offerings), were commanded in Deuteronomy 12 to be offered only where the LORD placed His name. But now, Mount Moriah is capped by the Islamic Dome of the Rock, God's *shekinah* glory was removed from it at Christ Jesus' crucifixion, and Pentecost has widely dispensed God's Holy Spirit, called by His Name, to the heart of every true Believer. All Believers, Christians and Jews (who are priests of the order of Melchisedec through Jesus Christ) are authorized by God to offer *minchot*. (*Minchot* is plural for *minchaw*.) Hebrews 7:12 reads, "For the priesthood being changed, there is made of necessity a change also of the law."

If the *minchaw* of fire is offered in the Diaspora, on the valid premise that God's name is present via His Holy Spirit in His temples (our bodies), there truly is grace for this. God wills adaptation of systematic theology to progressive understandings of the Godhead, rather than rote reconstructionist regression to Toraism and its admittedly-beneficial, radical, primitive godliness. Despite this, *every human violation of the Torah incurs some consequence, ranging from the imperceptible to the disastrous, according to the reality of God's grace through Christ Jesus.*

Contraindications?

Deuteronomy 12:11, in the Jewish TaNaK (the Old Testament), states, " . . . Then you must bring everything that I command you to the site where the LORD your God will choose to establish His name: your burnt offerings and other sacrifices, your tithes and contributions, and all the choice votive offerings that you vow to the LORD."

Photo 1.2: A pinched-off grain offering of fire loaf, consisting of flour, olive oil, salt and frankincense. One touch to such a *minchaw* loaf imparts ennobling holiness until the next sunset.

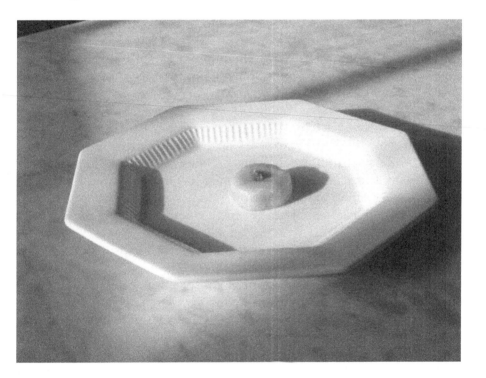

Deuteronomy 12:13,14 in the KJV reads, "Take heed to thyself that thou offer not thy burnt offerings [Heb., *olaw*, but possibly implying the wider idea of Jerusalemic ascent] in every place that thou seest: But in the place which the LORD shall choose in one of thy tribes, there thou shalt offer thy burnt offerings, and there thou shalt do all that I command thee." As we shall see, this geography-specifying commandment may or may not be yet applicable, post-Pentecost, to the *minchaw* (which, strictly, is not identical with *olaw*).

For rigid Old Covenant types, Deuteronomy 12:11-14 stipulated that *olaw* (Heb., burnt offerings or ascents) were only to be done in Jerusalem. The implication is, perhaps, that all "offerings made by fire" (Heb. *ishaw*) unto the LORD were to be done only at the place where He then placed His name. Then, that was on Mount Moriah in Jerusalem, Israel, now capped by Islam's Dome of the Rock. But, God removed His name from Mount Moriah when He took His *shekinah* glory from Herod's Temple at Jesus' crucifixion, although His commandments for feast-days' *ishaw* remain in force. (Leviticus 23: 8, 14, 18, 25, 27, and 36)

The huge exception to this geographic restriction is that, due to Christ Jesus and since the first Pentecost, God places His name in the heart of every true Believer in Messiah Jesus, no longer only atop Mount Moriah in Jerusalem, Israel. Nomenclative identity in Yahweh is easiest sensed in Christian fellowships and after restful Saturday-sabbath afternoons. New Covenant sound doctrine relaxes geographic permissibility of the *minchaw*.

No geographical restriction was ever specified for Firstfruits' day's grain offering of firstfruits (*minchawth bikkuwrim*) or Shavuot's bread of firstfruits (*lehem bikkuwrim*). Those two offerings are specifically commanded to be offered as a " . . . statute forever throughout your generations *in all your dwellings.*" (Lev. 23:14b, emphasis added) Neither of these two offerings are *olaw* (burnt offering), either. Hebrews' dwellings were obviously not all located at Jerusalem. The *minchawth bikkuwrim* and *lehem bikkuwrim* (of firstfruits and Weeks), neither of which are *olaw*, are commanded to be done at Hebrews' dwellings anywhere, presumably by anyone, on firstfruits Sunday and Shavuot Sunday, respectively. More about these, further on in this chapter.

God, in six verses in Leviticus 23 pertaining to the feasts of the LORD, commands the making of "offerings made by fire unto the LORD." These commandments, fulfillable now only by the grain offering of fire (Heb., *minchat h'esh*), indicate this offering for the seven days of the feast of unleavened bread, Yom Teruah, Yom Kippur, and the eight days of Sukkot. Firstfruits Sunday (which may follow, and be external to, Passover week) and Shavuot Sunday (the feast of Weeks) also require grain offerings. Specifically, they require the *minchawth bikkuwrim* (grain offering of firstfruits, for firstfruits Sunday) and *lehem bikkuwrim* (bread of firstfruits, for Shavuot Sunday). We'll cover these two types of offerings later in this chapter. They are important, but secondary to the *minchat h'esh* for temporary ennobling holiness.

The *minchat h'esh* (Heb., grain offering of fire) is the primary offering made by fire unto the LORD that is still acceptable to God, post-Calvary. Deuteronomy 12 specifies that the burnt offering (*olaw*, not *minchaw*) may only be done where God places His name. In Old Testament times, God placed His name upon Mount Moriah in Jerusalem, Israel. But, from the first Pentecost, He has placed His holy name, via God the Father's Spirit, within the heart of every single Believer in Messiah Jesus at the instant of his or her true saving faith.

Minchaw Theology

The next four points distill the essence of *minchaw* theology, regarding Believers' inner man, gatherings and bodies as loci of YHWH's sacred name, and regarding voluntary satisfaction of the completed Torah.

Firstly, each true Believer is named of Y'howah in his <u>heart</u>. "For this cause I bow my knees unto the Father of our LORD Jesus Christ, *of whom the whole family in heaven and in earth is named . . . That Christ may dwell in your hearts by faith . . .*" (Ephesians 3:14,15,17a, emphasis added) This means that the Temple Mount and an Aaronic priest are no longer the only repositories of Triune Elohim's sacred name, since He now places it in the heart of every single true, Holy Spirit-indwelt Christian or Believing Jew. God the Father's Holy Spirit is called by His terrible, holy, beloved name, *Y'howah*. He imparts this Word, His covenant personal name, to the hearts of tens of millions of Christian and Jewish Believers in Jesus, only because of our faith in God the Son. Believers are priests, and our bodies are temples of God's Holy Spirit. This is the first exception to the Deuteronomy 12 geographical restriction.

Secondly, Y'howah's covenant name is present at all Born Agains' <u>gatherings</u>. "For where two or three of you are gathered together in my name, there am I in the midst of them." (Matthew 18:20) Where Elohim the Holy Spirit is present, His name is, also. This is the second exception to the priestly-genetic and geographical restrictions on an offering made by fire unto Yahweh.

Thirdly, Y'howah's covenant name is present in each true Christian's and believing Jew's <u>body</u> via His Spirit, no longer only atop Mt. Moriah, beneath Islam's Dome of the Rock. "What! know ye not that *your body is the temple of the Holy Ghost*, which is in you, which ye have of God, and ye are not your own?" (I Corinthians 6:19, emphasis added) Since the first Pentecost, His name is present within each true Believer's body from His love, as a direct result of grace through New Covenant faith. His Spirit will not neglect to impart His name to the heart of a true Believer, making us priests, and our bodies temples of God the Father's Spirit. This is the third exception to the priestly-genetic and geographical restrictions.

How else than by His name may He identify such a Believer as His? The sign gifts are not yet widely re-sanctified, in the early 3rd millennium, as they will be by the latter-rain doctrinal reformation and revival. No, identity in Y'howah Elohim is by His name-bearing Spirit. Sanctification is first nomenclative. Religious universalism notwithstanding, other spirits, known by pagan names for Deity, cannot possibly impart true holiness to a worshiper.

Providing the presence of God's name, the infilling of God the Father's Spirit relaxes any Deuteronomy 12 geographical restriction upon offerings made by fire unto the LORD, while the blood-free nature of *minchot* simultaneously avoids the New Covenant prohibition (Heb. 10:17,18) against replication of Calvary's sin atonement.

Fourthly, *minchaw* grain offerings alone <u>satisfy the Christ-completed Torah regarding the feasts of the LORD</u>, without any offense at all to Adonai Jesus' New Covenant. Hebrews 10:17,18 teaches, "And their sins and iniquities I will remember no more. Now where remission of these is, *there is no more offering for sin*." (Emphasis added) Jesus paid it all! If anyone today intended a Levitical blood ritual to remove men's sins, then that would be offensive to God the Father, who accepted Jesus' sacrificial death for all mankind who believe. *Minchot* are the only type of Toraic offerings of the LORD made by fire that may ever again be offered in fulfillment of their intended purposes for the feasts of Christ, as commanded in Leviticus 23: 8, 14, 28, 25, 27, and 36.

The remainder of this chapter will examine these and related theses referring, for authority, to the Bible.

Photo 1.3: Second shot of a pinched-off pre-offering *minchaw* grain offering of fire, made of flour, olive oil, salt and frankincense. One touch to it sanctifies until sunset.

Background

Jesus of Nazareth, who is Adonai the Christ and Elohim the Son, first widely revealed the pre-existent other-two Persons of the Triune Godhead via His first-century personal public ministry. His revelation of the Triune Godhead dispensed wide new understanding of His Father and Holy Spirit. (Ephesians 3:5) This sudden widening of human understanding should encourage each Jewish Believer to learn systematic theology and Paul's sound doctrine, over and above observance of Toraic righteousness.

For example, Mark 1:9-11 recounts the revelation, to Jesus' associates, of His Father and Holy Spirit, at the time of His token water baptism. New Testament water baptism, that of repentance for the remission of sins, should be an once-in-eternity embarkation, not a periodic ritual immersion (as some assert from the related Old Testament Hebrew idea of *mikvah*). Rabbinic Judaism is a far cry from being the real-McCoy Protestant Christianity.

During the millennial kingdom of Messiah Jesus, when the lion lies down with the lamb and eats straw like the ox (and, according to some, killings will no longer occur), the bloodless *minchaw* grain offering will be the only licit offering made by fire unto the LORD that is acceptable by God for its Toraic purpose, throughout Messiah Yeshua's entire, future thousand-year millennial kingdom, because of God's appreciation, love and support for Christ Jesus' atonement and for Pauline sound doctrine. Paul wrote to the future of spiritual man.

The *minchaw* grain offering is the only offering made by fire unto the LORD that is yet licit, post-Calvary. Some theologians correctly argue that the ceremonial law was fulfilled in Christ Jesus. But, if there are Toraic ceremonial offerings accepted by God, now or in the millennial kingdom of Christ, they truly will be only these *minchot* (grain offerings). Triune Elohim will not repeal sound doctrine, to regress theology back to pre-Christian days. God won't nostalgically abolish awesome Calvary and sound doctrine's priceless truths, during Messiah Jesus' millennial kingdom, to revert theology to the pre-Christian era.

The Grain Offering of Fire

The main type of grain offering, the *minchaw* of fire (Heb., *minchat h'esh*), is by definition bloodless and voluntary. The offering consists of a small cake or biscuit compacted of fine wheat or barley flour, olive oil, salt, and sweet-smelling frankincense. This cake is then toasted, smoldered, or flamed in a pan over a heat source. If you are of Aaronic descent you may eat it. The *minchat h'esh* loaf is never to contain leaven or honey, or flesh or blood. It was never intended by God to atone for sins, because God said in Leviticus 17:11 and Hebrews 9:22, "Without the shedding of blood there is no remission of sin."

The *minchaw* presents no conflict with the perfect completeness of Messiah Jesus' awesome blood atonement. *The minchaw of fire is optional under the New Covenant, but indicated by the Torah for each day of the seven-day feast of unleavened bread, Yom Teruah, Yom Kippur, and the eight days of Sukkot. As the only yet-permissible offering made by fire unto the LORD, the minchaw of fire doctrinal loophole can uniquely fulfill six completed-but-perpetual ceremonial-law commandments in Leviticus 23, that affect seventeen feast days!*

The *minchaw* grain offering is a voluntary gratitude offering to God that He may still be pleased to receive, even during the church age. A *minchaw* of fire that is accepted by God encourages the heart, soul, and elastic psychic membrane (Heb., *sawkak*) of the offerer(s). God may use the resultant holiness to temporarily banish fear from the offerers' hearts. God may use it in conjunction with personal hopes to encourage offerers' souls to heal, reknit and reclaim space previously yielded to Satan.

If properly understood by academia, *minchot* may become a valuable adjunct to Biblical counseling, and become a great blessing to the larger Body of Christ, because they invite God's grace to bolster complex human personalities. The psalm of deliverance, Psalm 91, says in verses 11 and 12 "For He shall give his angels charge over thee, to keep thee in all thy ways. They shall bear thee up in their hands lest thou dash thy foot against a stone." Temporary holiness imparted by *minchot* of fire provides, for the asking, an ennobling one-day benchmark experience of relative spiritual well being, from which to reconsider one's heart and standing before *Yahweh h'Av*, the Father of lights.

Leviticus 2:9 says of the *minchaw* of fire, "It is an offering made by fire, of a sweet savor unto the LORD." Since they are bloodless and not a sin offering, *minchot* were not pre-empted by the LORD Jesus' sacrificial atonement. *Minchot* are righteous deeds that have been forgotten over the centuries, because of competition from human traditions. But, the Torah

31

obliges *minchot* (an offering made by fire), and the New Testament does not forbid them.

Minchot are the one and only type of the five ceremonial 'offerings made by fire' (Heb., *ishaw*) unto the LORD that do not contain animal flesh or blood. They are thus the sole licit priestly instruments for post-Golgathic fulfillment of the six perpetual Toraic commandments found in Leviticus 23: 8, 14, 18, 25, 27, and 36. These verses command offering made by fire unto Yahweh on Biblical feast days "throughout your generations."

Despite that many Christians suffer regrettable ignorance of it, the Hebrew word spelled *yud hay waw hay* (YHWH) is God the Father's terrible, holy, beloved *Name above all names*. Written throughout this text mostly as Yahweh (but phonetically pronounced Y'howah), this Word, His covenant personal name, was translated LORD throughout the Old Testament, and drew that honorific upon Yeshua of Nazareth, the LORD Jesus, who is Elohim the Son and Adonai the Christ.

The words for the God of the Bible used in this book are as follows. "Y'howah" is God's covenant personal name; "YHWH" is its acronym. "Elohim" is analogous to God's surname and is plural. "God" and "Yahweh" are titular. "Jesus," and "Y'shua" are His bodily names, and "Christ" and "Messiah" are His Son's titles.

From the plagues of the Exodus to the immaculate conception, the LORD God of Israel was normatively the preincarnate God the Son! His holy name is not to be spoken in vain vows, nor ever blasphemously. In Hebrew, the tetragrammaton is spelled YHWH [*Y'howah!*], with all consonants, for war. In Koine Greek, the tetragrammaton is spelled like Ia'oa [*Ia-hoa!*], with all vowels, for affection.

"Koine" is Greek for "common." Koine Greek balances tendencies to self-justified *chutzpah*. The Hebrew language has about one-half of the number of words that English or Koine Greek have. Hebrew is the language of praise. Koine Greek and English are the languages of theology. Heartsongs in Hebrew imply the End-time aparchic firstfruits mission, as the Tribulation then unwinds toward the Rapture of the un-marked. The Koine Greek word for 'body' (*soma*) is used throughout the New Testament. The Hebrew word for 'body' (*guf*) is not mentioned in either the Old or New Testament. Jesus' impartation of His Father's Spirit conveys new meaning to one's body.

Photo 1.4: A shot of a grain offering of fire, actively in progress.

Role of Grain Offerings

Leviticus 23:4-14 reads, establishing the roles of the *minchat h'esh* and *minchawth bikkuwrim* (during the feast of unleavened bread):

v. 4— "These are the feasts of the LORD, even holy convocations, which ye shall proclaim in their seasons.

v. 5— "In the fourteenth day of the first month at even is the LORD's Passover.

v. 6— "And on the fifteenth day of the same month is the feast of unleavened bread unto the LORD: seven days ye must eat unleavened bread.

v. 7— "In the first day ye shall have a holy convocation [Heb., *miqra*]: ye shall do no servile work therein.

v. 8— "But *ye shall offer an offering made by fire unto the LORD seven days*: in the seventh day is a holy convocation [*miqra*]: ye shall do no servile work therein. [Emphasis added]

v. 9— "And the LORD spake unto Moses, saying,

v. 10— "Speak unto the children of Israel, and say unto them, When ye be come into the land which I give unto you, and shall reap the harvest thereof, then ye shall bring a sheaf of the firstfuits of your harvest unto the priest:

v.11— "And he shall wave the sheaf before the LORD, to be accepted for you: on the morrow after the sabbath the priest shall wave it.

v.12— "And ye shall offer that day when ye wave the sheaf an he lamb without blemish of the first year for a burnt offering unto the LORD.

v.13— "And the meat offering [*minchaw*, or grain offering] thereof shall be two tenth deals of fine flour mingled with oil, an offering made by fire unto the LORD for a sweet savor: and the drink offering thereof shall be of wine, the fourth part of a *hin*.

v.14— "And ye shall eat neither bread, nor parched corn, nor green ears, until the selfsame day that ye have brought an offering unto your God: *it shall be a statute forever throughout your generations in all your dwellings.*" (Emphasis added)

The New American Standard Bible translates Leviticus 23:4-14 slightly differently. "These are the appointed times of the LORD [the Angel of Yah, the preincarnate God the Son], holy convocations which you shall proclaim at the times appointed for them. In the first month, on the fourteenth day of the month at twilight is the LORD's Passover. Then on the fifteenth day of the same month there is the Feast of Unleavened Bread to the LORD: for seven days you shall eat unleavened bread. On the first day you shall have a holy convocation; you shall not do any laborious work. But, *for the seven days you shall present an offering by fire to the LORD.* [Emphasis added] On the seventh day is a holy convocation: you shall not do any laborious work. Then the LORD spoke to Moses, saying, 'Speak to the sons of Israel and say to them, 'When you enter the land which I am going to give to you and reap its harvest, then you shall bring in the sheaf of the first fruits of your harvest to the priest. He shall wave the sheaf before the LORD for you to be accepted; on the day after the sabbath the priest shall wave it. Now on the day when you wave the sheaf, you shall offer a male lamb one year old without defect for a burnt offering. Its grain offering [*minchaw*] shall then be two-tenths of an *ephah* of fine flour mixed with oil, an offering by fire to the LORD for a soothing aroma, with its drink offering, a fourth part of a *hin* of wine. Until this same day, until you have brought in the offering of your God, you shall eat neither bread nor roasted grain nor new growth. *It is to be a perpetual statute throughout your generations in all your dwelling places.*'" (Emphasis added)

God would not have given the perpetual command "It shall be a statute forever throughout your generations in all your dwellings" (Leviticus 23:14b), for an offering made by fire unto Him, except with foreknowledge that it could be kept via faith in Christ Jesus and through *minchot*, even without a bricks-and-mortar Temple in Jerusalem!

Offerings During The LORD's Feasts, Part I

The LORD God of Israel, Elohim the preincarnate Son, commanded offerings made by fire unto Him, during His feasts, in the following verses.

In Leviticus 23:8, for Unleavened Bread, "But *ye shall offer an offering made by fire unto the LORD seven days*: in the seventh day is a holy convocation: ye shall do no servile work therein." (Emphasis added)

In Leviticus 23:21, for Shavuot and its offering of the bread of firstfruits: "... It shall be a statute forever in all your dwellings throughout your generations." A *minchat h'esh* (grain offering of fire) would be the "meat offering" for this day, such as is specified by Leviticus 23:18.

In Leviticus 23:25, for Yom Teruah, "Ye shall do no servile work therein: but *ye shall offer an offering made by fire unto the LORD.*" (Emphasis added)

In Leviticus 23:27, for Yom Kippur, "Also on the tenth day of this seventh month there shall be a day of atonement: it shall be an holy convocation unto you: and ye shall afflict your souls, *and offer an offering made by fire unto the LORD.*" (Emphasis added)

In Leviticus 23:36, for Sukkot, "*Seven days ye shall offer an offering made by fire unto the LORD*: on the eighth day shall be a holy convocation unto you: *and ye shall offer an offering made by fire unto the LORD*: it is a solemn assembly: and ye shall do no servile work therein." (Emphasis added)

And, in summary, Leviticus 23:37, "These are the feasts of the LORD, which ye shall proclaim to be holy convocations, *to offer an offering made by fire unto the LORD* ..." (Emphasis added)

The only permissible way to observe these multiple Toraic commandments, by offering an offering made by fire unto the LORD without abominable replication of Christ's atonement on Calvary, is via the theological loophole that is the *minchaw* grain offering! These feast day observances were to be " ... A statute forever throughout your generations in all your dwellings." (Lev. 23:21,31) They are still relevant today, in the early 3rd millennium, for us who are interested in true religion, undefiled. The ceremonial law is completely fulfilled in Christ Jesus, but "Whatsoever a man soweth, that shall he also reap." (Galatians 6:7)

Grain Offering Techniques

Pertaining to the *minchat h'esh*, a sample recipe for a grain-offering-of-fire doughball consists of: 3 cups of all-purpose flour, 3 teaspoons of table salt, and about 10 ounces of olive oil. Extra-virgin olive oil smells nicest.

The ingredients should be mixed in a bowl and kneaded by hand, until cohesive, elastic and softball-sized (a large doughball). Adapt quantities of ingredients according to consistency and texture. Small chunks may then be pinched off of the larger dough ball, and burned with a bit of frankincense, as offerings of the *minchaw* grain offering of fire. This fragrant, oily dough tends to become stiffer, with time, as the volatile molecules in the olive oil evaporate. You may pre-mix *minchaw* dough (flour, olive oil and salt), and store the large ball of it in a plastic bag until ready for use. Refrigeration is not required. Then, pinch off a small chunk, add frankincense to it, and heat in a steel pan over a propane torch, in order to offer a ten-minute instant *minchaw*. God probably applies sanctity to dough contactees only on the same day that their touching it occurs, until the next sunset.

Offering a so-called instant *minchaw* in a mere ten minutes is easiest if the small loaf is allowed to flame, which is a process not forbidden in the Torah. "Sons of Aaron" are the only persons authorized to eat the salty, bland, oily *minchaw* loaves, anyway. (Lev. 6:18) Genetic descent from Aaron is not implied by the LORD Jesus' Melchizedekian priesthood.

Since this author is not a genetic descendent of Aaron, he slowly flames his *minchat h'esh* and doesn't prepare it for eating. Per Leviticus 6:23, *minchaw* grain offerings for feast days or therapy should probably be wholly burnt, as introductory of you, the priest, to the LORD God of Israel, who is God the Son. Anyone descended from Aaron is welcome to prepare *minchaw* loaves as food and eat them. And, a *minchaw* loaf is not identical with shewbread. (I Chronicles 23:29)

The basis for the instant *minchaw* is that Israelite Levitical priests offered small portions of the total ingredients given to them to offer, and retained some for personal use. Leviticus 6:23 instructs that *minchaw* grain offerings should usually be burnt to carbon and not eaten, except by descendents of Aaron. Flaming the loaf is permissible to accomplish this, but smoldering of it may draw more angelic attention. By these methods an instant *minchaw* can be offered in as little as ten minutes. An instant *minchaw* is an instrument for requesting temporary uplifting grace from our Triune Elohim, for the offerer and his conclave of dough handlers.

If there is danger of Satan's demonic retaliation to a *minchaw*, it is probably because if ignorant that they're newly holy, offerers might react with volatility at the LORD's preemption, at His holiness-raised expectations for them. Offering *minchat h'esh* puts human existence in a starkly spiritual context that may be unsettling to those who yet yearn for foolishness or irresponsibility.

Grain Offerings Sanctify

What does the Bible say about holiness imparted by the *minchaw* grain offering of fire? What modern applications might it have? Leviticus 6:14-23 says:

v. 14— "And this is the law of the meat offering [*minchaw* grain offering of fire]: the sons of Aaron shall offer it before the LORD, before the altar.

v. 15— "And he shall take of it his handful, of the flour of the meat offering and of the oil thereof, and all the frankincense which is upon the meat offering, and shall burn it upon the altar for a sweet savor, even the memorial of it, unto the LORD.

v. 16— "And the remainder thereof shall Aaron and his sons eat: with unleavened bread shall it be eaten in the holy place: in the court of the tabernacle of the congregation they shall eat it.

v. 17— "It shall not be baked with leaven. I have given it unto them for their portion of my offerings made by fire; it is most holy, as is the sin offering, and as the trespass offering.

v. 18— "All the males among the children of Aaron shall eat of it. It shall be a statute forever in your generations concerning the offering of the LORD made by fire: *everyone that toucheth them shall be holy.* [Emphasis added]

v. 19— "And the LORD spake unto Moses, saying,

v. 20— "This is the offering of Aaron and of his sons, which they shall offer unto the LORD in the day when he is anointed; the tenth part of an *ephah* of fine flour for a meat offering [*minchaw*] perpetual, half of it in the morning, and half thereof at night.

v. 21— "In a pan it shall be made with oil; and when it is baked, thou shalt bring it in: and the baked pieces of the meat offering shalt thou offer for a sweet savor unto the LORD:

v. 22— "And the priest of his sons that is anointed in his stead shall offer it: it is a statute forever unto the LORD; it shall be wholly burnt.

v. 23— "For every meat offering for the priest shall be wholly burnt: it shall not be eaten."

Again, the NASB translates Leviticus 6:14-23 slightly differently. "Now this is the law of the grain offering [*minchaw* of fire]: the sons of Aaron shall present it before the LORD in front of the altar. Then one of them shall lift up from it a handful of the fine flour of the grain offering, with its oil and all the incense that is on the grain offering, and he shall offer it up in smoke on the altar, a soothing aroma, as its memorial offering to the LORD. What is left of it Aaron and his sons are to eat. It shall be eaten as unleavened cakes in a holy place; they are to eat it in the court of the tent of meeting. It shall not be baked with leaven. I have given it as their share from My offerings by fire; it is most holy, like the sin offering and the guilt offering. Every male among the sons of Aaron may eat it; it is a permanent ordinance throughout your generations, from the offerings by fire to the LORD. *Whoever touches them will become consecrated.* [Emphasis added] Then the LORD spoke to Moses, saying, 'This is the offering which Aaron and his sons are to present to the Lord on the day when he is anointed; the tenth of an *ephah* of fine flour as a regular grain offering, half of it in the morning and half of it in the evening. It shall be prepared with oil on a griddle. When it is well stirred, you shall bring it. You shall present the grain offering in baked pieces as a soothing aroma to the LORD. The anointed priest who will be in his place among his sons shall offer it. By a permanent ordinance it shall be entirely offered up in smoke to the LORD. So every grain offering of the priest shall be burned entirely. It shall not be eaten.'"

Quite interestingly, Leviticus 6:18c says that any human who touches the dough of a *minchaw* loaf itself, becomes "*holy*" and "*consecrated.*" God probably acknowledges such touch until the subsequent sunset, and imparts holiness if the dough is offered before then. Benefits of such ennobling benchmark holiness, sought from gratitude more than from ambition, should be studied and experimented with for advancement of therapeutic health science. There may be quantifiable benefits to human heart rate, blood pressure and stress hormone levels, resulting from offering *minchot*. Since the *minchaw* of fire, as the only licit offering made by fire unto the LORD acceptable to Him, imparts temporary benchmark holiness (until the next sunset), it can be valuable for therapy and for large-scale sanctification of entire congregations. The *minchaw* of fire truly provides dignifying benchmark holiness, a temporary interlude of grace. It can restore hope in life and interest in Jesus' eternal *Abba*, to darkened, panicky hearts. The blacker the pre-existing spiritual darkness, the more dramatic the ennobling sanctity resulting from contact with a *minchaw* loaf. "There, now you're holy!"

The more sin-ravaged, spiritually darkened and facial-brightness deficient a *minchaw*-dough handler, the more dramatic his or her temporary ennobling sanctity, resulting from a touch to a *minchaw* loaf that is then successfully offered by fire.

Minchot have the potential to remind darkened hearts and panicky souls of Elohim's patient, glorious goodness: the previously darker the heart, the more spectacular the bright-browed sanctification. Such uplifting benchmark holiness may raise sufferers' self-expectations despite trial and emotional turmoil. A holy evangelist's "Jesus loves you!", with direct smiling eye contact and a firm proper handshake, makes a genuine impression with the message of God the Father's earnest *agape* love, into recipients' hearts and souls.

Humans who become holy from a pre-offering touch to a *minchaw* loaf quickly notice ennobling facial brightness or clarion (a halo of clarity to the face and heart), which is not an altered state of consciousness (ASC). It is almost as though, for that day until the next sunset, their souls' angels look upward in heaven upon the face of God the Father, just like innocent children's angels do. "Take heed that ye despise not one of these little ones: for I say unto you, That in heaven their angels do always behold the face of my Father which is in heaven." (Matthew 18:10) And, God looks back. Holiness from a *minchaw* compliments intellect, but does not mix well with lust. *Minchaw* sanctity heightens and deepens cognition within Yahweh's Logos. It is worth noting that the ennobling holiness caused by handling *minchaw* dough is felt most wonderfully in proportion to pre-existing spiritual darkness.

Grain Offerings Ennoble Handlers

Grain offerings can be instrumental for asking God for temporary sanctifications of solitaries or large groups of people, for feast days or for counseling. Let's look at Leviticus 6:18 in various translations.

The King James Version translates Leviticus 6:18 as "All the males among the children of Aaron shall eat of it. It shall be a statute forever in your generations concerning the offerings of the LORD made by fire: every one that toucheth them shall be holy." By interpretation, the offered *minchaw* is an instrument of temporary sanctification to all who handle the loaf, until the next sunset. The "every one that toucheth them" refers back grammatically, in the same sentence, to "the offerings made by fire unto

Photo 1.5: Second shot of a grain offering of fire, actively in progress.

the LORD," not to the priests. Anybody who touches an offering made by fire unto the LORD becomes holy until the next sunset.

The New International Version translates Leviticus 6:18 as "Any male descendent of Aaron may eat it. It is his regular share of the offerings made to the LORD by fire for the generations to come. Whatever touches them will become holy." This translation also implies the narrow rule that holiness is transmitted to the contactee(s), until the subsequent sunset, by their touching a *minchaw* loaf prior to its being offered.

The New American Standard Bible translates Leviticus 6:18 as "Every male among the sons of Aaron may eat it; it is a permanent ordinance throughout your generations, from the offerings by fire to the LORD. Whoever touches them will become consecrated." This translation also implies the interpretation that touching the *minchaw*, as an offering of the LORD made by fire, sanctifies the offerer(s). The "them" being touched refers back grammatically, in the same sentence, to the offerings by fire unto the LORD, not to the priests.

The Jewish Publication Society's TaNaK (the Jewish Old Testament) uses a different numbering system for the verses of Leviticus 6. The equivalent verse in the TaNaK is Leviticus 6:11. It reads, "Only the males among Aaron's descendants may eat of it, as their due for all time throughout the ages from the LORD's offerings by fire. Anything that touches these shall become holy." This translation, too, addresses the priestly sons of Aaron to permit their eating the *minchaw* loaf, and states that anything touching "these," in context referring grammatically to the offerings of the LORD made by fire, shall become "holy." The Hebrew word used there for "holy" is *qawdash* (Strong's number 6942), meaning "be clean; appoint, consecrate, dedicate, hallow, keep, prepare, purify, and sanctify." Such temporary ennobling holiness produces a welcome state, but we mustn't let it puff us up with pride. In God's sight all have sinned and come short of His glory (Romans 6:23). Experimentally, *minchot* may elevate God's expectations for the offerer. They may raise the bar of His expectations for spiritual maturity, prompting heart- and soul-searching for the *minchaw* offerer who walks with Messiah Yeshua.

The New Living Translation translates Leviticus 6:18 as "Any of Aaron's male descendants, from generation to generation, may eat of the grain offering, because it is their regular share of the offerings given to the LORD by fire. Anyone or anything that touches this food will become holy." Thus, the NLT explicitly corroborates the narrow interpretation that temporary holiness is imparted to a man by his touching the *minchaw* loaf as an offering given to the LORD by fire, and that the "them" refers back grammatically to the offering loaves themselves, not to the priests.

Experimentally, the ennobling benchmark holiness from *minchot* remains until the following sunset. During this span of time, it pleasantly increases natural buoyancy, confidence and extroversion, while decreasing self-absorption and making any spiritual troubles more bearable than usual. The temporary holiness from *minchot* is 'benchmark' in the sense that it provides a Biblical peak experience for comparison to one's habitual state. The *minchaw* loaf's contagious benchmark holiness should prove valuable for pastors, elders, deacons, lay ministers, counselors, priests, rabbis, physicians, psychologists, prophets, psychiatrists, psychotherapists, and chiropractors: in short, to intercessors and healers.

Offering *minchot* develops any pre-existing spiritual gift of prophecy. The temporary sanctity from offering *minchaw* grain offerings probably develops all pre-existing spiritual gifts in the personalities of Believing offerers!

If offered in Jerusalem before the LORD, available Aaronic priests (not specifically Melchisedecian ones) were allowed to eat the cooked *minchaw* loaf. *Minchot* of fire were to be offered at the anointing of a new high priest (Lev. 6:20). Then, the loaf was to be wholly burnt, not eaten even by the sons of Aaron who alone, otherwise, are specifically allowed to eat it (Lev. 6:18a). Explicitly, genetic non-Aaronites are excluded from permission to eat *minchaw* loaves. Indweltness by God the Holy Spirit is not identical with Aaronic genes.

Male genetic descendents of Aaron, not priests of God in general, may eat a completed *minchaw* loaf. Non-Aaronic priests, such as Melchizedekian Christians, are not permitted by commandment to eat a *minchaw* loaf. Melchizedekian priests' flaming a of *minchaw* loaf, to expedite its offering, does not violate God's Toraically expressed will for it, although such flaming is certainly not mandatory. Time-consuming preparation of the *minchaw* grain offering as a foodstuff would be a sentimental statement.

Believers in Jesus Christ are indwelt with God the Father's Holy Spirit. Per Hebrews 7:1, Christians and Believing Jews are thus priests of the order of Melchisedec, who was not a Jew. This same Melchizedek, as described in Genesis 14: 17-24, was a Christophany, a pre-type of Christ Jesus. Melchizedek was a contemporary of Abraham the Hebronite (Genesis 13:18), who was the first man called 'Hebrew' (Genesis 14:13), and thus could not have been a Hebrew, himself. Melchizedek was not Abraham's descendent. His name means 'righteous, my king.' According to Pastor John F. MacArthur, Jr., Melchizedek was not an incarnation of the LORD God of Israel.[2] Melchizedek is the Old Testament spelling, Melchisedec is the New Testament spelling. Melchizedek was a pre-type of Adonai Yeshua, but was not Christ incarnate.

Believers in Jesus Christ, having faith that He is Elohim in the flesh and the only true Christ or Messiah, are members of the Melchisedecian priesthood by the indwelling *Paraclete* (Holy Ghost, Comforter), because Yeshua Himself is the high priest of the order of Melchisedec. Hebrews 7:11-14 states "If therefore perfection were by the Levitical priesthood, (for under it the people received the law,) what further need was there that another priest should rise after the order of Melchisedec, and not be called after the order of Aaron? For the priesthood being changed, there is made of necessity a change also of the law. For he of whom these things are spoken pertaineth to another tribe, of which no man gave attendance at the altar. For it is evident that our LORD sprang out of Juda; of which tribe Moses spake nothing concerning priesthood."

YHWH-indwelt Believers are priestly enough today, in the order of Melchisedec, to offer *ishaw* (the five offerings made by fire unto the LORD), but the only type of *ishaw* permissible, that doesn't offend the New Covenant, is the *minchaw!* The New Covenant lends grace to permit the canonic loophole that is the *minchaw*, for observance of the feasts of the LORD or for therapy.

Since Believers are indwelt by God the Father's Holy Spirit (Matthew 10:20), we are priests of God, of the order of Melchisedec, the same order as Jesus Christ. We are thereby sufficiently priestly to offer the *minchaw* of fire as an expression of faith in our Triune Yahweh.

Minchot should ideally be lovingly, gratefully offered and accompanied by scripture-based praise songs and prayers. *Minchot* of fire are neatly and handily offered using a propane torch and a steel pan. By this method, a *minchaw* of fire can be offered in as little as ten minutes with practice. The larger the pinched-off *minchaw* loaf, the more heating and longer time it takes to carbonize. Burnt *minchaw* ash should be disposed of, not left onsite. Care should be taken not to leave *minchaw* scent on local structures, to minimize sickening demonic retaliation. Such demonic backlash can be stressful, so don't be reckless in this righteousness.

Scent is a relevant aspect of the *minchaw* offering, so the implements should be kept clean. The *minchaw* grain offering is called "a sweet savor unto

Photo 1.6: Ingredients and equipment needed to offer a *minchaw* grain offering of fire. Counterclockwise from bottom left: a large flour-salt-and-olive-oil doughball, propane torch, igniter, frankincense, and steel pan.

the LORD." Just as Aaronic *cohenim* (Heb., priests) were commanded to wash their flesh and don clean linen garments to serve in the Tabernacle, a modern *minchaw* priest should probably shower and change into clean clothes prior to offering a *minchaw*, if he has strong body odor. Cleanliness is smart spiritual warfare. The *minchaw* grain offering's sweet-smelling frankincense symbolizes the radical purity due to God from each Believer. Radical faith is God's primary interest in human radicality.

The Diasporic *minchaw* grain offering is not sin to a modern day Believer, but may be marginally dangerous with regard to demonic retaliation, apart from grace, wisdom, and common sense. Satan does not like the ennobling *minchaw* grain offering; for it, angels desire to look into crannies of human hearts and souls.

Obstacles to Offering

If a man becomes ritually unclean through ejaculation, or dermal contact with a menstrous woman, unclean meats, shellfish, (or with a corpse, human bone, or grave), it would be better to for him to defer a day (or a week, depending) until he is again ritually clean, to offer a *minchaw*.

Levitical uncleanness that is contagious to other human bodies is called *primary uncleanness*. Levitical uncleanness that is not contagious is called *secondary uncleanness*. Ejaculation, menstruation, or dermal contact with a corpse, human bone or grave make a human primarily unclean: humans he or she then dermally touches, while so, become secondarily unclean until sunset. Dermal contact with a menstrous woman, unclean meats or an unclean animal's carcass makes a human secondarily, noncontagiously unclean. Levitical uncleanness can be cumulative. Levitical uncleanness invites ono-occlusion: Gr., *ono-* (name).

Mortality-derived primary uncleanness is contagious and lasts one week, with all subsequent dermal contactees during that week made secondarily unclean until the next sunset. Procreation-derived primary uncleanness produces temporary secondary uncleanness in others touched, but lasts itself (and in them) only until the following sunset. (Then, there is a return to psychical normalcy.) All dermal contactees until then are made secondarily unclean until the next sunset. Noncontagious, dietary secondary uncleanness also lasts until the next sunset after the *treif* (Heb., unclean meat) clears the gastrointestinal tract. " . . . Purging all meats." (Mark 7:19) During spans of Levitical uncleanness, shadows fall a bit denser than usual.

Seek ennobling benchmark holiness, by the grateful offering of a *minchaw* of fire, only while Levitically clean: it is possible at God's discretionary grace. He prefers *minchot* done in Levitical cleanliness. Without Triune Yahweh's overarching grace, it would be unwise for anyone to offer a *minchaw* in its complexity. For adults, benchmark holiness from offering a *minchat h'esh* brings on the feeling, 'You now have about twenty-four hours in which to completely grow up.' *Minchot* urge one to spiritually mature.

The transitory blessings seem to increase geometrically by *minchot* offered back-to-back on a series of consecutive days. Fourteen days was a Levitical priest's course of service. However, *minchot* of fire have been offered by at least one modern man upon at least fifty consecutive days, without adverse side effects. The ennobling clarion halo of temporary soul-brightness resulting from a *minchaw* heightens perceived trustability of God the Father, and thus blesses faith. Civilization relates to the set of societal forms which attest to the safety and authenticity of trust in Elohim the Father, the Abba of the *Logos*.

When is the best time of day to offer a *minchat h'esh*? In this author's opinion, just after sunset is the best time of day to offer a *minchaw* of fire. Sunset is the beginning of the new Biblical day. Most Levitical uncleanness ends at sunset. (Lev. 11:24, Lev. 15:16) "And the evening and the morning was the first day." (Genesis 1:5) Under the Toraic covenant, the preincarnate LORD Jesus commanded Moses to have the Levites offer at dusk and dawn, perpetually. The temporary blessing and grace for a *minchat h'esh* persist until the subsequent sunset. *Minchot* offered in direct sunlight during non-sabbath daylight hours are slightly more stressful than are those offered just after sunset or during pre-dawn grayness. If clouds obscure the western horizon, this author measures sunsets by published astronomical tables.

Due to the flesh nature, irritability, and over-familiarity toward the LORD could become concerns for a *minchaw* priest. While *minchot* make the body and soul to be holy for a while, they do not necessarily permanently improve the virtue of the heart or spirit regarding the LORD, nor do they remove sin. They elevate the LORD's expectations, and may make an offerer's complacency and satiety offensive to Him and set the inner man up for scourgings. *Minchot* urge their offerer(s) to expedite spiritual maturation.

In the words of David D. Burdick, "A man is righteous if God says he is righteous, not because of anything he does." Righteousness is imparted, not earned. *Minchot* are peak experiences of ennobling sanctity to remind us of hope in God, and are not identical with plateaus of personal victory. Even as Adonai (the preincarnate God the Son) angrily tried to kill Moses (Exodus 4:24, 25), until Moses' wife Zipporah circumcised their son with a sharp stone, the LORD Jesus may treat a *minchaw* priest with peremption, requiring that he sustain loving obedient submission toward Him.

Minchot transitorily raise the bar of the LORD's expectations for those ennobled and made holy by them. Consistent with this raised bar of expectations, Christ Jesus may relate peremptorily to a *minchaw* priest, out of sheer frustration at the man's stubborn flesh nature. Next to the need for scent control, possible irritation at the LORD's royal peremption is the greatest risk identified in offering *minchot*. It would not be proper for one to bristle in irritation against Elohim the Son, not even for any peremptory treatment. A *minchaw* priest regarded peremptorily by the LORD should not reply irritably, and should emphatically never blaspheme!

Exodus 23:2 commands "Do not join a crowd that intends to do evil. When you are on the witness stand, do not be swayed in your testimony by the opinion of the majority." (NLT) This prohibits sins of omission (of God's promptings), as well as sins of commission (of Satan's temptations, for inclusion in a corrupt group). Majority approval does not impart holiness. *Minchot* raise the bar of God's expectations for their offerers.

If a Believer, then, will not meet God's elevated expectations, he may be chastised by Him. If he cannot meet God's holiness-elevated expectations, then grace is required. *Minchot* raise the bar for the offerer's affection for Jesus Christ. Such essential affection may be difficult for a wounded spirit to achieve. "A wounded spirit, who can bear?" (Proverbs 18:14) Apart from the reality of New Covenant grace, the priestly rites of the *minchaw* would be inappropriate and unwise.

Offerings During The LORD's Feasts, Part II

A *minchaw* of fire is implicitly commanded, post-Golgotha, for each of the seven days of the feast of unleavened bread, Yom Teruah, Yom Kippur, and the eight days of Sukkot: seventeen feast-days of the LORD. "An offering made by fire unto the LORD" is commanded for each of those days in Leviticus 23. For firstfruits Sunday, the *minchawth bikkuwrim* (Heb., grain offering of firstfruits) is the proper offering made by fire unto the LORD.

For Passover, Leviticus 23:7,8 says, "In the first day ye shall have an holy convocation: ye shall do no servile work therein. But ye shall offer *an offering made by fire* unto the LORD seven days." (Emphasis added)

For Shavuot Sunday, the *lehem bikkuwrim* (bread of firstfruits) is the proper offering. A *minchat h'esh* (grain offering of fire) too, on this day, would fulfill Leviticus 23:18's commandment for a Feast of Weeks meat offering.

For Yom Teruah [Rosh haShannah], Leviticus 23:24,25 commands, "In the seventh month, in the first day of the month, shall ye have a sabbath, a memorial of blowing of trumpets, an holy convocation. Ye shall do no servile work therein: but *ye shall offer an offering made by fire unto the LORD.*" (Emphasis added)

For Yom Kippur, Leviticus 23:27 reads, "Also on the tenth day of this seventh month there shall be a day of atonement: it shall be an holy convocation unto you; and ye shall afflict your souls, and offer *an offering made by fire* unto the LORD." (Emphasis added)

For Sukkot, verse 36 reads, "Seven days ye shall offer *an offering made by fire unto the LORD*: on the eighth day shall be a holy convocation unto you; and ye shall offer *an offering made by fire* unto the LORD: it is a solemn assembly; and ye shall do no servile work therein." (Emphasis added.)

The minchaw is the only one of the five offerings made by fire unto the LORD that does not offer animal blood to improve the status of sin and, subsequent to Calvary, has uniquely not become abominable to God for this reason. The minchaw grain offering is the sole licit instrument for modern-day fulfillment of six completed-but-perpetual ceremonial-law commandments applicable to seventeen feast days of Yahweh each year, including the High Holy Days.

These commandments for an offering made by fire unto the LORD are found in Leviticus 23: 8, 14, 18, 25, 27, and 36. The *minchaw* is a theological loophole permitting these commandments to be kept, under the New Covenant.

The Torah about Firstfruits Day

How does a *minchaw* of firstfruits differ from a *minchaw* of fire, technically speaking? Leviticus 2:7-16 says:

v. 7—   "And if thy oblation be a meat offering [*minchaw*, or grain offering] baked in the frying pan, it shall be made of fine flour with oil.

v. 8—   "And thou shalt bring the meat offering that is made of these things unto the LORD: and when it is presented unto the priest he shall bring it unto the altar.

v. 9—   "And the priest shall take from the meat offering a memorial thereof, and shall burn it upon the altar: it is an offering made by fire, of a sweet savor unto the LORD.

v. 10—   "And that which is left of the meat offering shall be Aaron's and his sons': it is a thing most holy of the offerings of the LORD made by fire.

v. 11—   "No meat offering, which ye shall bring unto the LORD, shall be made with leaven: for ye shall burn no leaven nor any honey, in any offering of the LORD made by fire.

v. 12—   "As for the oblation of the firstfruits, ye shall offer them unto the LORD: but they shall not be burnt on the altar for a sweet savor.

v. 13—   "And every oblation of thy meat offering shalt thou season with salt; neither shalt thou suffer the salt of the covenant of thy God to be lacking from thy meat offering: with all thine offerings thou shalt offer salt.

v. 14—   "And if thou offer a meat offering of thy firstfruits unto the LORD, thou shalt offer for the meat offering of thy firstfruits green ears of corn dried by the fire, even corn beaten out of full ears."

v. 15—   "And thou shalt put oil upon it, and lay frankincense thereon: it is a meat offering.

v. 16—   "And the priest shall burn the memorial of it, part of the beaten corn thereof, and part of the oil thereof, with all the frankincense thereof: it is an offering made by fire unto the LORD."

The New American Standard Bible offers a slightly different translation of Lev. 2:7-16. "Now if your offering is a grain offering [*minchaw*] made in a pan, it shall be made of fine flour with oil. When you bring in the grain offering which is made of these things to the LORD [the LORD God of

Israel, God the *Son*], it shall be presented to the priest and he shall bring it to the altar. The priest then shall take up from the grain offering its memorial portion, and shall offer it up in smoke on the altar as an offering by fire of a soothing aroma to the LORD. The remainder of the grain offering belongs to Aaron and his sons: a thing most holy of the offerings to the LORD by fire. No grain offering, which you bring to the LORD, shall be made with leaven, for you shall not offer up in smoke any leaven or any honey as an offering by fire to the LORD. As an offering of first fruits you shall bring them to the LORD, but they shall not ascend for a soothing aroma on the altar. Every grain offering of yours, moreover, you shall season with salt, so that the salt of the covenant of your God shall not be lacking from your grain offering; with all your offerings you shall offer salt. Also if you bring a grain offering of early-ripened things to the LORD, you shall bring fresh heads of grain roasted in the fire, grits of new growth, for the grain offering of your early-ripened things. You shall then put oil on it and lay incense on it; it is a grain offering. The priest shall offer up in smoke its memorial portion, part of its grits and its oil with all its incense as an offering by fire to the LORD."

Authentic temple implements were, per the NKJV, made of silver, gold, and bronze, but the Torah does not forbid lesser materials. Various versions of the Bible differ on the bronze. The NKJV translates this Hebrew word *nechosheth* as bronze (chemically, $SnCu$: tin alloyed with copper); the KJV, as brass ($ZnCu$: zinc alloyed with copper); and, the TaNaK, as pure copper (Cu). This author thinks bronze is indeed the third, true temple metal. The three tabernacle metals were probably silver, gold and bronze. Bronze is heavier, harder, more corrosion-resistant, has a higher melting point, and was more-widely used by ancient cultures, than brass or copper. Bronze is a nobler metal than brass. More about metals in chapters three and seven.

The Grain Offering of Firstfruits

By interpretation of this passage, the yearly, early-spring *minchaw* of firstfruits, (Heb., *minchawth bikkuwrim*) consists of a (container holding a) small pile of barleycorns or wheat kernels (v. 14), salt (sodium chloride) (v. 13), olive oil, and fragrant frankincense (v. 15) that is then placed in a small pool of about one and a half quarts of red table wine (Lev 23:13c) poured out (upon the ground outdoors).

Regarding the second type of *minchaw* alluded to earlier, for the *minchawth bikkuwrim* (which is the grain offering of firstfruits (Gr., *aparche*)), a small memorial portion of the mixture of grain kernels, olive oil, salt, and all of the frankincense, is to be burned by the officiating priest (v. 16), but not on the altar (v. 12). Offerings of the LORD made by fire should never contain honey or leaven (v. 11).

The idea of *firstfruits* (Heb., *reysheit* and *bikkuwrim*; Gr., *aparche*) has four meanings in the Bible. Firstfruits is a Person, that of Yeshua of Nazareth. Firstfruits is a day, the Sunday after the only sabbath that always occurs during the weeklong feast of unleavened bread. Firstfruits is the second type of grain offering (Heb., *minchawth bikkuwrim*). And, firstfruits will be a group of missionaries, the hundred forty-four thousand missionary evangelists prophesied in Revelation 7:4-8, from twelve of the fourteen tribes of Israel. Fourteen, because Joseph produced Manasseh and Ephraim, but produced other children, as well, and his root retains its own latter-day tribal identity, per Revelation 7:8. The tribes of Dan and Ephraim are discluded from the firstfruits roster, probably for tribal idolatry in ancient times, when king Jereboam placed an idolatrous golden calf in those tribes' geographical areas. The hundred forty-four thousand firstfruits missionaries will need resurrection bodies, in order to "Follow the Lamb whithersoever He goeth." (Revelation 14:4)

The *minchaw*-variant early-spring grain offering of firstfruits (called *minchawth bikkuwrim* in Hebrew), consists of a measure of plump barley kernels (or hard winter wheat grains), olive oil, and salt, stirred in a vessel and garnished with a few chunks of fragrant frankincense. A container of this mixture is then placed in a poured-out puddle of about one-and-a-half quarts of red table wine or grape juice. A small portion of the grain-oil-and-salt mixture, containing all of the frankincense, is taken up and burnt to carbon. This may be done only one day per year, on firstfruits Sunday (Leviticus 23:11-14). It is to be perpetual, " . . . A statute forever throughout your generations in all your dwellings." (Leviticus 23:14,21)

This commandment applied to all the Israelites' dwellings, whether at the males' campsites at Jerusalem for a feast of the LORD, or at their inherited freeholds within the twelve tribal hinterlands. Since all the Israelite males were commanded to be in Jerusalem, other household members at the hinterland freeholds, such as Levitically-clean ladyfolk, may have been delegated to offer a *minchawth bikkuwrim*. It seems unlikely that there would have been enough Aaronic priests or Levites to service every single Hebrew household on the solitary day of firstfruits, thus these offerings may have been offered by laity.

Photo 1.7: Firstfruits day grain offering, seen on Firstfruits Sunday, April 24, 2011. This is *minchawth bikkuwrim*.

Firstfruits Offering Details

What may be called a man's dwelling? A place that is owned or rented residential real estate, also perhaps where one has spent a night since Nisan 1 of that year. (Nisan 1 occurs on the day of the first visible crescent moon in late March or early April. More about new moons in chapter two.) The sites of both hinterland tribal homesteads and Jerusalemic feast-day campsites as dwellings are implied. It may be that the males offered *minchawth bikkuwrim* for firstfruits, and *lehem bikkuwrim* for Shavuot, at Jerusalem, while kinfolk who stayed at home offered the same two offerings at their tribal freeholds, to fulfill "in all your dwellings."

If the Bible does not specifically prohibit an aspect of this offering, then it is worth exploring. *Minchawth bikkuwrim* (the grain offering of firstfruits) was designed to be offered by all heads of household, most of whom did not harbor a Levite to do it for them. Offerings of the *minchawth bikkuwrim* and *lehem bikkuwrim* are intended to be geography—(and possibly gender-) ubiquitous, to occur "in all your dwellings." If all males are to be in Jerusalem but some of their homes are in the hinterlands, who would have offered at all their dwellings? Levitically-clean ladyfolk, perhaps. The issue today is faith in Christ Jesus, demonstrable by Toraic ritual.

If the Bible does not specifically say a facet of the offering is prohibited, then it should be explored, lest oral-traditional fences warning of the Law unjustly encroach upon New Covenant freedom. The *minchaw*-variant firstfruits offering (Heb., *minchawth bikkuwrim*) was intended to be offered in all households, many of which did not harbor a Levite. The *minchat h'esh*, too, can be done by lay Believers in a manner acceptable to God.

The drink offering of the *minchaw* of firstfruits is a fourth part of a *hin* of wine. A *hin* is about six quarts.[3] Thus, a fourth part of a *hin* is about 1½ quarts or liters. It may be better (but not required) to offer a firstfruits *minchaw* outdoors, where the wine may soak into the soil, except in wicked neighborhoods where the lingering scents of the offering might, apart from grace, hold the attention of oppressive fallen cherubim and invite siege spiritual warfare. You can conceivably catch the wine in a large pan or tub, if demonic interest in the scent might cause stress.

According to God in the Torah, observant Hebrews are to fast from grain products on the day of firstfruits until the *minchawth* is offered, from the sunset beginning that Sunday after the one and only sabbath that always occurs during Passover week. If you would like to honor God with an unique gesture of righteousness, then you might set out a *minchawth bikkuwrim* in your backyard, this Passover week's firstfruits' Sunday. To gratefully invite the Father of lights to harmoniously and gloriously look down upon your home for a year, you might gently place a *minchaw* of firstfruits out in your backyard this firstfruits Sunday. Our God the Holy Tri-Unity (Heb., *Eloheynu ha Shiloosh haKodesh*) may remember you positively for it.

"And he shall wave the sheaf before the LORD, to be accepted for you: *on the morrow after the sabbath* the priest shall wave it." (Lev. 23:11, emphasis added) Firstfruits day is the Sunday immediately after Unleavened Bread's sabbath, which always occurs once during each year's Passover week. It is not either of the two, feast-bounding *miqra's* or holy convocations. Firstfruits day often coincides with Christianity's Easter Sunday.

Firstfruits Day Itself

The Torah calls the days of Pesach-1 and Pesach-7 *miqra's* (holy convocations), not *shabbats* (intermissions). Thus, for specificity, "the morrow after *the* sabbath" (Lev. 23:11, emphasis added) must refer to the Sunday after the one and only *sabbath* that always occurs during Passover week, as the one true day of firstfruits. Shavuot, the fiftieth day later, must also occur on a Sunday. Most rabbinic Judaism calculates firstfruits day and Shavuot incorrectly, from the first *miqra* during Passover's feast of unleavened bread.

For firstfruits day, Believers observing righteousness are to fast from grain products (Lev. 23:14), from the sundown that ends Passover-week's Saturday sabbath until the firstfruits day *minchawth bikkuwrim* is successfully offered. For those who touch a *minchaw* of fire, grace to the heart and soul lasts until the following sundown. For those who handle a yearly *minchawth* of firstfruits, the grace probably endures an entire year until the following Passover season, next spring.

Aptly, Jesus resurrected on a firstfruits Sunday, since He was the Firstfruits of the Spirit, offered for the holiness of all we who believe on Him. Romans 11:16 says, "For if the firstfruit is holy, the lump is also holy, and if the root be holy, so are the branches." As noted, the firstfruits *minchawth* offering in Toraic times blessed God for the grain harvest. Messiah Jesus, by cooperating with His crucifixion and allowing His lifeblood to be spilled to atone for sin, sanctifies all of mankind who believe in Him and His resurrection.

Parallels to Christ

Christ's blood ably does for mankind what *minchot* do not and were never intended to do: atone for sin. His blood atoned for mankind's sin, something God never intended *minchot* to do, since they are bloodless. Because God never intended *minchot* to atone for men's sins, they don't detract from Jesus of Nazareth's perfect blood atonement and are not yet obsolete. *Minchot* are offerings to God that do not compete with the fully-completed, awesome blood-atonement of the LORD Jesus, who is Adonai the Christ.

The bread of firstfruits (Heb., *lehem bikkuwrim*) is for Shavuot (in Leviticus 23:15-21). This lunar-calendar anniversary of Law-giving (traditionally) and of Pentecost, which occurs on the fiftieth day after the Sunday of firstfruits, obliges a ceremony that calls for loaves of leavened bread as a new grain offering. What is sought for the day of Shavuot are two new leavened loaves of bread. The two loaves are to be brought out of one's house, but are not specifically commanded to be made therein. One might conceivably purchase two new loaves, made recently somewhere else, and bring them into, then out of, one's dwelling in order to present them to the LORD, on Shavuot Sunday.

The offering of ceremonial *minchaw* of firstfruits points to Messiah Jesus in both the Old and New Testaments. The Torah, in Leviticus 23:14c, commands *minchot* with the exact same stringent language used to command observance of Yom Kippur. I Corinthians 15:20 reads, "But now is Christ risen from the dead, and become the firstfruits [Gr., *aparche*] of them that slept." Animal flesh and blood are no longer acceptable to God, as a sin sacrifice, because Yeshua haMashiach atoned more perfectly with his sinless blood. Messiah Yeshua resurrected from the dead on a firstfruits Sunday, the particular day after an only specific sabbath, such that always occurs during Passover's week of the feast of unleavened bread. Firstfruits Sunday's offerings bless God in anticipation of the grain crop, but Yeshua the Firstfruit blesses God for His harvest of the spirits of just men made perfect.

Cautions

The grain offering of fire (*minchat h'esh*), the grain offering of firstfruits (*minchawth bikkuwrim*), and the bread of firstfruits (*lehem bikkuwrim*) are three pivotal but widely overlooked means for expressing faith in our narrowly-true, set-apart, Triune, Hebrew-Christian God. Leviticus 23:14

Photo 1.8: Firstfruits day grain offering, post-burning of memorial portion, as seen on Firstfruits Sunday, April 24, 2011: a completed *minchawth bikkuwrim.*

commands the firstfruits *minchaw* with the exact same severe wording used in Lev. 23:31 to mandate fasting and rest upon Yom Kippur.

The limitations of the *minchaw* are illustrated by the fact that the word for Cain's offering of "the fruit of the ground" (Genesis 4:3) is *minchaw*. Cain's offering was similar to some sort of *minchaw*. No *minchaw* can compare to Christ Jesus' perfect blood atonement. Even as God rejected Cain's offering, He will reject any human offering not predicated upon faith in Messiah Yeshua's obedient death and glorious resurrection. The *minchaw* grain offering is a theological loophole left in place by God, so that Leviticus 23: 8, 14, 18, 25, 27, and 36 may be fulfilled, even under the New Covenant.

A *minchaw* loaf is not identical with shewbread. "Both for the shewbread and for the fine flour for meat offering, . . ." (I Chronicles 23:29) Shewbread and *minchot* are mentioned as distinct from each other.

The *minchaw* or grain offering has not been widely done in recent history, possibly because Orthodox Jewry has forgotten the *minchaw* doctrine in the Torah: Yahwehism obliges it, Christianity permits it without requirement, but Judaism has lost it in the Talmud.

Daniel 9:27 foretold the cessation of the Jewish national *minchaw*: ". . . In the midst of the week he shall cause the sacrifice and oblation [*minchaw*] to cease . . ." Nevertheless, the individual or household *minchaw* obliged for the feasts of the LORD, in Leviticus 23: 8, 14, 18, 25, 27, and 36, remains neither forbidden nor mandatory.

How long may a man minister, via offering *minchat h'esh*? In Biblical times during the Levitical priesthood, Aaron ministered into his old age, until the time of his death. (Numbers 20:22-29) Levites, by contrast, were commanded to serve only between ages 30 and 50. The Levites were like the porters and technicians of the Tabernacle, while the Aaronic priests directly interfaced with the LORD God of Israel, who was normatively the preincarnate Christ Jesus. Christians and Believing Jews are priests of the Melchizedekian order, not the Levitical order.

Summary

Now, Messiah Yeshua's ultimate blood atonement for sin eclipsed all Levitical offerings that involve animal flesh and blood to atone for sin of any sort, rendering them obsolete and abominable. No offering made by fire unto the LORD that involves animal blood to improve the status of sin will any longer find acceptance with God. Hebrews 10:17,18 states, "And their sins and iniquities I will remember no more. Now where remission of these is, *there is no more offering for sin.*" (Emphasis added) Forgiveness of sin is now by grace through faith in Christ Jesus and His resurrection. The bloodless *minchaw* grain offering represents the only one of the five types of 'offerings made by fire' (*ishaw*) unto the LORD that was uniquely not rendered obsolete by Messiah Jesus' superior atonement, since *minchot* were never designed to atone for sin. The other four types of *ishaw* all utilize new sacrificial blood to improve the status of sin. A *minchaw* is not a sin offering and cannot insinuate replication of Calvary. *Blood-free minchot may constitute the only offerings made by fire unto holy Y'howah that He will still accept for their Toraically-intended purposes, subsequent to Yeshua of Nazareth's crucifixion on Golgatha.* Only the blood-free *minchaw* grain offering can fulfill both six perpetual Toraic commandments (to observe the feasts of the LORD with an offering made by fire unto Him) and the New Covenant (to not ritually replicate Christ Jesus' blood atonement). Forgiveness of sin is predicated upon factual shedding of blood (Levitical animals' or Christ Jesus'), combined with faith in Triune Yahweh. Amongst *ishaw*, factual *minchot* will probably continue to uniquely find acceptance as the only Levitical offerings made by fire unto Elohim permissible by God for their narrow Toraically-intended purposes, throughout Messiah Yeshua's entire millennial kingdom. Modern-day Diasporic grain offerings find permissibility in New Covenant grace wherever God's name is present.

Chapter 1 notes:

[1]   Alfred J. Kolatch. *The Jewish Book of Why?* Middle Village, NY: Jonathan David Publishers, 1981, 148.
[2]   John F. MacArthur, Jr. *Hebrews.* Nashville: Thomas Nelson, 2007, 53.
[3]   Henry H. Halley. *Halley's Bible Handbook.* Grand Rapids: Zondervan, 1965, 35.

Chapter 2

Righteousness Recapitulated

The Torah may be classified into the civil law, moral law, and ceremonial law. The civil law does not apply to the church, since she is not a nation, but exists within sovereign national societies. The moral law (the Ten Commandments plus the commandments reiterated or first given in the New Testament) is yet binding upon all mankind. The ceremonial law and its requirements were technically fulfilled in Christ Jesus and His death and resurrection. The LORD Jesus' fulfillment of the Torah allows God the Father to selectively credit His perfect righteousness to Believers as grace. Adonai Yeshua observed His lifelong perfect righteousness with full comprehension that His Father would subsequently credit it to us, who are completely unworthy of Him.

While only the moral law is still binding, optional observance of ceremonial law makes true faith by sound doctrine perceivably directed only toward set-apart YHWH, and secondarily acceptable to modern Israeli's. Toraic righteousness' stabilizing primitive godliness catalyzes personal evangelism. If the ceremonial law is ever reinstated, the *minchaw*, exegeted in chapter one, will be the only permissible offering made by fire unto the LORD. The *minchaw* uniquely, among the five types of Levitical offerings made by fire, does not employ animal blood to try to improve the status of sin. Every violation of Torah has some consequence, varying from extremely minor to terribly major, depending upon the immediacy of God's grace.

If you observe due moral- and ceremonial-law righteousness, you may find John Bunyan's "River of Death" (when it's your time to cross it) to be only ankle deep for you. However, if commendable moral- and ceremonial-law righteousness is the lifelong sum of your response to Messiah Jesus' call to you, then you may wade into the River of Death without first having lived,

RIGHTEOUSNESS RECAPITULATED

but awaken with chagrin to find that you've missed the first resurrection. (Revelation 20:6) Toraic observance alone doesn't admit anyone to the kingdom of heaven. However, "Whatsoever a man soweth, that shall he also reap." (Galatians 6:7)

Righteousness originates either from Jesus-by-faith, oneself-by-Torah-observance, or vanity-by-imagination. God prefers the Jesus type, with men's Toraic earned righteousness running distant second. Toraic earned righteousness, distinct from righteousness by faith in Jesus Christ, ought be done in responsive gratitude to Yahweh, not ambition for spiritual advancement. It should imply neither self-justification (even righteous men need Christ Jesus) nor apostate Judaizing (the insinuation that God insists all Believers rotely observe the Law as precondition to relationship with Him, their consciences notwithstanding).

The Ten Commandments comprise part of the yet-binding moral law. The commandments given or reiterated in the New Testament also apply to modern man. But, Jesus Christ technically fulfilled the ceremonial Torah, via His life, death, and resurrection, as far as compulsion or obligation to observe it goes. Jesus' technical fulfillment of the ceremonial Torah allows God the Father to credit His comprehensive righteousness to any man He wills, at any time, for any reason: Jewish or Gentile, righteous or unjust—it's what He wills that is determinant. Jesus' righteousness technically satisfied God the Father's requirements for the human fraction of His creation. True faith in 'Jesus Christ, resurrected' suffices to save! David D. Burdick correctly stated, "Toraic righteousness should be done gratefully, not ambitiously." All righteousness is God-imparted, not automatically or permanently accrued for men's earning of it, apart from His will.

Toraic Background

One may keep every one of the 613 laws of the Torah yet still fall short of God's high standard. This is because Messiah Jesus, whose inner man is revealed in the apostle Paul's sound doctrine, set a higher standard of heart and behavior than that required by the Torah. In Paul's sound doctrine (Galatians 5:19-21), God forbids gratuitous sexual uncleanness (ejaculation) and lasciviousness (lewdness). This exceeds the comparable Toraic commandments (Leviticus 18:7-19), since it applies to all relationships, not merely familial ones. Paul's sound doctrine forbids *all*

RITE FOR THE TIMES

illicit lust, not merely lust involving near relatives of the opposite sex, as does the Torah.

The dispensation of law will not be exactly repeated during Christ's millennial kingdom dispensation, in which the Gospel and Pauline sound doctrine to the inner man will be more binding upon mankind than either the ceremonial or civil Torah. History is linear. Messiah Jesus' millennial kingdom will not be an exact repetition of ancient Israel! Sound doctrine and Torah observance will coexist in Christ's millennial civilization.

Toraic righteousness makes a great corrective to the liberal emergent church, if such righteousness is itself subject to Pauline sound doctrine. Toraic righteousness appeals to the set-apart, holy, narrowly-true Spirit who is Triune Yahweh of the Bible, about whom the liberal emergent church and the Talmudists are confused. Toraic righteousness orients one toward Y'howah Elohim, but He is not very impressed by it unless it's accompanied by Christlike obedience to the truth of the Father in heaven. Paul's sound doctrine countered the Phariseeism of his day, addresses rampant Talmudism in modern times, and modulates the *chutzpah* that so easily proceeds from Toraic self-earned righteousness. Righteousness calms and emboldens.

The Torah is to pro-evangelistic, earned, self-righteousness, as the Talmud is to rabbinic Judaism, as religious liberalism is to the emergent church. Paul's sound doctrine can improve all three systems. Apostasy primarily offends sound doctrine, but apostasy secondarily offends the Torah. Torah observance is not sin but, in the twenty-first century, it must advance evangelism in order to truly accomplish God's will for it. In the words of David D. Burdick, "The New Testament is the Old, circumcised." God the Father sacrificed His firstborn Son to make atonement ("covering") for millennia of Believers. Jesus Christ obeyed His Father to the death, by cooperating with His murderers. "Thanks be to God, for His unspeakable gift." (2 Corinthians 9:15) Yeshua of Nazareth obeyed His Father lifelong, to the death, to benefit us who don't deserve Him.

The essence of righteousness is to love God and your neighbor as yourself. But, benefits exist for those willing to express their faith through radical Toraic earned righteousness. Faith involves believing the Word of God and trusting Him according to the Bible, but *faith shown by works of the Law is harder to misinterpret than faith spoken of but never acted upon.*

Table 2.1: Categories of relationship with God.

Conscientious obedience to the truth of God the Father	3
Faith, that Jesus is YHWH and that He resurrected	2
Works of the Law (Toraic earned righteousness)	1
Works of tradition (Talmudist or romish; submission to authority)	0

The *righteousness-grace controversy* alluded to in the book of James reflects contention over full, co-equal, fraternal acceptance, of those who show their faith only by words compared to those who showed their faith by both words of truth and deeds of Torah. "Yea, a man may say, Thou hast faith, and I have works: show me thy faith without thy works, and I will show thee my faith by my works." (James 2: 18) "Be ye doers of the Word, and not hearers only." (James 1:22) "If ye love Me, keep My commandments." (John 14:15) The whole theme of the book of First John is that your true saving faith should be accompanied by hatred of your own sin, one antithesis of which is faith expressed as righteousness. Carnal-mind oriented Toraic earned righteousness relates to God's justice upon creation. The stricter the Toraic commandment, the greater the temptation to religious pride in an observer comparing himself to those who fulfill the Law merely by faith.

Basic Biblical morality should be a prerequisite to congregational membership and leadership, but not to attendance. Sympathy with human traditions or with Christian Zionism should not be prerequisites to attendance. Radical Toraic earned righteousness plus a personal testimony can distinguish sincere students of the WORD from agents of human tradition, be they romish or Talmudist. "And the dragon was wroth with the woman, and went to make war with the remnant of her seed, *which keep the commandments of God, and have the testimony of Jesus Christ.*" (Revelation 12:17, emphasis added) Evangelism of the Gospel combined with radical Toraic earned righteousness is hated by Satan, but has special significance to Triune Yahweh.

Nowhere does the Bible teach that God the Son loves all creatures equally, and nowhere are we His people commanded to love all others equally, feigning oblivion to differences between persons. Despite that the Torah was completed in Christ Jesus and is since mostly non-compulsory, God promised to bless righteousness (Deuteronomy 28:1-14), and never rescinded His promises. The moral law (the Ten Commandments plus the commandments first given or reiterated in the New Testament) is the basis for God's ongoing covenant with the Church and Israel. The Toraic carnal-mind covenant of ceremonial behaviors and ritual conscience has been supplanted by the new spiritual-mind covenant of relationship with Elohim the Father's Holy Spirit (Matthew 10:20), through Christ Jesus. Relational conscience mostly supplants ritual conscience. Ritual conscience is to the letter of the Law, as relational conscience is to the Spirit of the Law.

The Torah's Originator

In Psalm 146:8, the psalmist wrote, "The LORD loves the righteous." If you want to bless God and have expectation for a type of grace, believe in Jesus Christ resurrected, and demonstrate your faith by low-key righteousness. Children perceive flagrant unrighteousness as inauthentic, as concessions to the occulted groupthink mentality of the world. "And hereby we do know that we know him, if we keep his commandments. He that saith, I know him, and keepeth not his commandments, is a liar, and the truth is not in him." (I John 2:3-4)

The "He" we are to love is the LORD God of Israel, who, between the Exodus plagues and the immaculate conception, was normatively identical with the preincarnate God the Son. However, " . . . By grace are ye saved through faith; and that not of yourselves: it is a gift of God: Not of works, lest any man should boast." (Ephesians 2:8-9) Christ Jesus tends to dislike men's attempts to transact business with Him. He often spurns mutual obligations implicit to transaction, but demands obedience to His Father and deserves unilateral submission to Himself.

What obligates you to God the Father? For starters, your name does.

> "Your name.
> It came from your Father,
> T'was the best He had to give.
> So it's yours for you to cherish,
> As long as you may live.
> If you lose the watch he gave you,
> It can always be replaced,
> But a black mark on your name, son,
> Can never be erased.
> It was clean the day you took it,
> And a worthy name to bear.
> When I got it from my Daddy,
> There was no dishonor there.
> So make sure you guard it wisely.
> After all is said and done,
> You'll be glad your name is spotless,
> When you give it to your son."[1]

At great cost to the Triune Godhead, Christ Jesus can ameliorate black marks against one's name. Grace is costly, not cheap.[2] Can sound doctrine, evangelism, worship, and righteousness advance the hope which one holds in this life? Yes, by lifting a person's heart and conscience upward toward our Father in heaven, as on sabbath days.

Righteousness Defined

Toraic earned righteousness, distinct from righteousness by faith in Christ Jesus, instills an emboldening radical godliness. Torah observance foments fundamental recklessness for the WORD of God. Doctrinal reformation and revival should accompany this primitive godliness becoming widespread. Does ignoring sound doctrine, evangelism, and righteousness result in oppression and a downward spiral? "Where the Spirit of the LORD is, there is liberty." (1 Corinthians 2:2) This word "LORD" refers to YHWH the WORD of God, specifically to Elohim the Son.

The very basics of righteousness are to love the LORD God of Israel (Yahweh the Son, the preincarnate Jesus of Nazareth), love your neighbor, believe Yeshua of Nazareth is Elohim born flesh (the true Messiah), and that God resurrected Him from the dead. The New Birth is by faith and identity in Christ. Similarly, Toraic righteousness is a set of ceremonial behaviors that are rewarded with steadiness and calmness. "The work of righteousness shall be peace, and the effect of righteousness quietness and assurance forever." (Isaiah 32:17)

If radical Toraic earned righteousness intensifies algorithmic psychomotor earthiness, it contributes to psychological inertia, while steadying the soul. This is not categorically bad, but it may inculcate reliance upon the habitual, at costs to spontaneity and creativity.

Toraic earned righteousness [Heb., *tzedakah*] is observance of God's commandments beginning with "Love the LORD your God with all your heart, soul and strength," "Love your neighbor as yourself," the 10-Commandment Moral Law, plus others. Moses wrote, in Deut. 6:25 as a postscript to the Ten Commandments, "It shall be our righteousness, if we observe to do all these commandments before the LORD your God, as He hath commanded us." The LORD God of Israel was normatively the preincarnate Jesus of Nazareth!

Rigorous Torah observance is theologically conservative relative to Talmudism, but it is theologically liberal relative to Paul's sound doctrine. That is to say, compared to Talmudism, zealous Torah observance is theologically conservative; but compared to personable New Covenant sound doctrine, Toraic righteousness is theologically liberal but psychologically radical.

The LORD Jesus would "do righteousness" as scientifically as possible, were He to walk upon earth in the 21st century. His intellect surpasses all firmamental judicial degrees, and all fundamental chemical doctorates, ever conferred.

God's Commandments

Righteousness tends to bring the peace of shalom, but there is a higher purer peace available, from the inner man's conscientious obedience to the truth and will of God the Father in heaven, according to Christ Jesus' executorship with the indwelling Holy Ghost. "The testimony of Jesus is the spirit of prophecy." (Rev. 19:10c) The face-brightening door to this higher purer obedience opens with evangelism of the Gospel. Evangelism is, quite literally, ascent (Heb., *aliyah*). Evangelism is the best *mitzvah* (Heb., good deed).

Although many Christians suffer ignorance of it, the Hebrew word *yud hay waw hay* (YHWH) is God's terrible, holy, beloved *Name above all names.* Written throughout this text mostly as *Yahweh* (but phonetically pronounced *Y'howah*), this Word, His personal name, was translated *LORD* throughout most of the Old Testament, to indicate the LORD God of Israel. Rabbinic scribes coded this Word as Adonai (meaning 'Lord'), so that readers could not learn to pronounce it in vain. This translational device drew the honorific LORD upon Yeshua of Nazareth, the LORD Jesus, who is Elohim the Son and Adonai the Christ. The LORD God of Israel became the LORD Jesus Christ. His holy personal name is never to be spoken in vain vows, nor at all blasphemously. The Hebraeo-Christian *YHWH-the-Son* is the true living WORD of God, whereas the pantheistic-Hindu *AUM* is a satanic counterfeit of the WORD.

God listens to men's hearts on the seventh-day Saturday sabbath, then binds back oppressive evil spirits based on what He hears, making first-day Sundays to be especially peaceful as a consequence. He does not require human participation to do this, but personal sabbatic stillness facilitates His process. God sanctifies seventh-day Saturdays. Toraic earned righteousness assists with cognition, and emboldens evangelism if one loves to share the Good News. Righteous observance applies at least the Ten Commandments, found in Exodus 20 and Deuteronomy 5, plus a few others. There are a total of 613 commandments in the Torah, 248 positive and 365 negative, but the essence are as follows.

Deuteronomy 5:7—"I AM the LORD thy God. Thou shalt have none other gods [angels or demons] before me." *The speaker is the LORD God of Israel, normatively identical with the preincarnate Jesus of Nazareth (God the Son).*

Deuteronomy 5:8-10—"Thou shalt not make unto thee any graven image or any likeness of anything that is in heaven above, or that is in the earth beneath, or that is in the waters beneath the earth: Thou shalt not bow down thyself unto them, nor serve them: for I, the LORD thy God, am a jealous God, visiting the iniquity of the fathers upon the children unto the third and fourth generation of them that hate me, and showing mercy unto thousands of them that love me and keep my commandments." That is to say, No religious statues or figurines. Inference is that evil spirits set up shop in or around religious statuary. This commandment is omitted from the Vatican's Vulgate Bible, but is present in the original Hebrew. The Vatican unblushingly admits to changing or imposing thousands of religious laws,[3] replacing God's ways with traditions of men. Roman Catholicism is comparable, in this sense, to Talmudism.

Deuteronomy 5:11—"Thou shalt not take the name of the LORD thy God in vain, for the LORD will not hold him guiltless who taketh His name in vain." That is, Don't vow idly, or blaspheme, using the holy name of Y'howah, or that of *Jesus Christ.* Don't blaspheme God the Holy Spirit! "The LORD thy God" was the Angel called Adonai, and He became Jesus of Nazareth. His name is holy.

Deuteronomy 5:12-15—"Keep the sabbath day to sanctify it, as the LORD thy God hath commanded thee. Six days thou shalt labor, and do all thy work: But the seventh day is the sabbath of the LORD thy God: in it thou shalt not do any work, thou, nor thy son, nor thy daughter, nor thy manservant, nor thy maidservant, nor thine ox, nor thine ass, nor any of thy cattle, nor thy stranger that is within thy gates; that thy manservant and thy maidservant may rest as well as thou. And remember that thou wast a servant in the land of Egypt, and that the LORD thy God brought thee out thence through a mighty hand and by a stretched out arm. For in six days God made all that is in heaven and earth, and rested on the seventh day." Regardless of when you worship, Saturday rest is a good idea! Spirited fun is not work: "The sabbath is made for man, and not man for the sabbath." (Mark 2:27) God listens to living persons' spiritual hearts on the Saturday sabbath. From what He hears, He decides how to have mercy. He binds back evil spirits during the Saturday sabbath, then uses the cleared atmosphere of Sunday mornings to reason with our educated minds. The Bible says God sanctifies the *seventh* day, not merely any random weekday of rest.

Deuteronomy 5:16—"Honor your father and mother, as the LORD thy God has commanded you, that thy days may be prolonged, and that it may go well with you, in the land which the LORD thy God giveth you." That is to say, don't rebel against parental authority if you can possibly avoid it. Try to work with their system, even if they don't seem to be particularly godly, just, or excellent. God the Father can forgive you of parental sins, too, that otherwise might weigh down your heart. If they neglect faith and righteousness, don't you.

Deuteronomy 5:17—"Do not murder."

Deuteronomy 5:18—"Do not commit adultery." Adultery is fornication across the vows of marriage. Fornication (copulation outside of marriage) of any sort would bode disastrously evil consequences.

Deuteronomy 5:19—"Do not steal."

Deuteronomy 5:20—"Do not bear false witness." That is to say, do not lie.

Deuteronomy 5:21—"Do not covet." That is to say, do not enviously crave for yourself goods that the Father of lights in His infinite wisdom has bestowed upon your fellows. This commandment is split into two commandments in the Vatican's Vulgate Bible, to arrive at the correct total of ten, considering that the Vatican deleted from the Vulgate Latin translation the second commandment, which forbids religious statuary.

Deuteronomy 6:4,5—"Hear, O Israel: *The LORD thy God* is one LORD: Thou shalt love the LORD thy God with all thine heart, and with all thy soul, and with all thy might." (Emphasis added) This is the *Shema.* 'The

LORD thy God' during the days of the TaNaK (the Old Testament) was normatively the preincarnate God the Son, not all three Persons of Triune Elohim. The other two Persons of the Godhead, the Father and the Holy Ghost, were first widely revealed to civilization by Jesus of Nazareth's earthly ministry. Elohim the Son is indivisible.

The sense of the Shema is '*Elohim ha Beyn echad:*' the LORD God of Israel (God the Son) is one indivisible spiritual Person of three, and the holy Tri-Unity is one Spirit. The Angel of Yah is indivisible, even as Jesus' coat was gambled for, not ripped into parts, at Golgotha. The other two Persons of the Godhead were first broadly revealed by Jesus of Nazareth's personal ministry, which sparked extensive new revelation about the Godhead. "Which in other ages was not made known unto the sons of men, as it is now revealed unto his holy apostles and prophets by the Spirit." (Ephesians 3:5)

Leviticus 19:18 and Matthew 19:19—"Love your neighbor as yourself." Jesus of Nazareth promoted this ancillary Toraic commandment to much higher status as the second greatest commandment, as He uniquely has the authority to do. *Jesus' shift of emphasis represents a distinct change in God's provisions for His peoples, between the Old and New Covenants, from mostly-outer behavioral to mostly-inner relational acknowledgments of Him.*

Acts 15:20—The Jerusalem elders of the faith, in the first century, added "Abstain from pollutions of idols [religious statuary], and from fornication [sex outside of marriage], and from things strangled [resulting in meat retaining blood], and from blood [drunk in various pagan rituals]." These were appended to the Moral Law in response to the first-century spiritual environment.

I Thessalonians 4:11—Paul the apostle added, "Work with your own hands, as we have commanded you." The humble lowly social status of blue-collar work may inoculate against the pride of life. Skillful, callusing use of the hands disciplines use of the tongue, and confirms some fundamental concepts of language. That said, cleanliness and literacy are, truly, right up there next to godliness; both are difficult to sustain in hard manual labor. Manual trades, as tentmaker-support for controversial ministries, is intrinsically very difficult, due to the earthiness common to both sweaty manual labor and (mostly fallen) cherubim. Sweaty body odor profiles a workman to cherubim, most of which are fallen.

Exodus 23:2—"Do not join a crowd that intends to do evil. When you are on the witness stand, do not be swayed in your testimony by the opinion of the majority." (NLT). Apropos commandment for these days, when many are told that majority (read, media) approval of an idea, behavior, or policy means that it cannot be wrong. The logical fallacy *argumentum ad populum* has this antithesis in Biblical law. We are not to allow a majority to sway us to follow them into evil saying or doing. We are not to allow stage fright to deviate us from true judgment or testimony. Majority opinion does not sanctify.

God the Son, who is Adonai the Christ, rarely restores grace to a backslidden Believer on the basis of his positive 'righteousness : sin ratio,' but God the Father may notice such a man's righteous works and monitor his soul and progress, with the intention of having mercy upon him. "Whatsoever a man soweth, that shall he also reap." (Galatians 6:7)

Transgression?

The penalty for sin is worse sin, and yet greater difficulty obeying Jesus Christ. Someone once said, "Sin takes you farther than you want to go. Sin costs you more than you want to pay. Sin keeps you longer than you want to stay." Compared to the dreadful consequences of sin, God, His call, and His ways are a sweet, light, pleasant yoke to bear. Satan is not appeased by one's submission or by one's fear, only by worse and worse sin, unto complete destruction of one's conscience, heart, spirit, soul, and body. "Resist the devil, and he will flee from you." (James 4:7b) "Where the Spirit of the LORD is, there is liberty." (2 Corinthians 3:17b)

Toraic righteousness and its beneficial primitive godliness blesses Christians as well as Jews. It does not discriminate racially. Jesus of Nazareth said in John 14:15, "If you love Me, keep My commandments." Again, in Matthew 5:20, He said, "Except your righteousness shall exceed the righteousness of the scribes and Pharisees [predecessors of the rabbis, who are often pious men], you shall in no case enter into the kingdom of heaven." If you choose to sin, then your heart and soul may become degradingly submitted to a root (implying, to a cherub) of sin.

Dispensational antinomianism has led to fallacious traditions of men, just as did the rabbinic Oral Law. Loving intellectual assent to "Jesus is YHWH" brings *justification* unto resurrection hope, but without hatred of sin and a transformed life, does not assure *sanctification* unto freedom of heart and soul in this life, or *glorification* of private spirit and quickening resurrection unto eternal life. Heart belief plus vocal profession of faith justifies, per Romans 10:9,10. Faith lived out tends to sanctify. Should God reward diligence and indolence equally? For true Believers, Messiah Jesus' sacrificial death offsets the penalty for sin (eternal damnation) and many of the consequences of sin (chastenings to repent). Justification frees one from sin's penalty (eternal damnation); sanctification, from sin's power; glorification, from sin's very presence.

The apostle Paul found grace to make saving faith in Christ sufficient for salvation of Gentiles and of Jews. Due to this grace, the promised blessings for Old Covenant righteousness were subjugated to relationship with God the Father, instead of becoming automatic rewards for religious transactions. However, to say that because of grace we should make no pretense of righteousness would be a shameful breach of filial opportunity.

The ceremonial Torah is technically fulfilled in Christ Jesus, but "Whatsoever a man soweth, that shall he also reap." (Galatians 6:7) In the words of the respected Christian pastor, John MacArthur, "Faith minus works equals zero!" *These works may be purely relational, or they may be structured by Torah. Neither is wrong, but evangelism is right.*

Regarding righteousness, the primary tension in the Bible is between Yahweh and sin. This primary tension argues for set-apartness from the heathen by faith in Yahweh confirmed by sabbath rests and other righteous deeds. The secondary Biblical tension is between Jesus of Nazareth and the scribes and Pharisees. They had turned Toraic earned righteousness into self-justification, and a thing of pride, pomp, and envy, where the LORD Jesus wanted it to be for man, unto Himself in love. The tertiary tension in the Bible regarding righteousness is between the apostle Paul and the Judaizers of his day. Paul wanted Jesus' view of Toraic righteousness, as an expression of grateful faith, while the Judaizers tried to make Toraic earned righteousness into a thing of pride, of ethnicity, of 'the flesh,' of self-justification, and a precondition to salvation. And, the quartenary Biblical tension is between children of God and adults who are ruled by an earthy, radical 'old man' sin nature. (Ephesians 4:22, Colossians 3:9)

"Now the end of the commandment is charity." (I Tim. 1:5). The end of charity is evangelism. Toraic earned righteousness, distinct from righteousness-by-faith in Jesus Christ, causes a helpful primitive godliness.

This must benefit from Pauline sound doctrine to reveal the truth of Christ Jesus' inner man and avoid subsumation into Talmudism. Truth is enlarged by evangelism, if tradition will condescend to allow it.

Tradition and 'the flesh' are inter-related. In this new, 3rd millennial dispensation, the end of charity is evangelism. Levitical uncleanness (from unclean meats, ejaculation, menses, etc.) hinders evangelistic projection, to another human being, of God the Father-given conscientious brightness, which imparts freeing upward cognitive hope.

Christian-Jewish Contrast

True Christianity is to conscience and greatness, as rabbinic Judaism is to norming and submission. This requires decisions by Believing Jews. The word 'Judah' means *praiser*, while 'Christian' means *little Christ*. Praise is fine, but according to the Bible, we are saved by doing the will of the Father in heaven. (Matthew 12:48) In so doing we affirm filial conscience. The LORD God psychospatially (soul-atmospherically) inhabits the praises of Israel (Psalms 22:3), but praise is not exactly the same as true saving faith. Judaism implies, 'If you cannot authorize yourself, then you should submit to authority.' Christianity implies, 'If you cannot forgive your own sin and guilt, then you need a personal Savior.' The idea of 'Messiah' is to the Jewish nation, as 'personal Savior' is to Protestant exceptionalism. Obedience is preferable to submission, even as proactively conscientious decisions are less stressful than acute bendings of will. Corporate salvation is groupthinking myth.

One may Believe all he wants, but unless he is inwardly like a little Christ (a Christian) he's hopeless. Despite that some Messianics claim Paul's Christianity does not apply to Jews, the Father in heaven expects Christian charity, civility, meekness, unselfishness and obedience to His *Logos* until Christ Jesus returns and dons the crown of Yeshua haMashiach. Until then, Believers are to speak, decide and behave toward men more like Messiah ben Joseph than like Messiah ben David. More like the suffering servant than the conquering Messiah. We are to be Christlike and self-controlled, not full of ourselves in exuberant *chutzpah*, lest our consciences fail to discern and communicate the mind of our earnest Father in heaven. Faith in Yeshua is a high calling, more than a mundane business. Having an attitude cannot satisfy the requirement for having a conscience.

Evangelistic Ascents

An instance of evangelism of the gospel momentarily explains the evangelist to God the Father, because Jesus of Nazareth said, "Whosoever therefore shall confess me before men, him will I confess also before my Father which is in heaven. But whosoever shall deny me before men, him will I also deny before my Father which is in heaven." (Matthew 10:32-33) A word or gesture of evangelism invites instant welcome explanation of oneself and one's complexities to God the Father. Evangelism invites instantaneous explanation of oneself to the holy earnest heavenly Father of Adonai the Christ. Words of evangelism bring 'ascent' upon the heart and soul. Evangelism is true *aliyah* (Heb., a returning ascent (as though to the Land of Israel)). Evangelism is *aliyah*-at-hand. Evangelistic ascent invites explanation of oneself from the living WORD, to His Father. "Also I say unto you, Whosoever shall confess me before men, him shall the Son of man also confess before the angels of God . . ." (Luke 12:8)

Sabbath Days

The word *sabbath* means *rest* and *intermission*. It is a day that limits spiritual strife. Yeshua of Nazareth did much of his teaching and many of his miracles on sabbath days. Every Saturday that a human being rests from his bread-winning toil, the observant man becomes calmer and quieter in his being. The LORD is particular about not carrying heavy loads into or out of the doors of one's residence, from sundown Friday until sundown Saturday. Although grace allows for unavoidable sabbath toil, there is great blessing for resting and worshiping on it. God listens to spiritual hearts on the Saturday sabbath. God listens intently to men's hearts and sanctifies us on Saturday, that He may inquire of and reason with our minds on Sunday. The Saturday sabbath is to sanctifying rest, as the Sunday LORD's Day is to mathematical reasoning. God the Father's still small voice speaks to man's heart and mind during sabbath rests, teaching us to recognize Him.

Saturday rest is psychologically relevant because it is a blessing of health to the body and soul, and a weekly reminder of the Angel of YHWH's (God the Son's) covenant with Israel (and, optimally, also with the church). In this time of post-modern apostasy, as the Vaticanic spirit of Antichrist waxes and its doctrines filter into lukewarm apostate Elohim-alienated churches and synagogues, sabbath rests and knowledge of systematic theology become very helpful to growing close to the root and essence of Christ Jesus. Toraic righteousness reminds a Believer's conscience of Triune Yahweh, via his carnal mind and soul's root.

"If thou turn away thy foot from the sabbath, from doing thy pleasure on my holy day; and call the sabbath a delight, the holy of the LORD, honorable; and shalt honor him, not doing thine own ways, nor finding thine own pleasure, nor speaking thine own words: then shalt thou delight thyself in the LORD; and I will cause thee to ride upon the high places of the earth, and feed thee with the heritage of Jacob thy father: for the mouth of the LORD hath spoken it." (Isaiah 58:13) This was written at a time when generations of God's people had greatly angered the LORD God of Israel, who was normatively identical with the preincarnate God the Son. He was willing to be lenient to them on the basis of sabbath observances, alone. "The heritage of Jacob thy father" speaks of the Hebrew idea *seykel*, meaning "street smarts." Jacob the Patriarch was a schemer, and epitomized street smarts.

"Thus saith the LORD: Take heed to yourselves, and bear no burden on the sabbath day, nor bring it in by the gates of Jerusalem; Neither carry forth a burden out of your houses on the sabbath day, neither do ye any work, but hallow ye the sabbath as I commanded your fathers. But they obeyed not, neither inclined their ear, but made their neck stiff, that they might not hear, nor receive instruction. And it shall come to pass, if ye diligently hearken unto me, saith the LORD, to bring in no burden through the gates of this city on the sabbath day, but hallow the sabbath day, to do no work therein; Then shall there enter into the gates of this city kings and princes sitting upon the throne of David, riding in chariots and on horses, they, and their princes, the men of Judah, and the inhabitants of Jerusalem: and this city shall remain forever. And they shall come from the cities of Judah, and from the places about Jerusalem, and from the land of Benjamin, and from the plain, and from the mountains, and from the south, bringing burnt offerings, and sacrifices, and meat offerings [Heb., *minchot*], and incense, and bringing sacrifices of praise, unto the house of the LORD. But if ye will not hearken unto me to hallow the sabbath day, and not to bear a burden, even entering in at the gates of Jerusalem on the sabbath day; then will I kindle a fire in the gates thereof, and it shall devour the palaces of Jerusalem, and it shall not be quenched." (Jeremiah 17:21-27) God uniquely sanctifies seventh-day Saturdays, for resting and congregating.

Adonai, God the Son, is obviously not neutral on the subject of seventh-day rest. Regardless of whether you worship Him on Sunday or Saturday, it makes a great deal of sense to rest on Saturday, the day that He sanctifies. If life seems altogether too stressful, bed rest all day Saturday can have a profoundly restorative effect. But, salvation is by grace through faith, unmeritable by transactions of brute-force works. The Old Testament's Torah commands Believers to rest and congregate on Saturdays. During His earthly ministry as Jesus of Nazareth, the LORD God of Israel did not emphasize Saturday-sabbath rest, but also never tried to change the sabbath from Saturday to Sunday. That was the Vatican's misdeed.

"I am the LORD your God; walk in my statutes, and keep my judgments, and do them; and hallow my sabbaths; and they shall be a sign between me and you, that ye may know that I am the LORD your God." (Ezekiel 20:19,20) This was the message to God's people at a time of their gross rebellion. Saturday rest, diligently tracked over the centuries by mostly-pious Jewish sages, is an important matter in the sight of the LORD.

"The sabbath was made for man, and not man for the sabbath." (Mark 2:27).The sabbath rest is for the purpose of building a healthy personal relationship with God through Jesus Christ, not for conforming the inner man to religious traditions. Sabbath rest can increase Holy Ghost-revealing sanctity, quietness and assurance, by harmonizing one's biorhythms with spiritual election.

The Fourth Commandment, to rest on the sabbath day, is the only one of the Ten Commandments that is not quoted in the New Testament. The Hebrew religious elite, the Jews of that day, had turned sabbath rest into a means of conforming all men to their extensive human traditions. Their 'tradition of the elders' became transcribed as the Talmud, unto the spiritual bondage of almost all Jewry. That state of affairs Adonai Yeshua, preincarnately the LORD God of Israel, greatly dislikes. Outward Jewishness should not be a precondition for Twice-Born charity. "Jewishness requires faith in Jesus" is a true statement. "Faith in Jesus requires Jewishness" would be Judaizing.

God the Father is directly cognizant of Saturday worshipers' speech and hearts. He hears every syllable uttered on Saturdays, and the spirit behind it. God the Son reports to Him concerning Sunday worshipers. Saturday rest and worship are theologically preferable and richer in grace. The

RIGHTEOUSNESS RECAPITULATED

Saturday sabbath day of rest and worship was heinously changed by the Vatican to Sunday, centuries ago, but death penalties are no longer meted out by God for Saturday toil.

In a sense, Sunday LORD's Day worship approaches evasiveness of Triune Yahweh, who hears the spirit behind each syllable uttered by human beings on Saturdays. Worship of God is fine, but He sanctifies the seventh day. In the 1500's, the Protestant Reformers decided that the Vatican's Sunday rest and worship were too entrenched in the economy and in society to challenge, and acquiesced to that human tradition. In the 2000's, many Protestant Christian leaders feel tempted to think, 'New Covenant scripture is somewhat equivocal about the seventh-day sabbath, and Sunday rest and worship seem to work so well for so many, it must be God's will.' But, Sunday as a replacement for the Saturday sabbath is at best a tradition of men. At worst, Sunday rest and worship is a Vaticanic ploy to wrest honor from the WORD of God, to give it to His competitors for men's worship. 'Sunday-tarianism' avoids attentiveness to the still, small voice of God, from the firmament to Believers' hearts and minds.

If one asks, "How stringently to rest, on seventh-day Saturday sabbaths?", the following seven questions arise as a heuristic. Would a contemplated sabbath deed expend many calories? Would one be paid money in exchange for work? Would lifting a heavy item cross one's dwelling's threshold? Would the purchase of a food or drink item on the sabbath day nourish one's body on that exact same day? If one studies an academic subject on the sabbath day, is it a relevant aspect of God's mind and creation? Does it edify? Is it right now early (Friday night) or the fully-come sabbath (Saturday afternoon's *shabbaton*)? The sabbath day is unduly ignored Moral Law, but God intends it to be for man, not man for it. The Saturday sabbath is God's moral day, for heightening, de-stressing, and sanctifying man. Saying 'No' to worldly pursuits on sabbath days teaches one to attend to and wait upon God the Father's Spirit, and to say 'No' to the world, the flesh and the devil, 24/7/365.

Philosophy + Religion = Psychology

God the Father, omnisciently paternal, may forgive sins that God the Son, ego-to-ego, cannot in clear conscience forgive. God the Father learns about a man through the quality and steadfastness of his faith, including the testimony of his

77

righteousness. Your keeping a written journal helps God the Father to know you! What God the Father forgives, God the Son no longer begrudges. God the Holy Ghost does not forgive sins, but intercedes for the Believer with pleas.

Since "The sabbath is made for man," it is no great sin to rectify cosmetic imperfections then, that would cause personal anguish if left in stasis. Some non-virgins only have conscientious clarion intellect on 'high' days, but attribute their exalted psychological status on weekends to material or economic causes, not to divine grace. High day *angelic*, workday *occluded* is their sentence. Saturday is the sabbath, but Yeshua resurrected on the first day of the week, a firstfruits Sunday.

Toraic ceremonial-law observances prime the souls of men to suspicion toward papist tradition. In conjunction with Bible knowledge, ceremonial-law righteousness makes gross romish paganism feel wrong. The combination of New Covenant sound doctrine with due Torah observance is theologically conservative relative to sound doctrine that's only talked about. For example, ". . . The remnant of her seed, which keep the commandments of God, *and* have the testimony of Jesus." (Revelation 12:17, emphasis added) Sound-doctrine faith braced by due Torah observance is psychological conservatism, since "Whatsoever a man soweth, that shall he also reap." (Galatians 6:7) *However, religious radicalism mustn't be authorized to cloud inner-manly cognition.* If radicalism does so obscure personal cognition, then the man becomes theologically liberal and psychologically backward. He becomes less brilliant, cognitive and creative, and more earthy, externally-controlled and habitual.

Vocally-related New Covenant sound doctrine is theologically conservative, relative to only Torah observance. Torah observance is theologically conservative relative to Talmudic or romish traditions of men.

Christ the LORD's Feasts

The feasts of the LORD God of Israel, who was *Elohim ha Beyn*, and the preincarnate Adonai Yeshua and God the Son, are thrice-yearly appointed holy days according to the lunar calendar, and are described in the Toraic covenant. They are Unleavened Bread (Passover), Weeks (Shavuot, around Pentecost), and Tabernacles (after Yom Kippur). The Biblical feasts are not "feasts of the Jews" or "feasts of the Old Testament," but are "The feasts

Table 2.2: First sample determination of firstfruits day, random year.

Sunday	Monday	Tuesday	Wednesday	Thursday	Friday	Sabbath
						Nisan 15; (1st *miqra*, Passover 1)
Nisan 16: Firsfruits Day; the morrow after unleavened bread's sabbath; Passover 2	Passover 3	Passover 4	Passover 5	Passover 6	Nisan 21; (2nd *miqra*, Passover 7)	

Table 2.3: Second sample determination of firstfruits day, random year.

Sunday	Monday	Tuesday	Wednesday	Thursday	Friday	Sabbath
Nisan 15; (1st *miqra*, Passover 1)	Passover 2	Passover 3	Passover 4	Passover 5	Passover 6	Nisan 21; (2nd *miqra*, Passover 7)
Nisan 22: Firstfruits Day; the morrow after unleavened bread's sabbath						

of the LORD," who is the same yesterday, today and forever: "These are the feasts of the LORD, even holy convocations, which ye shall proclaim in their seasons." (Leviticus 23:4). Deuteronomy 16:16 says, "Three times in a year shall all thy males appear before the LORD thy God in the place which he shall choose; in the feast of unleavened bread, and in the feast of weeks, and in the feast of tabernacles: and they shall not appear before the LORD empty."

The LORD God of Israel, normatively identical with the preincarate God the Son, appoints seven feasts. First, the weekly sabbath days. (Leviticus 23:1-3) Then, the six yearly feasts of Unleavened Bread, Firstfruits, Weeks, Trumpets, Atonement, and Tabernacles. (Leviticus 23: 4-44) Observation of these feasts of Christ helps one to understand Him.

New Moons

The Biblical calendar is lunar, based upon the moon's 29½-day earth-revolution cycle. (Per Wikipedia, the moon has a 29.530589-day cycle.) The new moon hides overhead during daylight hours, then some fifteen days later the full moon sails overhead during nighttime.

At each successive evening, sunset catches the moon a little further eastward on its nightly perceived-westward journeys. The earth rotates west-to-east. The moon revolves, around earth, also west-to-east, but much slower than the earth rotates. The moon revolves around the earth at about 3.39% of the earth's rotational velocity, and thus traverses about 12° 12' of arc through the heavens, each 24 hours.

The Torah does not define precisely what delineates a new moon, such as is crucial to signaling the beginning of a month: it is totally silent on the subject. The first visible crescent moon, sighted from the land of Israel, would have been the only means available to ancient Hebrews, for them to positively ascertain the beginnings of months and commencements of the feasts of the LORD.

The barely-visible crescent moon occurs on the first, second or third evening after each invisible new moon event, which is the precise day, hour, and minute each month when the moon is most nearly between the earth and sun. Thus, it seems true that the LORD allows the first visible crescent, not the astronomical new moon event or the precalculated first

Table 2.4: Likely Passover Week of Jesus of Nazareth's Firstfruits-Sunday Resurrection. Biblical Days Begin at Sunset. (Genesis 1:13)

Sunday	Monday	Tuesday	Wednesday	Thursday	Friday	Sabbath
			Nisan 14: Post-sunset, Jesus of Nazareth's Last Supper with His 12 disciples, then Jewish leaders' Gethsemane arrest of Him afterward that same evening.	Nisan 15: *Pesach* 1, 1st *miqra;* Jesus tried by Jewish priests, Pilate, and Herod, then crucified & entombed this afternoon. This was His 1st [part-] day and night in the tomb.	Nisan 16: *Pesach* 2; the day of preparation; Jesus' 2nd day and night in the grave.	Nisan 17: *Pesach* 3; Jesus' 3rd day and night in the sepulchre.
Nisan 18: *Pesach* 4; Firstfruits Sunday: Jesus, the Firstfruit of the Spirit, resurrected from the dead early this morning.	Nisan 19: *Pesach* 5.	Nisan 20: *Pesach* 6.	Nisan 21: *Pesach* 7; 2nd *miqra* (Heb., holy convocation).			

RITE FOR THE TIMES

or second day after it, to be His standard for the beginning of months and the feasts of the LORD. Even though science now reveals a precise measurement of the invisible new moon event, the LORD God of Israel, who became Jesus of Nazareth, probably identifies beginnings of months by the first crescent moon visible with the naked eye from Israel. Ancient Israelites would have had to rely upon the first visible crescent for positive visual confirmation of the first days of the months. The absolute record for unaided first visual sighting of a lunar crescent, following a new moon event, is 15.5 hours elapsed time.[4] Thus, only a sunset-then-moonset that occurs more than 15.5 hours after the just-preceding new moon event produces an unaidedly-visible lunar crescent.

The precise, single, solitary day of the new moon is crucial for determination of the exact days of firstfruits, of Shavuot, and of Yom Kippur. A estimated generalization risks a serious astronomical error. "On *exactly* the tenth day of this seventh month is the day of atonement: it shall be a holy convocation for you, and you shall humble your souls and present an offering by fire to the LORD." (Leviticus 23:27, NASB, emphasis added) Determining "exactly" the correct day to begin a month, and from it to measure to the solitary day of Yom Kippur, can only be done by visual observation, from Israel, of a fleetingly visible crescent new moon just after sunset on the first, second or third evening after a new moon event. "An offering by fire to the LORD" can now only be the *minchaw* grain offering exegeted in chapter one of this book. *Minchot* alone, as offerings made by fire unto Yahweh, do not conflict with Calvary!

The new moon fleetingly appears visible on Israel's western horizon in the few minutes after sunset, but before moonset, on each exact day of true *rosh chodesh* (Heb., head of the month). The next morning, the crescent moon rises above the eastern horizon just after sunrise, and sails invisibly westward, until it becomes briefly somewhat visible again, after sunset but before moonset, above the western horizon.

Karaite Jews keep track from Israel of the first visible lunar crescent. The Karaites post their crescent moon sightings on their website, *www.karaite-korner.org*. Apparently, Elohim accommodates them in this, because the Bible does not record any commandment contrary to the Karaite belief that new months begin with the sighting of the first visible crescent. How else would ancient Hebrews have positively identified the beginnings of months? Talmudist Jews set beginnings of months by relatively generalized rabbinic estimations, that regularly diverge by a day or two

---

from the observed first visible crescent. Talmudist Jewry have viciously persecutedKaraite Jews, because Karaites derive religious authority from the Torah of God, instead of from the Talmud of Jewish traditions.

Passover

Pesach is the Passover anniversary, the feast of unleavened bread, which identifies firstfruits Sunday. This early spring feast coincided with Jesus of Nazareth's sacrificial death as the paschal Lamb to atone for the sins of all mankind who believe on Him, and is memorialized by the church as *Easter*. The word 'Easter' is derived from *Ishtar,* an ancient Babylonian fertility goddess of prostitution. Hence bunnies and eggs.

The scriptural injunction for *Pesach* is Leviticus 23:5-8. "In the fourteenth day of the first month at even is the LORD's passover. And on the fifteenth day of the same month is the feast of unleavened bread unto the LORD: seven days ye must eat unleavened bread. In the first day ye shall have a holy convocation [*miqra*]: ye shall do no servile work therein . . . in the seventh day is a holy convocation: ye shall do no servile work therein." The voluntary bloodless *minchawth bikkuwrim*, or grain offering of firstfruits, is commanded to be offered on the Sunday after the only sabbath that always occurs during the week of *Passover*, even to this present year. That Sunday is the day of firstfruits (Heb., *Yom haReysheit*). The feast of unleavened bread is designed to purge human homes and bodies of the influence of yeast, symbolic of sin but also potentially sickening.

The feast of unleavened bread's two *miqra*'s are not *shabbats*, making the correct calculation to specify the days of firstfruits and of Shavuot to be contrary to rabbinic tradition, which measures fifty days from the first *miqra*. Contrary to most of rabbinic Judaism, for specificity, the day of firstfruits must always occur on the Sunday after the one and only *shabbat* that always occurs during Passover's weeklong feast of unleavened bread, and cannot be the day after either of the two *miqra*'s.

Yeast symbolizes sin, but it is also a microbe that can potentially sicken a human. Ingestion of the prescription antifungal compound nystatin during the feast of unleavened bread kills intestinal yeast, purifying emotionality, and increasing personal quietness and assurance for the entire ensuing year. Otherwise, yeast can sicken later in the year. Strange as it may sound, a nystatin enema taken on the Friday preceding firstfruits weekend, just after the Passover anniversary, can have profound longterm health benefits.

Feast of Weeks

Shavuot is the feast of weeks, the early summer feast upon which the law was given and the first Pentecost occurred. Modern-day Pentecost occurs upon *Shavuot* each year that Easter falls upon the Sunday of firstfruits. The scriptural injunction for *Shavuot* is Leviticus 23:16, 21. "Even unto the morrow after the seventh sabbath shall ye number fifty days . . . and ye shall proclaim on the selfsame day, that it may be a holy convocation unto you; ye shall do no servile work therein; it shall be a statute forever in all your dwellings throughout your generations." This numbering is from the Sunday after the only sabbath that always occurs during Passover week, which is the Sunday of firstfruits.

Modern rabbinic Judaism errs in determining the day of the feast of weeks (*Shavuot*), in that it counts fifty days from the day after the first of the two *miqra's* (holy convocations) bounding the feast of unleavened bread, instead of correctly, from the day after the specific, one-and-only sabbath that always occurs during the feast of unleavened bread.

Feast of Tabernacles

Sukkot is the feast of tabernacles, the early autumn feast commemorating the Israelites' dwelling in huts under the stars in the wilderness, during the Exodus. A parallel meaning is that the spirit of man exists in a fleshly body, analogous to a man dwelling in a temporary structure. The scriptural injunction for *Sukkot* is Leviticus 23:34-36 and following: "Speak unto the children of Israel, saying, The fifteenth day of this seventh month shall be the feast of tabernacles for seven days unto the LORD. On the first day shall be a holy convocation: ye shall do no servile work therein . . . the eighth day shall be a holy convocation unto you . . . it is a solemn assembly; and ye shall do no servile work therein." The season of *Sukkot* is arguably the true time of year that Jesus of Nazareth was born, since He ministered from age thirty, the age for a Levite to begin temple service, for three and a half years and was crucified about the time of Passover. Passover occurs six months later than *Sukkot*. *Sukkot* is observed by the building of makeshift huts of leafy branches. Zion-born Hebrews are to dwell in those huts for eight days. Modern rabbinic tradition claims that that command is fulfilled by eating even a single meal in one. By discernment, the LORD God of Israel (Jesus Christ) makes up His jewels (dignified human beings) between Yom Kippur and Sukkot each year. (Malachi 3:17)

Blue Tassels

Numbers 15:37-41 records that Moses wrote God's words as: "Speak unto the children of Israel, and bid them that they make them fringes in the borders of their garments throughout their generations, and that they put upon the fringe of the borders a ribbon of blue: and it shall be unto you for a fringe, that ye may look upon it, and remember all the commandments of the LORD, and do them; and that ye seek not after your own heart and your own eyes, after which ye use to go a whoring." The idea is confirmed in Deuteronomy 22:12: "Thou shalt make thee fringes upon the four quarters of thy vesture, wherewith thou coverest thyself." The modern Hebrew term for the blue fringes or tassels to wear upon the quadrants of your garments is *tzit-tzit*. The only Biblical stipulations are that the threads be blue, that they be upon the four corners of your garments, and that they be of non-diverse material (e.g., not of wool and linen, both).

Some more-traditional types assert that *tzit-tzit* need to made of wool and dyed with the blue dye obtained from the (unclean) mollusk used in ancient times. A nice idea, but not required by the Torah. God may stabilize you for them even if they are made of four-inch long blue embroidery floss and sewn onto your tucked-in teeshirt's tetra-quadrantal hem. The author's term for such a teeshirt is a *Tzit*-Shirt™, made from camouflage, patriotic or uniform-issue teeshirts, as well as from A-shirts. The idea involves putting tassels of blue thread upon the four quadrants of the hem of a teeshirt. Wearing *tzit-tzit* seems to assist visual and mental chastity.

Tzit-tzit are to remind the wearer of the LORD God of Israel. That is, of Adonai, the Angel of Yahweh, who became Christ Jesus. The main purpose of prayer shawls (Heb., *tallitim*) is to mount blue fringes. Authority-fixated Talmudists changed God's commandment for blue fringes to white ones. The two prophets or witnesses, who will torment the globalists with their prophecies during the Great Tribulation (the final three-and-a-half years before Christ's return) may wear handmade prayer shawls made of rectangular swaths of coarse brown burlap, consistent with

85

mourning, adorned at their corners with fringes made of blue threads. This could fulfill the prophecy in Rev. 11:3, that they will be " . . . clothed in sackcloth."

What else does the Bible say about *tzit-tzit?* "And behold, a woman, which was diseased with an issue of blood twelve years, came behind him and touched *the hem of his garment:* For she said within herself, If I may but touch his garment, I shall be whole. But Jesus turned him about, and when he saw her, he said, Daughter, be of good comfort: thy faith hath made thee whole. And the woman was made whole from that hour," (Matthew 9:19-22, emphasis added). "And a woman having an issue of blood twelve years, which had spent all her living upon physicians, neither could be healed of any, came behind him, and touched *the border of his garment:* and immediately her issue of blood staunched. And Jesus said, Who touched me? When all denied, Peter and they that were with him said, Master, the multitude throng thee and press thee, and sayest thou, Who touched me? And Jesus said, Somebody hath touched me: for I perceive that virtue [Gr., *dunamis*] is gone out of me. And when the woman saw that she was not hid, she came trembling, and falling down before him, she declared unto him before all the people for what cause she had touched him, and how she was healed immediately. And he said unto her, Daughter, be of good comfort: thy faith hath made thee whole; go in peace." (Luke 8:43-48, emphasis added) This was a case where a *tzadique* or righteous man's subconscious mind, or angelic retinue, was tapped by the will of the Father, not by the will of the man, to effect a healing for the Father's glory. Current Messianic belief is that the hem and border of Yeshua's garment mentioned in this passage in Matthew and Luke were in fact blue-threaded tassels or fringes. Someone once said that *tzit-tzit,* or tassels of blue thread, were the WWJD bracelets [What Would Jesus Do?] of the First Century. The appeal of frayed demin to youth may relate to the pro-prophetic effects of blue tasselling.

By Old Testament theology, wearing *tzit-tzit* declares one's intention to keep oneself from fornication. Jesus of Nazareth upped the ante during New Testament times so that, from then on, *tzit-tzit* are a declared intent to also keep one's *eyes* holy, pure from lascivious sights. *Tzit-tzit* chastity went from the intention of sexual purity to the intention of perceptual, visuospatial purity, by the higher standard than the Torah, set by the exemplary life of Yeshua of Nazareth, in the sight of God's angelic witnesses.

Phylacteries

Phylacteries (singular, phylactery) are slips of paper bearing verses from the Torah or Pentateuch, tied as a set onto both a man's forehead and his right hand, as a symbol of faith during prayer. Chasidic Jewish phylacteries can be costly works of embossed leather. The idea is derived from the scripture, "And thou shalt bind them [the words of the Law] for a sign upon thine hand, and they shall be frontlets between thine eyes." (Deuteronomy 6:8) The obvious inescapable meaning of the commandment is to make Trinitarian faith to be one's first perceptual filter and a main topic of conversation and cooperatings. It is not a command to literally wear Jesus Christ's words like clothing, if we deny Him with our lips and hearts. According to SDA Pastor Michael Oxentenko, the looming VeriChip identity-management mark of the beast portends significance as a satanic anti-phylactery, occupying its victims' right hands or brows (the bodily sites where Elohim's phylacteries are worn).

Mezzuzot

A *mezzuzah* consists of a verse from the Torah copied onto a slip of paper, sealed inside a decorative container, and tacked onto a door frame or gatepost of one's house. The idea of the *mezzuzah* is found in Deuteronomy 6:9, "And thou shalt write them [the words of God's Law] upon the posts of thy house, and on thy gates." Some *mezzuzot* are designed as small decorative tubes, often decorated with the Hebrew letter *shin*, for Shaddai. *El Shaddai* was one of the names of the Angel of Jehovah, the Old Testament-revealed Second Person of the pre-existent Trinity. The idiomatic Hebrew language expression for the Holy Trinity is *ha Shiloosh haKodesh*, literally 'the Holy Trio.'

The obvious, inescapable meaning of the commandment is, again, that God intends godly conversation to predominate within our houses. He emphatically does not mean that we should be satisfied with external symbols of superficial piety. Knowledge of His Word is helpful to build mental purity and zealous heart attitudes. He did not intend that a mere architectural add-on should satisfy His call to be first in His peoples' dialog and hearts. Toraic Judaica amounts to aids for praying to Jesus of Nazareth, who preincarnately was the God of the Old Testament. Traditional Judaica, such as white *tzit-tzit*, can obfuscate this truth.

Jesus' Torah Scroll

Speaking of laws pertaining to scripture, kings of Israel were commanded by God to copy the book of Deuteronomy in their own handwriting. (Deuteronomy 17:18) This may mean that Jesus of Nazareth copied Deuteronomy in His own handwriting during the early first century, in order to be worthy to be the King of the Jews! Since He probably has already done so, one wonders, 'Where is this priceless scroll hidden?' Most of the LORD Jesus' quotations of scripture, to rebuke Satan, came from the book of Deuteronomy, a text He had laboriously transcribed by hand, not merely read and spoken. He may have quoted His own hand transcription to oppose Satan's propensity for mesmerizing psychic powers. Witness Adolph Hitler.

Diet

The ceremonial law, fulfilled in Christ Jesus, forbids eating unclean meats such as pork and shellfish, as well as all blood, all animal fat, all reptiles and a variety of birds (such as owls, vultures, hawks, ostriches, swans, pelicans and storks). For an animal to be clean for a Hebrew to eat, it must both chew cud and have cloven hooves. *This is another way of saying that dietary animal flesh should provide vitamin B$_{12}$.* Examples of clean animals include beef cattle, whitetail deer, stags, antelope, bison, and elk. Horses are not clean animals, since they do not have cloven hooves. Pigs are not clean animals because they do not chew cud. Vitamin B$_{12}$ is cobalamin, the red vitamin. The cobalamin molecule uniquely, among vitamins, contains a metal ion, the element cobalt. Metallic cobalt has a very high magnetization threshold. It takes an extremely-strong Gauss magnetic field to alter cobalt ions' magnetic polarity.

However, Jesus said, "Do not ye yet understand, that whatsoever entereth in at the mouth goeth into the belly, and is cast out into the draught? But those things which proceed out of the mouth come forth from the heart; and they defile the man." (Matthew 15:17,18) Jesus of Nazareth explicitly told his disciples, "All their works they do to be seen of men . . . And love the uppermost rooms at feasts, and the chief seats in the synagogues, And greetings in the markets, and to be called of men, Rabbi, Rabbi. But be not ye called Rabbi, for one is your Master, even Christ; and all ye are brethren." (Matthew 23:5-8) Fascination with hierarchized rabbinic radicalism may stunt brotherly love of the inner man for truth.

The King James Version of the Bible was translated by a professional bureaucratic effort decreed, staffed and funded by King James I of England,[5] during the lengthy zealous revival which was the Great Reformation. The King James Version Bible is the English translation that usually most-accurately relates the mind and holiness of God.

The Old Testament describes the preincarnate God the Son's dealings with Israel. The New Testament, the Trinity's relationship with the church and Israel. The word church is from the Greek *ekklesia*, meaning 'called out or separated from [the world].' It is supposed to be the same idea as *kadosh* in Hebrew, meaning 'set apart,' from paganism and obfuscatory human tradition. Toraic earned righteousness and Christian sound doctrine both synergize modern holy set-apartness.

Who Is The LORD?

Adonai (of the Jews) is God the Son (of the Christians). This is how Christianity and Judaism fit together. The LORD God of Israel was the preincarnate God the Son, and became Jesus of Nazareth. He was normatively the only person of the Triune Godhead revealed to pre-Christian Hebrews, between the Exodus' plagues and the immaculate conception. In the first century, He ministered as Yeshua of Nazareth and first extensively revealed the other two Persons of the Godhead to mankind. "Which in other ages was not made known unto the sons of men, *as it is now revealed unto his holy apostles and prophets by the Spirit.*" (Ephesians 3:5, emphasis added) This pivotal truth, involving dispensational knowledge about the Godhead, should instill eagerness within devout Jews to master theology and sound doctrine, in order to winsomely communicate narrow truths of Triune Yahweh to others. Profound life-changing decisions are reached by *eurekas* of mathematical-logical thought more than by self-satisfied rumination.

Normatively, Adonai Jesus reigned spiritually over the Israelites from Moses' time past the Babylonian captivity and the inter-testamental period. Then, He was miraculously born to Miriam, Joseph's espoused virgin wife, grew up, and toiled as a blue-collar worker, iconoclastic teacher, healer and prophet to teach of his Father. He first widely revealed His Father's Holy Spirit to mankind after His resurrection from the dead. He now reigns on high as King for His Father, and decides justice and mercy upon men, primarily according to Paul's sound doctrine and secondarily according to the Torah. *Paul's sound doctrine accurately relates the life of Jesus' charitable inner man corroborated by God the Father's Holy Spirit, who requires a new relational conscience exceeding (in depth, scope, and purity) the old ritual conscience instilled by the Torah's 613 laws. In Elohim's Spirit, New Covenant relational conscience finds affirmation in Toraic ritual conscience.*

Normatively, between the Exodus plagues and the immaculate conception, the LORD God of Israel was the preincarnate God the Son, who became the resurrected glorified Christ Jesus. This pivotal truth fits Christianity with Judaism, and the Old Testament with the New. The LORD God of Israel as the glorified Christ reigns with His Father and Holy Spirit through each man, woman or child who believes.

Ritual conscience is learned by going through Toraic motions, such as are biblically defined as righteous. Relational conscience is learned by interplay with the three persons of the Holy Trinity (Heb., *Eloheynu ha Shiloosh haKodesh)*, especially in evangelism and fellowship, and on sabbaths and high days.

The Law's Role

Righteousness steadies and stabilizes the soul. Quickening comes from health and Messiah Yeshua's grace, and from hope toward the pearl of great price (which means fulfillment of the desires of one's heart). "Even so, the Son quickeneth whom he will." (John 5:21) He knows the innermost thoughts of the heart, and uses His privy knowledge to gladden or deject any given man, according to His assessment of him, His grace toward him, and his utility to Him. His ruthlessness is gentled by the goodness of God the Father, if one's person has conscientiously emerged from the mists of sin to be recognized by Him. Being Born Again and showing accomplishments worthy of repentance invites recognition of oneself by God. He may pronounce His holy, terrible, beloved name, *Y'howah,* through the heart and soul of a sanctified man or woman, filling proximal spirits with either loving upward hope toward Him, or else with hostility.

Reformer-theologian John Calvin believed that the Moral Law is, for the Believer in Jesus, no more a reminder of sin or an instrument of death. Rather, through the activity of the Holy Spirit the Law becomes an active principle of the Believer's sanctification.[6] "The moral precepts of the Old Law are an obliging force to Christians, but not a compelling force, for what compels Christians to act well is the Holy Spirit, a gift to us through the Father's love." [7] If you are called of God, then graceful evangelism and lawful righteousness are synergistic, to becoming a son of God.

Toraic righteousness is one type of Hebraeo-Christian worship. If your heart is right toward God, then grace and will are synergistic, in grateful voluntary worship, to being an authentic man of God. No one would claim that upon accepting Christ you should stop making decisions and exerting your will, or allow others to do everything for you. No one would claim that, by indolence, the Word of God may be preached. Nor, that you can have the vitality of heart God intends for you to have, if your spirit is continually broken. The word *worship* implies the idea of *worth*-ship. Worship imparts worth, honor and respect to its recipient.

The moral law (God's Ten Commandments plus those reiterated or first given in the New Testament) is yet binding upon humanity. The remainder of the Torah is not sin to observe, but observance is no longer compulsory. It is the opinion of this author that there are recognizable personal benefits from righteousness (secondary to faith), such as are perceptible to children. In combination with knowledge of the Bible, voluntary ceremonial-law righteousness inculcates suspicion toward human religious traditions.

Religious liberalism and apostasy primarily offend sound doctrine, but secondarily they offend the Torah. Every violation of Torah or sound doctrine incurs some penalty, from minimal to disastrous, according to grace. Although some claim sound doctrine and Torah never conflict, if human interpretation conflicts them then sound doctrine and evangelism must triumph over the Law.

Charisma of the former rain began at Pentecost and will last until the conclusion of the church age, which began to transition to Christ Jesus' Messianic-kingdom dispensation on or around April 5, 2000 A.D. Charisma of the latter rain will begin before the onset of the Tribulation and extend to its midpoint, when the firstfruits missionaries will be caught up to heaven. The end-time latter-rain revival will set the nations of the world, especially Israel, alight with Yahweh's cognitive truth and clarion holiness. It will provide hope, sound eschatology and spiritual gifts for Believers to persevere through the Great Tribulation until the resurrection (of the dead in Christ and of un-VeriChipped living Believers) at Christ Jesus' only, and post-Tribulational, second coming. Hosea 6:3 refers to this latter- and former-rain revival of God the Father's Holy Spirit.

———

The latter-rain reformation and revival will bring cognitive clarion halos and Elohim the Father's Holy Spirit (Matthew 10:20) upon the true church and Believing Israel. We who keep ourselves un-VeriChipped will carry the brightness of it through the Tribulation to the Rapture, or be martyred in the attempt.

Most of the laws discussed in this chapter are of the ceremonial law. Even for Born Again Christians, the ceremonial law never totally goes away. If a Christian looks away from Jesus' face and stumbles into "the flesh," he falls under judgment via the ceremonial law. Men's ceremonial-law righteousness cannot remove the least of their sins. But, ceremonial-law righteousness discourages fecklessness and the bar culture. Ceremonial law righteousness serves as a reminder that one is not in submission to the bishop of Rome. God's Moral Law, comprised of the Ten Commandments plus New Covenant additions, approximates His terms of endearment to mankind.

Messianic Congregationalism

The next few pages are expressly intended as constructive criticism, to instruct beloved Messianics how to win more souls and bring greater glory to God. Any *pilpul* (Heb., peppery speech) to precious Messianics is from love of truth in a spirit of charity.

The complaint voiced by most who cycle out of the spiritually-charged Messianic scene after years of zealous contribution, is probably that while there, they weren't sufficiently fed, spiritually. For all Believers in Jesus, there is no substitute for pure unadulterated Christian sound doctrine. Without it, the inner man spiritually starves, rabbinic authority notwithstanding. The apostle Paul prefixed each of his thirteen epistles with the idea, "Grace and peace from God our Father and from the LORD Jesus Christ be with you . . ." Within God's grace and peace, the inner man adjusts and locates the authentic logical way for his person to learn to know and obey the truth of God the Father through the LORD Jesus. In the absence of grace and peace, that which is not ministry is manipulation. That which is not conviction is compulsion. Grace involves heartbeats, respiration and cognitive processes in-phase and harmonious with the living WORD of God and with elect nature.

A stumbling block from some Messianic pulpits is jesting, spoken to put a subset of congregants at ease. Humor is on the level of idiom, below that of cognitive logic. Paul the apostle wrote, "Neither filthiness, nor foolish talking, nor *jesting*, which are not convenient; but rather giving of thanks." (Ephesians 5:4, emphasis added) Other problems some Messianic congregations grapple with include: undue sympathy with the Talmud; temptation to regard the New Testament as mere commentary upon the Torah; congregational communion in outer-man traditions that preoccupy from truth; emphasis-shifts from New Birth theology to ethnic traditions; and, a Believer's lower-soul submission-to-authority as a prerequisite to his truth-dependent relationship with God and fellow Believers in Jesus. God chooses to be a Father, not a *Fuhrer*! Paul wrote to the future of spiritual man. Torah study does not counterbalance Talmudism; only the Gospel and Christian sound doctrine offset the manifold errors of oral-law Talmudism.

In their zeal to be real McCoy Jews, some Messianics still think the Holy Trinity is a paganized Gentile concept. But, *each Believer is indwelt by Yahweh the Holy Ghost, and is not to be taken advantage of by leaders in offices of authority.* God hates overbearing, self-serving leaders. (Ezekiel 24:1-10) This is why sound doctrine of our God the Holy Trinity (Heb., *Eloheynu ha Shiloosh haKodesh*) is especially crucial to Messianic congregationalism, with its ethnic opposition to some Christian theology. Believers in Jesus, indwelt by the Trinitarian Holy Ghost (Heb., *Ruakh haKodesh*) are to entreat each other with charity (Gr., *agape*). God longs for Messianics to teach reverent unashamed Christian sound doctrine, to Jews, too; similarly to the works of Michael L. Brown, Ph.D. and of Jews for Jesus. Some aspects of Judaizing are theologically of inferior quality to comparable Christianity.

The Gospel and Paul's sound doctrine will be more binding upon mankind than either the ceremonial or civil Torah, during Christ Jesus' millennial kingdom. With the New Covenant, God emphasizes Believers' inner man for truth, and heart attitude. Outward righteousness, although quieting, assuring, and focal upon Elohim, receives a secondary emphasis.

The secondary apostolic concept I acknowledge is that *God wants Christian sound doctrine accepted by Jews and moral Saturday-sabbath rests observed by Christians*, that there become "one new man" in Messiah Jesus. The Greek word *apostolos*, the root of the English word 'apostle,' means 'one sent.'

"Messicongs" should empower laity to countenance-brightening interactive verbal dialog in the written and living Word of God. In the interest of producing "one new man" in Messiah Jesus, Messianic congregations should discourage absorption with rabbinicism, oral-law tradition, or race.

———

In the epic struggle for the soul of Jewish evangelism, Messianic congregationalism is on the horns of a dilemma. The more Messianics appeal to traditional Jews via rabbinic forms, the less they edify the inner man via truth. The tail of ethnicity must not wag the sheep of truth. The means of Jewishness, to set unbelieving Jews at ease with the truth that the LORD God of Israel became Yeshua of Nazareth, must not become an end in itself.

Messianic congregationalism strayed in combining the offices of Jewish rabbi and Christian elder. Rabbis owe a debt to Judaism. Elders, to the Tri-Unity. Rabbis, to tradition, the people, and their own institution. Elders, to truth. The historic name "Hebrew Christianity" confers more truth and less confusion than does the relative neologism "Messianic Judaism," which came into vogue only in the 1970's. The rabbinic subset of Messianic congregationalists ought to ask each other, 'Are we Christ-like enough?', more than 'Are we Jewish enough?'

Submission to Authority

Rabbinic submission to authority is a tradition of men, and must not infringe upon Trinitarian grace to the inner man, as some imply that it may. Marital submission is in the truth of Christ Jesus, whereas military and rabbinic submission are to delegated authorizers. Marital submission is more fundamental to communion with Triune Yahweh, while military submission is more fundamental to the world. Women are not communal property. Matthew 20:25-28 reads, "But Jesus called them unto him and said, Ye know that the princes of the Gentiles exercise dominion over them, and they that are great exercise authority upon them. But it shall not be so among you: but whosoever will be great among you, let him be your minister; and whosoever will be chief among you, let him be your servant: even as the Son of man came not to be ministered unto, but to minister, and to give his life a ransom for many." Cognition of truth awards positional authority, whereas officialdom traffics in line authority. Exercise of religious authority primarily to effect submission of followers is not Biblical, but amounts to "the flesh" (the source of tradition).

God the Holy Ghost (Heb., *ha Ruakh haKodesh*; Gr., *ho Paraklete*) is God the Father's Spirit of Messiah ben Joseph (the suffering Servant), not of Messiah ben David (the conquering Messiah). The Holy Spirit has zero *chutzpah*, ethnic or otherwise. He loves or hates any given person, Jew or

Gentile, unsaved or Christian, on the basis of their inner man, history of cognitive decision making, and yieldedness to the truth of Y'howah as they know Him, from childhood. He cultivates the spirit of truth within men. He judges people on the basis of what they know and how they use it.

Messianic leaders who marginalize the relevancy to Jews of Paul's epistles deprive their flocks of most Biblical testimony about the Comforter. The *Ruakh haKodesh* does not know everything that God the Father knows: "But of that day and hour knoweth no man, no, not the angels of heaven, but my Father only . . ." (Matthew 24:36) And, the Holy Ghost opposed Paul's final-recorded journey to Jerusalem, which led to his first bondage and productive ministry in Rome. (Acts 21:11) The Paraclete may testify of a Believer's character to angelic election, for help, if he so chooses.

The LORD Jesus is Conservator for His Father's Spirit. (Matthew 10:20) If you have him, you must meet His standards, as a "little Christ."

Praise of Talmudic thought advances Antichrist, if it obfuscates the narrow truth that Adonai (of Judaism) is identical with God the Son (of Christianity), with all the need for Pauline sound doctrine that that implies. Oral religious traditions, whether Jewish or Gentile, invariably are affected by the flesh and admit occult thought. They are not reliable sources of theological knowledge. Some Christian doctrines, such as those proceeding from Trinitarianism and righteousness by grace through faith, are less incursions of paganism into God's true religion than they are valid theological responses to Messiah-Yeshua-denying Phariseeism. Obsession with human traditions distracts from God's mind, while failing to demonstrate zeal for narrowly-true personal Y'howah. If the Talmud is beautiful, then the Apostles wrote in vain.

Why Judaize? Truth is not ethnocentric: Two = 2 = II = *shtayim* (Heb.) = *deuteros* (Gr.). "Come out of her, my people" (Revelation 18:4), but don't throw the baby of Paul's priceless sound doctrine out with the bathwater of Vaticanic heresy. *Grace* is not a function of ethnopraxy, but corresponds to a conscience toward the truth of God the Father, by Christ Jesus. Evangelism is the best *mitzvah* (Heb., good deed). Words of evangelism of the Gospel are *aliyah*-at-hand, an inspiring fountainhead of instantaneous 'ascent' toward holy God the Father. The danger of Judaizing is that traditions which are not refuted become rabbinically authorized. Fondness for tradition at expense to the Gospel and Christian sound doctrine smacks of conceit and Judaizing.

It is true to say "Jewishness requires faith in Jesus," but it would be Judaizing to say "Faith in Jesus requires Jewishness." Apostate Judaizing (narrowly defined as Talmudism, rabbinicism, and racism) radicalizes its adherents. As a trend, radical motives cost men cognition. The remedy to Judaizing and its resultant radicalism is Christian sound doctrine, not outward shows of submission to any demagogic authority.

Beloved believing Jews should grow in faith according to Christian sound doctrine. The inner man of a true Born Again is Christian (a "little Christ"), whether or not his outer man is Jewish (a "praiser"). Faith is defined by Christlikeness all week, month, year and life long, not merely by weekly praise sessions. Twice Borns' inner men are one breath with God the Father's Holy Spirit. No one should let very-Jewish outer-manliness turn him against Pauline Christianity, for which there is no substitute. The neologism 'ethnopraxy' is from the Greek, *ethnos* (race or nation) + *praxis* (deeds or acts). Meek Christian reverence for face-brightening truths of God the Father, for His heart and mind, should become intrinsic to one's personality, not merely a veneer upon ethnic roots and bitter *chutzpah*.

If you have God the Father's Spirit (Matthew 10:20), you are called to be a "little Christ." The LORD Jesus acts as Conservator of His Father's Spirit. If you have him, you must meet His standards, as described in the Bible.

Oliver Wendell Holmes said a good catch phrase can stop thinking for fifty years. Case in point: rabbinic "submission to authority." It has stopped most Jewish thinking about the Messiahship of Jesus for centuries. Obedience to good judgment is a much safer concept than submission to authority. Any given authorizer may have ascended to office upon the ruins of former friends, for all anybody knows. It is better to obey truth than to submit to authority.

Speech on behalf of the Father in heaven, through the indwelling *Ruakh haKodesh* (Heb., Holy Spirit), is another thing God desires from us. "But it is not ye that speak, but *the Spirit of your Father* which speaketh in you." (Matthew 10:20, emphasis added) The Spirit of our Father speaks the mind of our Father. His mind encompasses logic, physical 'hard' sciences and mathematics, as well as theology and law.

Authorizers' any expectation of laity's radical servility, without adequate regard for servers' personal growth, creativity, genius understanding, or hope, makes submissionism extremely unwholesome, not to mention doctrinally unsound. Radical servility, wherein laity wordlessly submits to authority and puts on a outward show of submission to authority, can become as hopeless a rut to be in as outright incarceration: it doesn't free one according to clarion Christian hope.

Regarding authoring ideas, unto what does one ascend? To truth, or to control of one's fellows? Evangelism or self-satiety? Friends do not submit friends—they quicken and brighten them with truths of God's Word. As Baptist Pastor Gary J. Moritz ably stated, "Many with me, none beneath me."

Truth and tradition are like matter and antimatter. They ultimately annihilate each other, because "the flesh" takes refuge in traditions' ambivalence to Yahweh's *Logos*. Both Christians and Jews need to love truth more than tradition, be it Vaticanic or Talmudic. Human religious traditions disillusion men and drive them away from morality, because God is positively averse to man-made traditions and to their manifold obfuscations.

The blessings of godliness (i.e., grace) ought not make us arrogant, to rule suppressively over the less-sanctified. Per C.I. Schofield, the word *Nicolaitane* (a group hated by Christ Jesus in Revelation 2:6 and 2:15) derives from the Greek, *nikao*-(conquest) + *laos* (laity). According to Schofield, Nicolaitanism means conquest (domination) of the laity by an elite priesthood. Nicolaitanism practiced by truth-lovers would be oxymoronic. Conversely, Nicolaitanism practiced by tradition-lovers is ubiquitous. Born Again Christians know, as art, poetry and song imply, that "Truths are to your heart as facts are to your intellect and mind." Triune Yahweh prefers Believers who think for themselves, over people who automatically believe whatever religious authorities tell them. An alternative interpretation of Nicolaitanism is that the word refers to church leaders who err by condoning sexual sin within the body of Christ.

Christian Crowns of Judaism

Messianic congregationalism needs more Pauline sound doctrine and spontaneous evangelism, and less submission to earthy human authority. According to Stephen Katz of Jews for Jesus, *Yeshua haNotzri* is idiomatic Hebrew for "Jesus of Nazareth," quite apart from the Talmudic blasphemy *Yishu Nazri* ('may His name be blotted out'). As if the name of *Eloheynu haBeyn* (Heb., "our God the Son") may ever be blotted out!

97

Some esteemed Messianics insinuate that Christianity is a corrupted form of Judaism. But, contrary to Marvin R. Wilson's implication, in his book *Our Father Abraham: Jewish Roots of the Christian Faith*, across the chronology of history, Toraic Yahwehism preceded Gospelic Christianity, which itself preceded Talmudic Judaism. Almost all rabbinic Judaism proceeds from the Talmud: from the human oral tradition of the elders, codified as binding law. Apostate Judaizing may be narrowly defined as Talmudism, rabbinicism, and racism. Some beloved Messianics seem to prefer Jewish mistakes to Born-Again Christian eurekas.

The Torah was transcribed for God by Moses in the Paleo-Hebrew alphabet, not the Chaldean alphabet adopted by Jews centuries later during the Babylonian captivity. Many orthodox rabbis have yet to lay eyes on the Paleo-Hebrew alphabet, but it is published via the Internet.

Some blame Christians for the majority of Jews being unsaved. Precious Jews will believe on Jesus the Messiah when God removes the spiritual scales from their eyes and hearts, which He will do for many during the Tribulation. Narrow truth wins more souls than does commiseration in tradition. More lives are transformed by mathematical-logical theological reasoning than by postprandial rumination. By theological *eurekas* more than by formulaic liturgy. Christianity preceded Talmudic Judaism in the timeline of history. Blaming Christians for Jewish unbelief obfuscates the crucial truth that the TaNaK's (Old Testament's) *LORD God of Israel* was the Trinity's preincarnate God the Son. This crucial truth is not a secret.

Toraic earnable righteousness is a set of behaviors (less, attitudes) that is hard to misinterpret as pertaining to any spirit except to Adonai Jesus, the incarnate Elohim the Son. A modicum of emboldening, conservative Toraic righteousness, such as sabbath observance, is thus exactly what the theologically liberal emergent church needs. Triune Yahweh, holy and set-apart from the spirits of profane creation, recognizes Toraic righteousness as entreaty specifically to Himself, not to any creature spirit in competition with Him for human worship (such as Allah, 'Mary,' or Krishna). However, Toraic earned righteousness is susceptible to admixture of human tradition (case in point: Talmudism). Admixture of tradition with righteousness in the absence of sound doctrine invites the Talmudic error. If that occurs, faith becomes subsumed to an ethnopraxy that is peculiarly opposed to the truth of the Gospel and to freedom in Christ. Talmudism and romish heresy are both huge, albeit false, systems of authority. Neither is too big to fail. Talmudism is a worse obstacle to modern Jewish faith in Yeshua of

Nazareth than are the long-past Crusades or Inquisition. Salvation is of the Jews, but sound doctrine is of reformed Christianity

Christians elevate truth in situations where apostate Judaizers dote on ethnicity. The "one new man" in Christ Yeshua simply must love lofty truth more than he does ethnic radical authority – and the two often diverge. Every authentic teacher must love truth more than he loves his students, and vice versa, in order for there to be academic objectivity. Does God want "one new man in Christ Yeshua," or two old men in tradition?

Everybody is genetically either Jewish or Gentile; and, conscientiously either Christian or un-Believer. The appellation "Hebrew Christianity" imparts less theological and spiritual confusion than does the term "Messianic Judaism."

God the Father loves filial crowns more than He does human roots, and crowns come mainly from evangelism. Most Jewish evangelists disapprove of rabbinic forms of congregational order, especially of 'submission to authority.' Most who believe in Jesus as LORD, Adonai, and Messiah, do so from eurekas of truth, arrived at by thinking for themselves! Unbelieving authority has no percentage in approval of controversial, cosmic truth. Rabbinic forms risk becoming strange fire before God the Father, since the LORD Jesus consciously and vocally rejected the Pharisees' oral tradition of the elders. (Matthew 15:1-9) The LORD God of Israel, who is Jesus Christ, prefers to be a Friend via man's conscious mind, rather than a Master via natural subconscious-mind processes. (See Table 11.9.)

The Holy Tri-Unity's Import

If beloved Messianics yield to temptation to think that, based upon observance of the Mosaic covenant, their genes, their Jewish roots, and their radical Toraic earned righteousness, they have comprehensive knowledge of the full Godhead, they may not develop their evangelical crowns and theological minds in faith by sound doctrine, nor evangelize.

If Messianic congregations cater to precious Jews' sensitivities, to the extent of affirming a supposedly-superior extra-Christian relationship with Triune Yahweh, excused by genes or radical righteousness from any need for faith and charity by sound doctrine, then they do God and Jewry a disservice.

RITE FOR THE TIMES

The Holy Trinity [Heb., *Eloheynu ha Shiloosh haKodesh*] is a spiritual reality and to-die-for doctrine, not at all an incursion of paganism into Gentile theology. "And Jesus, when he was baptized, went up straightway out of the water: and, lo, the heavens were opened unto him, and he saw the Spirit of God descending like a dove, and lighting upon him: And lo a voice from heaven saying, This is my beloved Son, in whom I am well pleased." (Matthew 3:16,17)

The advent of Christ Jesus' earthly ministry began a dispensation of much new knowledge about the Godhead to mankind, while also technically fulfilling the entire Torah in God the Father's evaluation, for the first and only time in human history.

Inertia infiltrating Messianic doctrine, from tradition-oriented ethnic roots, will be a temptation for error until estimable Jews celebrate instant evangelizing more than they jubilate at ethnic traditions.

The LORD God of Israel, who was normatively the preincarnate Elohim the Son, "Behold, all souls are mine . . ." (Ezekiel 18:4) By this verse, all souls belong to preincarnate Jesus (the Angel of Yah). By the New Testament, we may choose in faith to also give Him our hearts. Imagine the iniquity, in His sight, of races of people insisting themselves to be captains of their own souls. Of themselves, human beings fleshlily rebel against Christ Jesus' spiritual rulership. By grace, we learn to love and obey Him, and in so doing, to live. Many precious unsaved Jews are doctrinal infants, despite any multigenerational chastity and Toraic earned righteousness.

For beloved Messianic congregationalists, evangelism should be to any and everybody, not only to unsaved Jews. Human traditions should be emphatically optional, since they tend to obfuscate the instant Gospel. Every time one replies 'No!' to temptation to sin, he nonverbally says, 'Abba, Father in heaven, I love you!'

Every Toraically righteous observance appeals uniquely to the holy, narrowly-true, set-apart Spirit who is Triune Elohim, but entails the risk of religious pride in one's own grace-sanctified root. Nobody needs his relationship with God micro-managed by a third party, be it pope, *guru*, *imam*, or rabbi.

Evangelical advantages exist for being more righteous than most rabbis, who are predisposed to listen to a more-righteous man. Although many are very pious, most unsaved-rabbinic righteousness is altered by Talmudic tradition, which counts for nothing with God. For example, Karaite Jewish lunar-sighted high holy days versus rabbinically-estimated beginnings of months, and Toraic blue *tzit-tzit* (tassels) versus Talmudic white ones.

Unsaved rabbis' righteousness need not be an insurmountable obstacle to Believers' creating a good impression for their words. No one respects overt mitigation (sycophancy). "Except your righteousness shall exceed the righteousness of the scribes and Pharisees, ye shall in no case enter into the kingdom of heaven." (Matthew 5:20)

Summary

Triune Yahweh is not a Talmudist who says one thing with His lips while denying it with His eyes. The Talmud is a study in self-opposition. Some Messianics also have turned righteousness into an instrument of submission, a turn of events God dislikes. Traditional "fences" around God's commandments do not enhance one's relationship with Him. Instead, they encumber grace and truth, while He looks positively askance at them.

Jesus of Nazareth's perfect righteousness means to God the Father that the Mosaic covenant with Israel did not totally fail: one man in all of history, Yeshua of Nazareth, conscientiously kept all 613 Toraic laws during His entire life, and even exceeded them, in obedience to Yahweh His Father. As a perfect Son, He obeyed both the letter and the Spirit of His Father's mind toward Him in carnal existence, knowing full well His Father would credit His righteousness to us, who are completely unworthy of Him.

Of any given spiritual leader's authority: does it derive from Biblical truth, or from tradition? Believers' proper attitude toward human religious tradition is, "For I determined not to know any thing among you, save Jesus Christ, and him crucified." (1 Corinthians 2:2)

Chapter 2 notes:

[1] Buzzy Killeen. *Cajuns of the Louisiana Bayous*. Metarie, LA: Authentic American Art, 1985, 49.

[2] Dietrich Bonhoeffer. *The Cost of Discipleship*. New York: Touchstone, 1959, 43.

[3] Danny Shelton and Shelley Quinn. *Ten Commandments Twice Removed*. Remnant Publications, 2004, 104.

[4] http://aa.usno.navy.mil/faq/docs/crescent.php. October 4, 2012.

[5] Adam Nicolson. *God's Secretaries: The Making of the King James Bible*. New York: HarperCollins, 2003, 70-83.

[6] Darrel Cole. *When God Says that War is Right*. Colorado Springs: Waterbrook, 2002, 68.

[7] *Ibid.*

[8] Stan Telchin. *Messianic Judaism Is Not Christianity*. Grand Rapids: Chosen, 2004, 148.

Chapter 3

Paganism and Penance

The LORD God of Israel condemned occultism at the giving of the Torah to Moses, shunned it in manhood as Jesus of Nazareth, and will ultimately suppress it wherever it breaks out. Occultism results from suggestion to the hearts and minds of men, by demons from the second heaven (the demonic dimension of nature), in direct competition with the Creator and His ways. Occultism is the latent phase of paganism. Paganism is the aggressive phase of occultism.

New Age occultists believe that 'the Christ' incarns within their bodies as they meditate, making them divine and their bodies due worship: *de facto* idols. They believe that such Christ-ing is an evolution of impersonal Cosmic Energy, corresponding to soul evolution toward godhood.

Definition of Terms

The term for meditative spiritual evolution toward godhood is *panentheism*. Friend, *Christ* means *anointed*, and is a reference to the Jewish Messiah, specifically to the LORD Jesus Christ. Any other man, woman or child who claims to have become the Christ is deceived, and is inviting judgment for trafficking with a spirit of antichrist.

Concerning the spirit of antichrist (Gr., *anti-* (in place of) + *Christos* (anointed, Christ, or Messiah)): "If any man shall say unto you, Lo, here is Christ, or there; believe it not. For there shall arise false Christs, and false prophets, and shall show great signs and wonders; insomuch that, if it were possible, they shall deceive the very elect." (Matthew 24:23,24) "Who is a liar but he that denieth that Jesus is the Christ? He is antichrist, that denieth the Father and the Son." (I John 2:22) "Hereby know ye the

Spirit of God: Every spirit that confesseth that Jesus Christ is come in the flesh is of God: and every spirit that confesseth not that Jesus Christ is come in the flesh is not of God: this is that spirit of antichrist, whereof ye have heard that it should come; and even now already is it in the world." (I John 4:2) "Then said Jesus unto them again, Verily, verily, I say unto you, I am the door of the sheep. All that ever came before me are thieves and robbers: but the sheep did not hear them. I am the door: by me if any man enter in, he shall be saved, and shall go in an out, and find pasture. The thief cometh not, but for to steal, and to kill, and to destroy: I am come that they might have life, and that they might have it more abundantly." (John 10:7-10) The whole chapter of John 10 shows that Triune Yahweh is opposed to the idea of a panentheistic Hindu anti-Christ.

In the introduction to his extremely interesting book *Unholy Spirits*, Dr. Gary North writes: "The rise of occultism as a cultural force in the United States began around 1965, and paralleled the rise of the counter-culture and the breakdown of the older . . . 'can-do' pragmatism."[1]

Further, "Occultism surfaces as a cultural phenomenon at the end of civilizations. It came at the end of Rome, at least in its more debased forms. Classical civilization had always been affected by occultism, but generally a more restrained form predominated, except at the annual chaos festivals. The consistent occultism of the late Roman Empire overwhelmed the rational, confident aspects of older classical civilization and weakened it sufficiently so that only the Christians had sufficient authority and self-confidence to take over and rebuild its faltering institutions. Occultism came at the end of the medieval world, not during it (contrary to popular opinion). It has now come at the end of Enlightenment humanism's civilization. While it always exists in the underground, such as during the French Revolution, it surfaces only when rationalism has lost its sense of destiny and its sense of power, and when humanists seek power from below. In the West, occultism has been a transitional phenomenon. It appears at the end of a civilization, and goes underground when the next phase begins to be built. It may become superficially civilized and absorbed into folklore and popular religion, but its more grotesque manifestations become illegal. If occultism is not at least partially suppressed, then no new civilization appears."[2]

God the Father dispenses authority and clarion cognitive light to the brows and hearts of Christians, via the Paraclete, elect heraldry, and literacy. *Can-do pragmatism* says, 'I may not know yet *what* I'm going to do: but I am going to do *something*!' And, does it courageously.

Civilization comprises the set of societal forms which reassure mankind that trust in the Father of the *Logos* (that is, in the Father of the LORD Jesus) is authentic and safe. This represents the Christian aspect of patriotism (Gr., *pater* (father) + *osis* (infusion)). Antitheses to this Christian aspect of patriotism are jingoism and New Age global governance.

The progressive meta-Left, consisting of varied proponents of global governance, strives to eliminate societal forms that recognize the truth of Jesus' Father in heaven. In rejecting Triune Yahweh's identity, mind and principles, they hope to appease Satan by politicizing submission to him.

The Vile 3 is a category of sins guaranteed to wreck a personality: fornication, occultism, or drug abuse. Fornication amounts to bodily idolatry: worshiping with your body an object that God has not consecrated to you. Occultism is the latent, symbolic phase of paganism. Drug abuse is sorcery: Gr., *pharmakeia*, origin of the word pharmacy. Those three types of sin bring tremendous future trouble and personal hardship, to one who stumbles and involves himself in them. Consequences are worse for persons of Hebrew descent.[3] Theology interprets spirituality. Spirituality either lovingly draws ever-loftier to God through Christ Jesus, or gravitates to cocky, radical self-absorption.

Why would occultism require suppression for civilization to progress? Because occultism involves an alternative false religion and worldview that demons, pretending to be gods, suggested to the minds of men. The demons rebelled against God the Father, the Creator. They directly compete with Him for worship from men. "Thou shalt have no other gods before me . . . I the LORD thy God am a jealous God, visiting the iniquity of the fathers unto the children unto the third and fourth generation of them that hate me; and showing mercy unto thousands of them that love me, and keep my commandments." (Exodus 20:3,5,6) Elohim deals with demons mostly by binding them back on Saturday sabbaths, thus lending glory and reason to Sunday mornings. Does our Triune Yahweh truly hate occultism that much? Consider what He says in His written Word, the Bible.

Biblical Prohibitions Against Paganism

The Bible contains many cautions against occultism or paganism. Sixteen such prohibitions consist of:

"There shall not be found among you any one that maketh his son or daughter to pass through the fire [a ceremony to a demon], or that useth divination [prognostication], or an observer of times [astrology], or an enchanter [an incanter of spells], or a witch [spell-caster for nature spirits]. Or a charmer [amulet maker], or a consulter with familiar spirits [trance channeller], or a wizard [male black-magician], or a necromancer [consulter of the dead]. For all these things are an abomination [greatly detestable] unto the LORD." (Deuteronomy 18:10-12) The LORD God of Israel was normatively the preincarnate God the *Son*, Jesus of Nazareth!

"Ye shall not eat anything with the blood [drunk in satanic rites]: neither shall ye use enchantment [incant spells], nor observe times [schedule business via astrology]." (Leviticus 19:26)

"Regard not them that have familiar spirits [spirit guides], neither seek after wizards [male black magicians], to be defiled by them: I am the LORD your God." (Leviticus 19:31)

"Thou shalt not suffer [allow] a witch [spell-caster for nature spirits] to live." (Exodus 22:18) Not to advocate executions, but be advised that Almighty God considers witchcraft to be an abomination, comparable with sodomy. Angelically, that death sentence is still enforceable, despite the lucrative media hype that the Harry Potter books and movies have received.

"A man also or woman that hath a familiar spirit [spirit guide], or that is a wizard [male black magician] shall surely be put to death; they shall stone them with stones: their blood shall be upon them." (Leviticus 20:27)

"For rebellion is as the sin of witchcraft [spell-casting for nature spirits], and stubbornness is as iniquity and idolatry." (I Samuel 15:23)

"Now [the prophet] Samuel was dead, and all Israel had lamented him, and buried him in Ramah, even in his own city. And [King] Saul had put away those that had familiar spirits [spirit guides], and the wizards [male black magicians], out of the land." (I Samuel 28:3,7) King Saul purged Israel of most occultism, but then . . .

"So [King] Saul died for his transgressions which he committed against the LORD, even against the word of the LORD, which he kept not and also for asking counsel of one [trance channeller] that had a familiar spirit [spirit guide], to inquire of it." (I Chronicles 10:13) Saul purged Israel

---

of occultism for a while, but then turned back to it, and for that sin was executed by the LORD.

"And he [King Manasseh] built altars for all the host of heaven [fallen demons (of the one-third of the stars that fell with Satan, Rev. 12:4)], in the two courts of the house of the LORD. And he made his son to pass through the fire [ceremony to a demon], and observed times [astrological scheduling], and used enchantments [incanted spells], and dealt with familiar spirits [spirit guides] and wizards [male black magicians]: he wrought much wickedness in the sight of the LORD, to provoke him to anger." (II Kings 21:5,6)

"And he [King Manasseh] caused his children to pass through the fire in the valley of the son of Hinnom: also he observed times [astrology], and used enchantments [spells], and used witchcraft [spell-casting for nature spirits], and dealt with a familiar spirit [ascended master], and with wizards [male black magicians]: and he wrought much evil in the sight of the LORD, to provoke him to anger." (II Chronicles 33:6)

"Therefore thou hast forsaken thy people the house of Jacob, because they be replenished from the east, and are soothsayers [fortune tellers] like the Philistines [a neighboring pagan tribe]." (Isaiah 2:6)

"And when they shall say unto you, Seek unto them that have familiar spirits [spirit guides], and unto wizards [male black magicians] that peep and mutter [trance channel]: should not a people seek unto their God? for the living to the dead?" (Isaiah 8:19)

"Therefore hearken not ye to your prophets [false prophets], nor to your diviners [fortune tellers], nor to your dreamers [soothsayers], nor to your enchanters [wiccan spell casters], nor to your sorcerers [psychedelic drug-abusers], which speak unto you saying, Ye shall not serve the king of Babylon." (Jeremiah 27:9,10)

"For the idols [religious statuary, foci of demons] have spoken vanity, and the diviners [fortune tellers] have seen a lie, and have told false dreams; they comfort in vain." (Zechariah 10:2)

"And I will come near to you to judgment; and I will be a swift witness against the sorcerers [psychedelic drug-abusers], and against the adulterers, and against false swearers, and against those that oppress the hireling in his wages, the widow, and the fatherless, and that turn aside the stranger from his right, and fear not me, saith the LORD of hosts." (Malachi 3:5)

"Now the Spirit [the Holy Ghost] speaketh expressly, that in the latter times some shall depart from the faith, giving heed to seducing spirits [ascended masters, fallen demons], and doctrines of devils [romish error, theosophy, Course in Miracles, New Age heresy]." (I Timothy 4:1.)

Bear in mind that the LORD God of Israel, the Angel of Yahweh of the Old Testament, was normatively God the *Son*, of the New Covenant. Then, as Jesus of Nazareth, He first widely revealed His Father and the Paraclete to humanity. The implications of this narrow truth are indeed staggering!

It means God changed the dispensation, with Jesus' life. It means that the New Testament is much more than a commentary upon the Torah. It means that Jews stand to benefit from studying Christian theology. And, it means that systematic theology and evangelism are the proper context for Toraic earned righteousness and its beneficial, primitive radical godliness.

Fertility cults, involving the likes of golden calves, phallic poles, and burnt incense on promontories, probably involved worship of fallen cherubim (chief of which is Satan).

Harry Potter irrespective, witchcraft cannot impart authority over one's own parents. Even a single attempt of parental cursing can incur savage, enduring judgment upon a spell caster. Any coupling of witchcraft with sexual sin usually results in long-term personal disaster.

More Against Occultism

According to leading authority on shamanism and comparative religion, Mircea Eliade, "All features associated with European witches are claimed also by Indo-Tibetan yogis and magicians." Some yogis "boast that they break all the religious taboos and social rules: that they practice human sacrifice, cannibalism, and all manner of orgies, including incestuous intercourse, and that they eat excrement, [and] nauseating animals, and devour human corpses. In other words, they proudly claim all the crimes and horrible ceremonies cited *ad nauseam* in the Western European witch trials."[4] Some turn from romish heresy to Eastern pantheism, going from the frying pan of Antichrist to the fire of paganism.

One false premise for New Age enlightenment as a means of regeneration is the induction of an ASC (altered state of consciousness) to try to dispel ignorance concealing supposed, latent godhood. Many disciplines for entering ASC presuppose this pantheistic idea, and involve the idea of *kundalini* arousal (spiritually-induced psychosis). That typically results in temporary states of insanity, radical changes in the physical body and possession by a spirit.

About *kundalini* arousal, Swami Narayanananda said, " . . . Many become insane, many get brain defects, and many others get some incurable diseases after much sorrow."[5] The aforementioned brain defects may include biochemical or genetic changes caused by spirit possession or drug abuse, and may result in spiritual depression or subject-object-dualism confusion. Possessing spirits for unforgiven sins can become like motes in one's heart's spiritual eye.

Occultism consists of the fallen demons' inter-related religions, rituals and disciplines that proceed from pantheism: Hindu yoga, Buddhist zazen, spiritism, astrology, witchcraft (wicca), trance meditation, mediumship (trance channeling), tarot, Ouija boards, fortune-telling, contacting the dead, Eckankar (tinnitus absorption), and psychic powers (telekinesis, clairvoyance, or prognostication).

Involvement with these brings guaranteed trouble farther on in life for the involvee, and temptation for his or her subsequent generation(s). (Deuteronomy 18:9-14) These may be "the depths of Satan" that Yeshua of Nazareth condemned in Revelation 2:24. Or, those depths of Satan may have to do with global governance and politicized investment banking. "The secret things belong unto the LORD our God, but those things which are revealed belong unto us and to our children forever." (Deuteronomy 29:29)

The myriad of New Age religions are outside of the pale of election. They do not result in true holiness or salvation, interfaithism to the contrary. A synonym for interfaithism is religious universalism. To avoid deception and great danger, spirituality should normally be vetted by theology.

The *occult* is a term for the rebellious, fallen demons and enslaved human beings who yield space to Satan or to the spirit of antichrist. The word 'occult' is derived from the Latin, *ob*— (in the way) + *culere* (to conceal).

A *cult* is a term for a group of often well-meaning individuals who submit their intellects, hearts, and wills to a charismatic leader or demagogue who turns them away from sound doctrine, to various forms of sin and/or occultism. From the Latin, *cultus* (to adore).

Ancient Bulgar society had a tradition to lynch the extremely talented among them, out of envy at their faces shining too brightly within the herd of society. The murder of intellectually brilliant people was a tradition of Bulgar paganism. Human sacrifice was done, by which the most intelligent among the population were offered as sacrifices to their pagan gods. This sort of ritual was likely conducted by the Bulgars' *tabibs* (shamans).[6] The idea is derived from Slavic paganism. The gifted are, yet, especial targets of Satan, via the culture war's temptations against our consciences and hearts.

Occultism strives to shift human psychology down into cherubic radicalism. Parallel to radicalism, the occult tries to evoke lawlessness from the naïve, that they deserve accusation.

Papist Heresies

Romish traditions of men have turned many to New Age spiritual disciplines, in search of truth. Romish traditions-*cum*-Laws may be more insidious than outright New Age doctrines, since they disguise gross doctrinal errors under a veneer of Trinitarianism.

Strictly speaking, the Vatican's Roman church combines egregious false doctrine, meaningless penance, and thinly veiled occultism, all whitewashed with the idea of Jesus of Nazareth, a presumption that must make Him extremely angry. The Roman church is a corrupt work. Reformers have thought for centuries that the Vatican will produce a pope who will become the End-time Antichrist. The Vatican unapologetically admits that, via papal authority it traces from Simon Peter to itself (the "living church"), it has altered from the Bible (or simply imposed) thousands of religious laws and human traditions. These include logical and thematic changes to the Toraic Law of YHWH,[7] even to the Ten Commandments.

Have the lessons of the Great Reformation been lost since 1965? Has the wariness of the Founding Fathers of the United States against organized religion supporting centralized government been obscured, in the tumultuous years since 1960 when John F. Kennedy, a Roman Catholic, was elected United States president?

Concerning romish error, occultism and sodomy are often related. The press have carried numerous stories of pederastic romish priests who sexually molested multiple tens of boys, even as many as seventy, over decades of years, despite numerous complaints to their bishops.

The LORD God of Israel was normatively the preincarnate God the Son, the Second Person of the Trinity. He said in Leviticus 18:22, "Thou shalt not lie with mankind as with womankind: it is abomination." That word *abomination* in Hebrew is *toweybah*, meaning (to the LORD God of Israel, homosexuality is) 'an abhorrence; something disgusting; an abomination.' Sodomy in the priesthood is plainly, grossly insulting to Triune Yahweh. Perversion haunts the steps of those who submit to and insist upon false doctrines or traditions, such as salvation by the Mass, purgatory, 'Mary' as co-mediatrix, patron-sainthoods, and papal infallibility, to name a few.

Jesus' mother Miriam (or Miri), the true Mary, is the possible angel of the resurrectable mother of Jesus of Nazareth. This Miri probably does not condone of the veneration of statuary, because Adonai Yeshua, later her Son, forbade the making and veneration of religious statuary, at the transcribing of the Torah by Moses, as recorded in the Bible. She may doubtless choose between holiness and vainglory as the basis of her offering to God.

Marism, or marianism, is veneration of actually *two* spirits that precious Roman Catholics identify as 'the queen of heaven,' a moniker deplored by the Hebraeo-Christian Jehovah-God in Jeremiah 44:15-19. One of the spirits called the queen of heaven may be Jesus' mother, but the other and more prolific is definitely the demon Ashtoreth.

"Then all the men which knew that their wives had burned incense unto other gods, and all the women that stood by, a great multitude, even all the people that dwelt in the land of Egypt, in Pathros, answered Jeremiah, saying, As for the word that thou hast spoken unto us in the name of the LORD [normatively Y'howah-the-Son], we will not hearken unto thee. But we will certainly do whatsoever thing goeth forth out of our own mouth, to burn incense unto *the queen of heaven*, and to pour out drink offerings unto her, as we have done, we, and our fathers, our kings, and our princes, in the cities of Judah, and in the streets of Jerusalem, for then had we plenty of victuals and were well, and saw no evil. But since we left off to burn incense to *the queen of heaven*, and to pour out drink offerings unto her, we have wanted all things, and have been consumed by the sword and by the famine. And when we burned incense to *the queen of heaven*, and poured out drink offerings unto her, did we make her cakes to worship her, and pour out the drink offerings unto her, without our men?" (Jeremiah 44:15-19, emphasis added.)

That queen of heaven was the demon Ashtoreth, which much of the Vatican's church is deceived into venerating via statues of 'Mary'. *Ashtoreth* in Hebrew means *she maketh rich*. The related Hebrew word *Ashtaroth* means *the statutes of Ashtoreth* or *the plural of Ashtoreth*. Both words are yet modern Middle Eastern locality names.

King Solomon's many wives corrupted his heart's purity toward the LORD God of Israel, who was normatively Elohim the Son, and turned him aside to venerate Ashtoreth queen of heaven. In the fifteenth generation after Solomon, young king Josiah of Judah read God's law, covenanted in his heart to serve Him, and during his reign nearly eradicated deeply entrenched paganism from the kingdom of Judah. "And the high places that were before Jerusalem, which were on the right hand of the mount of corruption, which Solomon the king of Israel had builded for Ashtoreth the abomination of the Zidonians . . . did the king [Josiah] defile." (2 Kings 23:13a)

In mythology, the study of the fabrications of demons, there is the Canaanite myth of two demonic sisters, one chaste and the other lewd. The chaste was called Ashtoreth, the queen of heaven, and the slatternly, Asherah. The former was a dominatrix; the latter, a slut.[8] Ashtoreth is the 'Mary' of mariolatry.

Triune Yahweh did not originate from a mother. That would position her as His creator, which would make *her* to be the Creator, and would become idolatry and blasphemy. In that sense, veneration of the queen of heaven (Ashtoreth/'Mary') is like the Trojan horse of Christianity, introducing erstwhile Believers in Christ to idolatry and witchcraft. Mariolatry controls much of the occult, within the civilized world.

The queen of heaven mentioned in Jeremiah 44:16-23 is a demon, possibly a fallen seraph, that seduced Israel and the nations into idolatry. It was idolized in Canaanite, Greek and Roman cultures by the popular names Ashtoreth, Astarte, and Diana, and was, in those cultures, associated with witchcraft, hunting, and altered states of consciousness (ASC's).

———

There may be a currently resurrected spirit, an angel, who was the mother of Jesus of Nazareth, but the demon Ashtoreth has built extensive tradition-laden romish heresy around her.

The true mother of Jesus probably doesn't call herself the queen of heaven, because she is not wed to her virgin kingly Son. Apparently, the spirit called the queen of heaven in Jeremiah 44:15-19 subsequently convinced unfortunate Vaticanic leaders that it is the resurrected angel of Miriam, the biological mother of Jesus of Nazareth.

According to the tradition of perpetual virginity, Mary remained a virgin all her life, despite the Biblical record that she gave birth to multiple children. The human tradition of immaculate conception expounds that Mary also was conceived of a virgin. Both of these views are apocryphal, mere traditions, rather than canonical, but hundreds of millions of dear deceived Roman Catholics believe them. The marist heresy teaches that Mary is a co-mediatrix, a co-intercessor to turn to if Jesus Christ won't hear one's prayers—perhaps for idolatry? The Bible, however, says "There is one God and one mediator between God and man, the man Christ Jesus." (I Timothy 2:5) No one should have a co-mediatrix.

Pagan mythology prominently echoes the theme of a perpetually virgin mother with child. The Greek word *parthenon* loosely means 'one, a virgin.' The same virgin-mother-with-child theme found use by demons in multiple cultures, such as Canaanite, Greek and modern. There exists what amounts to a wealthy sub-sect for the queen of heaven within the precious, deceived Roman Catholic community, complete with the real estate of multiple hundreds of shrines worldwide that contain God-forbidden graven images of religious statuary, such as were outlawed by Adonai the Christ, the preincarnate God the Son, in the second of the Ten Commandments.

In all candor, perhaps precious Roman Catholics believe that by venerating 'Mary,' they are joining Jesus' family, but there are two spirits called *the queen of heaven*, and the Vatican's 'Mary' is Ashtoreth the demon. Faith in Jesus Christ plus mariolatry is sin. That's the unvarnished truth. Mariolatry tempts its victims into mama's boys mindsets.

The Order of Jesus, the Jesuits, is a marist splinter group within the disparate Vaticanic community that pledges fealty to 'Mary, the mother of Jesus, the queen of heaven.' The Jesuits were founded in 1534 A.D. by the Spanish Basque, don Inigo Lopez de Recalde, who took the religious name Ignatius Loyola.[9]

Within civilized society, mariolatry rules much of the occult. Tradition-based Vaticanic forms of worship (and the errant theology that justifies them) distress and offend Triune Yahweh. To the extent that such religious forms infiltrate Protestant churches and denominations, God the Father is slightly less avid toward them. The demon Ashtoreth/'Mary' is to monetized society as the demon Baphomet is to fecund nature; both may be reprobate seraphim.

Solar Cult

Solar cult involves worship of the sun as a deity, and occurs in many animistic religions. Reformers identify solar cult as the doctrinal error of *helios christos* (sun christ), and found the Vatican's Catholic church rife with it. For example, the Roman Catholic mass typifies solar cult via a disk-shaped communion wafer (the host) placed by a priest into a radiantly-fashioned monstrance, in order to receive worship supposedly due to a fragment of Christ Jesus' fleshly biological body. Ancient Egyptians also worshiped the sun demon, which they called 'Ra.'

An altered state of consciousness (ASC; Gr., *pharmakeia* (Biblical sorcery)) under sunlight invites confusion. Many gentry of the largely Protestant Christian British *raj* customarily abstained from imbibing alcohol until after sunsets. "Mad dogs and Englishmen" thus tolerated the boiling-hot equatorial sunlight better than most natives, due in part to this discipline.

The late-Saturday afternoon (Heb., *shabbaton*) sunlight contains barely a trace of solar cult spirituality, because each Saturday sabbath God scatters solar cult spirituality, thus preserving societal homeostasis for another week.

Perspective on Paganism

To New Age theosophists, Jesus of Nazareth merely yogi'd His way into shamanistic miraculous powers. They allege that subject-object dualism is only *maya* [Skt., illusion], 'the cause of all human suffering.' The opposite is more true. Precious family-nurtured cognitive ego results directly from the sanctifying work of Y'howah's Spirit of truth within human hearts, one family at a time, according to the love of the Father of lights. Because of the blessings of the Almighty upon our civilization, for faith, we in the first world are usually able to stand off at a safe distance from problems, define them externally to ourselves, and solve them.

By contrast, pantheists such as Hindus are taught that they are helpless to overcome *karma*, life's ultimate problem. They learn that problems are only manifestations of illusion, *maya*, and that if they become personally involved in problem solving, it just makes things worse. That indoctrinated blurring of subject and object, coupled with fearful helplessness, keeps the lay pantheist passively innocuous in the hopes that trouble will leave him alone. That, instead of identifying problems and cognitively solving them, as filial honor invites. Pantheistic *gurus* think they've evolved into godhood, are above *karma*, and may sin as they will, since (for them, they think) sin equals non-sin.

Hindu *yoga* teaches that the conscious mind (i.e., the carnal mind) is the leading force of creation. By contrast, the Bible teaches that God the Father is the Creator, and that spiritual and material reality are totally subject to His will. Usually, God prefers to work through people or rational means.

Pretyping aspects of the modern culture war, rational egoistic West met pantheistic egoless East during Alexander the Great's campaign of conquest, and militarily triumphed over it. Elohim the three in One, who holds the hearts of kings in his hand, raised up Alexander to sow the Koine Greek language and esteem for reason throughout his known world, tilling the cultural soil for the dissemination of the Gospel and the apostle Paul's New Testament epistles.

East Indian culture differed greatly from Macedonian (originally pronounced "Makedonian"). "On the approach to Taxila [India] the Macedonians met the Indian ascetics [Skt., *rishis* or *yogis*] who sat immobile, naked, solitary, lost in meditation, indifferent alike to the burning rays of the sun and the icy cold of the night." [10]

"When in India, the Macedonians met a strange religious sect; naked, penniless . . . several of them approached Alexander and stood before him, striking the ground with their feet . . . Strabo tells how Alexander showed interest in another community of men who went about naked [and] practiced fortitude . . . Those who desired to speak with them were obliged to go to see them as they lay, stood or walked, ever unclothed, even on the warmest days when the ground was so hot that it caused pain to the bare feet. Alexander despatched Onesicritus as his messenger to converse with them . . . The life-denying principles of the Indian ascetics would appear strange indeed to the alert, inquiring minds . . . of the Greeks and the Macedonians." [11]

Himself a pagan, Alexander's nascent Western rationality contrasted sharply with the seminal pantheism of India. For all his bloodlust and paganism, Alexander of Macedon seems to have loved truth. Had he been born four hundred years later, Alexander might have believed in Jesus of Nazareth as the Christ. Such was his noble character. Despite Hollywood sophism, Alexander the Great was not homosexual.

Bible commentator C.I. Schofield believed that Revelation 2:6's and 2:15's reference to the hated *Nicolaitanes* referred to the idea of *conquerors of the laity*. He derived that conclusion from the etymology, in Greek, of *nikao* (conquest) + *laos* (laity). His interpretation implies the existence of a priestocracy deeming itself intrinsically holier and more authoritative than the laity they are supposed to instruct in the ways of God. The temptations are obvious; such a priestocracy would be uncorrectable from without. It might be uncorrectable from within, as well, if it became infected with witchcraft. Such as with the marist cult. *The priesthood of Believers, right down to the laity, is a fact, although the Vatican teaches that only its priestocracy is the church, per se.* Per Schofield's interpretation, Nicolaitanism relates to the religious tradition of submission to authority: "conquest of the laity." This duality, that of a commoner class governed by a superior elite class, occurs widely within reprobate creation. An alternative interpretation of Nicolaitanism is that it is the doctrine and practice of sexual promiscuity tolerated within Christ Jesus' church, by its leaders. In either case, Nicolaitanism is unacceptable.

The occult is constructed upon the philosophical ideas of pantheism and monism, both related to all-pervading consciousness and energy. Together, they are offered as excuses for worship of created spirits. In the words of Marcia Montenegro, pantheism [Gr., *pan*, (all or every) + *theos*, (God)] says, 'God is all, all are gods.' That is idolatry, since Yahweh states that He alone is God, and beside Him there is none other. Monism [Gr., *monos*, (one)] says, 'Mind is all, all is mind,' or 'That object out there blurs together with this subject in here.' Monism violates Aristotle's logical axioms of identity and exclusion. Pantheomonism combines the idolatry of pantheism with the impersonal boundlessness of monism. Tibetan or Hindu *yoga* and Buddhist *zen* urge identification of a man's heart with an Impersonal Absolute of pure consciousness (yogic *Purusa*) which would be a colossal mistake, not to mention sin.

Christianity and rational education impart priceless subject-object dualism, but spirit possession results in subject-object monism. Cognition or rumination. God prefers the former for His children, while theological liberalism foments the latter. "And it shall come to pass in that day, that the prophets shall be ashamed every one of his vision, when he hath prophesied; neither shall they wear a rough garment to deceive: But he shall say, I am no prophet, I am an husbandman; for man taught me to keep cattle from my youth. And one shall say unto him, What are these wounds in thine hands? Then he shall answer, Those with which I was wounded in the house of my friends." (Zechariah 13:4-6)

Occult psychology argues that all-pervading subtle electricity or tinnitus exists as an illusory dream of an impersonal *Purusa* or Cosmic Consciousness. The logical equivalent could be expressed as 'pervasive tinnitus creatively-imagines civilization.' That is a gross lie! It has never worked for residents of the Indian subcontinent, and it will never work for anyone else. Tinnitus may be related to magnetic resonance, and can be approximated by passing magnetic flux through (some) metal objects.

Comparable terms descriptive of yogic Samkhya metaphysics' impersonal *Purusa/prakriti* dichotomy are: *Impersonal Absolute/cosmic energy* and *Noumenon/phenomenon* dualisms. All three concept-pairings imply a sentient Impersonal Absolute as distinct from insentient energy and matter. That Impersonal Absolute of yogic Samkhya metaphysics is the philosophy upon which pantheism and most of paganism is based. It conflicts sharply with the personal God of the Bible. Both are not true, in the same universe. Witchcraft expediently identifies the supposed-Impersonal Absolute's cosmic energy as *spirits*. Meditative yoga (Skt., union) and witchcraft have much in common.

Tinnitus, yogic *nadam*, in occult philosophy is called the energetic substrate of the material and spiritual universe, but magnetic fields may induce tinnitus in humans. Hypothetically, cherubim may be able to induce some sort of magnetic field. Science has identified five types of magnetism: diamagnetism, paramagnetism, ferromagnetism, ferrimagnetism, and anti-ferromagnetism. Human flesh is faintly diamagnetic.

There may be other types of magnetism that are as-yet undiscovered by science. Interestingly, brass mutes magnetic resonance carried in magnetic fields passing through masses of that alloy. Jesus' feet are described as like "fine brass". (Rev. 1:15, 2:18) The Scots have a folk tradition that an upwelling induction of tinnitus presages a death in the household, so perhaps some tinnitus is truly of spiritual origination. New Age Eckankar has the yogic view of tinnitus.

According to the tetrapartite hypothesis of psychology, elect cherubim (such as a soul's cherub) need not penetrate down (or look) lower than sheet brass at a site where it is placed horizontal to the earth's surface. Sheet brass and limestone bedrock possess similar properties, regarding cherubim. If true, thin sheet-brass heel cups built into shoes, podiatric orthotics, or insoles, perhaps brand-named Serious Soles™, may provide bounded depth and improved foot respiration to superficial walks. See chapter eleven.

Religious universalism, also called interfaithism, is the theological error that Triune Yahweh, as God, identifies with all religions' names for deity. This error of religious universalism purports that this Elohim is the same spirit as Allah, Krishna, Shiva, or Buddha, etc., and that He identifies Himself with even pagan religions' names for deity.

Modern Occultism

My Sweet Lord, the song by the late ex-Beatle George Harrison, is an example of the theological error of religious universalism. In it, Harrison's lyrics alternate *Hallelujah* ("Praise Yahweh") with *Hare Rama, Hare Krishna* ("Praise [demonic] Rama and Krishna"). Harrison erroneously called all three, "*LORD.*" Concisely, the theological truth is that only Triune Yahweh is holy uncreated God; Rama and Krishna are created rebellious counterfeit deity. That is, demons. Only Yahweh-the-Son is LORD of lords, God of gods, and King of kings: the LORD Jesus Christ, who will return as Yeshua haMashiach. (Deuteronomy 10:17)

Thanks to Harrison and other hippie drug-abusive New Agers, religious universalism has become, to many, plausible on the level of urban myth, pop culture, and level two logic, but it is theologically false. Triune Yahweh, the God of the Bible, is a totally separate Spirit from the false deities of pagan religions, and does not identify Himself with their names. Righteous

Toraic behaviors appeal uniquely to Elohim, but even so man may approach Him only through a personal relationship with Jesus Christ.

Contrary to lyrical-*qua*-logical statements by The Moody Blues, another drug-influenced hippie rock band, *the living WORD of God is YHWH-the-Son, not AUM!* Street drugs open and paralyze the intellect to make a man more radical (more root cherubic). A major demonic theme of the 1960's sex, drugs and rock 'n roll was to exacerbate cherubic radicalism in the soul of our nation. Language and worship intersect at music. Rock 'n roll's pounding bass rhythm relates to fallen cherubic radicality (per chapter 11's multiple-intelligences metatheory). Satan was created to be the archcherub. The 1960's-relict 'party hearty' spirit of sex, drugs and rock 'n roll osmoses Mystery Babylon's silent confusion.

Binary Cosmological Paradigms

Pertaining to the culture war, pantheism and Eastern religions have significant problems trying to explain reality. They argue that knowledge (Skt., *jnana*) is analogous to a radiating radar-like soul-emanation from endocrine gland *chakras* (energy centers) developed by fixation (*darana*), suggestion (*dhyana*), perception (*samyama*), and identification (*samadhi*).

Suggestive processes were called *dhyana* by Hindus, *cha'an* by Confucians, and *zen* by Buddhists, as Satan migrated pantheism out from the Indian subcontinent. The equivalent idea is called *nasah* in Hebrew and *peismonay* in New Testament Koine Greek. Those words mean 'temptation to personally sin' in Greek and Hebrew, but 'the workings of impersonal *cosmic mind*' in the Far Eastern tongues. Eastern religions thus deny the earnest personality of God the Father, the filial opportunity to obey Him, and the corrupting influence of the demonic realm of nature (i.e., from theology's 'second heaven').

All five words for suggestion convey the idea of *rhetorical persuasion* so disdained by Socrates. The Judaeo-Christian usages imply temptation, but the sophist and pagan usages also imply internal or external mind control (not personal faith and prayer) as the means to solve life's problems. The superficial similarities between doctrine of temptation and rhetoric of suggestion identify a psychological cleavage plane, between the theology of our personal heavenly Father (Christianity) and the religion of Satan and his Impersonal Absolute (pantheism).

Another quirk of pantheistic thought relating to the culture war involves materials science. Hindu *Vedantic Ayurveda* describes pantheistic medicine. *Ayurveda* is a prolific cornerstone of much occult thought, mingling truth with error, and classifies all metals as *prithvi* (Skt., heavy). That is reductionist! There are profound physical and biological differences between chemically discrete metals. Though all are relatively dense and heavy, silver is not mercury, gold is not lead, cobalt is not cadmium, iron is not aluminum, and zinc is not nickel. Sodium is not beryllium, potassium is not plutonium, calcium is not radium, and magnesium is not arsenic. There is much, much more to chemistry and Western materials science than Eastern mysticism's fatuous generalization that metals are heavy. Similar profound differences exist in the spiritual and theological arenas, as well! Science identifies the orderly preexistent mind of God the Father and excludes myth, while mysticism flirts with diabolophilia. The two themes are inversely related.

Pagan religions worldwide bear certain similarities to each other, despite occurring in primitive cultures separated by vast distances. Similarities include: shamanistic initiation; ceremonial masks; statuary as foci of worship; and fornication, sodomy, or psychedelic drug use, as means of temporarily evading the Triune Elohim of Christ Jesus. The reason for these and other similarities is that pagan religions originate by environmental suggestion to the men or women involved, from demons striving for human slaves. The same is true, on larger, subtler and more systematic scales, of organized forms of paganism, including statuary marism. Neither submission nor fear placate satanic spirits of paganism and the occult: they want worse and worse sin, unto one's destruction.

Occultism's Progression

The following chronology of occultism within Western history illustrates the degree to which pagan spiritual nature has influenced societal and political trends. Any conspiracy that exists toward a one-world government is first spiritual and religious; second, political; third, socio-economic; and fourth, military and armament-related. The word *paganism* refers to the aggressive phase of occultism; *occultism*, to the latent phase of paganism. The following seven paragraphs contain analyses distilled from the research of Gary H. Kah, into the history of western occultism.[12]

Kabalism was the first systematic doctrinal attack against Triune Elohim's religion by Satan, in recorded history. It teaches that Moses was an occult figure sent to initiate the Israelites into Egyptian mystery religion. Kabalism presents Moses as an adept in the occult arts, and occult enlightenment as God's plan for Israel. Kabalism is to the Mosaic Covenant as gnosticism is to the New Testament.

Gnosticism was history's second large occultic movement identifed, and was problematic around New Testament times. Gnosticism presents the material world and the fleshly body as transient, unreal and evil, and thus inconvenient to a moral relationship with transcendent holy God, instead of the proving ground of faith and filial love that they truly are. Gnosticism insists, like *yoga*, Christian Science, and Silva Mind Control, that salvation comes through disciplined mind, instead of through faith in Jesus Christ's atoning blood and resurrection. It treats the root of the soul and body, material reality and procreation as tainted by materialistic evil. In reality, root materiality is heterogeneously affected by Satan, the fallen created archcherub, directly according to sins and inversely according to sanctification.

Knights Templar was the third major wave of occultism recorded in history. It involved Crusader knights of the order of Solomon's temple (hence, the name Templars). They were exposed to mystery religions in the Middle East, and co-opted by Satan and the occult. They became fabulously wealthy and influential in Europe, but were accused of satanism around 1300 A.D., and decimated by official fiat. Initiation rites to the order at one time included sodomy and urination on a cross. They served as a repository of occult knowledge and pagan practice from about 1100 AD to around 1300 AD, when Phillipe IV (Phillipe le Bel) king of France tried the leaders (including one Jacques de Molay) on charges of satanism and eradicated the order from France. The pope at the time reluctantly cooperated, and banned the Templars from most of Europe, excluding Portugal.

Rosicrucianism was Satan's fourth major organized doctrinal assault, against Triune Elohim's religion, in recorded history. It cropped up in Germany, after the suppression of Knights Templar. This variety of occultism was presented as non-religious in order to escape just censure. It was a recap of mystery religion promoting occult enlightenment. Purportedly, it is the teachings of a Franz Rosencruz, who traveled to Egypt and acquired occultic mystery knowledge. Symbol of the cult is a cross with a rose at the juncture of the stake and crosspiece. Rosicrucianism still exists today as an esoteric sect.

Freemasonry/Illuminati was the fifth systematic doctrinal attack by Satan, identified in the historical record. Speculative freemasonry has nothing to do with practical bricklaying, but is a mixture of occult ritual, secrecy, male bonding, and desire for spiritual power and political influence. The Illuminati conspiracy, developed through Adam Weishaupt in masonic lodges in Europe from the 1700's, had the stated intention of maneuvering freemasons into advisory and civil service positions with the major governments of the world in order to influence nations toward a pro-Luciferic society, such as is convenient to early 3rd millennial global governance. In the 19th century, former Confederate general Albert Pike, who believed that 'Adonai was not God, and that Lucifer (Satan) was,' rewrote much of freemasonic ritual and oath into Scottish rite freemasonry. The other main variety is York rite. From the 18th century until the present, freemasonry brings men and women under bondage to Satan through a variety of secret oaths and rituals which become more blatantly demonic the deeper an individual is seduced into the system. Many low-level freemasons believe their lodges are harmless charitable organizations. But, at the higher levels freemasons perform secret rituals invoking demons (such as 'Jahbulon,' an impossible alliance of holy Jehovah-YHWH with the demons Baal and Osiris). The freemasonic order for youth is called the Order of de Molay and is named for the condemned and executed leader of the occultic sodomitic Knights Templar.

Theosophy/Nazism was the sixth major movement of occultism against God's religion, identified in the historical record. Theosophy, between 1875 and 1949, grew out of the occultism of the Grand Orient Lodge of freemasonry, through the demon possession of several women: first, Helena Petrovna Blavatsky, then Annie Besant, then Alice Bailey. Those three women wrote many volumes of extremely-blatant occult literature. Among those influenced included Adolph Hitler, who kept a thickly annotated copy of Blavatsky's book, *The Secret Doctrine*, at his bedside.[13] Hitler believed that the world can only be ruled by fear.[14] At about the same point in history, the middle-to-late 19th century, a spate of other occult-influenced religions were released into the world, laying the groundwork for the New Age: Mormonism, Christian Science, and Unitarian Universalism. The theosophical writings were dictated to the three women by a fallen demon, which was supposedly an ascended master consistent with meditative evolution from manhood into co-equality and co-government with God—a familiar satanic theme. Those writings are larded with bizarre notions of Aryan racial superiority, salvation by disciplined mind, reincarnative evolution, anti-Semitism, occult enlightenment as the origin of all religion, *et cetera*. The young Hitler would have been called a New Ager, were he to have lived in the early 3rd millennium. According to Dr. Walter Stein, while Adolph Hitler was an art student in Vienna, Austria, before World War I, he read theosophy, studied astrology and yoga, immersed himself in pagan Teutonic and Greek mythology, and experimented with mescaline.[15] He opened himself up to Satan and his demons, which motivate the theosophists and all occultists, and brought about the Holocaust.

New Age movement/One World governance is the seventh, and most current, systematic doctrinal and political attack against Yahweh's religion and people, by Satan, in recorded history. Although New Age doctrine was described by Blavatsky and others since 1875, its blossoming was with the hippie youth movement of the 1960's, from the suddenly-widespread abuse of street drugs, fornication, Eastern religions, and extra-Biblical spirituality of many varieties. The hippie dream was to change the world, to alter it (as in *wicca*, which means 'to alter'). Since the mid-1960's it resulted in an explosive increase in the number of willing and unwilling victims of Satan exposed to and subverted by the kingdom of darkness. Street drugs popularized in the 1960's are what the New Testament calls *pharmakeia* (meaning 'sorcery') the root of the English word 'pharmacy.'

Sorcery would be a very severe sin, against Y'howah-God and against one's own soul and body. Pharmacologically-active chemical compounds can induce trance, an altered state of consciousness that results in long-term confusion about the transcendent set-apartness of Triune Yahweh. They can sensitize a man's nervous system to fallen seraphim and cherubim which can perpetuate a trance mindset and worldview. Ashtoreth (also called Astarte and Diana), possibly a fallen seraph originally local to the Mediterranean basin and propagated by mariolatry, is associated with ASC's (altered states of consciousness). The word *hypnosis* derives from Greek: *hupno-*, sleep, + *osis*, infusion.

The belief by many ex-hippie radical environmentalists, that the earth is a living organism pervasively infused with divine energy, is monism and idolatry—a mindset often resulting from drug-abusive sorcery. Occultic one-worlders use the lie of Goddess Earth to restrict rights, advance a pagan worldview, promote the global governance aspired to by Satan and his Illuminati, and coerce political and psychological submission. The Bible warns that, around the time of Jesus Christ's victorious return as conquering Messiah, the earth will be as in the days of Noah. Civilization will have become again widely pagan, likely involving mergers of mainstream Protestant doctrines with traditional Vaticanic heresies, mitigation toward sodomites, and esoteric Eastern spiritual disciplines. Faith plus occultism is, at best, lukewarmness, and at the worst, abominable apostasy.

In Gary H. Kah's words, the occult are like the Mafia, made up of factions that periodically fight against each other. In the third world, paganism and occultism correlate with disease, squalor, and spiritual bondage. But, "Where the Spirit of the LORD is, there is liberty." (2 Corinthians 3:17)

The pale-blue United Nations' flag depicts the continents of the world as imagined from the north. A Jewish tradition states that demons come from the north.

One of the goals of modern Believers needs to be to thwart, by a wise relationship with Triune Yahweh, futile submission to pagan leaders and the occult worldview that incepts the culture war pitting progressives against conservatives. The meta-Left versus people of Triune Elohim.

Such a perverse view of the universe results from incremental corruption of Western mind, by seemingly-harmless, media-condoned practices running the gamut from astrology, to tarot, to drug abuse, to witchcraft, to Eastern religions, to pornography and promiscuity, to trance meditation, or to satanism. Victims of the occult worldview descend toward death, by the mechanisms of spiritual excommunication, depression, and spirit possession. Submission to Satan doesn't appease him; he wants more and more sins, to multiply his authority over your soul and inner man. Whether or not you have specific knowledge that a decision would be wicked, the penalty for sin in worse sin. Even if you whole-heartedly rebel, you never totally escape from Y'howah-God. Deliberate sinning would make a miserable cry for help.

Conclusion

Being Born Again (justified by faith) in Messiah Jesus is the beginning of the objectivity, education and spiritual authority needed to successfully withstand paganism and occultism and the societal forms they induce. Within their own spiritual principalities, the fallen demons of paganism and their karmically proud human *gurus* have their way with every family wherein the new husband-and-wife couple fail to differentiate themselves from the false religious myths and superstitions of their in-laws.

Each new child born has the hope of being Born Again in Messiah Jesus, and through Him receiving the grace, peace and faith to purge his heart, mind, soul and home of occultism, and become the master of his own good God-given name.

The grip of paganism on humanity is challenged every time a new husband and wife couple finds the grace and peace to reject, and if necessary rebel against, the superstitions and spiritual bondage of their in-laws, by finding faith in Christ Jesus.

Families are as strong as their members' consciences before Triune Yahweh. Children's' consciences, in particular, are extremely precious in the reckoning of God the Father. The curse of occultism on society is as persistent as the sin legacy of the last three or four generations, and the influence of men and women currently in rebellion against the truths of the Triune God.

Chapter 3 notes:

[1]   Gary North. *Unholy Spirits: Occultism and New Age Humanism.* Tyler, TX: Institute for Christian Economics, 1994, 3.
[2]   *Ibid*, 13.
[3]   McCandlish Phillips. *The Bible, the Supernatural, and the Jews.* Camp Hill, PA: Horizon Books, 1970, 303-311.
[4]   Mircea Eliade. *Occultism, Witchcraft and Cultural Fashion.* Chicago: University of Chicago Press, 1976, 71.
[5]   Swami Narayanananda. *The Primal Power in Man or the Kundalini Shakti.* Rishikesh: Narayanananda Universal Yoga Trust, 1970, 356.
[6]   Arthur Koestler. *The Thirteenth Tribe.* New York: Random House, 1976, 40-41.

[7]   Danny Shelton and Shelley Quinn. *Ten Commandments Twice Removed.* Remnant Publications, 2004, 104.

[8]   William Dwight Whitney and Benjamin E. Smith. *The Century Dictionary: An Encyclopedic Lexicon of the English Language, Revised and Enlarged.* New York: The Century Co., 1914, 353.

[9]   Edmond Paris. *The Secret History of the Jesuits.* Chino, CA: Chick, 1975, 16.

[10]   Agnes Savill. *Alexander the Great and His Times.* New York: Barnes and Noble, 1993, 100.

[11]   *Ibid*, 224-225.

[12]   Gary H. Kah. *En Route to Global Occupation.* Lafayette, LA: Huntington House, 1992, 87-140.

[13]   Joseph J. Carr. *The Twisted Cross.* Lafayette, LA: Huntington House, 1985, 93.

[14]   Bob Rosio. *Hitler and the New Age.* Lafayette, LA: Huntington House, 1993, 113.

[15]   *Ibid*, 137.

Chapter 4

Church, State and Nature Worship

The United States' federal government must not fund neopaganism, which comprises the core religion of the United Nations. Pagan nature worship has distinct theological and philosophical characteristics. Thus, the United States federal government should not sympathetically favor the false religion of ecopaganism. If U.S. government policies advance an ecopagan state, they breach federalist separation of church and state, by cojoining a state of totalitarian globalism to a church of ecospiritual nature worship.

Limitations that United States' courts apply to Christian societal expressions should apply even more strictly to neopaganism than to Christianity. In the words of Ravi Zaccharius, religion drives politics; not politics, religion. Civilization is never a level playing field, because Satan is unethical and unscrupulous.

"Where the Spirit of the LORD is, there is liberty." (2 Corinthians 3:17b) The LORD is YHWH-the-Son, Jesus Christ, not any pagan deity. Losing sight of this eternal truth, in the glamour of ecumenical global governance, dooms the nations of the world to bondage to Satan, the father of lies. Not, 'where patriotism is,' nor 'where filthy riches are,' nor 'where weaponry is,' but where the Spirit of the LORD Jesus is, there is freedom.

Global governancers, comprising the 3rd millennial political meta-Left, strive to combine a church of spooky nature worship with a state of computerized one-world government. That monstrosity presently looms upon civilization, in these probably final few decades before Adonai Jesus-the-*Logos*' return. "Gay" is the Greek word for "earth." Satan wills for a pagan ecosociety, idolatrous in its earth focus and sexual abominations.

The disparate, progressive meta-Left advocates nature worship *cum* global governance, a spooky trend because Satan, the fallen created arch-cherub and author of occultism, is at the root of it. As decades of culture-war inroads into Protestant exceptionalism take their toll, the 3rd millennial New Age will see political victories of the radicalized, pro-global-governance meta-Left over Christian heritage in the United States, as well as Europe and elsewhere.

In United States' politics, the word 'Republican' derives from the Latin, *re-* (above) + *public* (the people). Above, as in 'more virtuous.' 'Democrat,' from the Greek *demos-* (people) + *cratos* (strength).

Demographic Shift

Many colonial and earlier settlers to North America came for religious freedom to worship Triune Yahweh as Jesus Christ, without a pope's or a king's micromanagement. Many modern immigrants venture to the United States, instead, to make money, shifting demographics away from Protestant Christian conservatism in the process.

Via his death tax, Barack Hussein Obama intends to redistribute wealth away from family ideals, and further shift demographics toward progressivist globalism and Roman Catholicism. Protestant exceptionalism brought God's highly conditional favor and prosperity upon the United States, but progressives vainly reject conscientious absolutes in an attempt to factor Adonai the *Logos* out of society.

Gaia Worship

Gaia was a pagan Greek goddess, the demon (in Christian terms) of the earth. Neopagans use the term 'Gaia' to refer to the idea that the earth is enlivened by an enveloping field of spiritual-and-cosmic energy, the intermingled spiritual-and-natural energetic *prana* of a pantheistic worldview. Neopaganism propagates eco-spiritual demonism.

Gaia worship is a coherent theological system, albeit loosely organized in terms of personnel and property. It has its doctrine, (false) deity, priestcraft, rites and rituals. It has the essential attributes of a religion and therefore must not be sponsored by the United States' government's federal policies, despite United Nations' advocacy of neopaganism at its root and core.

The Gaia hypothesis purports to venerate creation, the planet, as though it were a living female entity, consistent with wicca. That idolatry advocates removal of humans who offend occult systems of religion and ethics. In reality, any enveloping field of cosmic or magnetic energy imparts no holiness. The contents of any such field have no imparted holiness on that basis.

The Gaia hypothesis egregiously insinuates, 'Go green, and thereby incur divine blessing.' Hinduism notwithstanding, Christian-Jewish Yahweh cares somewhat about the natural environment, but His commands to humanity specifically focus upon the person of Jesus Christ. God the Son is revealed in the Old Testament scriptures as the LORD God of Israel, then in the New Testament books as Jesus of Nazareth.

Politicized Perfidy

Adolph Hitler said, "When you lie, tell big lies."[1] Hitler considered enormous lies more believable by the masses, requiring more time and effort to disprove, while the liar's policies enjoy the support of public hysteria. The error of man-made warming of the earth is being used exactly Hitler's way, to justify the financial ruin of the United States via scientifically shoddy treaties and policies. Anthropogenic global warming (AGW) is just such an enormous lie.

Anthropogenic (man-made) greenhouse gasses as the cause of global warming remain a very contested hypothesis. Advocacy of anthropogenic global warming falls more along emotional, theological and political lines than according to scientific evidence. Many in the scientific community absolutely deplore the poor quality of science that the radical environmentalists use to browbeat their agenda into the U.S. public and our legislative system. Anthropogenic global warming is a political red herring and a false-cause fallacy. The globalists have taken to calling global warming *climate change*, a complex question fallacy, since the atmosphere is naturally in constant flux. Unable to prove their point but wanting to change society, globalists want unproven anthropogenic global warming taught to secondary school students.

With an extremely high degree of probability, unavoidable solar flare activity is the cause of nearly all atmospheric warming.[2] The biosphere is in no danger of permanent harm from man-made greenhouse gasses.

Variations in atmospheric temperature almost perfectly correlate with solar flare activity. Nevertheless, globocratic agitators and politicians utilize partisan insider-owned major media to suggest to the populist citizenry, to work their policies. Anthropogenic global warming is being whipped into a political football to empower a pan-national global governance via eco-spirituality and the United Nations, to transgress the rights and sanctified freedom of middle-class Protestant exceptionalism and the United States of America. The result will be that some heretofore-free Americans may come to submit to the occultic United Nations and its pagan theology.

For more insightful reading on this topic, refer to Samantha Smith's cogent *Goddess Earth*, or to Dr. Michael Coffman's brilliant *Saviors of the Earth?* A clean natural environment is a laudable thing, if achieved for an ethical motive. But, if it is mandated for a pantheistic motive, then it's only a ruse and provocation in the epic conflict of the ages between Christ Jesus and Satan.

Dr. Michael Coffman wrote of the case of Judson Grant of Bangor, Maine.[3] Mr. Grant planned to build a car wash/restaurant/gas station complex in a developing area near Bangor. Beginning in 1989, over the space of a year he procured the requisite city and state permits, including from the Maine Department of Environmental Protection. The site he chose had, decades ago, been a wetlands, but had long since been filled in. There was no longer any standing water except briefly during spring and fall. Tag alder and bulrushes, both on the 1989 Federal Wetlands Species list, had taken root on top of the fill dirt. Near the halfway point of construction, a Fish and Wildlife agent chanced along and reported Grant to the EPA for a Section 404 violation of wetlands. The EPA promptly issued a cease and desist order, halting construction. After all the fines, delays and design changes were totaled up, and winter had delayed construction, entrepreneur Grant had spent $250,000 more than he had budgeted.

"Multiply Grant's experience by tens of thousands, and you can start to appreciate the financial drag these senseless regulations are having on our nation's economy, and each and every American. The cost is staggering."[4] The EPA might have saved a few mosquitoes, but impeded the progeny of several human families. Which have the more highly developed nervous systems and proper name, the humans or the mosquitoes? Which may contribute more to civilization, to *les beaux-arts*, to the advancement of science and theology: the human children or the mosquito larvae?

Founders' View

Patriot John Adams said, "The moment that idea is admitted into society that [private] property is not as sacred as the Laws of God, and that there is not a force of law and public justice to protect it, anarchy and tyranny commence. Property must be sacred or liberty cannot exist."[5]

Michael Coffman commented, "John Adams was correct. Property rights is a giant scale that balances the awesome power of the government with that of the people. Without property rights our remaining civil rights are an illusion. It is no coincidence that now that property rights are being assailed, tyranny [by the EPA] has resulted. Once America gives its property rights to the federal government [or to the North American Union, or the United Nations], we will have lost the only instrument that protects us from total control by the government. Like the feudal lords of medieval days, the federal government will have total control over every aspect of our lives. And the federal government is especially prone to rule by pressure groups."[6] The extent of this happening will be determined by ideology, policy, and their propagation in the U.S. judicial system. We need lawyers established in truth and holiness to transmit justice deep into the crannies of the judicial intellect.

"Professing themselves to be wise, they became fools . . . and worshiped and served the creature more than the Creator, who is blessed forever." (Romans 1:21,25)

Chapter 4 notes:

[1]   Bob Rosio. *Hitler and the New Age.* Lafayette, LA: Huntington House, 1993, 79.
[2]   S.Fred Singer and Dennis T. Avery. *Unstoppable Global Warming: Every 1,500 Years.* Blue Ridge Summit, PA: Rowman and Littlefield, 2008, 5.
[3]   Michael Coffman. *Saviors of the Earth?* Chicago: Northfield Publishing, 1994, 175.
[4]   *Ibid*, 176.
[5]   *Ibid*, 177.
[6]   *Ibid*.

Chapter 5

Crucial Messianic Doctrines

The LORD God of Israel = God the Son

SUMMARY: From at least the Exodus plagues until the immaculate conception, the LORD God of Israel was normatively identical with the preincarnate God the Son. He was born as Yeshua of Nazareth, then resurrected as the glorified LORD Jesus Christ. In pre-Christian days, all three Persons of Triune Elohim were not yet widely revealed, although a few prophets, priests, and kings glimpsed them.

Adonai (of the Jews) is God the Son (of the Christians). This is how Christianity and Judaism fit together. The LORD God of Israel was normatively identical with the preincarnate God the Son. He was born as Jesus of Nazareth, then resurrected as the glorified Yeshua haMashiach. He was the only Person of the Triune Godhead normatively revealed to pre-Christian Hebrews between the Exodus plagues and the immaculate conception.

During the 1st century A.D., the LORD God of Israel ministered as Yeshua haNotzri (Heb., Jesus of Nazareth) and first extensively revealed the other two Persons of the Godhead to mankind.[1] This idea of Adonai the Christ is the harmony of the Old and New Testaments. *This is the primary apostolic concept, that the LORD God of Israel became the LORD Jesus Christ.* This is why Jesus is called "LORD." Christ's words in the New Testament Gospels don cosmic profundity, in this context.

The Jewish religious leaders and Roman military authorities crucified the LORD God of Israel, in the Person of Yeshua of Nazareth. The Gospelic words of Jesus the LORD God of Israel contain cosmic significance, and impart galvanic faith to Christians.

"No man cometh unto the Father, but by me." (John 14:6) In the days of the Old Testament, this "me" was the LORD God of Israel (the preincarnate God the Son). In the years since the Advent and Calvary, this same "me" equals the lofty resurrected Jesus Christ. Preincarnation through Advent, this WORD remains the same true Individual, dispensing knowledge of His Father to men, to varying degrees, at various points in civilization's history.

In the words of David D. Burdick, "Jesus was the God of the Old Testament." Adonai of the TaNaK (i.e., of the Old Testament) was usually identical with God the Son. The LORD God of Israel was normatively Elohim the Son, and became Jesus of Nazareth. This is to say that Christ reigned as the LORD God of Israel, in Angelic existence as the eternal WORD of God, before He was born Y'shua of Nazareth.

The LORD God of Israel wasn't exactly identical with God the Father.[2] God the Father is in heaven (Matthew 6:9), but the LORD God of Israel dwelt for about seven centuries of Hebrew history near sea level, between the golden cherubim upon the mercy seat of the ark of the covenant. He did this first in the tabernacle, then in the temple. This distinction proves that the LORD God of Israel played a role for the Hebrew people that God the Father did not play. Biblical Israel's Angelic King became the King of the Jews. The LORD God of Israel became the LORD Jesus Christ.

"If you study the prayers of the Old Testament, you'll virtually never find people addressing God as their heavenly Father . . . . On those rare times in the Old Testament when God is referred to in fatherhood terms, it's almost always with respect to His authority or discipline . . . In John's Gospel alone, Jesus referred to God as His Father 110 times."[3] That's because the revealed LORD God of Old-Testament Israel was normatively identical with the preincarnate God the Son, not all three Persons of the Trinity.

The apostle Paul wrote, "All our fathers were under the cloud, and passed through the sea . . . they drank of that spiritual Rock that followed them: *and that Rock was Christ*." (I Corinthians 10:1,4; emphasis added) That ancient holy Rock was the LORD God of Israel, the WORD of God and preincarnate God the Son, who was eventually born Y'shua of Nazareth, then resurrected as the LORD Jesus Christ. The Koine Greek text for this verse literally reads, " . . . and that rock was *the* Christ." (Emphasis added) The Rock (the LORD God of Israel) equates to the Christ (Jesus).

Why do many Messianics not yet leap at this truth, taking initiative within the development of history? "Which in other ages was not made known unto the sons of men, as it is now revealed unto his holy apostles and prophets by the Spirit." (Ephesians 3:5) Elohim periodically dispenses new knowledge of the Godhead.

Usually, "the LORD God of Israel" was God the Son, preincarnate. This Angel of Yah was indivisible ("One," Deut. 6:4,5), like Jesus' coat (and soul) at Golgotha (John 19:23,34).

Outcomes of rejecting this doctrinal cleavage plane of "Adonai the Christ" include Talmudism and "opposing oneself." (Acts 18:6, KJV) Opposing oneself is one's heart and soul reactive in opposition to each other, if confronted by an awkward truth.

The LORD God of Israel, who was normatively identical with the preincarnate God the Son, interacted minimally with Hebrew laity, but more so with Jewish leaders, Hebrew kings, and prophets during Old Testament times. Later, in the New Testament, His dialogs with the scribes and Pharisees indicate His long egoic acquaintance with Jewish leaders and their bloodlines.

His intense frustration with them revealed Him as One who had intimate knowledge and experience with their forefathers. He watched them and interacted with them as the generations unfolded, for at least fourteen centuries of Hebrew history.

Poetically speaking, the LORD God of Israel was the immortal soul of the Jewish nation. For centuries, He observed the men, evaluated the character and logic of the leaders, and drew hard conclusions about families and the faith latent within their names.

During that time span, He stored within His soul temperament, even vehemence, concerning them, that was later divulged in Yeshua of Nazareth's Man-to-man dialogs with their descendents, the scribes and Pharisees.

Reprising His poetic role as the eternal soul of the Hebrew nation, and seemingly about to be accepted as Messiah, Jesus told the scribes and Pharisees, "Woe unto you! For ye build the sepulchers of the prophets, and your fathers killed them. Truly ye bear witness that ye allow the deeds of your fathers: for they indeed killed them, and ye build their sepulchers . . . From the blood of Abel unto the blood of Zacharias, which perished between the altar and the temple: verily I say unto you, It shall be required of this generation." (Luke 11:47,48,51)

His indignation toward them gives the distinct impression He had been nearby, maybe an Angel-to-men eyewitness, when Zacharias was murdered.

Denial that the LORD God of Israel became the glorified Christ Jesus obscures to unsaved rabbis and their flocks almost all understanding of the Father in heaven. "I am the way, the truth and the life: no man cometh unto the Father, but by me." (John 14:6) If you don't know Jesus, you don't know the Father in heaven, except through the limited means of natural revelation.

Natural revelation hints at the Father in heaven, but only acceptance of the truth of the Gospel message sweeps clear the starry horizons of un-Believing rabbis' hearts. Truths of Yeshua refresh torpors of left-brained myopia, like a fast-moving cold front blowing smoggy haze far over the skyline.

Unbelief in the Messiahship of Jesus of Nazareth impounds a firmamental torrent of grace and love from God the Father.

Triune Elohim

SUMMARY: Many Messianics downplay the Holy Trinity as a paganized Gentile concept, and doubt that there is even a way to say it in Hebrew. (According to Stephen Katz of Jews for Jesus, *Eloheynu ha Shiloosh haKodesh* is idiomatic Hebrew for Him.)

But, Tri-Unity is God's true nature, and is inseparable from Yeshua haMashiach's earthly and subsequent ministries. (Matthew 3:13-17; Luke 3:21,22)

The doctrine of the Trinity is essential sound doctrine, and provides the basis for Born Again conscience and, with it, identity, exclusion and community, under Triune Yahweh's protection. Christianity imparts subject-object dualism.

Marginalizing the pivotal doctrine of the Trinity puts Messianic leaders squarely at risk of violating Ezekiel 34:1-10, with its warning to shepherds who take advantage of God's flock.

This is because, by downplaying awareness that the same Triune Spirit and Name dwell in the hearts of leaders and laity alike, that which is not ministry is manipulation, and that which is not conviction is compulsion. Grace involves heartbeats, respiration and cognition being in-phase and harmonized with the living WORD of God and elect nature. The teaching of The Trinity is a caution against the rabbinocentric worldview that the apostle Paul deplored as apostate "Judaizing."

Believers in Jesus are indwelt by the Name (Ephesians 3:14,15) and Spirit (I Corinthians 6:19) of YHWH, and are not to be patronized to by self-justified leaders, who swerve from truths of God the Father toward religious traditions such as submission to authority, with its manifold temptations to subordinate truth to personalities. (Matthew 20:25-28)

If God had to choose between being a Father and being a King, He would choose to be a Father. Of necessity, He is God, first, and Friend, second.

Ha Shiloosh haKodesh (Heb., the Holy Trinity) is essential sound doctrine that enlarges the horizons of the heart.

Sound Doctrine's Standard Surpasses Torah's

SUMMARY: Jesus of Nazareth's Holy Ghost-revealed inner man, rendered into sound doctrine by the apostle Paul, sets a higher standard of personal conduct than the minimum required by the Torah. This higher standard may be commenced only by grace through faith in Jesus Christ and His resurrection.

The Torah does not forbid lasciviousness or masturbatory sexual-uncleanness toward a non-relative. Christian sound doctrine, by contrast, forbids all lasciviousness and erotic uncleanness outside of holy matrimony.

At the giving of the Torah to Moses, the preincarnate Christ forbade lasciviousness toward the nakedness of one's mother, father, stepmother, sister, granddaughter, niece, stepsister, aunt, uncle, daughter-in-law or sister-in-law. (Leviticus 18:7-17)

CRUCIAL MESSIANIC DOCTRINES

Centuries later, the LORD God of Israel as the glorified Christ forbade to the apostle Paul all lasciviousness and illicit erotic uncleanness. In Galatians 5:19, He called such 'the flesh,' commission of which would disqualify one from communion with God the Father and bring one under judgment by the Toraic law: not only by the Torah's moral law, but also by its ceremonial law.

God the Father's Holy Ghost (Matthew 10:20) exhorts the personal purity lived by Jesus of Nazareth, who exceeded Toraic requirements by obeying the Spirit, not merely the letter, of His Father's mind and will for Him.

It is safe to say that Jesus never gloated at the sight of any naked woman, nor ever once masturbated. Otherwise, the perfection of conscience that God the Father insists upon would be hypocritical. This perfection can only be approached by grace through faith, coupled with determination to apply the Bible to one's conscience.

Some apostate Talmudists opine that female masturbation is permissible by God, since it does not make anybody Levitically unclean. But, it inculcates the sort of lascivious thinking that Paul forbade! It may also involve the woman trafficking with a hateful incubus (a masculine seducing spirit).

Christians' indwelling Holy Spirit, the *Paraclete*, demands a higher standard of personal purity than that required by the Torah. In this sense, too, Christianity is far more than a corrupted Judaism.

Ritual conscience is to the letter of the Law, as relational conscience is to the Spirit of the Law. Righteousness-instilled ritual conscience seeks completion in Holy Spirit-inspired relational conscience, oriented to God the Father in heaven through the LORD Jesus.

Theological Newspeak?

SUMMARY: In some instances, theological ideas lose truth-content across translation or out of deference to hermeneutical approaches to it. Some Messianic congregationalists suggest that certain Christian theological words should be rephrased or revised to be more meaningful and sympathetic to Jews. Sometimes this can be done without cost to essential sound doctrine, but in other cases the resultant neologism errs from systematic theology's precise semantic nuance. Coupled with any

137

insinuation that semantic revision is owed to Jews, due to past Christian misdeeds against them, such doctrinal expectations may rankle.

First, "conversion" or "completion": Conversion (L., *con-* (with) + *vertere* (turn)) implies "sweeping, life-changing repentance," the idea of the Greek word *epistrepho*. Completion implies "adding something that had been missing." Conversion implies a complete departure from one's former sinful lifestyle, while completion connotes adding the missing piece. Neither is wrong, but conversion is more essential to sinful man than completion.

Second, "Christ (Savior)" or "Messiah": "Christ and Savior" imply individual forgiveness and sanctification through Jesus' atonement, while "Messiah" connotes Jewish national deliverance, redemption, and love. Across history, several men have been hailed as "Messiah," but "Christ" almost always means Jesus of Nazareth. The Savior's role is to intimately fathom one's heart, one's decisions, and one's guilt, unto God the Father's forgiveness. The Messiah's role is to come [back], for the benefit of the Jewish nation. "Christ" requires airing (if necessitated by being in-denial) and truly repenting of one's horrible sin-baggage, while "Messiah" connotes cause for celebration. Again, neither meaning is wrong, but their distinct semantic nuances ought be acknowledged.

Third, "baptism" or *"mikvah"*: Baptism, in Christian usage, implies what is supposed to be a once-in-an-eternity embarkation. God intends adult water baptism with confession of sins to be the beginning of one's official personal walk upon earth with Christ Jesus. The Jewish idea of *mikvah* (Heb., immersion) connotes a periodic ceremonial cleansing. Again, the two semantic nuances are not 100% congruent or interchangeable.

Fourth, "Christian" or "Believer": the word "Christian" means "little Christ"and becoming like Christ Jesus, obedient to God the Father in heaven, in one's inner man, radical outwardness, and heart attitude. "Believer" denotes loving mental assent to the deity and Messiahship of Jesus of Nazareth. The word "Christian" denotes and necessitates a more-sweeping life transformation than does the word "Believer." Neither is wrong, but "little Christ" is truer to God the Father's intentions for His faithful ones. Strictly speaking, relational "Christian" takes up where assentive "Believer" leaves off.

138

Chapter 5 notes:

[1] David Jeremiah. *Signs of Life: Back to the Basics of Authentic Christianity.*
Nashville: Thomas Nelson, 2007, 91.

[2] *Ibid.*

[3] *Ibid.*

Chapter 6

Logic: The Geometry of Reason

History reveals that during the inter-testamental period in ancient Greece, after Judah's Babylonian captivity but two or three generations before the life of Alexander the Great, professional rhetoricians lectured at the populace. Those rhetoricians, called sophists, considered gratuitous persuasion to be virtue. Like some modern trial lawyers, they would take any side of any issue and try to persuade debating opponents to their ideology. In his *Dialogs*, Plato recorded Socrates' opposition to their disingenuousness. Sophistry and logic thematically oppose each other.

Basis

During the inter-testamental period, while the Apocrypha was being written and after Judah's Babylonian captivity but before the birth of Jesus of Nazareth, Socrates the philosopher argued with the sophists to force them to admit that impartial pursuit of pre-existent truth embodies more virtue than does self-aggrandizing persuasion. Socrates made many enemies and eventually suffered condemnation to hemlock poisoning. However, his conviction prevails in most academia: candid dialectical truth-pursuing reason is more virtuous than sophistry, and sophistry is usually bad for philosophy and bad for civilization.

According to Christian apologist Ravi Zaccharius in a 2003 radio broadcast, Socrate's philosophy of logical reasoning was taught to his pupil Plato, to Plato's pupil Aristotle, and to Aristotle's pupil Alexander the Great. Alexander (aka, Sekundar) spread this philosophy of logical reasoning, by military and political conquest, eastward across the Middle East and Asia Minor into India. The philosophy of logical reasoning took psychological root in those cultures and passed by population migrations westward to

Europe, and finally to North and South America. Alexander spread the Koine Greek language and alphabet, and Macedonian-influenced classical civilization, as God's preparation for the letters of Paul the apostle of Jesus Christ. Clarion cognitive objectivity or lawless torpor: either one or the other of these springs from each human decision, to either stand up for Jesus or submit to temptation.

God used Alexander's conquests to create ready reading audiences for the subsequent proliferation of Paul's epistles. Aristotelian logic became authentic to the roots of Western civilization. The English word 'mathematics' derives from the Greek *mathematikos*, which means 'learning, mental discipline.' Mathematics is the language and science of measurement.

Agnes Savill writes, "The Greek word *sophos*, which originally signified skill and wisdom, had degenerated to indicate mere clever twisting of truth by trained oratory. In Greece a class of professional Sophists had aroused distrust because they taught their students to win arguments regardless of truth or lies. Speech had great power when printing was unknown and books were few. Direct, truthful, accurate, Alexander [of Macedon] had no use for the plausible oratory taught by the professional Sophists." [1] For all his paganism and bloodlust, Alexander seems to have loved truth.

Alexander detested sophistry, however. During the examination of Cassander over charges against him and his father, Antipater, Cassander defended himself cunningly. "Alexander, irritated, replied that such an explanation savored of sophistry; the Sophists could prove anything, true or false; he had had much experience of their unhealthy rhetoric and preferred to go direct to the core of a subject." [2]

Neither Alexander of Macedon nor Jesus of Nazareth admired sophists, scribes or pundits, due to such actors' habitual obfuscation to civilization of truth-acclaiming eurekas. Independently of each other, Alexander and Jesus furiously rebuked them, sophists and scribes, despite that literacy is dear to the heart of God the Father. Sophists' and scribes' self-serving pontifications imposed tempos of droning self-satiety, procrastination and phlegmaticism. That corruption sowed radicalism for passivity, cued to argument, contrary to hope's forward urgings. Incidentally, there is zero credible historical evidence that Alexander was homosexual, despite Hollywood's entrancing cinematographic sophistry. Alexander of Macedon was as straight as the arrows he shot, or he would have failed abysmally as a leader of men!

Greek sophists taught a deviated virtue. Contrary to Robert M. Pirsig's assertion in his influential novel, *Zen and the Art of Motorcycle Maintenance*, sophists sought their own prominence more than to teach true virtue (Gr., *arête*). On a culture-war level, the sophists taught unprincipled persuasion with disregard for impartial, preexistent truth: the *mythos* as greater than the *Logos*. Truth-bending to accomplish partisan agendas is common to sophists, global governancers, and some media moguls. East Indian pundits and ancient Jewish scribes occupied places in society similar to ancient Greek sophists.

Western knowing is according to verbal or visuospatial rationality: *reason*. Eastern knowing, by contrast, is more an intuitive conviction: a sudden, deep realization. In other words, Western cognition is typified by cerebral spatial and logical reasoning, while Eastern knowledge is typified by instantaneous holistic certainty.[3] God graces Christian conscience with Western cognition and objectivity. Pastor Steve Reynolds said, "Emphasis of love over truth risks liberalism. Emphasis of truth over love risks legalism." How may pre-existing absolute truth be reasoned about? Logical truth, either cognitive or holistic, produces an *eureka*!

Without the influence of Jesus the *Logos* and His Father (holy YHWH), societies lose indignation at lies. If that happens, people can't trust each other and soon spiritually hate each other. Impartation of respect requires a clear conscience. Filthy consciences' offerings of respect or honor amount to insults. Meta-Left progressives, in the early 3rd millennium, believe they are justified in lying, even under oath, to be entrusted with political authority and advance their satanic agenda.

Tenet

Pre-existent truth is supra-personal. It's not by whose authority that an idea is logical, it's by whether or not it's true. Nature, literature, materials, children, law and relationships contain instances of God the Father's orderly pre-existent mind, encoded as logical truths. Our belief in enduring transcendent truth bore fruit across the past twenty centuries as *systematic theology* and the *scientific method*.

Systematic theology explains the spirituality of the blessed 'I:Thou duality' that recognizes both the inner man and God the Father, of holy Triune Yahweh. Systematic theology explores the filial "I: Thou" duality between man and God, the holy Spirit who spoke the galaxies into existence and loves each human child.

The scientific method encourages a pragmatic 'I:that duality' for pursuit of nonsuperstitious scientific truth, within the paradigm of empirical universal reality. The scientific method supports the objective, rational "I: that" duality between a curious subject and an interesting object of study. The scientific method structures pursuit of peer-accountable scientific truth within the worldview of empirical universal reality, structured and navigable by the rules of *logic*.

Western objectivity is most prevalent in Protestant heritage nations: "Where the Spirit of the LORD is, there is liberty." (2 Corinthians 3:17) This is another way of saying, 'Where the Spirit of the LORD is, there is cognition; where cognition is, there are wise decisions made; where wise decision are made, there tends to be liberty.' Christianity tends toward subject-object dualism; pagan occultism tends toward subject-object monism. The former is pro-cognitive; the latter, pro-dementive. *Christianity imparts subject-object dualism. Toraic righteousness (Yahwehism) imparts quietness and assurance.*

Theological and scientific duality are essential to civilization's development and sustenance. Without them, men's minds tend toward superstition, confusion and lies. Logic and funding are essential to all organizational planning. God is not bound by logic, but condescends to it and most often honors it. Logic is to conscience, as emotion is to rumination. Conscientious absolutes are utterly essential to mental health, brightness of heart and unashamed hope.

The word *logic* derives from the Greek, *logos*, meaning "word, rational discourse, doctrine." The Bible refers to Jesus of Nazareth, Adonai the Christ, as "the *Logos* made flesh" (John 1:14). God the Father has an interest in the furtherance of Aristotelian logical reasoning. He dispenses clarion of the *Logos* to accomplished students of reality. The word *'clarion'* derives from the Latin *clarus*, meaning 'clear,' and originally alluded to medieval courts' heralds' high-pitched trumpet hails.

Logic is structured by a few handy rules by which statements and arguments may be evaluated for truth content, then understood, communicated and/ or discretely acted upon.

143

Aristotelian logic proceeds from two *axioms*. An axiom is a universally true, cosmologically-consistent definition. The first is: *Identity* (A is A, or, A = A), meaning "a thing is itself." The second is: *Exclusion* (A is not non-A, or, A < > A'), meaning "a thing is not its exclusion." Logical exclusion explains the relevance of the statement, "Difference is an absolute."[4] Psychological exclusion (most fundamentally, chastity) permits egoic identity. Without exclusion there can be no identity, nor excellence. Radically speaking, without chastity there can be neither personal identity nor romantic excellence. The word *radical* derives from the Latin, *radix*, meaning 'root.' *Psychologically, identity is to mathematical thinking, as exclusion is to chastity.*

In the English language, forms of the verb "to be" semantically imply logical equivalence, identity, and mathematical congruence, between subject and object. "A is A" means "A = A."

Logically, two binary states result from any proposition: true or false, yes or no, and right or wrong. Psychosocially, *three* states constitute valid response to any proposition: pro, con and neutral. This is an extremely important distinction, because it frees one from reaction, permitting discretion. Neutrality expands the inner man's discretion, while pro or con activate the outer man. A self-styled demagogue once said, *'Don't tell people what to do, tell them who they are.'* Motivation proceeds from identity. Identity consecrated to the *Logos* keeps safe. Non-servile coordinated hand-eye activity can help stimulate cognition, to thwart social-defeat stress and alleviate depression.

A *fact* is two dualistically-identified ideas equated in a verbal definition. For example, "The sky is blue" means "the sky = bluish air," a *conditionally true* statement. It is conditionally true because the sky can be opaque cloudy air, or earth-shadowed nighttime air, under different atmospheric conditions.

Cognitive epistemology identifies and classifies facts into coherent systems of science. A grammatical statement identifies a fact, which may then act as a premise in argumentive reasoning. *Facts are to your mind as truths are to your heart.*

The psychological state of one's actions contradicting one's understanding is called disobedience to conscience. It is the idea of living a lie, of being in denial. Logic connects human decisions and behaviors to cognition and conscientious absolutes. The inner man and logic intersect at the human conscience, which deals in conscientious absolutes.

Schematic 6.1: Syllogistic Venn Diagrams of Grammatical Conjunctions.

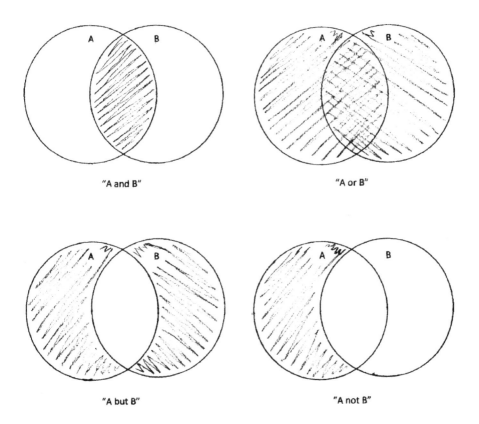

Logic may be *syllogistic* or *propositional*. *Syllogistic reasoning* uses graphics and symbols to convey premises, truths and arguments. *Propositional reasoning* uses linear sets of verbal statements functioning as premises and conclusions to identify, clarify, argue and prove rational truths. *Propositional reasoning* is, classically, a progression of premises from which is drawn one conclusion at a time.

Logical reasoning may be *deductive* (specific-to-general) or *inductive* (general-to-specific). *Deductive reasoning* is of the form, "Theory C is not disproven, therefore it is probably true in this instance." *Inductive reasoning* is of the form, 'Hypothesis D was true for the past ten tests, therefore it will probably be true for the eleventh test.'

An *axiom* is a proposition that is true by definition. A *theory* is a credible proposition not yet proven false. And, a *hypothesis* is a proposition undergoing exploratory testing for truth content.

Logical conclusions may be said to be either *sufficient* or *necessary*. In the case of the logical proposition "If A then B," a *sufficient* conclusion means "The existence of A implies a consequence of B." A *necessary* conclusion means "The existence of B implies a precondition of A."

According to Peter Rice of Jews for Jesus, Jewish sages developed *block logic* in which a set of premises is read, comprehended and individually weighted prior to the drawing of any of possibly several conclusions. To draw a hasty block-logic conclusion, before the entire premise set is identified, evaluated, weighted and understood, would risk an error.

Logical Fallacies

Logicians have identified at least twenty *logical fallacies*, or types of propositions that contain fatal internal flaws and cannot convey truth. Irving M. Copi[5] identified nineteen *informal logical fallacies*. Some of them carry Latin names familiar to scholars, lawyers and judges. You may recognize many of these intellectual non-dynamics from the verbal flounderings of some actors and politicians.

1. *Argumentum ad Baculum* (appeal to force): 'It's true because if you doubt or disagree with me, I'll beat you up!'

2. *Argumentum ad Hominem, Abusive* (slandering an opponent's character to disqualify his argument): 'It's a lie because so-and-so said it, and so-and-so is no good.'

3. *Argumentum ad Hominem, Circumstantial* (citing irrelevant circumstance to disqualify an opponent's argument): 'It's a lie because so-and-so said it, and he got a speeding ticket yesterday.'

4. *Argumentum ad Ignorantiam* (appeal to ignorance): 'It's true because you can't prove otherwise.'

5. *Argumentum ad Miseracordiam* (appeal to pity): 'It's true because you should feel sorry for me.'

6. *Argumentum ad Populum* (appeal to popular opinion): 'It's true because everybody else thinks so.' That is the mentality of political correctness and groupthink.

7. *Argumentum ad Verecundiam* (appeal to authority): 'It's true because Mr. Big says so.' That is the mentality of Talmudism.

8. *Reductio ad Absurdum* (reduction to absurdity; *non-sequitur*): Merely utilitarian premise. 'It's true because my claim hinders yours.' And, 'I don't care if you are free—Mr. Big is your master.'

9. *False cause: Post hoc ergo propter hoc* (chronological priority proves causation): 'The moon rose, then it rained, therefore moonrise causes rain.'

10. *False cause: Non causa pro causa* (wrongly identified cause): 'Moonrises cause rain.'

11. *Petitio Principii* (begging the question): Using as a premise the very conclusion sought to be proven. 'The sun went down, it started raining, therefore it is evening.'

12. *Ignoratio Elenchi* (irrelevant conclusion): A conclusion drawn from an unrelated argument cited as proof of a totally different argument.

'Moonrise brings rain, therefore I'll make an 'A' on my geometry exam.' Mythic.

13. *Complex Question* (two logical subquestions combined into an unanswerable or indemnifying compound question): 'Have you stopped beating your wife yet?' (A *yes* answer concedes unproven, perhaps nonexistent, guilt. A *no* answer implies facetiousness or cruel oblivion to imputed but unproven wrongdoing.)

14. *Accident* (general-to-specific *inductive* argument rendered invalid by oversimplified or accidental circumstances): 'Two days now, the moon came up, then it rained. Therefore, it will rain every morning this spring.'

15. *Converse Accident* (hasty generalization; choosing the example of an atypical case as a premise in a specific-to-general *deductive* argument): 'It rained three mornings this spring, therefore I can fire my gardener and sell my irrigation equipment.'

16. *Equivocation* (a word with multiple meanings used out of context in a premise): 'I can safely fire my gardener, therefore I should find some gasoline and matches.'

17. *Amphiboly* (grammatically ambiguous, loose or indeterminate premises used to argue specific conclusions): 'The lawn was damp this morning, therefore exactly 2.70 inches of rain fell last night.'

18. *Accent* (argument rendered deceptive by shift of grammatical emphasis in a premise; use of spin in an expression to imply a word has an imaginary or too-convenient meaning): 'Rain is *due* ['do'], therefore nothing further needs to be *done*.'

19. *Composition* ('what's true of the parts is true of the whole they compose'): 'I found two four-leaf clovers in my front lawn, therefore my entire lawn is composed of four-leaf clover plants.'

20. *Division* ('what's true of the whole is true of the parts'): 'I fertilized my entire garden with a generic, nitrogen-based fertilizer, therefore no individual plant comprising it needs any specialized watering or nourishment.'

Thesis

Logic structures the rationality upon which Western civilization is built. Logic is one human result of the spiritual leaven of Triune Yahweh. The Bible calls Jesus of Nazareth 'the *Logos*'. Poetically, Jesus Christ is the eternal Soul of both Western rationality and the Hebrew nation. Personal objectivity and intellectual detachment are conditional gifts to Christian-heritage civilizations.

Christian apologist Ravi Zaccharius stated over radio in 2002 that there are three philosophical levels of communication. *Level 1* of philosophic communication is the theoretical high ground of logic, where identity, exclusion, deduction and induction occur. It deals with 'Why we believe what we believe.' Peter Kreeft, in his book *Three Philosophies of Life*, as cited by Ravi, wrote that three things must go right with any argument: 1) The terms must be unambiguous, 2) The premises must be true, 3) The argument must be logical.

Level 2 is the realm of imagination and feeling. It deals with "Why we live the way we live." Ideas at this level may make belief-altering impact by capturing the emotions independently of cognition of the orderly pre-existent mind of God the Father encoded within reality. Such emotionality is often accomplished by secular music, movies, videos and television. Such ideation has, in Ravi's words, "historically molded the soul of a nation far more than solid reasoning has."

Level 3 is what Ravi calls "kitchen-table conclusions," where casual conversations structure and proscribe much of daily life. Level three is the sociological substrate, where ideas are applied to a model of reality, such as between a parent instructing a child or athletes critiquing political rhetoric between wind sprints. Level three encompasses loyalty to particular human beings and to their worldviews.

The credibility of anthropogenic global warming (AGW, or man-made climate change) is on philosophy's levels 2 and 3. It is almost certainly not true, but is becoming pop culture and urban myth, by sheer volume of the foundations, movies, advertisements, public policies and biased scientists leaping aboard its *ad populum* bandwagon.

Logical reasoning has an enemy, called syncretism (Gr., *syn*— (together) + *cretizein* (uncertain)). Syncretism is as insidious as sophism. Syncretism

---

is to intrapersonal, as sophism is to interpersonal. Syncretism declares that irreconcilable ideas, doctrines or philosophies are compatible—just don't evaluate them. Syncretism brazenly implies "*A* equals *A*-prime." Syncretism twists terminology using logical fallacies to claim that good is evil, and evil, good. Syncretism tries to claim sin is virtuous, lewdness is holy, and emotion is cognition. Syncretism purports that true patriotism and global governance are both good for the United States of America, and that deep-ecologic democide would be a socially beneficial form of earth cleansing.

Syncretism asserts that honorable uprightness and oblivious shame are equally desirable character traits. Syncretism presents systematic theology and occultism as equally truthful. Syncretism claims that even if I know an idea to be truly foul and evil but engage in it anyway, I cannot be called a hypocrite. Syncretism purports that there can be no real meaningful, absolute, philosophic or spiritual differences between persons.

Logic's relevance to psychology is that *conscientious absolutes* preserve personality, while conscientious syncretism invites calamity. Conscientious absolutes are angelic, but conscientious syncretism is demonic. Conscientious absolutes tend toward integrity and life, but conscientious syncretism tends toward debauchery and death. Conscientious absolutes structured by the Moral Law ascend toward prosperity and life, but conscientious syncretism descends to poverty, disease and squalor. Conscientious orthodoxy must not syncretize. Syncretism approximates Biblical double-mindedness (Gr., *dipsuchos*). (James 4:8)

Moral gentry construct their personalities upon reality-consistent conscientious absolutes. Human trash, upon conscientious syncretism. The former is loved; the latter, shamed. In this life, and into eternity.

Another enemy of the philosophy of reason, as a technique of truth seeking and didactic style, is *facilitation of an agenda*. Facilitation is defined as "The process of guiding a group toward a pre-planned consensus." It emphasizes harmony at the expense of reason, and is as such *a guided sophism*, like a college professor using a semester to sell a used car to his students. Resisters, who mentally hold out against facilitators, refuse to compromise truth for the cheap gratification of being hailed by the group. The rules for facilitation are: respect each member and their views; avoid argument or debate; communicate feelings, not contradicting facts or beliefs; and, willingly compromise to achieve unity. Obviously, a facilitated meeting, committee or conference conveys only the appearance of pursuing truth through reason.[6]

Anti-facilitative resister-type behaviors deemed unacceptable by facilitators include: *aggressing* (deflation of the status, egos, aplomb, or pride of others, or impugning their motives); *isolating* (obvious indifference or passivity, or resort to stand-offish formality; not voicing concerns during meetings, but undercutting agreement post-conference); *blocking* (over-arguing a point; rejecting ideas inconsiderately of others; unreasonable opposition and disagreement; exhuming dead issues after the group has resigned itself to them); and *special pleading* (introduction or support of suggestion related to one's own petty interests, biases or philosophies).[7]

Facilitation delves into *argumentum ad populum* and *ad vericundiam.* Facilitation delves into desire to be enfolded by a nexus' approval, be affirmed by groupthink, and submitted to authority. *Nexus* (L., knot) is Scottish anti-Establishment poet and psychiatrist R.D. Laing's term for a toxic, implosive group. Laing defined a nexus as "characterized by enduring and intensive face-to-face reciprocal influence on each other's experience and behavior." [8]

The neologism 'to nexate' means to gravitate into a nexus. 'Nexation' forms nexi. Community proceeds from shared interest in the *Logos* of Yahweh, but defaultive nexation lets apathy bind one to the herd. Nexation usually begins with desire for Mr. Big to provide cradle-to-grave satiation.

Facilitation depends upon thinking men lacking the grace or character to lambast an evil farce for what it is. The word 'facilitation' derives from the Latin, *facere*, "to do or make."

Corporate salvation, via mitigation, sycophancy, or submission toward an envious, bitter group, is theologically futile and philosophically loathsome. Nexus codependency is a real problem, but safely approachable only through systematic theology and cognitive psychology. Faith and reason.

Typically, the United Nations' Non-Governmental Organizational (NGO) cocktail-party legislature and ecologic earth summits are saturated with the facilitative mentality. Facilitation is designed to convey the impression of friendly agreement stemming from sincere quest for truth. But, facilitators bring to committees pre-determined conclusions, to guide members toward pre-set outcomes.

The facilitative dialectic implies that the end of group consensus justifies the means of biased sophism. This, instead of an unbiased Socratic method governed by *Logos*-fearing Aristotelian logic. Far from being candid, facilitation can be a tightly controlled collective sophism leading to downward-spiraling groupthink.

Summary

If the United States of America conforms to the level two media and ignores The Trinity's narrow logical truths, she will be told, 'There's no difference between what you want and what you don't want, therefore you shouldn't be upset when you are plundered for sinners' benefit.'

During the inter-testamental period prior to Jesus of Nazareth's earthly ministry, significant world events occurred. 'His-story' alludes to the purposes, within unfolding civilization, of Adonai the *Logos*, the LORD God of Israel, who became the LORD Jesus Christ. He enjoyed pre-existence with God the Father. He angelically gave the Torah to Moses, and exhorted the children of Israel to holiness. In the first century, He miraculously lived as Jesus of Nazareth, and first widely revealed God the Father and God the Holy Spirit. He will come again to fulfill prophecy.

God allowed world conquest by Alexander of Macedon, to propagate classical Greek logical reasoning and the Koine Greek language in preparation for the letters of the apostle Paul. Paul wrote to the future of spiritual man. The ministry of Jesus of Nazareth changed God's approach to the human conscience from access via the ritually-oriented carnal mind, regulated by the Torah, to the relationally-oriented spiritual mind, regulated by the indwelling Holy Spirit. "The law is spiritual," (Romans 7:14) because through the Torah God sought to spiritualize men's consciences, mostly via their materially-oriented carnal-mind behaviors.

Via Jesus' New Covenant, God spiritualizes men's consciences through relationship with Himself through the *Paraclete*. Paul's sound doctrine has ascendancy over both Hebrews and Greeks. Some in Messianic circles chafe at Paul's Christianity, but each, Jew or Gentile, will be judged by God according to Paul's sound doctrine. Sound doctrine takes up where the Torah leaves off, and is *revelation of Jesus of Nazareth's inner man*. It represents a mistake of incalculable proportion for anyone to jest about the apostle Paul's meek fraternal description of life via the inner man of Christ Jesus, by representing Paul as a vaguely jocular Rabbi Sha'ul. The New Testament is much more than a commentary upon the Torah.

Is one's basis for personal authority from his relationship to our excellent, holy Triune God, or from a social authority-centered hierarchy, should the two diverge by canon, logic, theology, or civil law? Is one too submitted-to-it-all to call a bad idea "A bad idea," against peer pressure and spiritual apathy?

Caveat

Groupthink means to agree with a social group's consensus because that is easier than persuading its leaders to become truly godly. If lies are too entrenched, vote with your feet. *Groupthink mentality* is the paradigm of habitually yielding to a consensus, to compensate for paucity of leadership within oneself. Those yielding to groupthink feel safe by the premise that if they collaborate in their decision, they can't all be wrong, or at least not all blameworthy.

'Too big to fail' makes a bad epitaph. The problem is that even privileged executive groups are subject to judgment. History does not exonerate the German NAZI high command, even though its component personalities commanded by some consensus, feeling safe in their civil legality and in their nexus.

In the future, holy people set apart for God may suffer exclusion themselves, from a market nexus enforceable by a VeriChip-based global identity management system. (See chapters nine and ten.) As Francis Schaeffer noted, Christians are not usually martyred for worshiping Jesus, who is Y'howah-the-*Logos*, but rather for rebelliously identifying Him as *The* Deity to the exclusion of emperor worship, paganism, or human tradition.

The set of societal forms which reassure mankind that trust in the Father of the *Logos* is authentic and safe, comprises true civilization. These civilization-comprising societal forms represent the Christian aspect of patriotism (Gr., *pater-*, father + *osis*, infusion). Antitheses to this Christian patriotism are New Age global governance and ultra-national jingoism. The

153

meta-Left, composed of 'progressive' proponents of global governance, strive to eliminate Christian societal forms, because YHWH-the-Creator and Satan the created arch-cherub are irreconcilably opposed.

Chapter 6 notes:

[1] Agnes Savill. *Alexander the Great and His Time*. New York: Barnes and Noble, 1993, 89.
[2] *Ibid*, 147.
[3] Mahesh Chavda. *Only Love Can Make a Miracle*. Charlotte, NC: Mahesh Chavda, 1990, 33.
[4] Felix Morley, ed. *Essays on Individuality*. Indianapolis: Liberty, 1977, 222.
[5] Irving M. Copi. *Introduction to Logic*, 4th Ed., New York: MacMillan, 1972, 72-107.
[6] Berit Kjos. "Homeland Security and the Transformation of America," *Hope for the World Update*. Summer, 2003, 4.
[7] *Ibid*.
[8] R.D. Laing and A. Esterson. *Sanity, Madness and the Family*. Baltimore, MD: Penguin, 1970, 21.

Chapter 7

Of Cells and Souls

Holistic health science is *ortho* if it doesn't utilize occultism. That is, if it doesn't invoke satanic sprits for the purposes of healing. Ayurvedic health traditions, by contrast, derive from Hinduism, which has no true Messiah in whom to resist Satan and 'the old man.' The word 'holistic' is from the Greek, *holos* (meaning 'whole, every whit, complete').

Where did Hindu Ayurveda go wrong? In addition to its pantheism, by confusing partisan spirits (heralds, seraphim or cherubim) with *prana*, the impersonal mechanistic energy of the cosmos. Hinduism makes much of supposedly-impersonal cosmic energy, calling it *prana*, *shakti* or *kundalini* in Sanskrit.

Worship of demons or angels, or of oneself, is sin in the sight of The Holy Tri-Unity. If a person imagines himself a Deity-in-training or a co-Creator consistent with pantheism, and tries to psychically imagine and apply impersonal cosmic energy to demonstrate his supposed Deity, those sins of idolatry and sorcery may consign his soul into bondage to Satan. Stretching and breathing exercises aren't intrinsically sinful, without pantheistic theology, chanting, solar cult or submission to a *guru*. Noninvasive acupressure therapy can be healthy.

Because of the intense spiritual temptations involved, naivety regarding meditation invites temptation to commit idolatry and sorcery, prompting God in His holiness to pronounce judgment. Occult medicine may occasionally result in some cures, because Satan has a certain amount of power, but such ends do not justify the means. The end result of a person healed by pagan spirituality, such as *santeria* (Brazilian witchcraft), may be worse than if he had turned to the true God, or if nature had taken its course. Submitting to occultism in search of healing is analogous to pouring gasoline on a house fire. A debt owed, or a soul sold, to Satan would be a totally unacceptable cost. However, if a type of treatment appeals to one's imagination and soul, at-least-brief healing may occur.

Permanent healing of a soul originates with mercy and grace toward the person from his or her Maker, Yahweh the Father. Occultism cannot heal a wounded spirit, because it proceeds from Satan, the Enemy of God and man. The word Satan derives from *ha satan* (Heb., the Enemy). Seek healing by believing in your heart that Yeshua haMashiach (Jesus of Nazareth) is Elohim born flesh and that He resurrected from the dead, and invite his Spirit of truth to dwell in your heart (Gr., *kardia*).

Such a decision of sincere belief *justifies* you in God the Father's sight, which sets you free from sin's eternal penalty, and begins the process of *sanctification*. Sanctification sets one free from sin's power, both inwardly and outwardly. Sanctification is sustained by grace, and catalyzed by faith. Perseverance with sanctification leads to *glorification*, freedom even from sin's presence.

Physical Science Basis

Regarding natural revelation, some theologians think that angels are drawn from the stars, which emit energy. The orderly pre-existent mind of God the Father is encoded within physical science. To verify that we're thinking in the same context, here are a few hard-science facts.

Electrons flow from electronegative to electropositive, and in so doing comprise electric current. A cathode is the negatively-charged, reducing electrode of an electrolytic circuit. In electrolysis, the negative cathode attracts positively-charged cations. An anode is the positively-charged, oxidizing electrode of an electrolytic circuit. In electrolysis, the positive anode attracts negatively-charged anions.

In respiration, pulmonary blood cells' hemoglobin molecules are oxidized (lose electrons), via reduction-oxidation reactions, while pulmonary atmospheric oxygen atoms are reduced (gain electrons). Human respiration involves reduction of breath with oxidation of blood. The form is "Lose electrons, oxidation; gain electrons, reduction."

Earth's upper atmosphere has slightly-north magnetic polarity. Magnetic flux travels from north to south poles, i.e., from magnetonegative to magnetopositive. Biologically, north magnetic flux revolves electrons counterclockwise to the axial direction of flux, soothes inflammation, dilates blood vessels, and heals wounds. South magnetic flux revolves electrons clockwise to the axial direction of flux, inflames tissues, constricts capillaries, and proliferates microbes. North magnetic flux heals, oxygenates, tones and anabolizes living biological flesh. South magnetic flux sickens, hydrogenates, inflames and catabolizes living flesh. Human flesh is faintly diamagnetic.

Viewed from the North, the Earth rotates counterclockwise. Viewed from the South, the planet rotates clockwise. A human being produces about one-hundred watts of energy. One gallon of gasoline contains about five-hundred times one human's daily biological energy production.

The word 'oxygen' derives from Greek *oxus-* (sharp, acid) + *-geneys* (producing). 'Nitrogen' derives from Latin *nitrus-* (nitre, salt) + *-gen* (producing). 'Hydrogen,' from Greek *hudor-* (water) + *-geneys* (producing).

Red light travels faster than blue light, and blue light travels faster than purple light. This is why low angle sunlight is reddish, because faster-moving red light is reflected away slightly less by earth's atmosphere, compared to other visible wavelengths. Red and infrared light travel faster, but contain less energy, than purple light. Purple and ultraviolet light travel slower, but contain more energy, than red light.

Digestion of food and assimilation of nutrients has more in common with chemical cracking and fractional distillation, of food's biotic fraction, than with putrifaction or rotting. Food's biotic fraction is composed of the assimilable calories and grams of protein, fats, carbohydrates, minerals, vitamins, enzymes, etc., comprising dietary intake.

Materialistic science erred by excluding the soul from study. The soul is a valid topic for systematic theology, but (according to Laurence E. Kennedy, Jr. PhD) cognitive psychology is the only branch of psychology that is compatible with Biblical Christianity. Almost all parapsychology is completely incompatible with sound doctrine and holiness.

Psychic Powers?

New Age physics, promoted by physicist Fritjof Capra and others, purports to meld parapsychology with science. Certain psychics, such as Uri Geller, claim to bend metal spoons using telekinesis and psychic powers. New Age physics involves the idea that a human mind is part of a huge, energetic, magnetic field (called *prana, chi, ki* or *wa* in various occultic disciplines), that supposedly infuses all space and matter. Within the bounds of that energetic Cosmic Mind, one's soul purportedly (by New Age physics) interacts with quantum mechanics of atomic reality, according to the visualizations of a meditator. *Psychic powers come with a curse, and obstruct mental hygiene.* Occultic *yogis* call the soul 'the subconscious mind.'

Scientists who believe pantheistic New Age physics accept the idea of psychic powers by the cunningness of its argument. New Age physics proceeds from two physical science theories. The first is the theory of relativity ($E=mc^2$), which states that matter and energy are points on a continuum. The second is the Heisenberg uncertainty principle, which states that the act of observing an electron alters it orbital position or velocity. In other words, according to the New Age interpretation of these two theories, matter is energy, but one's observation of either alters its properties. As though matter is energy, and vice versa, but fixation of meditative attention upon either alters it. This suggests to some a scientific basis for pantheism and sorcery. *New Agers deduce from these two physical science theories that man's mind has telekinetic power over proximal and future energy and matter, a worldview advocated by black occultists!*

This deceptive idea is that meditative trance obliterates subject-object duality (self and not-self). The myth of superconsciousness implies that subject is the author of object and Impersonal Absolute is the author and essence of subject, but it's not! Living persons are not figments of an Impersonal Absolute's imagination. New Age occultists claim that meditative trance makes the meditator intuit subatomic, atomic, ionic, molecular, cellular and massive matter and energy. That, then, supposedly conforms to the imagination of the meditating scientist by the power of Cosmic Consciousness (the Impersonal Absolute). But, such pantheistic meditation tempts the meditator to claim divinity for himself, which would be idolatry.

Psychic powers (sorcery) may or may not be possible by a mystic's soul's augmentation with Satan's demons, but should be shunned, not sought. *Either cognition or psychic powers may be cultivated, not both, in Yahweh's reality.* New Age physicists tolerate the idea of psychic powers, the pseudoscientific insinuation that *meditative alpha brain-waves alter objective reality*: beta brain-wave cognition doesn't alter objective material reality either (regardless of how many minutes one may wait for an occult miracle to happen), apart from dialogic or tactile involvement.

Satan uses the concept of all-pervasive spirituality, consistent with impersonal Cosmic Consciousness and cosmic energy, to discourage men's hearts from the Spirit of truth. He tempts ignorant pantheists with, 'You have no choice but to submit to lies, because you're already permeated by an alien being. Don't fight me, because the game is already lost. Your side was defeated before you realized you were contesting.' Satan can muster the authority to bluff and discourage men with half-truths or lies, more easily than the authority to weaken us or destroy our personal power. Satan doesn't like proactive conscience in the truth of Christ Jesus, and uses lies, when possible, to discourage men into apathy. If lies fail him, then he buffets to effect depression. Or worse.

The occult dogma that 'All subconscious minds are connected' reflects the pantheistic concept of universal infusion. Perhap's gross sinners' subconscious minds (souls) are connected, nexated and soul-tied to the extent that Satan ". . . hath [something] in" them. (John 14:30) Satan's pantheistic lie of a universal diffusion of spirituality and energy reveals his opposition to living souls' spatial integrity. Within the conscience- and warrior's imagination-fueled psychic membrane, heartsongs and spatial integrity prevail in blessed personalities. The lie of universal diffusion suggests another lie, that 'Resistance to evil is already futile, since the cosmos is pre-existently infused by Impersonal Absolute and its energy, in rebellion against personal Yahweh the Father.' Space yielded to satanic infusion costs rulership by man's dangerous heart, whether from decisions to rebelliously sin or from heartbroken submission to The All.

A pantheistic meditator stands in relation to the Creator, Elohim the Father in heaven, but may be chargeable with intention to commit idolatry and sorcery. Meditative trance is neither a law unto itself nor the ultimate reality. Meditation should not be trance. Cognitive meditation occurs if God invites a thinker to look up and allows his soul's angels to look upon His face, and He reciprocates the look. Contrary to *raja yoga*, invited cognitive meditation does not induce trance, nor introduce post-hypnotic suggestion, nor obliterate subject-object dualism, nor join conscious and subconscious minds, nor immerse a meditator in a motionless ocean of tinnitus. *Theology interprets spirituality.* Upward-looking invited cognitive meditation relates oneself and one's soul to Yahweh the Father, and integrates one's being beneath Him.

Eating, drinking, meditation, fasting, tinnitus-absorption, mind-control or orgasm – none of these take away sin. Not even death removes sin, unless it is Yeshua of Nazareth's death and you believe upon His Messiahship and resurrection.

Extreme openness to suggestion is some positive function of personal or ancestral sin. "I the LORD thy God am a jealous God, visiting the iniquity of the fathers upon the children unto the third and fourth generation of them that hate me, but showing mercy unto thousands of them that love me and keep my commandments." (Deuteronomy 5:9b) This LORD God of Israel was the preincarnate Jesus of Nazareth, the *Logos* of Yahweh. Rebellion against Yahweh's *Logos* is neither fashionable nor witty.

Another aspect problematic with New Age physics: it encourages a magical worldview by the label of science, and is thus antithetical to Christianity. The strivings of Western chemists in the 18th and 19th centuries to discard the systemic myths of alchemy are challenged by advocates of Easternized meditative physics. The alchemists believed that all space and matter are pervasively infused with *phlogiston* (a supposed fiery change-of-state ingredient to chemical reactions). They also believed in pervasion of *ether* (a supposed lighter-than-hydrogen gas that conducts light throughout space).

Alchemists' universal diffusions of phlogiston and ether are comparable to Eastern religions' views of an all-pervasive Impersonal Absolute and its cosmic energy. Occultic Eastern religions claim that the universe is infused with supra-dualistic, all-pervasive energy (the *prakriti* of yogic Samkhya metaphysics) and with Consciousness (*de facto* spirits, the *Purusa* of yogic Samkhya). This makes the occult worldview simultaneously that of a false impersonal deity and of sorcery, from the psychic powers of meditators.

A main difference between witchcraft and yogic Samkhya metaphysics is that witchcraft candidly identifies some of the prana as spirits. Fundamental to Western science is a purging out of the influences of paganism and reliance upon pantheistic ideas like pervasive phlogiston, ether, *prana* and spiritualism. Witchcraft cannot impart authority over one's parents. Power without authority tends to fail. Even one attempt at parental cursing invites severe, potentially-longterm judgments upon the imprecator. Destructive spells against one's parents can incur even crueler judgments. A combination of witchcraft with sexual sin can level extensive personal disasters against its perp(s).

Physical science got it partly right: the universe consists of matter and energy. But, the universe also consists of heterogenous discrete spirits. Systematic theology correctly asserts that God is uncreated light, a holy Person, and a Spirit who is distinct from His varied creation, and that spirits are heterogeneously distributed. *Occultic pantheism incorrectly claims that the spiritual and energetic components of the universe are impersonal and relatively homogenous.*

The appeal of the theory of evolution stems from materials science. The seemingly gradual uprighting of skeletal biology into modern man relates to cherubic spheres of competence: dense materials comprise the skeletal system. How have earthy psychological themes shaped scientific perspective? Physical science deigns to consider only matter and energy that can be empiricized in a laboratory environment.

The opposite principle from universal diffusion is self-absorption, that classroom bane of secondary-school teachers. Self-absorption can have biochemical correlates. Certain toxins, such as heavy metals, can produce a psychological state of self-absorption, the opposite experience of permeative infusion. Lead toxicosis can retard mental function to the point that self-absorbed emotions seem the only trustworthy alternative to ego death.

Metals and Spirituality, I

Medieval alchemists believed magic could transmute lead into gold. But, post-Reformation scientists, graced with the dualistic objectivity that God dispenses into Protestant Christendom, formulated chemistry's theory of electron valence to explain why some chemical reactions occur exothermically and others endothermically. They then discarded *phlogiston* and its monistic all-pervasive fire from science's model of the universe. A scientific mini-revolution occurred that incrementally freed Western civilization from the mires of occult thought. Those same scientists could find no experimental evidence of the *ether*, and discarded it too from theoretical chemistry. Thus, the scientific model of the world corrected slightly, and Western civilization was invited upward toward the mind of God the Father, of His *Logos*, and further freed from occultism. *Chemistry's periodic table of the elements is to engineering, as Elohim's Ten Commandments are to the judiciary.* Purified chemical elements symbolize ideal non-confused set-apart radicality within science, just as God's 10-Commandment Moral Law defines His unambiguous terms of endearment to mankind. A judiciary that abandons Biblical law is like an engineering that renounces materials science.

Multiple-Intelligences Metatheory

Science and religion overlap on the subject of metals. The Toraic temple metals were silver, gold and bronze. The LORD God of Israel, who was the preincarnate Jesus of Nazareth, called only silver and gold "His" in Haggai 2:8. The temple metals (silver, gold and bronze) correlate to the three angelic orders, of the seraphim, heralds and cherubim, and to the three colors of linen thread holistically woven into priestly garments (blue, purple, and scarlet). Multiple-intelligences metatheory (the tetrapartite theory of psychology), holds that the human soul consists of one crown herald, one left-hand and one right-hand seraph, and one root cherub.

According to Pastor David T. Moore in a 2003 radio broadcast, Gabriel is the archherald, Michael is the archseraph, and Satan was created to be the archcherub. The Hebrew name "'Michael" means "Who is like unto God?"; "Gabriel" means "man of God." According to the multiple-intelligences metatheory, the Levitical colors of purple, blue, and scarlet represent the heraldic, seraphic, and cherubic orders of angels. Linen threads of these three Levitical colors, woven together into priestly garments, symbolize holistic harmonizing of the trimodal tetrapartite human soul's crown herald, left-hand and right-hand seraph, and root cherub. Per this multiple-intelligences metatheory, each human soul is created by Elohim from such four spirits, sent by God from their three orders. The heart spirit is the essential man, distinct from his soul. More about this cutting-edge psychological metatheory in chapter 11.

Metals and Spirituality, II

Daniel's vision of Daniel 2:32-38 mentions gold, silver, bronze, iron and clay. Revelation 1:15 and 2:18 liken Jesus' feet to brass. The New King James Version identifies the third metal of the Tabernacle as bronze (SnCu). The JPS Tanach (the Jewish Old Testament) identifies it as copper (Cu). The King James, as brass (ZnCu). This author thinks bronze is the true third Tabernacle metal. The LORD God of Israel, who was the preincarnate Jesus Christ, as the LORD of hosts, said "The silver is mine and the gold is mine . . ." (Haggai 2:8) And, to reassure His Babylon-submitted people,

OF CELLS AND SOULS

"For brass I will bring gold, and for iron I will bring silver . . ." (Isaiah 60:17) God the Son claims silver and gold, out of all the chemical elements, as uniquely His.

Trace metals, minerals and metalloenzymes in human bodies have great effect upon health, strength, sanity, temperament, and stamina. Mineral molecules (containing metal ions) are built into the cells of the human body, in the form of metalloenzymes. A toxic metal ion reacted into a human metalloenzyme molecule can greatly retard its many reactions. But, a nutrient metal ion in a human metalloenzyme molecule enables it to instantly perform its multiple cellular reactions, in biological perpetuity.

The limbic system in the human mid-brain governs mood, motivation, scent processings and emotional memories[1], and is the most-heavily metalled organ in the human body. Somatic toxic metal tare causes oxidative stress via elevation of free radical levels. Oxidative stress accelerates aging, unless prevented by chelation or neutralized by antioxidants.

Envirotoxins

Metallic lead toxicosis factored into the collapse of the Roman empire's senatorial class, from leaded wine and lead water pipes. Lead dust is so virulent an enzymatic poison that it prevents grape juice from fermenting. The twentieth century saw lead pollution much more widespread than that which hindered ancient Rome. Lead is presently found in the soils and food chain because of its use as an anti-knock agent in gasoline, from about 1920 to the 1990's. During the 20th century, in the United States alone, some 560,000 cubic meters of that dense toxic metal were atomized into the atmosphere as metal aerosol through internal combustion engines, to condense with rain and fall onto soils. That pollution occurred more, downwind of cities and of landmasses such as on the eastern United States, but also quite significantly in the Rocky Mountain region. Lead ions lodged in soil become, to some extent, plant and animal tissue, and are so introduced into the food chain. Body lead chemically interferes with cellular respiration and metabolism.

Tragically, the same poison that stupefied and retarded the Roman empire's patrician leadership has reemerged on the scene to widely affect modern man. During the 20th century, seven million tons of metallic lead were vaporized into the atmosphere as a metal aerosol from tetraethyl lead[2] (an additive to gasoline), in the United States alone. Lead residue settled onto soils and drainages downwind of major roads and cities.

Tetraethyl lead was developed by General Motors, DuPont Chemical, and Standard Oil of New Jersey.[3] (Standard Oil became Exxon, and then merged with Mobil Oil, to form Exxon-Mobil.) The loss to productivity from the resulting national I.Q. deficit must be truly staggering. Violent crime rates have dropped sharply in the United States since lead was removed from gasoline here around 1990. *Childhood lead levels are the best-known statistical predictors for a juvenile criminal record, which is in turn highly predictive of adult criminality.*[4]

Lead is a neurotoxin, a pro-oxidant, and an enzymatic poison. It has zero nutritional benefit. Lead is non-biodegradable, and if not immediately excreted via urine, or bile into stool, is stored by the body in bone, where it has a 22-year half-life under average conditions. Thus, one-half of bone-stored lead excretes in 22 years and three-quarters in 44 years, given average nutrition and exercise. Vigorous exercise moves and vibrates cellular lead through molecular kinetics, catalyzing its excretion. If one does some form of metal chelation, lead can be steadily removed. Oral metal chelation with DMSA, EDTA, and N-acetyl cysteine is recommended, but intravenous EDTA can also be successfully utilized. DMSA (dimercaptosuccinic acid) and EDTA (ethylenediaminetetraacetic acid) chelate better in combination than separately. They synergize toxic-metal tare chelation.

Lead deposited in the bone of fleshly bodies causes free radicals, inflammation, and oxidative stress. Those damage cells and organelles (such as mitochondria), accelerate aging, rob energy, interfere with health, and predispose one to chronic diseases. Lead-related diseases include anemia, lowered intelligence quotient, hypertension, tremor, depression, cancer, memory loss, fatigue, headache, gout, male infertility, gingivitis, behavioral and cognitive changes, irritability, sociopathic behavior, and possibly Alzheimer's disease and multiple schlerosis.[5]

One-tenth part-per-million of lead in human blood begins brain damage. "According to internationally accepted benchmarks, drawn up by the U.S. Center for Disease Control and Prevention, 10 mcg of lead per deciliter of blood causes the beginning of brain damage."[6] Somebody known to this author recovered from 13 ppm of lead in his hair shafts, a toxic tare found in the sickest 3% of the population, and equal to 130 times the blood-level lead threshold for the beginning of brain damage, by grace and by urgent oral chelation.

Toxic-Metal Tare Chelation

Metal chelation stokes appetite for dietary fats. The best fats, per human biology, are omega-3 fatty acids, which are necessary to balance nearly-ubiquitous omega-6's. Cell walls are built of lipid molecules (fats). Omega-3 fatty acids are found in flaxseed oil and in cold-water fish oils. Fish oils (especially from large fish) can be a source of mercury, another toxic metal. Feminine curves store omega-3 fatty acids, and thereby boost curvy women's brain health and help them gestate healthier smarter babies.[7] This author trusts nutritional supplements by Twinlab and Jarrow brands.

Scientific methods for orally chelating lead out of the human body include the following. Over-the-counter water-soluble DMSA introduces assimilable reactive sulfur capable of crossing the blood-brain barrier and circulating into soft and skeletal tissue. EDTA was developed during World War II to treat sailors sickened by chipping lead paint off of ships. Chelation techniques such as chelating while lying relaxed upon an inclined plane, face down, with one's head lower than one's feet, while reading, during fasts, or interspersed between distance runs, all improve removal of toxic metal tare from crucial body structures.

N-acetyl cysteine (NAC) is a critically important amino acid, necessary for the human liver to react toxins, including lead, from tissues and put them into water-soluble organic salts for excretion via urine. N-acetyl cysteine precursors L-glutathione, which reacts toxic ions detained in the liver into water-soluble organic salts. DMSA, EDTA and NAC are the methods-of-choice for long-term, non-invasive, oral chelation of body toxic-metal tare. They synergize each other, working best in combination, but nutrient mineral supplementation becomes essential.

Biological metal chelation imparts new meaning to the Scripture, "And I will bring the third part through the fire, *and will refine* them as silver *is refined*, and will try them as gold is tried: they shall call on my name, and I will hear them: I will say It is my people: and they shall say, The LORD is my God." (Zechariah 13:9, emphasis added) Biological cellular metalloenzyme refinement via metal chelation fits the theme of Jesus Christ's orthodox intellect for chemistry. 'Perception is reality' does not usually apply to chemists.

The best known chelation strategy is to chelate heavily, once or twice per week, to remove, from soft tissues, lead leached from one's bones. "Typical rebound increase in blood lead concentration after DMSA therapy is largely complete after one week."[8]

Supporting nutrients, to move lead out of bone storage, include thyroid hormone and vitamin B_6. Exercise, utilizing molecular kinetics, helps mobilize lead from cellular and bone storage, to react in the bloodstream with oral metal chelators. The lead-intoxicated may want only to eat and sleep, but that would be unwise.

Human bodies with a significant body lead tare broil in oxidative stress caused by its free radicals, barring effective metal chelation or constant antioxidant quenching. Somatic toxic metal tare causes oxidative stress from elevated free radical levels and results in accelerated aging, unless quenched by antioxidants or prevented by chelation. Lead-affected tissues experience inflammation and are more susceptible to malignancy. The element selenium prevents some cancers, but correlates to dental caries.

Lead introduces to human beings a craving for food, and for heightened sensory stimulation, while making them mentally stupid and temperamentally volatile. Does widespread twenty-first century lead pollution contribute to senseless violence and paganism? Leaded wine and lead plumbing were factors in the failure of the senatorial class of the Caesars' Roman empire. There may be a lead-toxic psychical archetype (according to body mineral composition), a type of old nature, that reacts to stimuli with predictable emotionalism. Lead toxicosis makes men stupid, sensual, and violent.

The running fad of the baby boomers and later generations may be partly a subconscious countermeasure against low-grade lead toxicity from leaded gasoline, to treat it with exercise-invoked molecular kinetics. Exercise combined with oral metal chelation offers new hope. "Bodily exercise profiteth little," (1 Timothy 4:8), but little is better than nothing.

Advanced Health Tips

The human brain weighs only about 3 pounds, but metabolizes 20% of a man's intake of oxygen and nutrients. Cognitive nutrients can repair mental deficits caused by senesco-accelerative oxidative stress (such as from digestion, toxic metal tare, smoking, aging or alcoholism). The three main state-of-the-art over-the-counter cognitive nutrients are acetyl L-carnitine arginate (ALCA), phosphatidylserine (PS), and *alpha-*

glycerophosphocholine (*alpha*-GPC).[9] ALCA increases fatty acid transport into mitochondria and potentiates dendrites, thus improving mental energy and neurological complexity. PS improves neuronal plasticity, making synaptic gaps fit more efficiently. And, *alpha*-GPC boosts brain levels of ACTH, a crucial neurotransmitter[10] for short-term memory, that comprises 30% of grey matter. These three main over-the-counter cognitive nutrients are relatively inexpensive, and really do work according to the science.

Another new state-of-the-art over-the-counter nutrient with promise to extend health is pyrrholoquinolone quinone (PQQ). Mitochondrial DNA is contained within the mitochondria, and is separate from, and less-protected than, nucleic DNA. The mitochondrial theory of aging posits that vulnerable mitochondrial DNA suffers damage before nucleic DNA does. Then, damaged mitochondria inefficiently undersupply cells with energy, so that fatigue predominates and cellular wastes accumulate. PQQ causes mitochondrial biogenesis and improved mitochondrial gene expression, comparable to the effects of prolonged calorie restriction and vigorous exercise. Cellular mitochondria utilize 85% of the oxygen that a human breathes in, for production of adenosine triphosphate (ATP), the fundamental energy molecule of the human body. The human heart and brain are dense with mitochondria. The human heart is one-third mitochondria by mass.[11] Each human cell contains between one and several-thousand mitochondria.[12] Human liver cells contain between 1,000 and 2,000 mitochondria each.[13] Mitochondria produce ATP from oxygen, thyroid hormone, Co-Q_{10}, and nutrient lipid and protein molecules. R-alpha-lipoic acid is a unique water-and-fat-soluble mitochondrial antioxidant. Generally speaking, more and healthier mitochondria mean better energy levels, but don't exceed safe dosages with PQQ. PQQ is to the mitochondrial theory of aging, as vitamin C was to the free radical theory of aging, fifty years ago.

Another health tip is to take nystatin, a bitter yellow prescription powder that kills intestinal yeast, orally and as enema, during Passover week's feast of unleavened bread, when yeast is to be removed from one's body and home.

Odd as it may sound, a nystatin-and-tepid-water enema self-administered to eliminate intestinal yeast during Passover week can have amazing longterm health benefits. This preventative technique improves health, immediately and for the remainder of the year. A Passover-week nystatin enema can dramatically improve emotional peace, immediately and for the coming year.

Dietary caloric restriction most-effectively extends health and life, as a strategy for youthfulness. Holistic health is a legitimate, secondary concern for pastors, elders, deacons, counselors, psychologists, psychiatrists, teachers, rabbis, and laity.

Is there a health science basis for God calling some meats clean and others unclean? Unclean animals such as pigs and horses do not fix much vitamin B_{12} (cobalamin) into their flesh from their digestive tracts. Cobalamin, the red cobalt-containing vitamin, is essential for hemoglobin production, for more than seventy human enzymes, and for nervous system health. The cobalamin molecule contains cobalt. It's the only vitamin that contains a metal ion. Metallic cobalt has an extremely high magnetization threshold, meaning that it takes a very very strong magnetic field to repolarize cobalt ions. God has His own reasons for specifying these Toraic prohibitions, but they are relatively easy to follow. The elaborate orthodox Jewish traditions of never mixing meat and dairy products are men's interpretations, and evangelism-encumbering Talmudic fences around the written Torah. They are extrapolated from one single verse in the Torah which says, "Do not seethe a kid in its mother's milk." (Exodus 23:19) Boiling a calf in its mother's milk was a pagan fertility rite and a cruel idea.

If you eat meat, the Torah doesn't forbid cheeseburgers, since dairy cattle, such as Holsteins, are not often raised for the beef market, which is dominated by breeds like Black Angus. In any case, a slice of cheese with a beef patty is not the same as boiling the burger in milk. The cow that gave the milk probably isn't the heifer that birthed the burger's beef. The God of the Bible does not require traditional strict separation of all dietary milk and meat. The Torah emphatically and explicitly forbids eating or drinking blood or eating animal fat, so it makes sense to drain your meat and cook it thoroughly. An Israeli study seen on the Internet in the late 1990's found a correlation between low human vitamin B_{12} levels and louder tinnitus (Skt., *nada*, the pagan yogic-supposed substrate of manifested structure). Kosher meats, from animals that divide the hoof and chew the cud, provide dietary vitamin B_{12}, but pork, horsemeat, poultry, or fish do not supply much of it. Adults low in B_{12} have trouble seeing their feet while walking.

Red meat increases appetite for food, and men with a paunch ought not eat much of it. Commercially grown animals are fed estrogens to fatten them, which wreak havoc with men's hormones. Heavy meat eating skews identity of the heart toward radical themes. Dietary animal protein hinders detachment from earthy root themes and their limitations upon the human heart. God has sympathy with fasters, who factor phlegmatic self-absorption from out of their heart, soul, and body each day that they fast. (Matthew 6:16-18) Ethnic foods aside, hard brown visceral fat urges the lower soul to commence metabolic syndrome against emergencies. Metabolic syndrome correlates to visceral fat and an overstimulated lower soul. Visceral fat causes insulin— and leptin-resistance, and correlates to self-absorption and emotionalism. Obesity correlates positively with dementia. By gluttony and hard brown visceral fat, men armor their abdomens against fear from without. There is no substitute for fasting, to refine torpid gluttony and its character structure, which are such tempting medications for fear and shame. Habitual sympathy eating may temporarily help one possess his soul, but can harden self-absorption.

Chapter 7 notes:

[1] Daniel G. Amen. *Making A Good Brain Great*. New York: Random House, 2005, 41-43.

[2] John Pakkanen. "Why Is Lead Still Poisoning Our Children?" *Washingtonian Magazine*. August, 2006, 78.

[3] *Ibid, 112.*

[4] *Ibid*, 114.

[5] http://www.thorne.com/altmedrev/fulltext/3/3/199.pdf, 199-207. May 15, 2013.

[6] Malcolm Garcia. "Everyone is Poisoned Here: Gypsy Families in Kosovo Abandoned on Toxic Land." *The Washington Times Sunday Read*. Washington, DC. May 3, 2009, 4.

[7] Will Lasek and Steven Gaulin. "Eternal Curves." *Psychology Today*. August, 2012, 70-77.

[8] S. Bradberry, T. Sheehan and A. Vale. "Use of oral dimercaptosuccinic acid in adult patients with inorganic lead poisoning." *QJMed Oxford Journals*, Oxford University Press, 2009. *http://qjmed.oxfordjournals.org/ content/102/10/721.full*, December, 2010.

[9] Amen, 193-216.

[10] Mark Schauss. "Nutrients for a Vibrant Brain: The Big Three." *Vitamin Research News*, September, 2010, 1, 5, 15.

[11] Michelle Flagg. "Reverse Brain Cell Death by Growing New Mitochondria." *Life Extension Magazine*. November, 2011, 43-49.

[12] en.wikipedia.org/wiki/Mitochondrion. December 10, 2011.

[13] *Ibid.*

Chapter 8

Mathematical Conscience: Jurist or Perp?

Conscientious absolutes preclude random lusts. Pornography temporarily elevates testosterone levels, but estranges men from Him who gives victory over evil. Jesus Christ said, "A house divided cannot stand," (Matt. 12:25) and "No man can serve two masters: either he will love the one and hate the other, or he will cleave to the one and despise the other." (Matt. 6:24)

Lust after pornography instills vanity, foolishness, and emptiness. A man who focuses his mind's eye on pornography will be tempted to believe the foolish prideful lie that the individual who posed for the camera actually feels anything for him. The truth is, she was probably paid to bare her flesh, and if she thinks of his type at all it is to despise him for being a lecher. As someone once said, Ninety percent of attraction occurs above the nose.

Conscience and Leadership

Christian churches and Jewish *schuls* should hold virginity clubs as a category of youth group, and should preach openly about God Almighty's hatred of illicit promiscuity and insistence upon either virginity or chastity. This will help instill the spirit of prophecy through evangelism, that they may make God to be their boast. With due proactive leadership and encouragement, youths can be educated to be snobs for God the Father, instead of to mitigate toward sinners. Youths evaluate and idealize adults either for virtue and conscience or for corruption. If the former, well, unto respectable maturity; if the latter, evil, unto darkness-fraught rebellion. Youths who are denied authorization of conscience to evaluate the morals of bigger teens and adults will be tempted to mitigate to them, which leads to evil. Winners with intact consciences become leaders for Yahweh's *Logos*. The word *aristocrat* derives from the Greek, *aristos* (best) + *cratos* (strength); loosely speaking, aristocrat means "[moral and genetic] best strength." As in, the best strengths within each new generation, such as are uncorrupted by the lowest common denominators of adulthood. For all the blue blood ascribed to ancestored aristocrats, that hasn't prevented some of them from behaving like human trash.

God the Father can reinstate a human male's virginity. Although God alone can forgive sin, a virgin's face and hands may at-least-temporarily deliver himself and others from possession by evil spirits. Virginal deliverances occur as functions of grace or of Toraic attainment. By contrast, a slattern's coveting of a virgin and his freeing power, heedless of proper moral legal status, threaten utter ruin to both personalities. Monogamists retain virginity of their spiritual hearts.

World-weary adults should defer graciously to virgin youth. Virgins should be in no hurry to join the generation of so-called grown-ups, since fornicative defilement of virginity introduces spiritual trouble to the human psyche. "Hear this word, ye kine of Bashan, that are in the mountain of Samaria, which oppress the poor, which crush the needy, which say to their masters, Bring, and let us drink." (Amos 4:1)

Chastity is to intellectual, as hormones are to teenager. The word "chastity" is defined as abstinence until monogamy. Qualities of adolescence persist, while chastity and righteousness prevail. God's will for a man and the man's volition intersect at the man's conscience. The penalty for Biblical sin, *including violations of one's conscience*, is worse temptation and worse sin. Someone once said, 'Sin takes you farther than you want to go. Sin costs you more than you want to pay. Sin keeps you longer than you want to stay.' Pastor Steve K. Reynolds said, "You can choose your sin, but you cannot choose your consequences." He also said, "The way it usually works is for a man to sow until he's thirty years old, then reap thereafter." Adolescence remains longer in chaste persons. Promiscuity instills 'the old man.'

Don't leave your youths in a moral vacuum. Proactively equate locker-room vulgarities to Biblical precepts and commandments, to authorize their consciences to judge bigger teens and adults. Aristocratic, relatively-innocent youths would rather judge adult behavior than submit to sinners! If you fail to define the terms of adult virtue to your youths, you commit neglect. There can be truly draconian consequences for gray-area

171

promiscuity. Those gifted with youth leadership should strive for the character and integrity of Joseph, as when he refused Potiphar's wife's seduction. (Genesis 39:7-14)

Authorize youths' consciences by equating locker-room vulgarities with applicable Biblical precepts and commandments, then meet their eyes, and invite (and ask) hard questions! Candor is crucial to trust. If they question, 'Which rules – your next-to-God conscience or your generational libido?', then they should walk warily of altered states of consciousness. Authorize youths with orthodox knowledge of maturation equated to Biblical precept and commandment, as something to brace their developing consciences against and to judge adult behaviors. Define the words of adult sexual behavior to your youths while they are logical words to them, before they as slang acquire emotional momentum in competition for spiritual allegiance.

Among those of their generation and older, your youths will tend to judge them, appropriately and according to knowledge and cognition, or to join them. To call it sin, or mitigate to it as 'normal.' Authorize your youths to judge bigger teens and adults authentically, to not become submitted to their moral inferiors. Talk straight with them, without hilarity, narcissism or crookedness. Teach critical thinking about moral (procreative) semantics and orthodoxy. Unambiguously define the language of sexuality according to Biblical precept, to authorize conscientious judgment. Youths becoming adults will tend toward either the *Logos* or self-absorption.

The "old man" of "the flesh" nature hates judgment by spiritual youths. "But he that is spiritual judgeth all things, yet he himself is judged of no man." (1 Corinthians 2:15) For this reason, Christian and Believing Jewish youth need cognitive dialogic authorization of their consciences. They need this in order to levelly judge bigger teens and adults, including their parents, lest Satan unjustly shame them to submit to corrupt aspects of adult society, which envies their relative purity of root. Youths tend to either judge generational deviants, or join them in rebellion. In a vacuum of conscientious absolutes, "the world" would have relatively pure-hearted youths feign shame for their innocence as though this were ridiculous inexperience, to set guilty adults' minds at ease. Inexperience with fornication is commendable and dignifying, not ridiculous. But, as long as God loves their innocence, they enjoy exceptionalism. All of God's love is charity, but some things He hates.

172

Submission to Satan does not appease him, it merely intensifies his authority over your soul. Neither man's submission, his bitterness, nor his fear appease Satan; only worse and worse sin does, unto destruction of conscience, spirit, soul and body. Satan is a liar and a murderer, and the fallen created archcherub. But, in God the Father there is neither darkness nor confusion. He is holy and earnest. Someone once said, 'Those who can, may learn from theology; those who can't, may learn from psychology; those who yet can't, may learn from psychiatry.' If Satan is truly cherubic and radical, then human radicality should be per knowledge and specification, not rebelliously reactive.

Mens' Hearts

John Eldredge wrote that, in contrast to playboyism, every boy's heart searches for ongoing positive answers to two questions:

Am I am man? [1] *Do I have what it takes?* [2]

For affirmative answers to the two questions, holy love and respect must exist somewhere for the man's heart, that he not need to cringe from life. There comes a season in every boy's life, somewhere between the ages of eleven and fifteen, when his father or guardian must enact plans to convince him of "Yes!" answers to both of these questions. The boy's heart never stops asking them, from pre-puberty until death. If his father fails in that capacity, then a teen is set up for disaster, because he will be tempted to answer those questions by illicit sexuality, instead of through dialectic with rational sanctified male authority. Beginning at adolescence, emerging soul earthiness and the Tempter will try to answer with shallow sexual relationships. Development of a dangerous, authentic man's heart will be impeded by frozenness and emotional unavailability.[3] This is a *huge* issue! The lives of quiet desperation that Henry David Thoreau said most men live happen because their pride puffs them up too much to truthfully answer these two questions. The world suggests to youth, 'Darken your heart with sin, like us, to obliterate the pessimism of unsaved existence.' Pastor Steve K. Reynolds said, "Men need respect: if they don't get it, they become angry. Women need love: if they don't get it, they become depressed." Every man yearns to draw a line, that of his life work within civilization and of his walk upon the geosphere. Youth need examples and instruction: the Baby Boomers had sex, drugs, and rock 'n roll as temptations (and yielded ground), but the Millennials face enticement by witchcraft, sodomy, and pagan globalism.

If a boy never answers those questions outside of lasciviousness and uncleanness, or worse, then the personality and spirit of man within him will experience inexorable destruction. A boy's conscience must be rationally authorized, by critical interaction on the subject of conscientious orthodoxy, to evaluate bigger teens and adults, by an authority figure, preferably his Dad or some comparable man. The resultant level playing field of moral orthodoxy and conscientious ideals should imply to a youth, regarding bigger teens and adults, "I'm not proud, you're not stupid!" *Authorization of conscience must define and impart to a youth the terms of adult virtue, and why and how to keep the vessel of his body, and equate locker room vulgarities to applicable Biblical commandments and precepts.* The point is to demystify *eros*, so that the Tempter cannot imply he and his slaves have superior understanding of relationships and sexuality. Good character should be emphasized over and above competitive academic or athletic performance. We should beware the risk of embarrassing Jesus Christ for the last time.

Adults can keep themselves either bright faced and intellectual, or promiscuous and earthily radical, not both. All adolescents become more or less radical for someone or some cause, because the word 'radical' derives from the Latin *radix*, meaning 'root.' During puberty, a soul's root begins to integrate into human personality. The ideas imparted to youths' consciences develop their radicality, on into adulthood. Radical purity is God's primary interest in radicality. The word "erotic" derives from the Greek *eros* (lusty beauty) + *osis* (infusion). To us of authorized consciences, promiscuity should not be a rite of passage, lest it sow seeds of personal ruin.

A precocious Protestant teen can hardly shame bigger teens with his judgment, unless an esteemed adult has imparted verbalized words of knowledge, authority and maturity to his or her heart and conscience. Teens suffer temptation to despair that lofty ideals originating within their generation are merely self-absorption (like so much else), and are thus not credible. While teachers and classes of students learn to trust cognition more than rumination, their any involvement with the Vile 3 would work to reverse this intellectual emancipation, substituting spirit possession, depression, or possibly much worse.

174

Girls' Hearts

Conjunctively, every girl's heart yearns to find the answers to four questions:

Am I lovely? Will you pursue me? Will you delight in me? Will you fight for me? [4]

These questions are fundamental to the heart of a lady. They are difficult to acknowledge, let alone answer, in the business world and the cultural *ethos* that proceeds from it. But, 'yes' answers to them are crucial to respect between the sexes, for life. Every man's and woman's heart needs a larger mission than mere fleshly existence. An intelligent, dangerous heart presumes a sanctified soul, and that presumes grace by faith found in Jesus Christ. Intelligence presumes personal refinement, that of both filial integrity and of biosomatic mineral profile.

God designed beauty to be a minor litmus test of conscientious trustworthiness. In the age of photographic and video pornography, beauty has lost many unique moral connotations. Prior to the technological age, facial beauty, neat handwriting and quick accurate mental mathematics served as minor outward indications of personal sanctity. Girls, like boys, need their consciences authorized to keep the vessels of their bodies, by equating vulgar words to Biblical commandments, to levelly judge bigger teens and adults. By yielding to temptation, many beautiful girls accrue to their roots impending dire judgments, that sniff at their heels for the rest of their lives, unless they reconcile with holy Triune Elohim through Christ Jesus.

Conscientious Orthodoxy

Human nature being what it is, men who let their eyes and hearts dwell upon pictorial or literary pornography experience temptation by evil spirits to believe lies. The lust-soaked actors seem to enjoy with impunity the pleasures of sin, and magnanimously offer the same to voyeurs who view them. Pornography does not make a man a better son. Lust makes him unstable, suggestible, and immature in God's sight. At worst, it makes him a lecher, a fornicator, an adulterer, a homosexual or a pedophile. Yeshua of Nazareth said, "Whosoever looketh on a woman to lust after her hath committed adultery with her already in his heart." (Matthew 5:28)

175

Home-wrecking adultery would be an extremely serious sin in God's sight. Adultery means violation of the seventh of the Ten Commandments ("Thou shalt not commit adultery." (Exodus 20:14)). The word "adultery" means "Sexual intercourse that transgresses marital fidelity." Adultery stores up tremendous spiritual fear in those guilty of it. That fear eventually finds expression through the two partners' psychological and physical natures, apart from grace. If one cannot avoid, some year, becoming an old man, then at least through grace, mental hygiene, faith, and godly character and integrity, he may prevent himself from becoming a bitter dirty old man. Shame diminishes depth perception.

Sexual sin is insidious. It may seem like a victimless crime, but it darkens the heart and destroys human spirit. "If therefore the light that is in thee be darkness, how great is that darkness!" (Matthew 6:23b) For fornicators and idolaters, smaller and smaller a total volume of personal heart-space. If you can't imagine her bright brow and face, you shouldn't desire her voluptuous body. God judges homosexuality more like a felony than like the traffic ticket homosexualists deny it to be.

Men who fuel lust via pornography feel a misguided sense of power over women. But, *what lechers do is worship with their bodies an object that God has not consecrated to them.* The second of the Ten Commandments says, "Thou shalt not make unto thee any graven image [religious statue] or any likeness [venerated painting or photograph] of anything that is in heaven above, or the earth beneath, or the waters under the earth." (Deut. 5:8) Statues or photos kept as foci of worship, adulation or lust violate this commandment and are sin.

Pornographic photographs assume the role of idolizable likenesses. If a man fastens his mind's eye upon a porn actress, then yields his self-control to a seductive evil spirit hypnotically fascinating his imagination, he commits a type of idolatry. In the words of Pastor Steve K. Reynolds, "If I can't help the first look [at a lascivious sight], I *can* help the second." If you are addicted to pornography, it may be argued that you are involved with the occult.

God's will is for a man to court and ravish in lifelong courtship the one true love of his life. God as *ha Shem* (Heb., *The* Name, *Y'howah*) desires each man to make marriage work for life, for the honor of his name, something that pornography (lasciviousness), masturbation (uncleanness), fornication, adultery, homosexuality, or pedophilia actively scuttle. If a man strays into pornography and masturbation (the "lasciviousness" and "uncleanness" of Galatians 5:19), or worse, God can let spirits offended by the sin possess the man unto his great discomfiture. Biblically, lasciviousness is lewd undress, and sexual uncleanness results from ejaculation. Outside of marriage, they are un-Christlike and 'the flesh.' Your career is as interesting to true authority as your conscience is clean before God

Is recreational sex ever permissible? It depends: If a heterosexual married couple both decide it is, then for them moral recreational sex is permissible. Is contraception between marrieds ever permissible? It depends: How many children do they already have? About how many fertile months remain to them? The married couple stands in relation to the Person of God the Father, who loves children.

"For the works of the flesh are manifold, which are these, *adultery, fornication, uncleanness, lasciviousness*, idolatry, witchcraft, hatred, variance, emulation, wrath, strife, seditions, heresies, envyings, murder, drunkenness, reveling, and such like, of the which I tell you before, as I have told you in time past, that those which do such things shall not inherit the kingdom of God." (Galatians 5:19-21, emphasis added)

Jesus of Nazareth's Holy Ghost-revealed inner man, transcribed into sound doctrine by the apostle Paul, sets a higher standard than the minimum required by the Torah. The Torah, by contrast, does not forbid lasciviousness or masturbatory sexual-uncleanness toward a non-relative of the opposite sex. For that matter, some Talmudists opine that non-unclean female masturbation is permissible by God, despite that it inculcates the sort of lasciviousness that Paul forbade, and may involve conscious response to a hateful incubus (a masculine seducing spirit). Jesus of Nazareth's inner man was revealed to the apostle Paul by God the Father's Holy Spirit, who is entrusted to Christians. The heavenly Father's indwelling Holy Spirit, the *Paraclete*, demands a higher standard of personal purity than that required by the Torah.

Sexual Idolatry

In ancient Israel, the Canaanites plagued the Hebrews with the religion of their demons, false gods, that suggested sexual idolatry to them as the stuff of fertility cult. Suggestion, from the demon Asherah (possibly a cherub), persuaded the Canaanite idolaters to set up phallic poles and conduct orgies round about them. Perhaps the demon would descend from the second heaven and impale itself upon the pole, and the pagan revelers, heterosexual or homosexual, would suffer intense spirit-possession. The net result was that the pagan idolaters incurred judgment by YHWH, the true God of gods, for indulging in idolatrous worship of demons. He also judged them for violating vows of marriage and other commandments pertaining to moral sexual conduct.

Many of those same ancient sexual spirits exist today. A succubus is a feminine erotically-seducing spirit, while an incubus is a masculine erotically-seducing spirit. Such spirits plaguing a person's dreams signify trial and temptation. *Homosexual behavior results in spirit possession by an incubus, a masculine seducing spirit, and causes ravening, uncontrollable, damnable libidos.*

The spirit of Canaanite Asherah finds expression in those who dress lewdly in public. The spirit of demonic Ashtoreth finds expression in abusers of authority to suppress evangelism, which is the spirit of prophecy. Asherah is to lust, as Ashtoreth is to altered states of consciousness (ASC's). Denigration of the consciences of virgin youth is of the spirit of Asherah, sometimes called a Delilah spirit. Domination of the conscientious intellects of virgin youth, especially with doctrinal error, is of the mariolatrous spirit of Ashtoreth, sometimes called a Jezebel spirit. A masculine spirit of false love is called an Ahab spirit. These spirits may be rebuked in the terrible, holy, beloved name of YHWH, as when Michael the archseraph said to Satan the created archcherub, "The LORD [*Y'howah!*] rebuke you." (Jude 1:9)

Canaanite fertility cult, such as involving golden calves, phallic poles, and burnt incense on promontories, probably involved idolatry of fallen cherubim (one of which is Satan). Per the tetrapartite hypothesis of psychology, a living soul's cherubic root relates naturally to the lower body and feet, but is adversely affected by the fallen, created archcherub, Satan.

Impartation of respect, worth and honor is the essence of worship (i.e., the idea of 'worth-ship'), and requires a clear conscience. Attempts to offer respect from a rebelliously filthy conscience constitute an insult. This is the danger of merely-cultural Christianity: each must be a leader or risk subversion. Conscientious orthodoxy mustn't syncretize. Your conscience is your soul-herald's imploring you, via your intellect, to conduct yourself with moral fastidiousness. Moral, as in the Ten Commandments and Christian moral law.

Leadership Traps

Human sluts resemble what the intelligence community calls 'honeypots,' in the spiritual war of the ages between Christ Jesus and Satan. The Devil tries to use sluts and lechers as *anti-leaders*, to drag down godly gentlemen and ladies to disgrace, depression and desperation, through temptation to defile their bodies and consciences with promiscuity. Temptresses targeting leaders to entice them into sexual sin resemble what the intelligence community calls 'mata-hari's.' Both types of seductresses express spirits dedicated by Satan to the downfall of godly leaders. The Reverend Billy Graham said, "There's not a man alive that cannot be seduced." During his ministry, Reverend Graham would not even eat lunch alone with a woman who was not his wife. Leaders, guard your consciences and testimonies! Leaders develop the outward character and inner integrity to reject sinful generational solutions, while brainstorming about Yahweh's *Logos'* solutions. All true leadership proceeds from moral leadership. Saturday sabbath rests impart moral leadership needed by most Christians. The word *synagogue* derives from the Greek, *syn-* (together) + *gogue* (lead). Moral-law morality tends to impart leadership.

Human trash are men and women who will not draw the sharp distinction between illicit promiscuity and chastity unto Jesus' Father. Human trash identify with promiscuity and the culture of debauchery and dissipation. If lamentable human trash become tempted by Satan into sin's Vile 3 (fornication, occultism, or drug abuse), their lives go from bad to worse. Only Jesus can rescue them. A poet once wrote,

> "When the words have been spoken, and my life is done,
> true love or lust, which will have won?
> "May I look up, with hope I'll be welcome above?
> Jesus or Asherah, who will have won?"

If you, too, need to stand up for Jesus, and if you aspire to not be corrupted by the coming global governance, then you should purge your mind's eye, heart and home of pornography and illicit lewdness. Smut will only make you suggestible in a crisis, and less of a man of truth, discretion, and action. Moral orthodoxy is defined by the God of the Bible and confirmed within the space between Believers. Conscientiously orthodox decisions (or oblivion to them) stratify generations, from true aristocrats ranging on down to immoral trash.

———

The pagan worldview has influenced the culture to twist interpretations of U.S.' First Amendment guarantees of free speech and religion. The major media so ruthlessly exploit libido to sell products, so unrestrainedly glorify 'the flesh,' that many an otherwise-virtuous American man no longer hates his own sin. That is a great pity. God will not let us get away with unrestrained lust.

Pagan or excommunicated men, cut off from *zoe* (Gr., vital aliveness in Christ), lack the spirit and grace to win admiration and true love from spiritually-free women. They may connive to prey upon impressionable teens or even children, to take power over them. Such men may be incapable of hating their own sin, and therefore have serious long-term spiritual problems. Their strength will do them no good in the end. The only way that a man's heart can be authentic, dangerous, and rule over his corner of nature is to find Jesus and His truth: this is the way our holy Triune Yahweh remedied the fall of creation.

Holy Manhood

Jesus of Nazareth said, "The light of the body is the eye. If therefore thy eye be single, thy whole body shall be full of light. But if thine eye be dark, thy whole body shall be full of darkness." (Matthew 6:22) There's an old saying, 'The wheels of God grind slow, but they grind exceeding fine.' If you harden your heart to His call to repent, consoling yourself that 'everybody does it,' or 'I'm no worse than average,' then God is quite capable of exacting judgment. He is the God of the spirits of all flesh. (Numbers 16:22) He can consign you to evil spirits that can submit your soul to sin and cause you tremendous suffering, to teach you to repent or even to terminate your life. If your conscience pricks you, be glad! Find accountability with a trusted pastor, and confess to God in his presence the sins that you've done! Confession truly is good for the soul. Your family, congregation and nation need your able body, heart, soul and mind. You are worth far more to us confessed-out and prayed-up than you are waiting in dread for the axe of God's judgment to fall.

During the Great Reformation in England, in the 17th century, Oliver Cromwell's roundhead Puritan army defeated the long-haired Anglican cavaliers of King Charles I. [*Roundhead* was a reference to short haircuts. Hair contains metals, the domain of (mostly-fallen) cherubim.] At forty-three, Oliver Cromwell, despite his age, raised his first military command, a cavalry troop. Cromwell demanded strict codes of moral and ethical conduct and purity of speech from his soldiers. Swearing was prohibited, let alone theft, lewdness, or rape. His sound doctrine and severity paid off, as his New Model Army conquered the royalist forces supporting the hierarchized liturgical state church. Cromwell's New Model Army became the standard for the British military for generations thereafter. Applying criteria that would bear fruit for the remainder of his career, Cromwell commanded that his officers and enlisted men meet high standards of moral uprightness. He demanded instant response to commands. Religious fervor, zeal, and the conviction that the cavaliers subservient to the king and the state church did not have God's blessings, continued prominently in Cromwell's military strategy.[5]

Tribulation-era Israeli Defense Forces (IDF) may resemble Oliver Cromwell's New Model Army for true faith, conviction, and zeal. During the three-and-a-half-odd year Tribulation revival in Israel (which may exhibit aspects of the six-month Welsh revival of 1904), many Israeli youth will believe the suddenly-obvious truth that Yeshua of Nazareth is the true Messiah, and receive God the Father's *Ruakh haKodesh* (Holy Spirit). As the Army, possibly minus the VeriChip identity management mark of the beast, they may pitch battle, during Jacob's Trouble, to defend The Land against United Nations troops taking revenge upon Zionists for the dekapartite global government's fiat currency collapses of those years. Reformation-alight Israel will be saved by the post-Tribulational glorious return of Jesus of Nazareth, but by then some two-thirds of Jews may have perished for the national guilt of Israel. (Zechariah 13:7-9)

Men quite normally want evil to fear them but in the New-Agey, early 3rd millennium apocalyptic evil fears little except the living agenda-partisan *Logos* of God, who is Yahweh-the-Son. Evil waxes bold as an inverse function of protagonists' sanctity, because God the Father watches us from above through elect heraldry.

Sodomitic Defilement

Notorious pederasty (boy molestation) scandals have plagued the Vatican's hierarchy. To a lesser extent, sex scandals have also rocked the Protestant community. Multiple accounts of romish priests sodomizing sometimes scores of boys who trusted them for counsel and prayer, only to be protected by a bishop who hushed up the atrocities, must greatly grieve God the

Father. Triune Y'howah (Heb., *Elohim ha Shiloosh haKodesh*) abhors the sin of sodomy. If it occurs within the ranks of romish priests naming Jesus Christ as their truth and authority to minister, it reveals glaring doctrinal and spiritual problems within their sect.

"And he cried mightily with a strong voice, saying, Babylon the great is fallen, is fallen, and is become the habitation of devils, and the hold of every foul spirit, and a cage of every unclean and hateful bird. For all nations have drunk of the wine of the wrath of her fornication, and the kings of the earth have committed fornication with her, and the merchants of the earth are waxed rich through the abundance of her delicacies." (Revelation 18:2,3) Beloved Roman Catholics can believe unto salvation, and may have God the Holy Ghost in their hearts. Their problem is that God hates the Mass, while romish traditions perpetuate false doctrines via the Vatican's priestocracy, which claims itself, only, to be the sum of the Church. Gary H. Kah, however, opines that the United States of America may be becoming 'mystery Babylon' of Revelation, and New York City, 'the whore of Babylon.'[6] Both interpretations may be true, given recent demographic trends.

The Vatican's priestly hierarchy's tolerance of sodomy within its ranks is apostasy. While the Bible does not forbid priests to enter into heterosexual holy matrimony, it states that the LORD God of Israel (who is the Angel of Yahweh and who became Jesus of Nazareth) finds sodomy abominable. Most of the church fathers were married men. "Now the Spirit speaketh expressly, that in the latter times some shall depart from the faith, giving heed to seducing spirits and doctrines of devils; speaking lies in hypocrisy; having their conscience seared with a hot iron; *forbidding to marry* and commanding to abstain from meats." (I Timothy 4:1-3, emphasis added)

Precious Roman Catholics are told by their priests that the Vatican's priestocracy is the sum of the Church, and that the romish laity are thus excused from evangelism of the testimony of Jesus (which is "the spirit of prophecy," Revelation 19:10c). Consequently, some unfortunate Roman Catholics more-or-less subconsciously impede water-cooler style evangelism, as though evangelism were solely the domain of ordained romish priests and not that of the priesthood of all Believers, which is in truth the case.

Occultists, also, have been plagued by sexual sin. Pantheistic *gurus* don't admit that lust is an offense against the Creator, because they believe that they are divine manifestations of the Creator. Although that's not true, they think it means they define moral high ground as whatever they, the enlightened, prefer it to be. Their consciences, seared by sin, are inured to nagging guilt by the false theology of pantheism, which claims that enlightened souls are so spiritually evolved that they have become godlike. United Nations' globalists insist that the moral pretentiousness of pantheism authorizes them to global governance.

We find a growing need to empower Christian and Believing Jewish youths to retort to those less fervent toward God the Father than they are, and with it a need to encourage virginity. Evangelism sorties can introduce youths to instant obedience to the spirit of truth. Paralegal internships can help youths connect words with authority. Carpentry employment with Born Again Christians, as summer jobs, can offer progression of material facts, quickening male ethos and humility, and connect language with power. However, manual-trades tentmaking support of controversial personal ministry is intrinsically very difficult, due to its earthiness in relation to spiritual warfare.

Homosexuals are typically abhorrent to tradesmen at the journeyman level. Many manual tradesmen more-or-less openly jeer at gays, sensing their demonic components but not forced by their jobs to share close quarters with them. Conversely, in confined-space office jobs, gays tend to be feared for their demonic retinues and perfunctorily supported, according to groupthink. Passivity toward sin results in spiritual torpor. It's neither fashionable nor witty to flaunt the *Logos* of Yahweh. The homosexual lobby vilifies the Boy Scouts of America as a hate group for excluding pederasts [boy-molesters] from leadership, in order to preserve boys' authentic personalities.

Alternatives

Within the realm of neologisms, a *theophile* (a lover of God) isn't necessarily a *homophobe* (someone fearful of homosexuals). A more accurate word for homophobia would be *diabolophobia* (fear of demons). Homosexuals suffer worse temptation to *diabolophilia* (love of demons) and *theophobia* (fear of the Creator). *Fornication and sodomy are two sides of the same coin, although sodomy is the worse of the two.* Those sins tend to foment diabolophilia. Everyone should keep himself from both illicit heterosexual and homosexual lust. Pastor Michael Youssef ably stated, "I'm not phobic, homo or otherwise."

183

The same should be true for all Believers. "Open homosexual" means "notorious homosexual."

In the immortal words of Born-Again Jewish comedian Bert Rosenberg, "Fools say of illicit *eros*, 'Let's go *in there!*'" Prior to 15 December 1973, the American Psychiatric Association officially classified homosexuality as a mental illness.[7] However, on that date, the APA's fearful board of trustees capitulated to homosexual activists' raging hateful harassment of their persons and disruption of their meetings, and lessened their accurate former diagnosis to "unhappiness with sexual orientation." Wearied and literally fearful for their persons, those professional psychiatrists mitigated to the enraged perverts. Lofty clinical submitted to raunchy radical. Sexual sin is the root cause of much, if not most, mental illness.

What constitutes mental health? Cognition implores God's intervention, entreating Him for deliverance. Elohim watches over cognitive persons of faith, meeting their souls' angels and delivering their hearts and bodies from spirit possession. Untrammeled heralds have a special relationship with God the Father. By contrast, yogic 'cognitive trance' brings curses. Dynamic cognition implies "thine eye be[ing] single," a state of grace. (Matthew 6:22, Luke 11:34) Cognition implies a viable psychic membrane, such as is envied by hopeless theophobes and diabolophiles. Depressives seek joviality from cognitive people, because they're uncomfortable communing with moral judgment. Cognition and a dirty mind (one obsessed with illicit eroticism) are opposing trends. The fruit of God the Holy Spirit tends toward highly-conditional cognition, while the works of the flesh tend toward depression and dementia.

Don't 'mirror' crookedness or gluttony, to placate a Mr. Big's diabolophilic ambition. Mirroring an interrogator displays back to him a disarming kinesiological body-language semblance of passive candid submission, according to survivalist author Ragnar Benson.[8] Nonservile hand-eye activity can help free cognition from social-defeat stress and depression.

Gay Problems

Concerning sodomy, the LORD God of Israel [the preincarnate Jesus of Nazareth] said, "Thou shalt not lie with mankind as with womankind: it is abomination." (Leviticus 18:22) The Hebrew word for abomination is *toweybah* (Strong's number 8441), meaning [that, to the LORD God of Israel, sodomy is] "an abhorrence; an abomination; something disgusting." Sodomy, the male homosexual sex act, represents an ancient sin that is extremely offensive to our Triune Elohim. The God of the Bible loves precious homosexuals and desires that they repent of immorality and be saved in eternity; but, He positively hates the behaviors and spirits of homosexuality. "And there were also sodomites [gays] in the land: and they did according to all the abominations of the nations which the LORD [the preincarnate God the Son] cast out before the children of Israel." (I Kings 14:24)

Vulnerability to sodomy relates to a conscience weighed down with unconfessed, unforgiven sin. Proclivity to homosexuality would be suggested to the inner man by demonic spirits, instead of being only genetically transmitted. Poor gays want to believe that homosexual desire originates only from genetic heredity, instead of from spirituality, but that is a myth. For homosexuality to be genetic, it would have to be an anti-procreative mutation, and would rapidly become extinct, by atheism's own logic. Homosexuality is a vice that may be transmitted along a guilty family tree by suggestion from evil spirits. Sensual titillation may tempt experimental sinning that can result in spirit possession. Sinful urges, acted upon, justify worse possession and become part of a human personality, subject to divine judgment.

God punishes sinful words, decisions, and actions! The penalty for sin is worse sin, a downward spiral effect. Homosexuals complain that they are suppressed by societal bigotry from godly humans, but what suppresses them most is spiritual opposition from the vast dynamic elect angelic realm, on behalf of Elohim the Three in One. Triune Yahweh of the holy Bible loves homosexuals and yearns for them to repent, but absolutely hates the ancient vice of sodomy.

The preincarnate Jesus (Elohim the Son) commanded Moses to write, "There shall be no whore [prostitute] of the daughters of Israel, nor a sodomite [gay] of the sons of Israel. Thou shalt not bring the hire of a whore [harlot], or the price of a dog [male prostitute], into the house of the LORD your God for any vow: *for even both of these are abominations unto the LORD thy God.*" (Deuteronomy 23:17,18, emphasis added) A prostitute of either sex would be an abomination to Triune YHWH, but sodomy would multiply abomination, even to prostitution.

The apostle Paul, writing to the future, wrote "Beware of dogs." (Philippians. 3:2, KJV). The Hebrew word for "dog" is *chelev*, written in the Old Testament (Deuteronomy 23:18) as a metaphor referring to a male homosexual prostitute. The equivalent words in Greek are *kunos* (Septuagint) and *kunas* (New Testament); both words translate as "homosexual." The Greek text of Philippians 3:2 literally reads "See to dogs," implying that Elohim- or Christ-naming congregations are to exclude or remove from office unrepentant homosexuals. Unfortunately, the predominant spirituality that will support unrepentant gays is demonic, and to some extent homosexuals involuntarily submit to and serve their strategizing demons. The neologism *kunonoia* (Gr., *kuno*— (homosexual) + *noia* (mind)) describes "homosexualist libidinous rapacity," while *pornonoia* (*porno*— (prostitute) + *noia* (mind)) connotes "the playboy mindset toward women as sex objects." Kunonoia and pornonoia represent opposite sides of the same troublesome coin.

The United States' Episcopal, much Lutheran, and some Presbyterian churches' early 3rd-millennial doctrinal positions, that Triune Yahweh is anything but fiercely opposed to homosexuality, are at best totally un-Biblical and at worst egregious lies. Sodomy causes submission to Satan. The Bible says, "For this reason, God gave them over to degrading passions; for their women exchanged the natural function for that which is unnatural, and in the same way also the men abandoned the natural function of the women and burned in their desire toward one another, men with men committing indecent acts and receiving in their own persons the due penalty of their error." (Romans 1:26,27 NASB) Triune YHWH Elohim loves precious gays, in hopes that they will repent of homosexuality, but He emphatically loathes the gay and lesbian lifestyle.

Eschatosexuality

The latter-day first spiritual beast (Gr., *thayrios*) of Revelation 13 is believed to be a compound entity of multiple fallen cherubim, that relates to money, violence, weapons, promiscuity and sodomy. It is believed to be capable of possessing thousands of humans simultaneously, and of strategically nudging their careers toward Satan's plan for society.

Straight men and women fraternizing with homosexuals endure oppositional psychospiritual suggestion that any forcefulness of conscience deserves marginalization, vilification and disenfranchisement.

Fraternization of straight men with homosexuals tempts straights to flinch forcefulness of conscience away from progressivist malefactors. If there is too much opposition to speaking the truth, hold your tongue, but don't condone sin. Gays' demons deplore the fear of God (Gr., *maranatha!*), and don't want it breathed (let alone spoken) in their presence, atmosphere or ambience. Proud gays blur lofty ideas with inner wretchedness, into ribald humor derisive of straights' forcefulness of conscience. The same ribald humor aimed at straights' forceful consciences pressures their souls' roots to habitually enfold evil. That is, to abdicate exclusion of evil from psychological identity. However, root-enfoldment of evil tends to be incompatible with personal holiness.

The spirit of sodomy tries to sicken or corrupt the beauty of pro-angelic man's dangerous, vocal, active heart. Why would sin-acquiescent speech indict a relatively-innocent bystander? "Do not join a crowd that intends to do evil. When you are on the witness stand, do not be swayed in your testimony by the opinion of the majority." (Exodus 23:2, NLT) "Not that which goeth into the mouth defileth a man, but *that which cometh out of the mouth, this defileth a man.*" (Matthew 15:11, emphasis added) Verbalized approval of severe sin osmoses some guilt onto the approver.

In a sense, homo-occultists act like Satan's shock troops in the culture war against the family, the economy, and Protestant exceptionalism. Occult-influenced, sexually-immoral Adolph Hitler said, "Where we are, others must leave." Video displays do not convey root vibes or scents to viewers, that might otherwise warn them of wickedness within actors. Bright secondary-school students' derisive "That so *gay* . . ." cognitively identify and judge homosexualists' inauthentic intrusions into academia, art, and society.

Sin-altered societal mores desire to punish speech that identifies sodomy as sin. But, if Believers mis-speak to tacitly authorize spirits of sodomy in other men, they risk drawing judgment from God upon themselves. Sodomitic spirituality is especially rough on unmarried straight men who still have a need to prove themselves in courtship and parenthood. Parents of young children enjoy relative immunity to much demonic oppression.

Homosexuals inevitably suffer susceptibility to demons that want to propagate their vice, in order to influence civilization for Satan. The net effect is that gays are pressured to obey Satan and the occult, to corrupt the innocent and to propagate paganism. If actively unrepentant gays become philosophical or political allies, beware, because (even if they try to) they cannot avoid transmitting diabolical influences. Triune Elohim excludes active unrepentant homosexuals from communion with Him, and they think and decide through a diabolophilic gestalt. Unless gays Biblically repent and cease all sodomitic activities, and their repentance is accepted by holy Y'howah Elohim, they have no part in Him.

Acting-out according to "the flesh" (Galatians 5:19-23) lands one under judgment according to the ceremonial Torah, the oral law, romish spirituality and/or the occult.

Dogs of Earth

Educated guess as to how the term *gay* came to be applied to the homosexual lifestyle? The Greek word for "earth" is spelled *gamma-eta* and is pronounced "gay." Gay homosexuality implies demonic earth-religion incurring ultimate eternal hopelessness for objectively-sanctified personality. Sodomitic spirituality reeks of earth worship: of bodily idolatry of creature creation. Christian subject-object dualism advances personal and societal improvement via conscience and intellect. Rampant sodomy pressures for societal and personal devolution via noxious radicality.

Regional Sins

Some regard sodomy as a victimless crime between consenting adults. The truth, however, is that sodomy does violence, over entire geographic regions. And, God's justice in reply, directed at the geographic region, affects straights and gays alike. For example, the city of New Orleans, Louisiana hosted Southern Decadence, a crowded yearly homosexual festival, held each Labor Day weekend during the 1990's and early 2000's. On Labor Day weekend, 2005, God reluctantly allowed Hurricane Katrina to directly strike New Orleans, submerging eighty percent of the city. In 2010, the Deepwater Horizon oil spill occurred, and spewed some one-hundred sixty million gallons of crude oil into the Gulf of Mexico, adversely affecting southern-Louisiana fisheries. Holy Triune Elohim considers sodomy more like a felony offense than a traffic ticket. Homosexual behaviors amount to allegiance to Satan, because the LORD

Jesus Christ, who is the LORD God of Israel, will tolerate none, zero, of them.

The neologism *cardiospatiality* refers to atmosphere and space harmonious for cardiac rhythms. Shared atmosphere promotes osmotic intersuggestibility between Christians or pagans, between sanctifieds and sinners. Cardiospatiality is hindered by frictionless passive emulation, and submission to, others. A population's sexual orientation factors in regional cardiospatiality. Space sanctified for cardiac rhythms occurs, in any given person or region, inversely to regional oppression for severe widespread human sin. Historically, Elohim rejects and turns His back on flagrantly-corrupt civilizations, and what comes next to them can be truly horrific. "Come out of her, my people, that ye be not partakers of her sins, and that ye receive not of her plagues." (Revelation 18:4)

Homo-Occultism vs. Youths

Homosexuality and occultism often occur together, as Scott Lively and Kevin Abrams cogently discuss in their book, *The Pink Swastika*.[9] One prominent homosexual occultist was Alistair Crowley, a pederast and author of *The Satanic Bible*. Sodomy was one rite of initiation into the occultic Knights Templar, a secret society in Medieval Europe. *Entrenched societal sodomy relates closely to a soul of a nation characterized by timidity of conscience, obduracy to evangelism, and siege mentality against prophets of Triune Elohim.*

A pederast is a male homosexual so degenerate that he resorts to sexual humiliation of a young boy, sodomizing him into a *catamite*. The word "catamite" means "A boy detained as a sex slave to an adult male homosexual." Pederasty damages the authenticity of a boy's developing male ego, in relation to girls of his generation. The aggressive, butch, older male says in effect, "I despair of being who and what I was created to be, so out of spite you'll be dragged down too, through the abomination of pederasty." Inner-man desolation tempts submission to sugardaddy sexuality.

Pederasty violates a boyhood soul's psychic membrane. It forces the will of his inner man. It lies to him that his pro-angelic inner man is helpless to thwart demonic violation by aggressive, butch, older males. Pederasty pressures a boy to submit to the lie that he does not have what it takes.

Pederasts do the work of Satan by pressing a boy to abandon his psychic membrane and eternal hopes, to aggressive, butch, older males. The pederast slang word 'chicken' refers to young boys, comparing their little bodies to tender morsels of food, like succulent delicacies just begging to be abominably savored.

There exists a well-documented relationship between homosexuality and occultism. About occultic societies, George Grant writes, "Rome was a perpetual satyricon. Egypt, Persia, Carthage, Babylon, and Assyria were all steeped in pederastic traditions. And the ancient empires of the Mongols, Tartars, Huns, Teutons, Celts, Incas, Aztecs, Mayans, Nubians, Mings, Canaanites, and Zulus likewise celebrated depravity, degradation and debauchery."[10] Many pagan societies were steeped in homosexuality. J.K. Rowling, author of the Harry Potter series, identified her youth-fiction character Dumbledore as gay, implying the latent sympathy between homosexuality and occultism.

Many occultic societies still practice pederasty. Such societies are found worldwide, in locales such as Brazil, New Guinea, Morocco, sub-Saharan Africa, and Malaysia. In such societies, male homosexual relations are structured according to generation and age. The older partner takes the male, controlling, butch role, and the boy is forced to take the female, responsive, femme role. Anthropologist Gilbert Herdt reports that "ritual homosexuality has been reported by anthropologists in scattered areas around the world [revealing a] . . . pervasive link between ritual homosexuality and the warrior ethos . . . We find these similar forms of warrior homosexuality in such diverse places as New Guinea, the Amazon, Ancient Greece and historical Japan. In these societies, the process of a boy's homosexual initiation is horrific: he is deprived of sleep, starved, beaten and raped over several days, until he is completely 'resocialized' as a homosexual."[11] Until he and his conscience permanently submit to the power of sin.

Warrior Homosexuality

Warrior homosexuals may perceive pederastic power over boys as power over mankind in general. *Brutalization and humiliation by an older male damages the boy's inner man, psychic membrane, and active will to oppose aggressive radical earthiness! Such horrific violation would have the effect of a shamanistic initiation into occult spirituality.* To true soldiers, a military career is a pro-angelic patriotic ideal. To warrior homosexuals, a military career is a paying job within their sexual fantasy. Siege mentality dogs the feet of warrior homosexuals.

A warrior has forcefulness of conscience, but media-embellished gays address ribald raunchy humor at straight men's forceful consciences, pressuring them to verbally compromise them. It is no sin to keep silent, if the moment to speak is not at hand, rather than tacitly mitigate to the promiscuous and to their vice.

In the early 3rd millennium, the spirituality of homo-occultism attempts to disenfranchise (or sicken) personal power and conserved wealth supporting forcefulness of conscience. Homo-occultism toils to sabotage Protestant exceptionalism, and to 'progress' the meta-Left agenda through religiopolitical events and demographic attrition. Satan probably wants a nation of spiritual catamites, to channel submission to him throughout civilization.

'Finished' Men

John Eldredge, in *The Way of the Wild Heart*, writes that each man goes through six, more-or-less sequential, overlapping stages. He identifies them as Beloved Son, Cowboy, Warrior, Lover, King, and Sage.[12] New Age spirituality hates the Warrior in the dangerous heart of man, to whatever extent that Warrior-hood empowers interjection of forceful true conscience into the culture war. Accomplishing each stage puts a finish on the man.

The words of adult virtue and sexual morality must be logically defined to youth, before and during the teachable adolescent years, to spiritual Christian and Believing Jewish children as allegiance in the culture war between godly conservatives and pagan-humanist progressives. Most youth would choose to become judges of adult behavior, rather than perpetrators of horror. Verbally instill the ideas "Honor bright? Hero or goat?" to authorize and integrate youths' consciences in the safety of their families, against temptation, lewdness and perversion outside them. Descent to vice should be taught as shaming: 'My soul is neither for sale nor for the conquering.'

Thus-empowered, spiritual Christian and Jewish children may be tempted, apart from knowledge of sound doctrine, to be judgmental of the adults in their lives. This may be temporarily humbling and uncomfortable for the parents, but their refusal to define for their children the terminology and logic of why and how to keep the vessel of their body would be neglect. It would stunt children's consciences, subject them to unutterable terrors, and predispose them to trouble with our just and holy God, further on in life. Parents should cognitively instruct their Believing children to confirm their consciences with the morally orthodox terminology, theme, and logic of why and how to keep the vessels of their bodies. Not refrain from instruction in order to enshrine their reputations with their children, or obtain superficial respect from them. "But he that is spiritual judgeth all things, yet he himself is judged of no man." (I Corinthians 2:15) Authorize your youths to discretely judge morals of adults and bigger teens, in the context of Christian sound doctrine, starting with their parents, their pastors, and their teachers. Anti-leaders (and Satan, their god) don't want there to be any authentic judges, particularly not young blameless ones, because virgins' bright faces can deliver themselves and others from evil-spirit possession.

Business people suffer temptation to despise evangelism, the testimony of Jesus, which is the spirit of prophecy (Revelation 19:10c). But, God calls all Believers, businessmen too, to spread the good news of Yeshua of Nazareth. Evangelism is an ever-present fount of grace and truth. Evangelism is also an instantaneous 'ascent' (Heb., *aliyah*), and the best good deed (Heb., *mitzvah*).

Men "darkened of heart" [Romans 1:21] for unthankfulness to God [or worse], struggle facelessly, because clarion light departed from their heart, for sin. Sinners darkened of heart are not invited by God into upward-looking cognitive meditation. The neologism *skotocardiac* describes a man darkened of heart, from the Greek *skotos*-, (dark) + *kardia*, (heart). Sexual sin is the root cause of much, if not most, mental illness.

John Eldredge said, If courtship between a man and a woman he truly loves is told and prospers, and succeeds to holy matrimony, the groom offers his bride his honorable name, and the bride reciprocates with her pure heart. This is God's plan for the relationship encompassed by holy matrimony: one man and one woman, vowed together into partnership for life. His desire is that sin mar neither the groom's name nor the bride's heart, in order that the husband's heart be authentic, dangerous, and able to rule nature. During their honeymoon, for the first time, a bride and her groom become one flesh, within a sanctifying relationship eternally blessed by God the Father.

As long as the bride and groom are true to Jesus Christ and to each other, they enjoy more resistance to temptation and spirit possession. Clarion cognition, discretion, and elegance can be imparted by God's grace into the new family, in ways that make the couple a blessing to the community of Believers in Jesus, salt and light to the nations, and that subject-object-dualistically seal out most evil spirits.

Politicized Sanctity

Legalized same-sex marriage may cost the United States of America divine protection on the order of what she lost from the removal of the Bible from public schools in the early 1960's. That disaster precipitated the generational drift away from her patrician Protestant Christian middle-class heritage, from the playboys to the hippies, to the New Agers, to the gays, to the globalists, to the witches, to the forthcoming Gaia-troopers, into progressive global-governancing politics.

President Barack Hussein Obama's 2010 authorization for homosexuals to serve openly in the U.S. military will incur torpor and garrison mentality upon it, that high technology will not fully compensate for. Garritroopers nervously dread invasion.

Procreation in holy matrimony is a trustworthy means for personal establishment (loosely, 'established of mind'). Sexual propriety cannot be taught by denial or by bad example. If a father has an unrepented-of pornography addiction, then his teenage son is going to perceive him as a total phony if he tries to proactively impart true Born Again virtue.

Deuteronomy 23:2 says, "A bastard shall not enter into the congregation of the LORD; even to his tenth generation shall he not enter into the congregation of the LORD." A bastard is a man born outside of wedlock. The implication is, that if you impregnate your girlfriend, you have nine months to marry her. If you don't during that time, your child is born into trouble with Triune YHWH Elohim, and you will probably have more problems raising him. This said, God can completely forgive the sin of even entrenched multigenerational bastardy. If God says so, the sins of one's fathers, including any paternal-line bastardy, can be completely forgiven *in this life*. If a man discerns bastardy as a problem in his life, and confesses to God, and God forgives it, then bastardy is no longer resident in the man's body or soul. It is as though a layer of subconscious shame is peeled off of his heart and mind, like the skin of an onion, freeing his heart and soul. God can apply Christ Jesus' perfect righteousness to any true Believer; then, as long as he walks in the Spirit and not in 'the flesh,' he enjoys Jesus' grace.

American men, repent! Trash your pornography! Too many men have befouled their families with illicit lust. The people of God need *holy* men, positive for sanctification and engaging, not passive. *The psychological vaccination for apathetic faceless moral syncretism is proactive, candid, verbal instruction and discussion.* We need godly pedagogues, not dissipated self-absorbed debauchees.

A technique that may increase beneficial primitive godliness is a Numbers 15:37 *Tzit*-Shirt™, which is a teeshirt or A-shirt with blue tassels, of threads or embroidery floss, looped through minute slits in the four quadrants of the shirt's hem. The reader can make his or her own, or some enterprising entrepreneur may manufacture them for sale, complete with the appropriate scripture quotation.

A *parthenovindicator* is a bride whose being corroborates virtues her husband has admired from his virginity. Parthenovindicators make the best mates. A parthenovindicator bride retains deep spiritual links to both Triune Yahweh and her human husband. The hundred forty-four thousand endtime Hebrew missionaries (the firstfruits) will be like parthenovindicators to Jesus Christ (Heb., *Elohim ha Beyn*). Romantic love involves two life stories authentically paralleling then ceremonially uniting, into one Christ-honoring future hope. Mere meshing of body parts fails to convey romantic love. For his parthenovindicator, a man would be elegantly upright, dangerous to evil, and cogently romantic. Via stalwart clarion cognition, one pledges troth to his parthenovindicator. One's bride is not communal property.

Three Vile Blunders

The more victory-wrecking temptations can be briefly addressed with 'Avoid the Vile 3 as though they are HIV.' The Vile 3 consist of fornication, occultism, or drug abuse.[13] Deliberate involvement in the Vile 3 invites shamanistic initiation into satanic spirituality. Commoners-by-the-Vile-3 instinctually attempt corruption of the set-apartness of virgins and the chaste, but virginity and chastity are terribly precious to the heart of Y'howah.

Commoners-by-the-Vile-3 spitefully act out as anti-leaders bent to the corruption of younger or more-excellent youths. Virgin adolescent youth desire either to be *better than* bigger corrupt teens (in confidence that God and His reality will stratify adult society), or to brokenly, appeasingly *emulate* them (to desensitize primal dread of being submitted to a root of sin). Left in a vacuum of virtue, some youth simply emulate those who are momentarily powerful. *If the less-excellent fellowship with the more-excellent, they are to learn from them, without tempting them.*

Whether or not you have certainty that a decision would be wicked, the penalty for experimentation with sin is worse sin, and worse difficulty obeying the LORD Jesus and His narrow perfect will. Jesus is always right! Erring, one's resultant failures in life make it more difficult to love and obey Him. Each stripe or buffet then becomes temptation to distrust Him. Each disobedience or lawlessness becomes an obstacle to one's (and one's progeny's) obedience and ascent. Born Again Christian children yearn, 'How to be better than the big boys?' Most of the answer is complex dialectical candor with his Daddy, unto excellence founded upon chastity and good judgment.

Summary

Failure is an event, not a person, unless the failure is one of chastity. *Fornication fractures ideals.* Chastity is essential to personhood and intellect, as hormones are crucial to parenthood. Promiscuity, if consummated, incurs submission to 'the old man,' to the flesh nature and to its root of sin. That is, to Satan. In the transition from academia to the business world of adult consensus reality, a student's chastity adds, as it were, about 1.5 to his lifetime cumulative GPA. Longterm chastity is a huge competitive advantage in every aspect of the adult civilized world.

Systematic theology's *Traducianism* is the doctrine that the souls of children are created from the bodies of their parents,[14] and are thus susceptible to their parents' sins. A *soul tie* results from two adults coitally becoming "one flesh" (Matthew 19:5). By an unforgiven soul tie, former lovers eventually suffer comparable cherubic incursions into each other's cardiac rhythms, to average their moral virtue and spiritual experiences. A soul tie to a partner by fornicative coitus would operate like alimony payments transactable in scarce guardian angels, payable for life (or until God says otherwise). Ideally, only one's spouse should share one's vitality. Neither adolescence, nor coitus, nor death (except Jesus') takes away sin. This is one advantage of virginity, and another reason why to be sexually abstinent until marriage and chaste thereafter.

At great cost, God the Father can reinstate a human male's virginity. Virgins' bright faces can deliver themselves and others from spirit possession, as some positive function of grace or of attainment in Toraic righteousness. A virgin's clarion-bright countenance repels evil spirits. A slut's coveting of a virgin male and his power to deliver bodes terrible danger to both.

The outworkings of apostasy, of earthy radical rebellion against Yahweh the Son, are such that homosexual behaviors are poised to define the next protected minority. If voters and legislators believe dross earthiness and decide they needn't acknowledge Triune Elohim in the definition of marriage then teaching the full Bible, with its sound doctrines contrary to sodomy and religious universalism, may become misidentified as a hate crime. Politically correct hate-crime legislation may criminalize truths that otherwise can prevent incalculable heartbreak and anguish. Biblical instruction cautioning against sodomy and interfaithism can prevent much suffering. Promiscuity cannot bring respectability! Triune Y'howah of the Bible calls sodomy, abomination (Leviticus 18:22 and 20:13), and interfaithism, apostasy (2 Timothy 4:3). The day will probably come soon when churches will be legally forced to acquiesce to heretical homosexualist doctrines, or even to employ unrepentant gays, in order to retain tax exempt status. Sodomy is God-loathed perversion, not a basis for legitimate minority status. Homosexual 'marriage' is the direct sociospiritual antithesis of Christ Jesus as Bridegroom to His church.

The dismantling of the United States' Protestant Christian institutions is very painful to watch. Because the preincarnate God the Son (Adonai, the LORD God of Israel) said "Behold, all souls are mine . . ." (Ezekiel 18:4), the progressive meta-Left rebelliously attempts to dismantle every societal institution derived from Him. It tries to alter sound doctrine to make the church, too, abominable to Triune Elohim. The world attempts to prove that the ways of the LORD don't work. But, He cannot fail.

———

196

A temptation with counterculture movements, from the playboys to the hippies, to the New Agers, to the gays, to the globalists, to the witches, to the yet-to-be Gaia-troopers, is to exult in the myth that rebels against Yahweh's *Logos* are above judgment. They're emphatically not!

As persons mature and years roll by, God expects a higher and higher standard of chastity and godliness. Mistakes of youth, by an adult, are much harder and costlier to forgive. Souls are real. Oozing religion is only as helpful as one's indispensable fasting to minimize the "old man." Cultivation of opposing traits[15] helps in thinking outside the box. Genius-singer Frank Sinatra sagely advised his daughter Nancy, "Keep a written journal. Study languages. Retain the rights to your own creative work."

A key belief of each new generation is 'I don't have the problems of my seniors.' Given chastity unto holy matrimony and parenthood, barring the Vile 3, this is mostly true. Exceptions include ancestral sin and looming one-world government. God usually will not scourge a man without provocation, nor scourge twice for the same repented-of sin. But, in a futile rush to immunize the herd against Yeshua haMashiach's divine judgment, socialites and media sophists wantonly destigmatize both spiritual felonies (e.g., homosexuality) and misdemeanors (e.g., conscientious syncretism). Don't you become their victim!

Sodomy within church or synagogue leadership comprises one of the vilest blemishes on the Roman and Episcopal churches, in the sight of Triune Yahweh. Over this issue, during the 1980's, Britain became like Aholah. The U.S.A. now approaches to become like Aholibah. (Ezekiel 23:1-21) During the last days, sodomites will probably receive civil authority to demand office, even employment, within churches seeking to retain tax-exempt status. If that happens to your church, God the Father can suddenly subtract His Holy Spirit from those leaders' hearts and occlude their minds, leaving them at risk for myopic left-brained kunonoia. Man tends to either mental-math-cued visuospatial cognitive intellect, or left-brained verbosity. Society will further devolve into militant, purity- and holiness-hating post-Christian multiculturalism, affecting Protestant finances and exceptionalism. In the Diaspora, we should study Dutch Reformed congregational order for ideas on how to handle militant post-Christian society, and we will need many doctrinally-sound lay pastors for covert house churches.

We must beware theological liberalism supportive of seeker friendliness, excused by politically-correct modern translations of the Bible. Conservative pulpits build bigger, brighter congregations.

Societal morals endure abasement. United States' World War II conscripts were questioned "Do you like girls?", with the intention of identifying problem homosexuals. So many of those boyhood-Christian farmhands answered "No [I love Jesus more than fornication]," that military brass had to change their question. Due to President Barack Hussein Obama's moral rebellion, such screening would not even be attempted in the early 21st century. Rather, U.S. armed forces' officer cadres follow civilians' orders to submit to homophilic sensitivity training, boding terrible evil for our nation.

Chapter 8 notes:

[1] John Eldredge. *The Way of the Wild Heart*. Nashville: Thomas Nelson, 2006, 196.

[2] John Eldredge. *Wild at Heart*. Nashville: Thomas Nelson, 2001, 62.

[3] *Ibid*, 90.

[4] *Ibid*, 182.

[5] Michael Lee Lanning. *The Military 100: A Ranking of the Most Influential Military Leaders of All Time*. Secaucus: Citadel, 1996, 77.

[6] Gary H. Kah. *Hope for the World Update*. Winter, 2010. 1-6.

[7] Scott Lively and Kevin Abrams. *The Pink Swastika: Homosexuality in the NAZI Party (3rd Edition)*. Keiser, OR: Founders Publishing, 1997, 189.

[8] Ragnar Benson. *Ragnar's Action Encyclopedia of Practical Knowledge and Proven Techniques*. Boulder: Paladin, 1995, 180.

[9] Lively and Abrams, 57.

[10] *Ibid*, 59.

[11] *Ibid*, 62-63.

[12] Eldredge. *The Way of the Wild Heart*, 10-15.

[13] McCandlish Phillips. *The Bible, the Supernatural and the Jews*. Camp Hill, PA: Horizon, 1970, 305-307.

[14] Louis Berkhof. *Systematic Theology*. Grand Rapids: Eerdman's, 1932, 1938, 1996, 197.

[15] David H. Freeman. *Corps Business: The 30 Management Principles of the U.S. Marines*. New York: HarperCollins, 2000, 155.

Chapter 9

Latter-Day Islam

Where does Islam err? By misidentifying Jesus of Nazareth as a mere prophet, instead of the Son of God, and by then demanding submission to Allah, a false god that is not identical with Elohim. Too, Muslims are taught erroneously that Yahweh the Holy Spirit is identical with the Vatican's 'Mary.'

The word 'Islam' literally means *submission*. Islam's prophet, Mohammed, was born in 570 A.D. At that time Arabs, the descendents of Ishmael, worshiped an assortment of deities, including the Judaeo-Christian Yahweh. Until the rise of Mohammed, the Arabs had 360 gods represented as idols, one for each day of the lunar year. They were housed in the *kabaa* (literally, 'cube') in Mecca, which was supposedly built by Abraham. When Mohammed incepted Islam after 610 A.D., he declared Allah the moon god to be the one true deity from among that pantheon of 360, and in 630 A.D. destroyed the idols that had been housed in the *kabaa*.

There are two main sects within Islam. The Shi'ites believe that Islamic leadership is transmitted along the bloodline of Mohammed through his son-in-law Ali. The Sunni's believe that succession of Islamic leadership is by spiritual anointing. The two sects have fought bloody wars with each other over the issue.

Revolutionary Islam has been called *Islamism*. It can be summed up as 'Islam is the solution (whatever the problem).' For Islamists, Islam is far more than a religion, it is a political ideology. Destroying Israel is, post-Iranian revolution, a sub-objective for the Islamists. Destroying the United States of America is their primary attempt at world domination. The Iranian revolution inspired Osama bin Laden, Hamas, and Hezbollah. Osama bin Laden died at the hands of U.S. Navy SEAL Team Six, on

May 1, 2011, which raided his secret compound near a Pakistani military installation in Abbottobad, Pakistan.

For all the problems inherent to it, Islam is but a ruse in the spiritual chess match of the nations between Christ Jesus and Satan to usher in global pagan socialism and one-world governance. *In the early 21ˢᵗ century, every major political action will tend to result in a pro-globalist reaction.* This is the new dispensation.

The strategy of the Islamists is diabolical and simple. According to Yosef Bodansky, author of *Bin Laden: The Man Who Declared War On America,* reviewed by WorldNetDaily in 2001, they hope "to lure the United States into an attack on Muslim nations that will unite Islamic peoples into toppling regimes in Saudi Arabia and other Arab gulf states so that radical Islam will possess a world monopoly on oil."

Bin Laden considered oil his ultimate asset. He did not think the United States is determined to wage a long, costly war, but that we will lash out angrily, antagonize larger Islam, hand them the Persian Gulf oil fields, and "be forced into submission to Allah due to the overwhelming economic pressure of revolutionized oil states." The attacks occurred, with the U.S. invasions of Iraq and Afghanistan. In winter, 2011, popular uprisings against long-standing demagogues in Egypt, Yemen, Syria and Libya threatened to destabilize the Middle East, polarizing oil states against the U.S., just as Osama bin Laden hoped.

9/11 Infamy

The conflict is chess-like, as were the propaganda-fueling, collusion-beset, *kamikaze*-like airplane impacts that mass-murdered some 2,997 Americans in the World Trade Center and Pentagon, on September 11, 2001. Those strange very-complex attacks benefited many monied-elite entities whose privy interests conflict sharply with those of justice, of the United States of America, and of Protestant exceptionalism.

Some argue competently from engineering evidence that the destruction of the World Trade towers involved demolition charges. If true, it implies a false-flag covert intelligence operation designed to draw the United States into expedient but unjust wars. The World Trade Center complex was a real estate white elephant, and lost millions of dollars per year in operating costs. Due to its high asbestos content, the WTC could not have been conventionally demolished. Media suppression of alternative explanations remains egregious.

Oddly, World Trade Center 7, which housed the Security and Exchange Commission and its many open stock- and bond-market fraud investigations, collapsed abruptly and symmetrically into its basement, in some six-and-a-half seconds, at about 5 PM on 9/11/2001, some seven hours later that day than the plane strikes, after sustaining only minor damage from debris and fire. It is likely that any Islamists' plot for September 11, 2001 was discovered, anticipated, and enhanced, by parties unnamed, to cause a flagrant new Pearl Harbor and fling the United States into convenient wars against certain countries. World Trade Center 1, 2, and 7 collapsed by an energy much more potent than merely kinetic impact and fire, combined with gravity. Who had motive? Who had opportunity? 9/11 is a window to eschatology, to those who understand.

According to Architects and Engineers for 9/11 Truth (www.AE911Truth.org), WTC 1, 2 and 7 collapsed due, in large part, to nanothermitic cutter charges pre-set as controlled demolition. More than 1,700 architects and engineers, with more than 25,000 years of combined work experience, have signed the AE911Truth petition, crying foul and demanding a new independent investigation. The National Institute for Standards and Technology (NIST), the primary U.S. federal government investigative agency in the case, admitted that it did not even test for explosive residue in the WTC debris. "And ye shall know the truth, and the truth shall make you free." (John 8:32) Truth heals. The inveigling of respect and love, under politically-correct false pretenses, rankles.

Truly, the subsequent wars in Iraq and Afghanistan became disadvantageous to the Bush administration and the United States' Republican party. As it turned out, Iraq did not even possess any weaponry of mass destruction. Islamic states' enemies, who colluded to put the blame for 9/11 solely onto radical Muslims, by so doing gravely damaged their own partisan agenda, because Triune Yahweh is earnest and just. Barring repentance, their lamentable infamy concerning 9/11 may make much of their agenda boomerang back at them, for decades to come. The unprecedented Homeland Security and USA Patriot Acts emerged from the intricate tragedies of 9/11, as the progressive globalist elite utilized the crisis to consolidate authorization for one-world government.

Bluntly, 9/11 was a false-flag op. Unfortunately, 9/11 will incur contempt and indignation upon its intended beneficiaries. Elohim's Biblical provisions for repentance are confession and restitution. (Exodus 22:5, Numbers 5:7)

Most major media engines in the United States will not seriously discuss 9/11 truth, nor have they ever. "Therefore whatsoever ye have spoken in darkness shall be heard in the light; and that which ye have spoken in the ear in closets shall be proclaimed upon the housetops." (Luke 12:3)

It's what Y'howah Elohim says that matters, not merely what rich influential men say. "Lying lips are an abomination unto the LORD: but they that deal truly are his delight." (Proverbs 12:22)

Cultural Islamism

Funded by the vast resources of Arab oil money, Muslims are buying abandoned Anglican churches in England and converting them to mosques. In the 1980's, there were about 150 mosques in England, but in 2001 there were thousands. In that year, there were between three and seven million Muslims in the United States, with a nascent lobby in Congress.

In order to control Islamism, we must demythologize the theology that motivates radical Muslims to commit suicide in the murder of infidels. We must reverse the major media's syncretist whitewashing of the religion of Islam as godly within the pale of religious universalism (interfaithism).

Islamists are taught by the *mullahs* from the Koran that anyone who does not submit to Islam (literally, to submission) is worthy of death. The Hebraeo-Christian Bible says, "Do not murder" and "Whosoever will be great among you, let him be your minister." Both cannot be the voice of the Creator. They are not, *because the Triune Spirit named Elohim is not the spirit called Allah.* Y'howah Elohim and Allah are two separate spirits. Yahweh tempers submission with personality.

202

Diagram 9.1: Cautionary Binary Outcomes of 9/11.

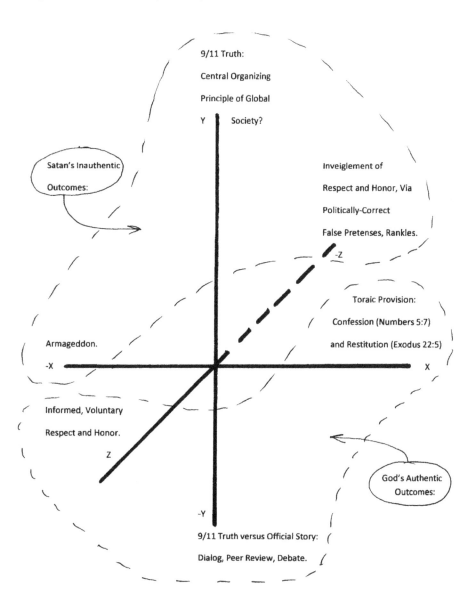

Pan-Religious Deity?

Interfaithism is a totally false doctrine. It is sometimes called religious universalism, and is the idea that a monolithic God identifies with all names for deity. However, Y'howah is not Allah, nor is He Krishna, nor Buddha, nor Shiva, nor 'Mary.' Those are disparate spirits, despite that some men confuse them with each other as monolithic deity or as pantheism's Impersonal Absolute.

American progressives have generated media pressure to give credence to the myth of interfaithism. Interfaithism, or religious universalism, claims that God is the same by all names for Him: that the God of the Bible, holy Jehovah-Yahweh, is the same Spirit as profane Allah, Krishna, Shiva, or Buddha. But, that is completely untrue. Triune Yahweh is a narrowly-true Spirit who is distinctly separate from the spirits of created pagan deities. Debunk interfaithism and confusion evaporates over who holds the moral high ground. Jesus Christ's Triune Yahweh is a Spirit distinctly separate from pagan deities. When moral high ground is evident, prudent courses of action become conceivable.

Precious Muslims are taught by the *mullahs,* on behalf of Mohammed and Allah (a moon god), that if a *jihadist* kills an infidel, then he will be awarded seventy-two virgins in the afterlife. The Koran promises rewards for cruelty and murder, as long as the victims are relatively infidel. The Bible, which contains the words of holy Elohim, teaches that if a man murders another, for that sin he should die and at death be banished from the holy presence of God the Father and consigned to eternal torment in hell. The two outcomes are logically exclusive.

Both simply cannot be true in the same universe. This is because YHWH Elohim is our holy Creator, and He is not Islamic Allah. They are totally different sprits. In order to defend against Islamists, we need to debunk their flawed theology, intelligently and compassionately, to show them that a murderous faith is a misguided one. Then, perhaps, they will live more peaceably.

The real shame in the *kamikaze*-like attacks of September 11, 2001 is not the terror that they caused, but the sin that produced it. The liberal progressive media has tried to selectively define the problem to the globalists' advantage by, from the outset, labeling the offenders 'terrorists.'

But, that only defines the terms for future crackdowns on worthy deviants from the herd of society.

Islamic Roots

The true miscreants are the false-flag colluders who created a new Pearl Harbor. The 9/11 attacks on the World Trade Center were complex and devious, and designed to draw the United States into foreign wars.[1]

Esteemed Muslims often have better chastity than many Americans of the baby-boomer and following generations. This fact bodes ill for the United States in its elite-contrived conflict with Islam. However, many dear Muslim women have suffered forcible clitorectomy. "Seventy-five percent of Muslim women worldwide have undergone female circumcision," according to radio pastor David T. Moore in a sermon entitled *Islam—In Your Face*, broadcast around autumn, 2001.

According to Christian missionary Faysal Sharif, female circumcision is prevalent in some African and Asian countries, but is not mandated by the Koran. However, Shari'a law does not forbid the practice. Clitorectomy is medically unnecessary. It involves cutting out or abrading away the tissue of a female's clitoris and the immediately surrounding areas. Clitorectomy vastly decreases an adult woman's enjoyment of sexual intercourse with her husband. The effect upon such a girl is to traumatize her, and pressure her to yield space to the religion of Islam and its 7th-century *ethos*. The word 'Islam' means *submission*.

Islamic Kilotons

Jihad is sobering as a provocation to global governance. Islam foments a 7th Century culture. Islam proceeds from warping of human spirit to an occultic medieval worldview. It is constructed upon fatal internal flaws and will ultimately fail.

An alternative strategy, that Satan might use Islamism for, is to develop an Islamic atom bomb. The mere availability of Islamic kilotons for nuclear *jihad* can be used to incite a mass media frenzy to trade rights for peace, and turn to the United Nations for mediation in order to forestall nuclear holocaust. If the major news and entertainment media have their way, some

Baby Boomer and Gen-X'er urbanites might submissively trade rights for peace to secure a few more years of *pax romana* under the U.N.

According to Yosef Bodanshky, author of *Bin Laden: the Man who Declared War on America*, as published in 2001 by WorldNetDaily, bin Laden was in possession of chemical weapons and of suitcase-sized nuclear weapons obtained from covert sources in Russia.

Osama Bin Laden's *al Qaeda* was believed by intelligence organizations to possess as many as ten suitcase-sized nuclear weapons, portable by one man, and to know dirty bomb technology. These threats have not materialized.

A dirty bomb consists of radioactive material packed around a conventional high explosive charge, to render a locale's ground and atmosphere uninhabitable by explosive distribution of radioactive dust. A dirty bomb can be built as a car bomb. Many rogue Islamic states spend up to one half of their gross domestic product (tens of billions of dollars) on weaponry, although the U.S. spends more on defense than the rest of the nations of the world, combined.

Culture War, I

Radical Islamist leaders hate United States citizens' Yahweh-given rights, ingenuity, entrepreneurship, and freedom of speech, because we defy submission to Muslim *sharia* law and its 7th century culture, and because the U.S. government condones pornography, alcohol abuse and sodomy.

Political globalists fan the flames of third-world jealousy at United States citizens' standards of living, claiming that U.S. industries use disparate quantities of raw materials purchased on the free market, leaving less raw material for future generations of third-worlders. Islam represents a long-term problem,[2] especially as a dire provocation for global governance. The multi-trillion dollar U.S. backlash against the 9/11 false-flag op makes global peace much less likely.

The worst material threat facing the United States is high altitude nuclear airbursts or super-intense solar storms, which can destroy millions of microchips *in situ*. Its worst politico-economic threats are devaluation of the dollar into the *amero* (in order to dominate the economy and pay off the national debt with devalued currency), a disastrous Constitutional convention, and demographic attrition away from middle-class Protestant exceptionalism. And, its worst spiritual threat is the dispensation of global ecopagan socialist world governance that God is reluctantly allowing, in order to usher in the return of Jesus Christ.

The super-wealthy global elite responsible for 9/11 will probably contrive other major false-flag operations, with blame placed on Islamic agents and states. They may allow a plot to nuke New York City, and provoke more expedient warfare. Problematically for the guilty, secrets cannot be kept forever. "That which ye have spoken in the ear in closets shall be proclaimed upon the housetops." (Luke 12:3b) Despite its problems, Islam amounts to a ruse and provocation for global governance in the contest between Jesus Christ and Satan for the outworking of prophecy.

Islamism: Foil for Globalism

The globalists want to form a North American Union, patterned after the European Union, with the *amero* for its unit of currency. The huge debt burdens carried by most governments worldwide, in the early 3rd millennium, will likely be paid off at a fraction of market value, with devalued national currencies pegged against a global-state currency—possibly called the *uno* or *unica*. This will preserve public confidence in globalist leaders.

The globalist monied insider elite may arrange for tensions between the United States and Islamism to rise so high that a U.N.-brokered armed peace might win the approval of the gullible masses. Americans may be conned into trusting a paganized organization and trade rights for a convenient peace, striving to retain the prosperity that we have come to regard as our national birth right.

Our prosperity is the consequence of our religious freedom. Our judicial code results from our heritage in Hebraeo-Christian moral law and English common law, and has made it safe to succeed in the U.S. Our historic willingness to acknowledge Jehovah God in our customs and dealings, and in our national and state policies, is one reason that He has blessed us with peace and prosperity. Middle-class Protestant exceptionalism has been under intense culture-war siege in the United States for some fifty years.

God is the same yesterday, today and forever. He loves His Hebrew people, yet when they refused to acknowledge Him and observe His ways, He dispersed them to the Assyrians and the Babylonians. He will not long tolerate contented sinning, not even if excused by hackneyed political correctness. Fifty-two million aborted babies (and tens of millions of wounded women), since 1967, argue against perpetual United States' freedom. Cosmetic abortion amounts to murder for pride's sake. Triune Elohim is an ethical God.

The author's perspective on the United States' controversy with Islam, is that eventually the Islamists are going to chance upon The Bomb, if they have not already. When they do, global governancers will use Islamists' aggression as an excuse for expansion of United Nations' authority. Predictably, the progressive meta-Left will employ major media engines to advocate compromised U.S. national sovereignty.

The United Nations and its agenda (served by votive veneration of nature, by microdisarmament of U.S. citizens, and by occultism as the moral high ground for world governance, *et cetera*) is the message that the globalist monied elite churn out via their major-media propaganda engines. Just, holy Elohim would probably prefer that the pleasant land currently governed by Zionist Israel not become contaminated by radioactive fallout.

The global governancers anxiously seek to increase their political authority. Not only are United Nations' globocrats appointed, not elected, they have a flauntedly pagan world view and agenda, and they respond to partisan, globalist-funded lobbyists called non-governmental organizations (NGO's). They claim pantheism as the moral sanction to override the Protestant-exceptional United States of America's national sovereignty.

The United Nations is neither smarter or more virtuous than the United States' national, state or local politicians. Neither do U.N. morals have the sanction of Triune Yahweh. Nor does the U.N. have a viable plan for the perpetuation of civilization. *The U.N. is based upon satanic religion that doesn't work for India and will never work for America.* The U.N. is the vehicle that Satan wants to use to forcibly apply occult religious principles to the population of the world, with the authoritarianism of a computerized gobal ecopagan socialist one-world state to enforce them. A VeriChip-based global identity management system's mark of the beast would appeal to the demonic, naïve, and irreligious alike, but will be the beginning of the Tribulation.

Ideologues of the globalist elite include outright Luciferians, freemasons and New Agers. Their monies come from wealthy foundations and international investment bankers buoyed up by anonymous shareholders in the privately-held central-bank corporation called the United States' Federal Reserve.

Economic Globalization

The Federal Reserve, or Fed, is a European-style central bank, established by insiders, that pays anonymous private stockholders the first six percent of interest on funds borrowed by the United States federal government. That globalist monied elite funds foundations and charities that in turn fund lobbyists, writers, educators and artists who earn their living radicalizing and altering U.S. national culture and legislation. That globalist monied elite outright owns the overwhelming majority of U.S. and overseas newspapers, television stations and radio stations. The monied elite have such a near-monopoly upon mass-communications media that, for about the last sixty years, political correctness has become more core a virtue than personal uprightness and faith according to sound doctrine.

There is danger in overdoing security organizations. Only three countries in recorded history have formed unified national security organizations. Two of them are NAZI Germany and Stalinist USSR. The third is the United States of America, with the Homeland Defense Agency under the Homeland Defense and USA Patriot Acts. In the hands of the right men, the Homeland Defense Agency may be a good thing, but under the control of the wrong men with the backing of the wrong laws, it has the potential for extreme evil. With existing information technology, a totalitarian government can bring to bear terrible pressure upon Protestant Christians to submit to an occult worldview and surrender to the unjust authority of a charismatic tyrant bent upon democide.

With the potential for abuse implicit to the USA Patriot and Homeland Defense Acts, and with existing computer technology, the Internet, and VeriChip implanted-microchips, a pan-national socialist United Nations eco-state may be only a generation away.

Mark of the Beast

There was a company called VeriChip Corporation (*www.VeriChipcorp. com*, November 12, 2009) that developed a glass-encased subcutaneous implantable microchip, first invented by Digital Angel Corp. Called the VeriChip, that invention ostensibly met needs for veterinary identification of pets and identification of geriatric wanderers, and for linking bodies to their medical information.

The U.S. Food and Drug Administration approved the VeriChip for subdermal human implantation in June, 2004. The glass-encased VeriChip is about the size of a grain of rice, and can be read using a scanner wand, similar to card-reader access systems in modern secure office buildings. The VeriChip can function similarly to a credit or debit card, linking any given body to a bank account.

The United States' Food and Drug Administration refused to allow VeriChip Corp to market people-tracking implantable RFID chips with global positioning satellite (GPS) circuitry included, but a future variant may have both RFID *and* GPS circuitry, and either way may form the basis of a digital global identity management system. That technology is nearly COTS (commercial off-the-shelf) in 2010 A.D. Upon scanning, the VeriChip returns a pre-programmed binary 16-digit decimal-equivalent identifying number, which acts as a primary key of digital identity that can be processed against relational databases via a wide-area network. The chip-reader can query the digital record and input it to a wide-area network to a regional site: FBI? Homeland Security? NAU? United Nations? Then, an order could come back from the career globocrat on duty, 'Yes, that individual is on our list as a dissenter. Arrest him.'

By April, 2010, VeriChip Corp. merged with Steel Vault Corp. to form PositiveID Corp. (*www.positiveidcorp.com*) VeriChip technology imparts far too much population management power into the hands of appointed officials. In the words of Lord Acton, referring to the Vatican, "Power corrupts, and absolute power corrupts absolutely." With that merger, a series of confusing re-brandings occurred. The VeriChip has been variously called the BioChip, the MediChip, and the PositiveID, but the basic, glass-encased, FDA-approved, subcutaneously-implantable, radio-frequency identifier microchip is known as the VeriChip.

The glass-encased subdermally-implantable RFID VeriChip stores, in binary format, a 16-digit decimal number capable of digitally identifying 10 quadrillion unique bodies.[3] The U.N., with an atmosphere of contemptuous hegemony evidenced by cocktail-party legislating, may fulfill prophecy by providing Satan with the one-world government foretold in the Bible. Evil's ascent may happen very quickly, but can't until God the Father lets it.

Computer programs can be written to daily sort the identification numbers and other vital facts of any VeriChipped buyer or seller who does business in any store of any city, nationwide or worldwide. Other computer software can parse off into files the world-ID number, SSN's, names, addresses and vital facts of all business-transactors with suspected or proven Jewish DNA or with public unrenounced Christian-fundamentalist faith.

At a whim of appointed global-governance potentates, with the emotional support of a populace indoctrinated with the logical fallacy that if authorities say so then it must be true (*ad verecundiam*), the United Nations that once seemed sympathetic to Zionism will become its enemy. History, as the saying goes, tries to repeat itself upon those who refuse to learn from it.

If the monied investment-banker elite (some of whom are Jewish) fund a global VeriChip-indexed identity management system, thinking they can thereby regulate international markets and thwart anti-Semitism, Satan will take control of the global state away from them and use it against Zionist Israel. Per systematic theology, this will occur during the Great Tribulation, also known as Jacob's Trouble.

With a physical VeriChip-based global identity management system in place, with existing technology but not with existing leaders or laws, a world government of Satan can digitally identify every human body in every civilized market-nation.

Culture War, II

Some law-enforcement professionals would go through the motions they have been trained in without reasoning why. Career advancement, retirement accounts, college educations and *status quo* are not evil things, unless they blind men to the responsibility to reason godlily and logically, to decide right and wrong, and behave uprightly and forthrightly.

The middle-class treasure that we in the United States enjoy from God is preserved in our Constitution and judicial code, derived from God's Torah and from English common law, that permits living, free worship of our Triune God, (Heb., *"Eloheynu haShiloosh haKodesh"*). "Where the Spirit of the LORD is, there is liberty." (2 Corinthians 3:17b) Whether or not the LORD is present depends upon men's hearts and choices of words: is *Yeshua haNotzri* of the Bible invited within? The LORD God of Israel, who is Yahweh the Son, doesn't favor cultures that suppress sound doctrine in favor of pagan, Vaticanic or Talmudic traditions of men or demons. Sound doctrine of Triune Yahweh is essential to the priesthood of Believers.

The future will not go quite the way that the monied global-elite want. This author doesn't expect totalitarianism from any current or foreseeable U.S. administration. However, Satan the created arch-cherub understands human nature well, and men will do strange things for the sake of prosperity. The Germans who did the butchery of the NAZIs were by all accounts mostly respectable unassuming citizens who coveted the prosperity that the NAZIs promised, and in return refused to challenge the decisions of the ruling elite.

The Bible says that no one will be able to buy or sell, during Jacob's Trouble (the Great Tribulation) except he has the "mark of the beast in his forehead or right hand." (Revelation 13:17) Will that apocalyptic mark turn out to be a glass-encased RFID VeriChip or some similar product? That is the expectation. The return of Jesus Christ is the means that God the Father has chosen to glorify Himself. Techno-totalitarianism may occur before then. *Buying* may come to be defined as everything from paying mortgages to purchasing food. *Selling*, as everything from gainful employment to roadside stands offering garden produce.

Conclusion

The United States' founding fathers foresaw as evil any entanglement of our nation with heathen totalitarian regimes across borders and oceans. That same evil has dragged us far into dialog with proud satanically-deluded men who believe it is their endowment or *karma* to rule an underclass. Sheer inertia of political correctness and groupthink paralyzes the unchurched public into cocksure submission to Mr. Big and proffered cradle-to-grave security. Such demagogues would drag us into dull-witted placation of radical, envious, embittered groups, deceived into believing that by Satan's lies they can evade Yahweh's *Logos'* judgment.

A nation of television couch-potatoes must choose between finding a conscience to vote at every election and being allowed to live as drones. The virtue to speak and act intelligently is rarely touted by TV or movie producers, due to wealthy power mongers who want ever-more authority and with it men's worship. Many men have had their psychic membranes so altered by histories of vice that they partake in vanity. Such vain pride is foolish, just as is their evil ambition for prestigious roles in a global pagan socialist state under United Nations' authority.

When global governancers' plans succeed, for God will allow that, in part, to fulfill prophecy, it will be very brief, chronologically a blip in the context of history. Our Triune Yahweh will not tolerate His plans to receive honor, glory and worship, to be thwarted by His creation.

The globalists' any success will be because world governance is reluctantly tolerated in God the Father's plan to glorify Himself through the return of Jesus Christ, who is Yeshua haMashiach. In so doing, He will deal permanently with the problem of evil, temptation and sin. Men need to acknowledge Jesus of Nazareth as the Messiah and believe that God raised Him from the dead, but this may become a forbidden truth in the global governancers' VeriChip-controlled market nexus. "Be not deceived, God is not mocked." (Galatians 6:7)

Chapter 9 notes:

1   *www.911WeKnow.com*, August 3, 2010; *www.AE911Truth.org*, May 15, 2013.
2   Joseph Farah. "The War Comes Home." *The Whistleblower*. WorldNetDaily. com, November, 2001.
3   http://en.wikipedia.org/wiki/VeriChip. January 3, 2012.

Chapter 10

Tribulation-Era Global Identity Management

Urged by the Council on Foreign Relations (CFR), the Trilateral Commission (TC), and the Bilderbergers, the United Nations desires global ecospiritual socialism enabled by compulsory worldwide microdisarmament of privately-owned firearms. The U.N. is pagan in its doctrine and intentions, with much potential for totalitarianism. Pagan pantheism is the theological basis for U.N. globalists' claim that they are authorized to govern the world.

The United Nations intends to save the environment from man and man from himself, by uniting a church of ecumenical nature worship with a state of computerized global governance. That plan is the most liberal radical thing imaginable, and the goal of progressive politics. Exclusive faith in our Triune Elohim by sound doctrine, expressed as righteousness, freedom, and evangelism, is not welcome in the United Nations' worldview of the 21st century.

In the New Agey early 3rd millennium, every major political action tends to produce a pro-globalist reaction. Global governancers comprise the progressive meta-Left. They are turned in heterogenous unison against the truth of Christ Jesus and His ways, determined to evade His judgment. Molding the world in their likeness will produce global ecospiritual socialism.

Rejecting guilt and conscientious absolutes in favor of conscientious syncretism, the meta-Left opposes true civilization, which is the set of societal reminders that the Father of the *Logos* may be safely, authentically loved and trusted. This is the Protestant Christian meaning of patriotism (Gr., *pater-* (father) + *osis* (infusion)), a state of grace distinct from both jingoism and globalism.

Progressives or Regressives?

Global governancers such as Barack H. Obama decry American exceptionalism, but the correct term is *Protestant exceptionalism*. Each legislative turn that United States' politicians take away from God's Word (living and written), the more tenuous becomes our highly-conditional Protestant exceptional middle class, which frames the basis for our any national greatness! The New World Order, or New Age, corresponds to a waxing of Satan's strategy for civilization and to an increasing severity of grace to Protestant Christians and Believing Jews. The Archenemy wants events of the End-time described herein to catch Protestant Christians and Believing Jews by surprise. He wants one-world government and the mark of the beast to be a non-issue until after the fact. But, God wants these problems of the End widely discussed and thoroughly understood, well ahead of time.

Wealth and manufacturing infrastructure have flowed out of the United States since 1994, under then-president Bill Clinton's Global Agreement on Tariffs and Trade and the North American Free Trade Agreement (GATT and NAFTA). Progressives want to compensate for the economic damage by inflating the money supply.

Progressives, yielding to Luciferic influence, try to factor Jesus the *Logos'* influence out of education and society. Should they succeed, civilization will descend into Satan's control.

The corollary of change is risk. 'Too big to fail' is a bad epitaph. In this early 3rd millennial New Age, God grants Satan a higher percentage of *ad hoc* requests, for permission to try the faith of the upright. Satan wields more societal influence now than in recent decades.

How to combine true faith with a reckless sporting spirit? Tolerate the possibility of your own martyrdom for your personal public testimony. A mid-Tribulational select Rapture will probably catch the firstfruits hundred forty-four thousand Hebrew missionary evangelists up to heaven, to receive their glorified bodies. Then, nearly forty-two months later, at the resurrection of the dead at Jesus Christ's post-Tribulational second coming, *un-VeriChipped Believers will be raptured up to heaven* and receive their glorified bodies.

The pre-Trib Rapture theory bears the taint of liberal Vaticanic theology. Faith in the pre-Trib Rapture theory is not identical with faith in Jesus

RITE FOR THE TIMES

Christ of Triune Yahweh. While it may be tempting to yearn for a miraculous rescue, historically God usually lets Believers' faith be tried.

Context

Take ownership of your hope in Christ Jesus by conscientiously giving your personal public testimony, then stand by it to the death. People usually try harder for their ideals than for their intimidated conformities. Mathematical conscience reasons its way to productive ideals. Corporate salvation is a myth.

The mid-Trib select Rapture of the hundred forty-four thousand firstfruits will be followed by the three-and-a-half year prophesyings of the two witnesses. The theme seems to be Christ's bride tried like gold in a fire, prior to the post-Trib second coming of Christ Jesus.

The following discussion of an identity management system as an instrument of apocalyptic pagan tyranny is an educated scenario, not "Thus saith the LORD." Subcutaneous-implantable RFID-microchip technology, already in existence at this juncture in the outworking of global governance, represents a tremendous temptation to those in authority. If authorized and used by politicians in a global identity management system, subcutaneously implantable RFID microchips can fulfill Biblical prophecies about the mark of the beast.

The U.N.'s Destiny

At United Nations' headquarters on Manhattan Island, New York, politically-appointed globocrats ensconced Sri Chimnoy, their own Hindu *guru*, as a slap at the western world's Protestant Christian heritage. The United Nations' basement meditation room is maintained by The Lucis Trust, which was formerly named The Lucifer Publishing Company.[1] That organization internationally advances occultic theosophical principles in society through arcane schools and U.N. policies.

The Lucis Trust is an influential non-elected special-interest non-governmental organization [NGO] intent upon advancing its partisan agenda at the United Nations. The United Nations makes no secret that fundamentalists (Protestant Christians, Jews and Muslims) are *persona non*

216

grata in its New World Order, arranged as it is according to theosophical New Age occultism. These people of the Book don't submit to pantheistic leaders' claim to authority. New Age spirituality driving the meta-Left's New World Order discourages warriors' hearts within authentic men, because a warrior's heart empowers his conscience into outspokeness for truth. Meta-Left spirituality tries to provoke socially-indemnifiable reactions from warrior-hearted men, by contrivance of outrageous situations. Reaction to outrages comprises progressives' primary weapon.

Theosophy was a formative influence upon prominent NAZI leaders, as well as upon modern United Nations ideologues. While politicizing the philosophies of religious universalism and pantheism, the U.N. stalks its critical strategic milestone: authority over the United States' educational, judicial and governmental systems, in order to factor Protestant Christian heritage out of society, and with it Triune Elohim's protection. It would like to corrupt human worship of our holy Hebraeo-Christian Triune Elohim by introducing elements of paganism into Christian cultural forms. Religious universalism to the contrary, faith in Christ plus paganism is unsound.

Contrary to religious universalism, all paths to God do not lead to Him, since Triune Yahweh does not identify with pagan names for deity. *Pagan names for deity refer to distinctly separate spirits, not to Jesus Christ's set-apart, narrowly-true Y'howah Elohim, whose name and triune Godhead are uniquely holy!* The error of religious universalism is also called interfaithism.

The United Nations has published its willingness to sacrifice personal freedoms for a pantheistic utopia. It touts votive veneration of the environment as justification for restrictive global governance, and as a central organizing principle for society. In a VeriChip-based identity management system (or population management system), globalists will have the technology for totalitarian global pagan socialism, regardless of fundamentalist Hebrews and Christians, who love the holy Tri-Unity of Elohim more than they love His creation. The pagan U.N. can never produce freedom while it rebels against the narrowly-true *Logos* of YHWH. (2 Corinthians 3:17)

In order to redistribute the earth's raw materials between industrial Christian-heritage nations and pagan earth-friendly indigenous peoples, the United Nations and its advocates argue that sovereign nations should submit to the authority of pan-national governance, amounting to global pagan socialism.

United Nations' officials are appointed by the influence of a monied elite. They are not popularly elected. Therefore, they attempt to govern without a valid moral mandate or democratic vote to authorize them into power. The United Nations has the mood of an insiders' elite. It legislates with the contemptuous hegemony of cocktail-party lobbyists.

World Judiciary

The United Nations invites lobbying by non-governmental organizations (NGO's) in a clubby, old-boy, status-talks atmosphere. With the establishment of the International Criminal Court (the ICC), the globalists have been authorized to violate some national sovereignties by writing and expert-interpreting international law, with zero accountability to the governed. Expert-interpretation of evolving writ is an Oral Law administrative form that minimizes input from an educated middle class.

A globalist judiciary will start with obvious issues like war crimes, and proceed to complex environmental issues. The United Nations wants to apply radical environmentalism, based upon the false premise of anthropogenic global warming of goddess earth, to micromanage every sovereign nation, community, school, and household upon the globe, to regulate markets into zero evangelism, and introduce and enforce paganism. A wholesome environment is a moderately commendable goal, but faceless global pagan socialism is not the right way to accomplish it. That end does not justify those means!

U.N. Summit, I

The United Nations adopted, during the Earth Summit at Rio de Janeiro between 3 and 14 June, 1992, a mammoth comprehensive document called AGENDA 21 [as in 21st century]. In order to save Mother Earth, AGENDA 21 attempts to mandate U.N. oversight of the environment, by strict regulation of the planet's atmosphere, streams, lakes, coastal waters, rivers, oceans, wetlands, jungles, swamps, forests, deserts, grasslands, mountains, tundra, urban areas, rural areas, education, health care, agriculture, nutrition, labor, consumption and production. A pantheistic filter, for the viewing of nature, imparts no moral high ground to either its leaders or slaves.

AGENDA 21, heartily endorsed by Rio Summit chief, environmental activist, and Canadian billionaire, Maurice Strong, broadly and specifically indicts itself by staggering, unblushing admissions of malevolence. "AGENDA 21 proposes an array of actions which are intended to be implemented by every person on Earth . . . It calls for specific changes in the activities of all people . . . Effective execution of AGENDA 21 will require a profound reorientation of all human society, unlike anything the world has ever experienced—a major shift in the priorities of both governments and individuals and an unprecedented redeployment of human and financial resources. This shift will demand that a concern for the environmental consequences of every human action be integrated into individual and collective decision-making at every level." [2] With a VeriChip-based identity management system, global tyranny of that sort is technologically feasible.

Phrases such as 'every person on Earth,' 'all human society,' 'every human action,' 'every level,' 'demand,' and 'require' reveal the totalitarian intentions of the paganized globalists in charge of the United Nations.

The NAZIs politicized the influence of theosophic and Teutonic occultism to stir up their masses for world domination. The United Nations politicizes the influence of theosophy, pantheism, deep ecology, and globalism, and yearns to apply computer microchip technology to empower global pagan socialism. The NAZIs' and U.N.'s final solutions will eventually be revealed to be similar in result if not in method, because predictable satanic spirituality incepted and energized both organizations.

Vaticanic ecumenicism and its political arm, globalism, strive to effect reversals of Protestant Christian faith and exceptionalism. They try to couple this with a *de facto* covenant with Satan, disguised as veneration of nature. The theological essence of such a covenant will be de-emphasized by United Nations leaders, to make the abomination palatable to the masses.

Such eco-occultism may be cunningly spun by the media and couched as votive veneration of nature spirituality. But, if current United Nations' philosophy continues, and it likely will, an earth manifesto will come along containing language and principles that Satan can argue is a binding pact between him and most of the population of the world. Those who submit to it will be pressured to yield further ground to him. Inhabitants of first-world industrialized Protestant-heritage nations may suffer comparably to the population of the mostly-pantheistic Indian subcontinent. Not accidentally, politicians regularly emerge who shift United States' policies farther away from highly-conditional Protestant exceptionalism, toward a pagan one-world government (1WG).

Dr. Dixy Lee Ray, a former Washington state governor, enjoyed recognition as a world-class scientist, and provided a rare voice of sanity at the Rio Earth Summit.[3] In her 1993 book, *Environmental Overkill*, Dr. Ray writes, "The objective, clearly enunciated by the leaders of UNCED [the Rio Earth Summit], is to bring about change in the present system of nations. The future is to be world government, with central planning by the U.N ... If force is needed, it will be provided by a U.N. green-helmeted police force."[4]

U.N. Summit, II

The United Nations' 2002 World Summit on Sustainable Development (Earth Summit II or Rio+10, held 26 August to 4 September, 2002, in Johannesburg, South Africa) resulted in an Action Plan[5] that included points such as the following:

Replenishing Global Fisheries, to be attempted by layering on radical new treaties, instead of abiding by adequate, existing ones.

Drinking Water and Sanitation, upgrades to be attempted to provide drinking water to 550 million additional people by 2015, paid for with largely U.S. monies.

Renewable Energy, attempted by a call by the summiteers to transfer to renewable energy sources as quickly as possible, despite its inefficiency and capital-sapping expense.

The Precautionary Principle, the idea that there ought to be overbearing governmental restriction of anything that the organized environmental lobby says presents a risk to humans or to nature. By that travesty of prudence, development or implementation of new foods, medicines, housing or commercial developments, industrial chemicals, pesticides, energy plants, etc., might be stopped dead on the basis of mere suspicion by the radical environmental lobby. The U.N.'s Precautionary Principle is wholly un-American: instead of innovating, inventing, adapting, and overcoming (the can-do American way), globalists want the authority to stifle ingenuity by withholding the U.N.'s stamp of approval. Think the U.S. federal government is inefficient and expensive? The U.N. will be a thousand times worse, without even a pretense of accountability to the governed.

James S. Shikwati, director of Inter Region Economic Network (IREN) in Kenya, was also at Rio+10, and said, "To take people out of poverty, the focus needs to be on safeguarding their economic freedom. Less government intervention in private economic initiatives and securing property rights will act as incentives for economic growth. But the poor populations will remain poor if the rest of the world, through the vehicle of the United Nations, decides to plan and intervene in personal enterprises. And that is what some people here at the summit seem keen to achieve: limiting people's productivity."[6]

Temenos Means Earth Worship

United Nations occultism reached heightened levels of infamy in 2002. At the U.N. Earth Summit in Johannesburg, South Africa, in autumn of that year, Mikhail Gorbachev's Earth Charter was prominently presented. Replete with New Age rhetoric, the Summit exalted the occult through consecration of the Ark of Hope, an imitation of the Toraic Ark of the Covenant. The Ark of Hope consists of a painted wooden chest carried on two long poles carved as spiral unicorn horns to render evil ineffective. The U.N.'s Ark of Hope contained a copy of the Earth Charter hand-scribed upon papyrus, to imply dignifying antiquity. The Ark was then paraded to various points around the globe.

The Earth Charter represents another glaring example of United Nations' occultism. Global governancers tout the Earth Charter's sixteen commandments as the cure for earth's ills. They want them to serve as replacements for Jehovah God's Ten Commandments and Moral Law. The Ark of Hope contained occult writings of "collaborative prayers and affirmations for Earth." Those pseudo-sacred writings are called the Temenos Books. (*Temenos* in Greek means 'a sacred grove, devoted to idolatry,' implying the idea of goddess earth as an idol.) "The Temenos Books were created by 3,000 artists, mystics, teachers and students with an obvious knowledge of astrology, ceremonial magic, and earth worship,"[7] all doctrines related to spirituality that is abhorrent to Triune Yahweh. In Deuteronomy 16:21, the LORD God of Israel as the preincarnate Christ Jesus told Moses, "Thou shalt not plant thee a grove of any trees near unto

221

the altar of the LORD thy God . . ." Votive tree groves relate to pagan nature worship, such as is antagonistic to true Christian-Jewish religion.

Counterfeit 10 Commandments

The Earth Charter is designed to become the crowning document of the contrived-for globalist governance. The Earth Charter and it's ilk will be the pantheistic religious basis for international political authority, to save the biosphere from ostensible destruction, and man from himself, at great expense to Christian-heritage economies. Various globalist leaders laud the Earth Charter as crucial to implementation of pagan New Age theology, from which they derive their moral mandate to work their earthy wills upon the masses of humanity. Occult theological affirmations and pledges may amount to binding national covenants with Satan. They bode evil for the international community. However, "Where the Spirit of the LORD is, there is liberty." (2 Corinthians 3:17b) Triune Yahweh is uniquely holy. He imparts freedom to us who love Him and His ways.

Maurice Strong, Canadian billionaire and co-chairman of the Earth Charter Commission, said of the Earth Charter, "It will in fact become like the Ten Commandments." Mikhail Gorbechev, leader of Green Cross International and co-chairman of the Earth Charter Commission, said "My hope is that this charter will be a kind of Ten Commandments, a 'Sermon on the Mount' that provides a guide for human behavior toward the environment . . ."[8]

What the United Nations offers the United States of America is a giant step backwards toward pagan government-without-representation, wherein legislators are appointed by insiders in power, not chosen by democratic popular vote or republican selection. It utilizes cult of personality, more than truth-loving collegial cooperation.

The United Nations pantheistically-filtered utopia, one wherein the overarching constitution is geared toward domination of familial, religious, and personal rights by a central government, has distinct potential for horrible abuse. Where Triune Yahweh is demeaned and His deity is confused with fallen created spirituality, spirit possession and suffering become common. It remains progressively needful: "Get the United States out of the United Nations, and the United Nations out of the United States." In the words of Ravi Zaccharius, "Religion drives politics, not the other way around."

Photo 10.1: A Glass-Encased VeriChip Compared to a Human Fingertip.

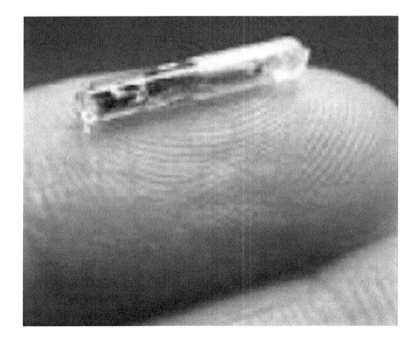

U.N. Summit, III

On December 7, 2009, United Nations' globalists convened the Copenhagen Climate Change Conference (COP15) in Denmark. Most conference attendees had the attitude that only scientists backward enough to believe in a flat earth doubt that global warming is anthropogenic (man-made). The leaders of many nations attended, as did those of thousands of NGO's.

Many attendees voiced criticism of capitalism as the engine of climate change, resources depletion and species eradication. Hugo Chavez, president of Venezuela, spoke derisively of the [now minimally Protestant exceptional] United States as if it criminally steals more than its share of natural resources, when in fact they are purchased.

The theme of climate debt was prevalent, the notion that industrialized countries' carbon dioxide emissions damage developing nations and incur a debt to them. President Barack H. Obama pledged $100 billion per year of United States taxpayers' monies to developing countries to offset that supposed climate debt. The progressive international press at COP15 overwhelmingly sympathized with the globalist agenda, and reported that global governance is necessary to thwart supposed anthropogenic global warming (AGW).[9] In 2010, the U.S. federal government borrowed 41 cents of every dollar it spent. Will the wealthy elite holding its purse-strings demand a catastrophic Constitutional convention, to move them to forestall default on the national debt?

Adolph Hitler said, "When you lie, tell big lies."[10] Hitler learned from Satan that big systemic lies require much more time and effort to refute, during which interval public hysteria assenting to the lies fuels the liar's radical agenda and devious policies. Anthropogenic global warming is just such a big systemic lie. Anthropogenic climate change has become progressivist urban myth, parroted by tame scientists and most major media.

Mark of the Beast, I

A device known as the VeriChip was invented from tracking technology developed by Digital Angel Corp. In the early 21st century it was marketed by VeriChip Corporation (*www.VeriChipcorp.com*). As of April, 2010, VeriChip Corp. merged with Steel Vault Corp. to form PositiveID Corp. (*www.positiveidcorp.com*[11]) PositiveID Corp trades on the NASDAQ stock exchange under the symbol PSID.

A series of confusing rebrandings followed, but the device's basic idea remained that of the VeriChip. It's been called the BioChip, the MediChip, and the PositiveID, but the glass-encased, FDA-approved, subcutaneously-implantable, radio-frequency identification chip is yet best known as the VeriChip.

The VeriChip or a similar device may become the apocalyptic mark of the beast (Gr., *charagma de ho thayrios*). A VeriChip-based identity management system can provide credit or debit card functionality, relating any given human body to a specific bank account, thus regulating buyers and sellers. Such a VeriChip-based identity management system can provide combined credit card, driver's license, and passport functionality, by primary-keying any given human body to umpteen records in an Internet-accessible relational database.

The glass-encased VeriChip (as in 'veracity chip') is a rice-grain sized, digital, radio-frequency-identifiable, subcutaneously-implantable microchip. It stores in solid-state circuitry, in binary form, a 16-digit decimal number capable of uniquely identifying 10 quadrillion bodies.[12] (That's 1.0×10^{15}.) At its approval for human implant in 2004, the VeriChip was not allowed by the United States' Food and Drug Administration to contain global positioning satellite circuitry. But, prototypes have had that and, per regulation, may again.

A future VeriChip variant may be developed and re-regulated to incorporate transpondable GPS circuitry in conjunction with scannable RFID functionality. Either way, the VeriChip can be used for a high-speed, digital identity management system. Would electromagnetic pulse (EMP), from a high-altitude nuclear detonation, fuse VeriChip circuitry, as would occur with most extrasomatic microchips?

Implantable-RFID VeriChip functionality can be designed into merchant-account credit-card readers, Internet logon and building access-egress systems, and firearm safeties. What if well-to-do Christians and Jews must someday all-too-soon choose between living their faith and utilizing the purchasing power of their money? All those who take an occult world government's identifier mark will forfeit the post-Tribulational Rapture of the true church, and a glorified body.

Such a RFID/*GPS* global identity management system can enable a tyrant to effect worldwide house arrest, to enforce a contra-evangelistic market nexus, to lock dissidents out of commerce and armament, and to militarily pinpoint a fleshly body's location to within a couple of meters anywhere upon the surface of the earth, for a missile strike. United States' drone-launched Hellfire missiles homed in on Afghani Taliban vehicles' GPS chips, circa 2006. The same may someday be done to subcutaneously implanted microchips, if they achieve GPS functionality.

In 2011, GPS functionality would require a much larger antenna and implant than those needed for only RFID. Instead of rice-grain size, a GPS chip would need to be paperclip-size or even pager-size.[13] And, even at that, layers of flesh over a GPS/RFID chip's antenna would tend to absorb transmissions upward to a satellite, and to cause system problems. But, research and development (R&D) tend to advance functionality.

If the VeriChip or a similar device becomes the mark (Gr., *charagma*) of the beast (*thayrios*), then bodily purity from any such mark will become a major concern of mid-Trib-Rapturable missionary firstfruits and post-Trib-Rapturable Believing un-Chipped Christians and Jews. Bodily purity from such a mark will also become a concern of traditional Jews, and may escalate into a cause for the invasion of revival-alight End-time Israel called the battle of Armageddon.

The papacy of that year will probably deny that an implanted-microchip identifier is the mark of the apocalyptic beast, and an earthy old-school within the rank and file of Believers will desire not to reject it. Refusal to accept the RFID implanted-microchip mark, in order to answer the Christian or Messianic Jewish calling, may be derided as insanity. Refusers of the RFID mark, on religious grounds, may be wrongly charged with religious paranoia, constituting grounds for confinement in order to facilitate treatment. VeriChip acceptance may be propagandized as patriotic, earth-friendly, sustainable, and the next step in sociotechnical evolution.

Global Identity Management System

Global house arrest capability will tempt political leaders to infringe upon human rights and civil liberties. *A VeriChip identity management system can enable body-specific social justice, by pagan standards of judgment.* The first beast, of Revelation (Rev. 13:1), is described as having seven heads and ten horns. It is described first as uncrowned but secondly as crowned, representing an End-time consummation of mystery Babylon's Roman empire. The beast's ten horns correspond to the ten toes of Nebuchadnezzar's dreamed-of image (Daniel 2:31-45). The ten components are thought to prophesy a dekapartite End-time global state.

A global identity management system may manifest the beast (Gr., *thayrios*). Some theologians think Revelation 13's first beast (with seven heads and ten horns) relates to the Diaspora, and the second (with two horns like a lamb), to the land of Israel. Possibly, the latter beast will have authority to turn many Jews' hearts toward the Vatican.

In those days, police, military, and the few tame licensed gun owners may receive an RFID implanted microchip in their right hands, to electronically activate trigger-enabling circuitry within their issued or personal firearms, making their guns usable only by authorized chipped right hands. The herd of hapless humanity, forbidden by the pantheistic totalitarian United Nations to own guns, may be chipped in the muscle under an eyebrow, necessitating a submissive bow to activate building-entry access systems or log on to the Internet (such as for cued idolatry of a leader's streamed image). RFID scanners may be built into personal computers' logon functionality, so that the lack of a RFID mark might mean being shut out of Internet commerce. Active-duty military personnel will almost inevitably endure orders to receive a VeriChip, as identity management systems are developed.

Global governancers are being let to coalesce a dekapartite one-world state. They would like to meld the United States, Canada, and Mexico into a North American Union (NAU), patterned after the European Union (EU) and economically unified by a common central bank and a new currency, the *amero*. The Club of Rome advocates, also, Japanese, Austral-South African, Russian, South American, North African-Middle Eastern, Central African, Indo-Maylasian, and Chinese unions.[14]

Globalists can't accomplish this until God authorizes changes to demographics, political personnel and laws. *Once He does, it seems likely that global governance and a VeriChip-based identity management system to enforce it will be a mathematical outcome.* The tragedies of 9/11/2001 and the economic crisis of 2009 are contrived shakeups to increase the authority of centralized government.

RITE FOR THE TIMES

Global governance depends upon the peoples of nations accepting its leaders' authority. Despite that they couch their authority in doctrinally narcissistic ways, the authority for global governance is false-religious and pagan. Exposure of globalists' inauthenticities, per Yahweh's *Logos*, deflates their suitability to rule, and galvanizes oppressed masses to debunk and defy globalists' pretensions. When God removes public confidence in globalist leadership during the Great Tribulation, their fiat currencies and civilization will abruptly collapse. Such a global fiat currency collapse may become a cause for a pagan United Nations invasion of Israel and the prophesied battle of Armageddon.

Metals of Prophecy

The End-time global governance is prophesied in Daniel 2. In that passage, it is symbolized in Nebuchadnezzar's dream by a tall metal image. Babylon was its head of gold. Medo-Persia, its chest and arms of silver. Alexander's Greece, its abdomen and thighs of bronze. And Rome, its legs of iron. The Roman empire divided into two, based at Byzantium and Rome, just like a man's legs are separated, left and right. Ancient Rome will re-emerge, consummated like an occultic Phoenix, into pro-Vaticanic End-time global governance, symbolized by the image's feet of clay and iron, with the ten toes symbolizing the Club of Rome's dekapartite world economic unions.

That dreamed-of statue's ten toes of harsh iron, set in two feet of brittle clay, correspond to the ten crowned horns of Revelation's first beast and to ten economic and political End-time global states, unified by fiat currencies accounted to VeriChip database-keyed buyers and sellers of the world. That global state will have the brittleness of clay, with the ruthlessness of iron. That world state will have the ruthlessness of post-Christian multiculturalism, with the brittleness of silicon semiconductors. The image in Nebuchadnezzar's dream was destroyed by a tumbling boulder not cut by human hands, which struck it in its feet, symbolic of the return of meek Jesus of Nazareth as conquering Yeshua haMashiach.

Mark of the Beast, II

The one-world government's mark of the beast (prophesied in Revelation 13, 14, 15, 16, 19 and 20) may take the form of that scannable, transpondable implanted microchip injected into the muscle under a victim's eyebrow

Table 10.2: Descents of Political Authority [Adapted from *The Glenn Beck Show* on Fox News TV, Winter 2010].

	The historic European model of society ➔	The U.S.A.'s Protestant—exceptionalist model of society ➔	The New World Order model of society [civilization submitted to U.N., Vatican, Talmudism, and Satan] X
Attributed Authority	God: personal Holy Trinity	God: personal Triune Yahweh	god: nature's Hinduistic 'Impersonal Absolute'
Administrators/ Executives	popes/kings	you, the middle class	the United Nations
Servant(s)	you, the *bourgeoisie*	U.S. constitutional government	you, the next under-class

or under the skin of the back of his right hand. The technology to digitally micromanage vast populations in this manner currently exists. If the NAZI's had had existing information technology, they would not have hesitated to implant microchips into the conquered populations of Europe. The VeriChip's 16-digit RFID output can be used as the primary key to an aggressively pagan totalitarian government's relational database of authorized buyers and sellers. This currently available commercial-off-the-shelf technology works as described: political authority and scalar affordability are the main variables.

VeriChips can be mass produced for a fraction of a cent each. If it costs an average of $100 per body in infrastructure, labor, and materials to inject a VeriChip into each buyer's or seller's body, $700 billion to chip most of the world is small change to the global elite. By some estimates, the globalist elites have amassed about $32 trillion with which to accomplish world government.

In those not-too-distant future days, at cash registers, checkpoints, airports and train stations, a brief scan of a person's right hand or eyebrow can bring up on a laptop computer screen the individual's name, bank accounts, address, family associations, club memberships, religious affiliation, genetic profile, financial records, political leanings, gun ownership, vehicle registrations, and employment history, for abuse by whatever on-duty globocratic thug. Evangelism may be punishable by exclusion from economic markets or by martyrdom. Via implantable microchip technology, conscientious dissidents may become GPS-targetable.

About the mark of the beast, the Bible says, in Revelation 13:16, 17: "And he causeth all, both small and great, rich and poor, free and bond, to receive a mark [Koine Gr., *charagma*] in their right hand, or in their foreheads: and that no man might buy or sell save he that had the mark, or the name of the beast, or number of his name." Injected into these bodily locales, the VeriChip's spiritual significance includes its acting as a satanic anti-phylactery, occupying the right hand or brow of its wearer, where Elohim's phylacteries would otherwise go.

Revelation 14:9-11. "And the third angel followed them, saying with a loud voice, If any man worship the beast and his image, and receive his mark in his forehead, or in his hand, the same shall drink of the wine of the wrath of God, which is poured out without mixture into the cup of his indignation; and he shall be tormented with fire and brimstone in the

Photo 10.3: A Glass-Encased VeriChip Compared to a Rice Grain.

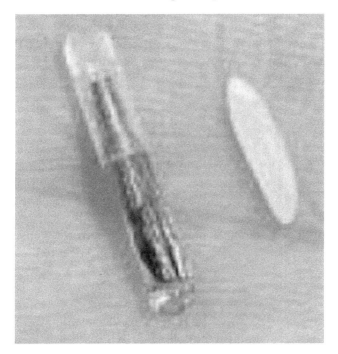

presence of the holy angels, and in the presence of the Lamb: and the smoke of their torment ascendeth up forever and ever: and they have no rest day nor night, who worship the beast and his image, and whosoever receiveth the mark of his name." The beast's image may possibly be streamed online over the Internet, enabling simultaneous real-time global idolatry, web-cam'd for humans with the VeriChip mark to display their idolatry as official.

Revelation 16:1,2. "And I heard a great voice out of the temple saying to the seven angels, Go your ways, and pour out the vials of the wrath of God upon the earth. And the first went, and poured out his vial upon the earth; and there fell a noisesome and grievous sore upon the men which had the mark of the beast, and upon them which worshiped his image." In 2007, between 1% and 10% (depending on which study) of animals' bodies experimentally implanted with a VeriChip developed a malignant soft-tissue tumor at the site of implantation.[15] What if that miraculously becomes 100%, in humans?

Revelation 19:20. "And the beast was taken, and with him the false prophet that wrought miracles before him, with which he deceived them that had received the mark of the beast, and them that worshiped his image."

Revelation 20:4. "And I saw the souls of them that were beheaded for the witness of Jesus, and for the word of God, and which had not worshiped the beast, neither his image, neither had received his mark upon their foreheads, or in their hands; and they lived and reigned with Christ a thousand years."

In three of these five passages in the Authorized King James Version Bible, the mark is described as being *in* its victims' hands or foreheads. The VeriChip is designed for injection *into* living flesh.

Selling may come to be politically defined by those in authority as monetary remuneration for one's time, education, sweat or leadership. Similarly, *buying* may come to be defined as payment of one's mortgage, rent, groceries, utilities or fuel bills.

If it truly becomes the mark of the beast, those who receive a VeriChip, if it is the mark of the beast, will suffer terrible sores, and will not be caught up at the post-Tribulation Rapture. They will be left to fend for themselves or die or, surviving, possibly rebuild a shattered civilization to the LORD

Jesus' specifications. Scripturally, no one tormented for receipt of a mark of the beast can expect to be raptured and receive a glorified resurrection body from God.

The Rapture

Will the general Rapture of the true church occur pre-Tribulationally or post-Trib? *Historical premillennialism* teaches a post-Tribulational rapture, a single second coming of Christ, and an unitary people of God. *Dispensational premillennialism*, a doctrinal newcomer proceeding from Vaticanic influences,[16] teaches a pre-Tribulational Rapture prior to Jesus' post-Trib second coming, and disparate treatment by God of Christians and Believing Jews, with the church waning in influence but Jewish evangelism waxing in effect. Historical premillennialism is to conscience, as dispensational premillennialism is to optimism.

Where else is the Tribulation mentioned in the Bible? "And at that time shall Michael stand up, the great prince which standeth for the children of thy people: *and there shall be a time of trouble such as never was* since there was a nation even to that same time: and at that time thy people shall be delivered, every one that shall be found written in the book." (Daniel 12:1, emphasis added)

Although some Bible scholars consider both to be theologically-valid views, historical premillennialism and dispensational premillennialism are mutually exclusive. The Bible nominally supports both views. Sabbatarian Believers tend to give credence to historical premillennialism and a post-Trib general Rapture. Mainstream Christians tend to believe in dispensational premillennialism and a pre-Trib general Rapture.

Many sabbatarians, such as Seventh-day Adventists and Messianic Jews, doubt that an unanticipatable pre-Trib rescue Rapture will occur. Some object to cocky attitudes associated with that doctrine, such as 'So many believe it, it must be true.' Many sabbatarians think pre-Trib rescue-Rapture doctrine incites apathy. Rescue-Rapture doctrine, as a tantalizing hope, is particularly cherished by 1st-world evangelicals. However, most Christians in the world today suffer if persecuted, to prove their faith. Why won't 1st-world Christians? Those who take the mark of the beast, whether it's a VeriChip or some similar technology, will almost certainly abdicate the Rapture of the church and forfeit their glorified resurrection body.

All Christian revivals from Pentecost to the year 1999 or so were of 'the former rain.' The mega-revival called 'the latter rain' will commence near the beginning of the Tribulation and continue until its midpoint, when the select mid-Trib Rapture will catch the firstfruits missionaries up to heaven. The latter rain is intended to prepare Christ's bride for the Great Tribulation, and charismatically and angelically equip her to stand up to the death for her personal public testimonies, until the post-Trib general Rapture.

We, God's people (true Christians or Believing Jews), then ought to evangelize, prepared for martyrdom. We should give our personal public testimonies from our mathematical consciences, and stand by them to the death. If we strengthen ourselves to withstand as valorous missionaries (such as the firstfruits), hoping for our mid-Trib select Rapture, we may do so either within the land of Israel with less of the RFID microchip mark, or upon our habitual coasts where global governance and its digital marker chip will be entrenched in the economy.

Will the general Rapture be pre-Trib or post-Trib? Will the church be proactively rescued, or tried like gold in a fire? The widely-held pre-Trib Rapture theory originated from Vaticanic theologians. "And the ten horns [dekapartite world governance] which thou sawest upon the beast [a composite of fallen cherubim], these shall hate the whore [the Vatican or possibly New York City], and shall make her desolate and naked, and shall eat her flesh [take her goods]." (Revelation 17:16) *With apologies to dispensational premillennialists, the pre-Trib Rapture theory originated from liberal Vaticanic theology and questionable charismata, and is a false hope.*[17] If government mandates a VeriChip identity management system, will that really precipitate a rescue Rapture? God usually lets Christians suffer, to prove their faith.

Papism

Theologians and reformers historically hold the Vatican to be the seat of the Antichrist. According to Gary H. Kah, the United States of America, with its virulent Hollywood and Internet pornography and pro-sodomitic politicians, may be developing into Mystery Babylon, turned away from the Triune Yahweh of her founding. According to Gary Kah, the whore of Babylon may be New York City. The words "Mystery Babylon" loosely translate from Greek as "silent confusion."

Photo 10.4: A Subcutaneously-Injectable, Glass-Encased VeriChip with Canula Needle.

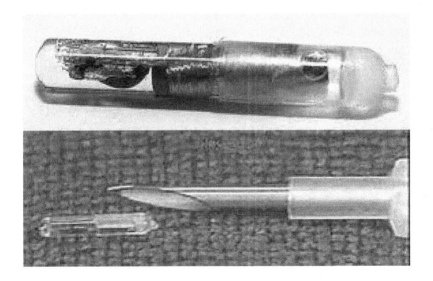

By discerning of spirits, God gave the Diaspora to the ten-horned first beast of Revelation 13:1-10 around the first day of the Biblical first lunar month of the year 2000, i.e., around April 6, 2000 and its subsequent sabbath, April 8, 2000. That spirit is believed to be a unitary hierarchy of multiple fallen cherubim, a composite demon that relates to violence, weapons, money, promiscuity and sodomy. It is intolerant of conscientious power within straight men, and it tries, Saul Alinsky-like, to strategically influence straight men's reactions to the meta-Left's outrages, as the primary weapon to hasten world government. It doesn't like Bible prophecy about Satan's immanent one-world government. In the early 3rd millennial New Age, it is as though Triune Yahweh has said to Satan and his men, "You may accomplish what I've prophesied, without immediate consequences."

Considering this, the only place where establishment can be even slightly permanent will be in or near the land of Israel. In Israel, there will probably be minimal influence of the first beast and the global government's identity management system. Believers in Jesus who live in Israel, however, will have to evangelize within an orthodox-Jewish influenced society that is aggressively antagonistic to evangelism, while a major revival occurs. The lamblike second beast of Revelation 13 will become an intensified culmination of mystery Babylon.

Probably, a covenant between Israel and a charismatic world leader will occur, coinciding with the global identity management system's rollout. Concurrently, the hundred-forty-four-thousand firstfruits Hebrew missionaries will evangelize in Israel and elsewhere. After forty-two months (a span of time equal to 180 weeks or three-and-a-half lunar years), the firstfruits missionaries will be caught up to heaven at the select Rapture and receive their glorified bodies. Then, the Great Tribulation will commence. At its end, at Jesus Christ's glorious return, the dead in Christ and un-Chipped living Believers will be Raptured upward to receive their resurrection bodies.

The Hundred Forty-Four Thousand

Candidates for the firstfruits missionaries and their supporters ('the woman' of Revelation 12:1-11) will be regarded by spiritual election (angels) as valorous, for their tenacious instant evangelizing, against great opposition. The two witnesses (Revelation 11:1-13), whom some theologians think will be Enoch and Elijah, will prophesy against the global regime for nearly forty-two more months during the Great Tribulation.

Photo 10.5: X-Ray Imagery Showing an Implanted VeriChip.

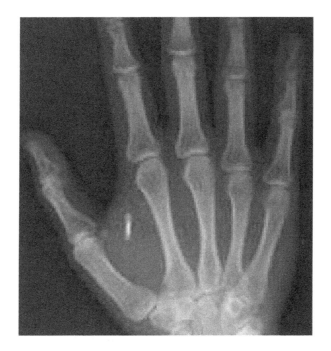

Then, Yeshua of Nazareth will return in glory, and the dead in Christ *and un-VeriChipped living Believers* will be caught up (Raptured) to meet Him in the air, and receive their glorified bodies.

The firstfruits will blend in with Israeli society, and evangelize until the midpoint of the Tribulation, amidst jubilant, convicted Born Again revival in Israel. God calls them the *first*fruits (Revelation 14:4), not the *last*fruits. The firstfruits' Rapture will be mid-Tribulational and 'select', 3 ½ years prior to elect Christendom's post-Trib and 'general' Rapture. The firstfruits will be harvested first, preceding the bulk of election. The hundred forty-four thousand will need resurrection bodies to "Follow the Lamb whithersoever He goeth." (Revelation 14:4)

Beginning at that time, the two witnesses (Gr., *martus*, prophets or martyrs) will prophesy for God, during Jacob's Trouble (the nearly three-and-a-half years of the Great Tribulation).

Jacob's Trouble will culminate in the martyrdom and resurrection of that duo and the return of Yeshua of Nazareth to Jerusalem, Israel. The theme of this eschatological scenario is escalation of Satan's authority. There will likely be a steady buildup of demonic authority until a VeriChip-held global identity management system is built, then an explosion of paganism. Predictably, there will be many unprepared disappointed pre-Trib Rapture-expectant Christians tempted to resignedly take the mark to stave off economic disenfranchisement and starvation.

The firstfruits (Heb., *bikkuwrim;* Gr., *aparche*) will be one hundred forty-four thousand missionaries who are lyrical, guileless, blameless, moral males from twelve of the fourteen Hebrew tribes. The tribes of Dan and Ephraim do not contribute to the membership of the firstfruits, probably because Adonai Jesus, who is the LORD God of Israel, hated Danite and Ephraimite tribal idolatry dating from the reign of Jeroboam. Assimilated genetically-dilute Hebrew-Christians may qualify.

Jeroboam placed the two golden calves, for backslidden Israel to worship, in Dan (to the extreme north in Israel) and in Ephraim (just to the north of Jerusalem). The tribes of Dan and Ephraim are excluded from the Revelation 7 firstfruits' roster, but retain tribal land inheritance in millennial kingdom Israel. The tribe of Joseph is included in the Revelation 7 firstfruits roster, making the sum of tribes there to be twelve. This is possible because the patriarch Joseph probably produced additional children after the births of his sons Manasseh and Ephraim.

VeriChipped Abdicate Resurrection Bodies

Worldwide, Believers in Jesus who don't receive a VeriChip mark for the nearly seven year period of the Tribulation, will be caught up at Christ Jesus' post-Tribulational return and the resurrection of the dead, to participate in the marriage supper of the Lamb and receive their glorified bodies. VeriChip refuseniks will risk internment in concentration camps and execution. Christians or Believing Jews who submissively receive a VeriChip-type mark of the beast will very-probably forfeit the post-Trib Rapture and abdicate their glorified resurrection bodies. Believers in Jesus who submissively and rebelliously receive a glass-encased RFID VeriChip mark of the beast to ensure subsistence will almost certainly abdicate the post-Trib Rapture of Christ Jesus' bride, the church, and eternally forfeit a glorified resurrection body. God alone knows who is truly elect.

To reiterate: the likely scenario is that concurrent with a covenant between Zionist Israel and a charismatic world ruler, and the rollout of an United Nations VeriChip-based identity management system, the firstfruits missionaries will escalate evangelism. After forty-two months, a mid-Trib select Rapture will catch the firstfruits up to heaven to receive a resurrection body. Beginning then on earth, the two prophets (Gr., *martus*, martyrs or witnesses) will prophesy for God during Jacob's Trouble (the second three-and-a-half year period of terrible trouble called the Great Tribulation).

During that second nearly-forty-two month period, those two men will prophesy rapidly-fulfilled cataclysmic disasters, to the unbridled horror of globalist leaders. They will then probably be shot dead in the streets of Jerusalem. Globalists will gloat over their unburied bodies for three-and-a-half days, until God resurrects them bodily before worldwide television audiences. Then, Jesus Christ's return, the instantaneous resurrection of the dead, and the general Rapture of un-VeriChipped Believers will occur. Gloriously, Christ Jesus will bodily descend to Jerusalem, Israel, halt the battle of Armageddon, and dismantle the Vatican, the United Nations, and Talmudist investment banking. The theme of the End will be trial-by-fire of Christ's bride, not miraculous sparing of the church from Satan's hatred. Only un-VeriChipped-marked Believers in Jesus will be Raptured. Those who die for refusing to receive a VeriChip-style mark of the beast will be rewarded by Elohim. (Revelation 20:4)

Sociopolitically, in the End we may see a market nexus: an autocratic, group-thinking cabal, enforced by global governance, consolidated by a VeriChip-marked identity management system, threatening disenfranchisement (or martyrdom) against anyone who dares evangelize the truth of Messiah Yeshua haNotzri and sound doctrine. *Global governancers will try to 'do a number,' with a VeriChip, on all buyers and sellers in all nations' economies.*

End-Time Semitics

Talmudist investment bankers, who fund global governance at usury to achieve favorable regulation of international markets and to promote Zionism's' triumph over anti-Semitism, wittingly or unwittingly serve Satan from subliminal zeal to suppress the evangelism which is so abhorrent to Talmudism. Talmudist investment bankers may be " . . . The synagogue of Satan which say that they are Jews, and are not, but do lie." (Rev. 3:9)

The wealthy elite, some of whom are Jewish, want one-world government. Perhaps they're tempted to think that via a VeriChip-based global identity management system they can pre-empt future anti-Semitism, by more-or-less-officially excluding anti-Semites and neo-NAZIs from employment, markets and economies. Talmudist-style expert interpretation of evolving writ precludes much argumentative input by an educated middle class, which has historically exerted theological, political, economic and social conservatism. Dichotomization of humanity into either a chic progressive class or a bewildered-herd underclass characterizes both occultic Nicolaitanism and communism, and is assiduously cultivated by major media engines. Inner-circle elitism typifies satanic temptation.

If a Jewish person says "No" to his covenant Adonai, who is Elohim the Son and was miraculously born Jesus of Nazareth around 4 B.C., he often ends up indirectly serving Satan.[18] Some Jewish people have historically functioned as Satan's unwitting servants, in that they have furthered various unethical trends via notably ungodly methods. What would Pauline sound doctrine say about the treatment of Palestinians in Israel? What about the treatment of Sephardis by Ashkenazis?

Paul's sound doctrine of Messiah Jesus' inner man will be more binding than will be the ceremonial Torah, during Jesus of Nazareth's millennial kingdom dispensation. The Bible teaches that two-thirds of Jews will die during the Great Tribulation (Jacob's Trouble), for the national guilt of Israel.

"And it shall come to pass, that in all the land, saith the LORD, two parts therein shall be cut off and die: but the third shall be left therein. And I will bring the third part through the fire, and will refine them as silver is refined, and will try them as gold is tried: *they shall call on my name, and I will hear them: I will say, It is my people: and they shall say, The LORD is my God.*" (Zechariah 13:8,9, emphasis added.) This has yet to occur in the annals of history.

It is ironic and sad that Jews' errors are nearly a *verboten* topic. If even constructive criticism is derided as 'anti-Semitism,' who may chide them? How will their consciences be pricked, that they learn to repent?

During the latter rain revival, many young Israeli Jews will '*eureka!*' and believe Yeshua of Nazareth is the true Messiah. This three-and-a-half year, cognitive truth-alight, end-time revival in Israel may be reminiscent of the comparatively brief, six-month Welsh revival of 1904. Millions of bright young Jews will joyously believe the suddenly-obvious truth that Jesus Christ is the true Messiah: *Yeshua haNotzri haMashiach.* They will rejoice to say with us, "Blessed is Jesus of Nazareth who comes in the name of Y'howah!" (Heb., *Baruch ha Ba b'Shem Adonai.*)

The latter-rain alight, Tribulation-era Israeli Defense Force (IDF) may wind up resembling Oliver Cromwell's New Model Army for true faith, conviction, and zeal. During the forthcoming three-and-a-half year Tribulation revival in minimally identity-managed Israel, millions of bright Jewish youth in the Land and worldwide will believe the truth that Yeshua of Nazareth is the true Messiah, and receive the clarion cognitive halo of His Paraclete.

As the Army, that generation of beloved Jews may pitch battle to defend Zion against Satan-coopted United Nations troops possibly seeking revenge upon Talmudist bankers and Zionists for global fiat currency collapses in those years. After the latter-rain revival, precious Israel will only be rescued by the post-Great-Tribulational second coming of the LORD Jesus Christ (the true Messiah), but by then two-thirds of Jews will regrettably have perished for the national guilt of Israel. (Zechariah 13:7-9)

241

Latter-Day Civilization

The New World Order's pagan governance will probably consist of three legs, tripod-like. Those likely three legs will be the Vatican, the United Nations, and Talmudist investment bankers, corresponding roughly to the Antichrist, his instrument the Beast, and the False Prophet.

The Vatican wants to be the religious-authority and spiritual leg of the global-governance tripod. The United Nations wants to be the political-authority and military-power leg of the apparatus. Super-wealthy Talmudist investment bankers, financing world government, guaranteeing its fiat currencies, and funding its VeriChip-based global identity management system at usury, want to be the monetary and economic leg of the End-time governmental apparatus, probably to prevent another Holocaust. They do not yet apprehend that Satan will take control of the completed system and direct it against Zionist Israel. To some, Holocaust-proofing civilization may argue for a VeriChip-based global identity management system. Collapse of global state fiat currencies may incur End-time pagan vengeance against Zionist Israel.

A pope may be to the eschatological Antichrist, as Rome's instrument the United Nations may be to the Beast, and as Talmudist investment banking may be to the False Prophet. Commercialized Talmudism is to the culture war against Born Again Protestant exceptionalist values, as the Vatican's hierarchy is to the impetus for one-world government. The culture war involves balkanization of morality, shifting focus onto aspects of the flesh and outer man, instead of upon inner men's community in faith by essential sound doctrine.

Within the culture, corruption of youth (via the Vile 3 (fornication, occultism, or drug abuse)) and theological liberalism (such as ecumenicism, or homosexualism's supposed holiness) attempts reversal of Protestant exceptionalism. Satan's purpose in the culture war is to incriminate society and default divinely-protected middle-class Protestant exceptionalism down toward an occultic one-world government and a pagan ecosociety.

Unbelieving, Toraically-righteous, ritually-conscientious Jews will have an easier time than inveterate pagans at the great white throne judgment but, unlike Believers, will not live and reign with the LORD Jesus in glorified resurrection bodies during His thousand year millennial kingdom.

Two Prophets

From the Tribulation's midpoint for nearly forty-two months, the two witnesses (martyrs or prophets) of Revelation 11, perhaps clad in home-made blue-fringed burlap *tallitim* (Heb., prayer shawls) consistent with mourning, will continue alone on earth for God. They will vex globalists with promptly-fulfilled cataclysmic prophecies for another forty-two months, until they are shot dead on the streets of Jerusalem. God will then resurrect those two men's bodies, after three-and-a-half days, and catch them bodily up to heaven on worldwide television, to the unbridled horror of globalist leaders.

Theologians think the two witnesses may be Enoch and Elijah, for "It is appointed unto man once to die and after that the judgment." (Hebrews 9:27) Those two men were taken to heaven by God without their dying. (Genesis 5:24; 2 Kings 2:11) Satan probably expects the two witnesses to be contemporarily-living Believers, of either the Baby Boomers or a later generation.

Quickly at the witnesses' resurrection, Christ Jesus will descend from heaven to Jerusalem, halt the battle of Armageddon, bind Satan, and dismantle the Vatican, the United Nations, and Talmudist investment banking. He will put a stop to every wicked, evil thing upon the face of the earth.

As noted, the two witnesses or martyrs may wear *tallitim* (Heb., prayer shawls) handmade of coarse jute burlap, consistent with grieving, adorned at the corners with fringes of blue threads. Such attire could fulfill the prophecy in Rev. 11:3, that the two will be " . . . clothed in sackcloth." An entire suit made of burlap would be itchy. Talmudic tradition tries to change the blue threads of *tallitim* to white ones, but *Eloheynu haShiloosh haKodesh* (Heb., our God the Holy Trinity) said 'Blue.' (Numbers 15:38) Talmudists are as guilty as the Vatican, for imposing false laws and human traditions upon trusting followers, in the name of God.

Approach of Armageddon

How may we recognize this endtime mega-revival when it draws near? One way will be by watching RFID implantable microchip technology and legislation. The early-tribulational revival amongst Jews may

243

commence simultaneously with the rollout of a nearly-gobal VeriChip identity management system enabling a digital economic and ecopolitical nexus. *Orthodox Jews may succeed in politically nixing mandatory, world-ID, subcutaneous RFID microchip implants within the nation of Israel, on grounds that the chips would defile human bodies, regarded by them as sacred.* Such traditional human sacredness prompts the Orthodox to patrol bomb blast sites in Israel with tweezers, to collect and bury fragments of sacrosanct human flesh.

This Tribulation revival in Israel will occur despite any doctrinal glitches remaining in Messianic congregationalism. However, it remains narrow truth, not mere ethnopraxy or jubilation, which sets men free. That is, it is obedience to the Father in heaven, via the truth of Yeshua of Nazareth described in the Gospels and Pauline sound doctrine, which frees the hearts and souls of Believers. Such obedience imparts, with God the Father's Spirit, characteristics of Christ Jesus' inner man, which He successfully offered to Y'howah His Father.

Recognition of the approach of the eschato-reformation in Israel may also occur by watching world politics. According to Bible prophecy, the one-world, end-time governance will have seven heads and ten crowns (Revelation 13:1), corresponding to seven geographic landmasses and ten political-economic regional unions of a Club of Rome-advocated one-world state.[19] In 2011, the European Union, only, exists, while plans are fomented for a North American Union, pending formation of eight more political-economic unions, to set the stage for realization of the Apocalypse. There should be unmistakable warnings of the end, as these vast political modifications are made by men of the beast, devoid as they will be of most spiritual worry or bothered conscience.

A North American Union (NAU), which globalists and their financiers advocate to usurp the free, sovereign United States of America, may (along with the existing European Union) presage the end. That wicked generation may unify Protestant church lands under the Vatican, to rationalize their spooky global state and stifle authentic evangelism of the testimony of Jesus. State nationalization of ecclesiastical lands was done in France during the French Revolution, to fund that ruthless government. The world government to come will be more overtly satanic than France's was.

An additional criterion for discerning the approach of the endtime revival in Israel and the Rapture is to watch the scope and magnitude of converts won by yearly Jews for Jesus[20] summer evangelistic campaigns. There is truth, authority, and power intrinsic to evangelism of the Gospel. "The testimony of Jesus is the spirit of prophecy." (Revelation 19:10c) Evangelism's cessation upon earth would incur cognitive torpor to mankind and propel humanity toward paganism. The penalty for sin is worse sin, and worse difficulty obeying Elohim the Son, Adonai the Christ, who is Jesus of Nazareth.

Freedom, Guns and Eschatology

Considering the United Nations' penchant for civilian firearm microdisarmament and the latitude dispensed by God to spiritual wickedness in these latter days, in the End the only legal private gun ownership may be within the state of Israel. Gun ownership imparts a higher quality of life plus the temperament to rebuke extreme earthiness. Despite this, the armed-prophet-of-Yah personality type, overtly antagonistic to the United Nations' apocalyptic ecospiritual socialism, will probably be angelically supported by God only in endtime Israel. It may not be supported anywhere in the Diaspora, despite Protestant nations' extensive Christian heritage.

The term 'global pagan socialism' refers to pan-national eco-spiritual collectivism. It will be apocalyptic enough, international enough, occultic enough, and communistic enough to fulfill Biblical prophecy.

Martyrdom for one's personal public Christian testimony invites eternal honor, but victimhood of a mere murderer for unreasoning envy, hate or greed, is relatively pointless if not suicidal. Keeping ones own self and possessing one's own soul implies the right and freedom to defend one's personal boundaries and space from bullies or other violent aggressors. God the Father usually gives grace for His sons in Christ Jesus to defend themselves. He is earnest, as well as holy. Man quite normally wants evil to fear him but, in the early-21st-century New World Order, neither apocalyptic nor mundane evil fear much except the agenda-specific *Logos* of God, Yahweh the Son. Evil waxes bold inversely to protagonists' sanctity, because God the Father usually upholds us whom He watches over, mostly via heraldic clarion.

Missionary martyr Jim Elliot, in 1956, carried guns with God's approval into the Ecuadorian jungle mission field, but faithfully refused to defend himself with them (as he and his missionary friends had pre-agreed), when attacked by the very Auca Indians he toiled to convert.

Non-violence during active evangelistic efforts is strongly advisable for Believers in Jesus. Outside of Believers' active missionary work, justice-supportive violence by Christians may be tolerable by God, if it truly is just and if it doesn't destabilize society during the descent to Biblically-prophesied global government.

Weapons ownership can impart to one the ability for him to possess his own soul. Rejection of genius adaptations to reality, such as the right to keep and bear arms (guns), regresses the spirit of man toward stone-age psychology. Satan is radical for man's unconditional submission to him and his earthy servants. Gun ownership potentiates psychological polarization against radical aggressors. Renunciation of genius adaptations to reality, such as gun rights and firearm technology, amounts to regression to stone-age psychology, wherein a Mr. Big dominates. Nonservile, coordinated hand-eye activity, such as properly-done shooting, can stimulate cognition to thwart social-defeat stress and ease depression.

However, much as some might wish it, God will not bless armed rebellion in the Diaspora, against the tyrannical wicked end-time one-world government, by interpretation of Daniel 7:19-25. If God the Father were to decide that United States' patriots are to fight and defeat United Nations-loyal occupation forces during the End-times, then He would say so and Christ Jesus would bring it to pass. Then, true patriots most assuredly would prevail militarily against the U.N. But, prophetically speaking, He is not likely to decide or say that! Biblical prophecy indicates that that wicked one-world government is going to have its brief, three-and-a-half-odd years span of fame under the heavens, prior to Christ Jesus' bodily return. Painfully, Christian-heritage radicalism is on a collision course with a beastly spiritual movement that enjoys a temporary but strategic prophetic sanction.

Sporter firearm usage is fine with God for the time being but, painfully, God will very probably not support even true Christian patriotism, in the Tribulation Diaspora, armed against the United Nations' beastly global governance. Until the End, God will support sporter, not insurrectionist, uses of guns. In the Tribulation, true Jesus people will be non-insurrectionist, as far as political paramilitarism goes. Until the End, privately-owned guns of non-insurrection will be tolerated by Elohim, as long as they are legal. If guns become unjustly outlawed, then even we true Christian patriots must not insurrectively destabilize civilization's prophesied descent into global neopagan socialism.

We are not to submit to presumptive doctrine, authority or power, but to keep uncorrupted the clarion moral conscience imparted by grace through faith in Christ Jesus. Unless God reluctantly slackens constitutional institutions that hold wickedness in check, such as the right to keep and bear arms, evil men will not hope enough in unmitigated gall to prevail against godliness. Provocation of illegal reaction to outrages is Satan's method for evoking public clamor for less liberty. When he has world government and its VeriChip-based global identity management system, Satan will intensify siege spiritual warfare against Protestant-exceptionalist values and forcefulness of Christian conscience.

About the End-times world government, Daniel 7:25 records that the spirit of it " . . . shall speak great words against the most High, *and shall wear out the saints of the most High*, and think to change times and laws: and *they shall be given into his hand* until a time and times and the dividing of times." (Emphasis added) "And they worshiped the beast, saying, Who is like unto the beast? Who is able to make war with him?" (Revelation 13:4) These verses are interpreted to mean that Christian patriots will not prevail against the one-world government, up to and including the three-and-a-half-odd crucial years of the Great Tribulation (Jacob's Trouble).

In Daniel 7, the fourth beast in Daniel's vision, representing the endtime one-world government (1WG), is described as prevailing against the saints, as devouring the whole earth and treading it down and breaking it into pieces, and as wearing out the saints of the most High. This description of the End-time world system fits with the idea of God testing the faith of Christ's bride until a post-Trib Rapture, a rude awakening contrary to the soporific pre-Trib Rapture theory, which was influenced by questionable charismata and liberal Vaticanic theology.[21]

In this early 3rd millennial New-Agey 21st century, wise gun ownership should be more sportsmanly than patriotic. This, because the prophetic significance of the End-times and Satan's looming world governance is greater than the current significance of the United States of America and its partially-ecumenized Protestant-Christian heritage. It remains very painful to watch the United States morph toward Mystery Babylon, with its aggressive porn industry and national politicians sycophantically pandering to sodomites and earth worship in the causes of progressivism and defiance of supposed bigotry. Monied-elite politicians are playing chicken with an earnest holy God, who will destroy their works while winning out mightily, Himself. *The 21*st *century will probably become a perfect storm for wickedness, then asymptote into a perfect storm for truth.*

Men who take up arms to oppose the beast-energized global pagan socialist governance risk being delivered by Christ Jesus to, and reduced by, that same beast-spirit. That is how serious Triune Yahweh is about letting the End-times happen, with much vocalized comprehension, but zero maverick martial interdiction from godly patriots! Generally speaking, any sinner who militates against beast spirituality concerning its patent issues (money, violence, weapons, lust or sodomy) can expect spiritual warfare intended to submit him, in direct proportion to his guilt before God. Christian-heritage radicalism in opposition to apocalyptic global pagan socialism, while both upright and historically favored, has become prophetically doomed to defeat, in these last times. (Daniel 7:25)

Make-do un-marked survivalism or immigration to the Middle East will be better outcomes than martyrdom, but martyrdom, a far better outcome than submissively receiving a glass-encased VeriChip to secure subsistence.

Although the United States of America was founded to encourage an armed populace to depose tyrannical leaders via armed rebellion, as an absolute last resort to a democidal tyrant, the onset of the 3rd millennium brought a sea change to society. Nobody wants to be dictator of an armed populace. Compulsory microdisarmament of firearms causes and intensifies chronic social-defeat stress. The early 3rd millennium will bring a consummation of Mystery Babylon and the sacrifice of some holy people. Although this is insult added to injury, to watch freedom's subsumation into abomination, our beloved God the Father wills it to prove His WORD. Violent overthrow fo the political forms of Mystery Babylon and the meta-Left is no longer supported by grace.

Beast spirituality lusts to humiliate and destroy holy people, by aggressive conquest and defilement of hearts. God's protection will be pulled back, probably first from the domain of freedom's power (the 2nd Amendment), then from social vitality (economic prosperity), and finally from free speech against abominations (the 1st Amendment). In the early 3rd millennium, pagan spirituality strives to ruin, through deception or sickness, those of us capable of resisting one-world government, softening up the citizenry for it. Lawbreakers and guilty consciences suffer worst risk for that.

In the year 2000, a prescient patriot known to this author burned a pale-blue United Nations flag, indignant that the occultic U.N. demands ascendancy over the Protestant-exceptionalist United States of America. Anguished, he cried out in his heart to Triune Yahweh, 'Who are these uncircumcised Philistines?' But, as we shall see, our holy God will reluctantly allow even corrupt globalists to ascend to political authority, for their brief three-and-a-half-odd years of fame. To make a statement, the man bought a two-foot-tall cement religious statue, an Ashtoreth, and publicly smashed it to rubble. Then the man, a competent big-game hunter, accurate metallic-cartridge reloader, perennial National Rifle Association member, and long-time concealed-carry permit holder, exercised his constitutional rights as an United States citizen to protest looming one-world government. He protested by law-abidingly exercising with regional citizens' line militia, a totally-legal, perfectly-normal 20th-century-and-earlier solution to impending political wickedness. But, such earnest saber-rattling against one-world government is a solution that God, as of the early 3rd millennium, will no longer bless, because it may hinder fulfillment of Biblical prophecy, which foretells that Elohim will authorize global tyranny to usher back the LORD Jesus.

Despite that that iconoclastic radical Born Again patriot was in-fellowship, prayed-up, tithed-up, confessed-up, instant-evangelistic, Toraically righteous, and had much treasure in heaven, God then authorized satanic New-Age spirituality to do unthinkable violence to his health and personality. God authorized Satan and pagan spirituality, including 'beast' spirituality, to break his health. Through grace, the man endured the lengthy painful ordeal mostly stoically, but stunned with perplexity, heartbreak and horror. "It is a fearful thing to fall into the hands of the living God." (Hebrews 10:31) Mercifully, like Job, the man refrained from blaspheming God's name.

The uniqueness of these times militates against armed patriotic opposition to the blatantly wicked End-time global governance. Armed defiance that was Christianly filial throughout preceding centuries has become quasi-anathema, in the early 3rd millennium. Would-be radical patriots should acknowledge God's prophetic purposes within this age's spiritual intensity, and refrain from destabilizing insurrection.

Social activist and progressive strategist Saul Alinsky said, 'Your enemy's reaction is your primary weapon.' Atheist H.L. Mencken said, 'For every problem there is a direct pragmatic solution that is one-hundred percent wrong.' Don't allow just outrage at the meta-Left's political diabolophilia react you into hard-heavy emotive judgment. Justice will come from God the Father, after He lets Christ's bride be tried like gold in a fire. Strive for orthodox economic authority (for administrative offices) and for holistic health, instead of intimidating the progressives and their homo-occultist culture-war shock troops.

Despite that United States citizens' rights to keep and bear arms are historically a blessed check against totalitarian democide, Elohim is reluctantly allowing the United Nations and its variety of occultic totalitarianism (apocalyptic global pagan socialism) to ascend to international authority, at great cost of future human suffering. Satan will incite demoniacs to break laws, resulting in furor against liberty. The U.N.'s eco-state may become several times as occultic as the NAZI's were, with a digital VeriChip-rooted global identity management system to micromanage the economy. Even so, don't let your reaction to outrages become Satan's primary weapon against freedom!

If Triune Yahweh were to will that the one-world governance be resisted with arms, then true patriots would prevail as we did during the American Revolution, but Daniel 7:19-25 indicates that God will permit global ecospiritual socialism to prevail upon earth for a historically short season. For this reason, wise gun interest should be sportsmanly, more than patriotic, from now on.

In this early 3rd millennial New Age, God the Father won't extend much grace to armed Diasporic resisters against traitors advocating satanic global governance. God gave grace around 1776 for mostly-Protestant Christian American patriots to defeat King George of England, but He is very unlikely to repeat it even for Christian patriots armed for rebellion against the United Nations' New World Order.

In this New Age, the LORD Jesus grants more of Satan's *ad hoc* requests to ruin Christian patriots, by His refusal to defend us if we are off on a tangent to His will. God wants prophecy fulfilled, even to the allowing of a satanic one-world government and to the removing of angelic protection from Protestant heritage nations and patriots. Holy people who descend into radicalism, or otherwise detach from The Vine (Christ Jesus), more than ever risk scattering of their power. It is not that Jesus Christ Himself actively opposes or scatters the power of His holy people. He simply withdraws His protection from the tangential.

Satan and the occult probably want a U.S. federal government to preside over rescission of our 2nd Amendment rights, because U.S. patriots will fight a U.N. more readily than we will a superficially-licit U.S. government. However, when that profound year arrives, the LORD Jesus will prefer that we patriots then stack our arms and report for martyrdom, cruelly unjust though that may seem. God the Father does not want His Sons to be passive, or belly-up to The All, but our just defiance of evil mustn't hinder outworkings of Bible prophecy.

Action Plan

As the Endtime intensifies, don't submit to evil authority, doctrine or spirituality. Live each day willing to be martyred for your personal public testimony. What God wants of His men will then be un-cowed, upright non-insurrection. Neither submit nor insurrect! Neither submit to, nor insurrect against, the sin of a U.N. world government. Scathingly cooperate. Vehemently comply. Tell them cogently that their service to Satan will bring them to damnation and Hell. Bear up: "Play the men." (2 Samuel 10:12) Don't get soft: "By peace shall destroy many." (Daniel 8:25) Possess your own soul: "Take every thought captive." (2 Corinthians 10:5) Don't submit to all authorities equally. All creature authority is limited in scope. Limited authority obliges limited submission.[22] This same 21st century very probably will usher back Christ Jesus, after an implosion of the world's economic and political systems amid homo-occult sparked hostility to true Christians and Believing Jews.

The spiritual reason for a RFID global identity management system, which seems like foolishness to the world, will be to regulate an interdependent market nexus. Such a mega-cabal will punish evangelism and enforce popery and Talmudism. It will want citizens' submission to a one world-religion under Rome and to a global state funded by Talmudist investment bankers trying to prevent another Holocaust. Those who sow a world devoid of instant evangelism will reap a governance controlled by

Satan. Popery and Talmudism are both false, albeit enormous and wealthy, hierarchies of authority.

Pending the endtime revival, Messianic congregations should campaign to win every possible soul, of whatever race and nationality, with the truth of Christ Jesus and His Father, rather than whiling away the weeks like Jewish country clubs. Not only Jews will be saved by the firstfruits missionaries, but also many Gentiles, beloved of God.

These are the times in which we live. The personal greatness fostered by God in earlier generations within the body of Christ, that of cognitive truth authorizing personal power, may be limited in the wicked Endtime. During the church age and in fairly recent times, great men such as Dietrich Bonhoeffer and Richard Wurmbrand found the grace to oppose (not merely withstand) wickedness (in their cases, NAZIsm and communism) with truth, authority and power. In the immanent endtime, peace will scarcely evoke courage, apart from grace and faith in the truth. Since about April 6, 2000, we are in transition to a new dispensation of God, that of Christ Jesus' millennial kingdom.

VeriChip-based identity management technology will make it difficult to commit anonymous civil disobedience. The earthy human tendency to placate a group-thinking herd mentality may, in those days, be reinforced by a sophisticated information infrastructure giving immediate access to detailed personal data. Minor acts of civil disobedience may incur (at least) socioeconomic disenfranchisement, and (at worst) martyrdom, retaliation for demon-enraging evangelism of Jesus Christ. Triune Elohim does not require Believers to unconditionally submit to corrupt tyrannical civil authority. If obedience to civil authority means sinning against Yahweh, then Believers in Jesus are obliged to obey God, not men. Martyrdom is a better outcome than taking the beast's mark. Survivalism or *aliyah* (Heb., ascent) to the Middle East is preferable to martyrdom, and martyrdom, to any VeriChip markedness. In these last days keep your heart a warrior's heart, but be socially gentle.

Stellar Examples

Dietrich Bonhoeffer, a German Lutheran pastor and martyr to the NAZI's, was firmly and justly convinced that it is a Christian right and duty towards God to oppose tyranny. That is to say, Christians are not to submit to governance that ceases to be based upon natural law and the law of God.[23] As a representative of the this-sided confessing evangelical church in Germany during World War II, Bonhoeffer rebelled on behalf of God against Adolph Hitler, but paid with his own life for that conscientious uprightness, receiving a martyr's eternal honor. Bonhoeffer wrote that costly grace is preferable to cheap grace. Similarly, grateful righteousness is preferable to ambitious righteousness.

Richard Wurmbrand, a "Christian Jewish" (his term) pastor, was an imprisoned activist in NAZI— and Communist-occupied Romania, and co-founded *Voice of the Martyrs*. He espoused intelligent beliefs, similar to Dietrich Bonhoeffer's. He correctly rebuked fellow Christians who rotely submitted to NAZI authority. "One could not help admiring some of the brethren who, in these circumstances, carried out their civic duties and were unwilling to break a single one of the rules imposed by the Fascist government . . . I had to explain to them that according to Scriptures the authorities were instituted to punish evil and reward good, but if the authorities did the very opposite, then we were absolved from our duty to obey them."[24] This grace to defy evil still exists under Triune Elohim, with two *caveats:* that the demonic apocalyptic beast's authority, within civilization, is tending to increase with the passage of time; and, that we mustn't disrupt Triune Yahweh's prophetic gameplan, with insurrection.

The endtime one-world government and its apocalyptic global pagan socialism will be unique and unprecedented within the annals of history. There will be no free nation to flee to, unless the state of Israel opens its borders. Some think the Jordanian plateau to the east of the Dead Sea may one day harbor some of the firstfruits' supporters. That region was part of Biblical Israel.

Summary

If you are Hebrew or a supporter and opt to remain in the Diaspora, read *Foxe's Book of Martyrs* with consideration of your own possible martyrdom. "It is sown in corruption; it is raised in incorruption." (I Corinthians 15:42) If you cherish Bonhoeffer's vision of the this-sided church then prepare as a survivalist, or emigrate to Israel and successfully meet the economic, linguistic, cultural and evangelistic challenges implicit to going there, before the firstfruits' mid-Trib Rapture.

Should a human body be chipped as the price of admission to a global pagan socialist economy? Biblically, the answer is emphatically '*No!*' "What? Know ye not that your body is the temple of the Holy Ghost which is in you, which ye have of God, and ye are not your own? For ye are bought with a price . . ." (I Corinthians 6:19,20) "Render therefore unto Caesar the things which are Caesar's; and unto God the things that are God's." (Matthew 22:21) The human body is Triune Yahweh's. He intends Believers' bodies to be the temples of His Holy Spirit by rational conversion, mathematical conscience, and public testimony, according to faith in the identity and resurrection of the true Messiah, Jesus of Nazareth.

You should adamantly never covenant your name with one-world governance, nor let it inject its marker chip into your body. Historically, Christians are not martyred for worshiping holy Triune Elohim. Christians risk martyrdom, instead, for rebelliously not combining worship of Jesus-Y'howah with that of Caesar, Krishna, Allah, Shiva, 'Mary' or other pagan deity, via false religion or compulsory human tradition. Christians and Believing Jews face martyrdom for exclusively worshiping Elohim the Father through Jesus Christ. They risk martyrdom for rebellion against human organizations that require combined worship of Triune Yahweh plus that of profane creation.

When the once relatively-moral United States federal government becomes co-opted by the aggressively—pantheistic United Nations into an early-3rd millennial, eco-socialist global governance, we should neither submit to it nor insurrect against it. This is because submission to other agents comprising creature creation compromises theological, psychological and spiritual executorship, shifting it outward. Submission to a root of sin would be antithetical to the inner man and to love of truth. As far as God is concerned, all that will be due from Believers toward that prophesied tyranny is non-submissive non-insurrection. Upright neutrality.

If evil men legislate away the YHWH-given right to keep and bear arms, their next goals may be to impoverish the middle-class, topple the Constitution's First Amendment guaranteeing free speech, and declare a one-world government supported by a VeriChip-rooted global identity management system.

As that one-world state approaches, we should keep our eyes lifted toward truth and the starry deep firmament beyond the cobalt blue sky, and not react militantly against that satanic government.

Competing latter-day themes include the aparchic ("of the firstfruits"), the patriotic, or the demonic. Let rebellion against Satan take the forms of evangelism, authentic affection and righteousness.

May true Christians' and Believing Jews' boldness for our faith and mathematical consciences, in the context of our personal public testimonies, elicit grace to avert and, if necessary, slake ecopagan bloodlust.

Chapter 10 notes:

[1] Gary H. Kah. *En Route to Global Occupation*. Lafayette: Huntington House, 1992, 77.
[2] William F. Jasper. "Eco-Agenda for Planetary Control." *The New American*. September 23, 2002, 18 (19), 17.
[3] *Ibid.*
[4] *Ibid.*
[5] *Ibid*, 18.
[6] *Ibid*, 19.
[7] William F. Jasper. "The New World Religion." *The New American*. September 23, 2002, 18(19), 12.
[8] *Ibid*, 13.
[9] William F. Jasper. 'From Copenhagen: Obama Fails to 'Seal the Deal.'" *The New American*. January 18, 2010, 26(2), 10.
[10] Bob Rosio. *Hitler and the New Age*. Lafayette, LA: Huntington House, 1993, 79.
[11] March 1, 2013.
[12] http://en.wikipedia.org/wiki/VeriChip. January 3, 2012.
[13] Katherine Albrecht and Liz McIntyre. *The Spychip Threat: Why Christians Should Resist RFID and Electronic Surveillance*. Nashville: Nelson Current, 2006, 171.
[14] Kah, 42.
[15] *www.antichips.com/press-releases/verichip-cancer-report.html*, February 23, 2012; *www.antichips.com/press-releases/chipped-pets.html*, March 11, 2012.
[16] Shawn Boonstra. *The Appearing*. Ontario: Pacific, 2005, 94-107.
[17] *Ibid.*
[18] McCandlish Phillips. *The Bible, the Supernatural, and the Jews*. Camp Hills, PA: Horizon, 1970, 303-311.
[19] Kah, 42.
[20] *www.jews-for-jesus.org*, March 16, 2012.

[21] Boonstra, 96.

[22] Tim Baldwin and Chuck Baldwin. *Romans 13: The True Meaning of Submission*, 2nd Ed. Kalispell, MT: Liberty Defense League, 2011, 44-45.

[23] Dietrich Bonhoeffer. *The Cost of Discipleship*. New York: Touchstone, 1959, 29.

[24] Richard Wurmbrand. *Christ on the Jewish Road*. Bartlesville, OK: Living Sacrifice Book Co., 2002, 161.

Chapter 11

Multiple-Intelligences Metatheory

Definition of Terms

Multiple-intelligences metatheory is an interdisciplinary model reconciling aspects of theology and psychology. It reconciles personality theory with systematic theology. Multiple-intelligences metatheory, also known as tetrapartite psychology, systematically explains human personality in concepts conducive to victorious living. Multiple-intelligences metatheory (MIM), also known as tetrapartite psychology (TP), is an internally consistent, Biblically-supported theory of personality. Diagrams and tables in this chapter are included to stimulate right-brained *eureka's* about personality. Psychology is to biologically living souls, as theology is to spiritual eternity. Multiple-intelligences metatheory is a model, a simplified explanation of highly-complex human personality. MIM is a comprehensive system relating Scripture with psychology.

As a hypothesis of psychology, multiple-intelligences metatheory proceeds from two systematic-theological tenets. The first tenet is that the three Levitical colors of blue, purple and scarlet symbolize the three orders of angels: the seraphim, the heralds, and the cherubim.

The second tenet is that the human soul is symbolized by the Levitical priestly garments. These were stitched together from minimally-sweaty linen cloth woven from blue, purple or scarlet flaxen threads. Thus symbolized, a human soul is commissioned and harmonized by God from four elect spirits of three angelic orders. That is, from two seraphim, one herald and one cherub cooperating to form a human soul. Hence, tetrapartite soul.

The term *tetrapartite* means 'four-part,' and *psychology* is from the Greek, *psuche* (soul) + *logia* (science). Tetrapartite psychology explains human personality as influenced by and sustained from the four spiritual parts of its unique soul. Tetrapartite psychology analyzes human personality as sustained and expressed through a set of four created spirits. *Even as Levitical garments were woven of purple, blue and scarlet linen threads into priests' clothing, so God intends holistic weaving and harmonizing of each living soul's trimodal tetrapartite component spirits: one herald, two seraphim and one cherub.* The whole is greater than the sum of its parts.

The Bible usually sequences the Levitical priestly colors as blue-purple-scarlet, but the heralds (symbolized by purple) are the highest order and have a special relationship with God the Father. The sequence of *shekinah*-glory descent is heralds-seraphim-cherubim, symbolized by purple-blue-scarlet. The Bible usually focuses attention upon blue before purple, and silver before gold, although purple and gold are the loftiest within the two series.

What, exactly, is a soul made from? According to the multiple-intelligences metatheory (i.e., tetrapartite psychology), each human soul is created by God from four spirits drawn from three angelic orders: one crown herald, two seraphim (a left- and a right-hand seraph), and one root cherub. These four angels of each proper name keep heart and respiratory rhythms, and endocrine energetic fields, bioreponsive and onoresponsive (Gr., *ono*- "name"), and induce electrical impulses in nerve cells. A person's soul is the engine of his metabolism, the wings of his heart, and the eye of his intellect.

A popular belief is that the soul consists of the *mind*, the *will* and the *emotions*. But where do the mind, will and emotions originate from? Are they merely mechanistic biochemical or biomagnetic phenomena, or are they uniquely spiritual, angelic and personal? Are they material or spiritual in origin? Tetrapartite psychology hypothesizes that each human soul is created and woven together, from four spirits.

The spirit of a man is the essence of his true individuality. Man's spirit consists of graceful, focused instantaneity of his hands, spiritual heart, breath, speech, intellect and imagination. The spirit of man cannot be imposed top-down, from compulsion by an overbearing authoritarian demagogue. Some dualistic, affectionate respect remains essential to spiritual growth, because man is formed in the image and likeness of Elohim, who is a person, not a beast of burden. Abusively denied authenticity, junior participants tend to shun judgments against them from their seniors, by whatever tragic means happens along. Avid partisan interest makes for a longer, more-positive attention span than does fearful loathing.

Theological Ramifications

Personality and psychology relate to spirituality, and spirituality relates to the angelic or demonic realms. According to the Bible, angels and demons have a certain amount of power. Biblical evidence of demons interfering with men include: purposeful deception (Genesis 3:1-5:13); disguise as good spirits (2 Corinthians 11:14-15); instantaneous projection of a false reality (Matthew 4:8); apparent ability to remove and implant thoughts and manipulate men's minds (John 13:2, Matthew 13:19, 38-39); deception, blinding minds (2 Corinthians 4:4); oppression (Acts 10:38); possession of humans (Matthew 8:28, John 13:27); causing of physical ailments (2 Corinthians 12:7); defilement through occult practices and human sacrifices (Deuteronomy 18:9-13); communicate by speech to humans (1 Kings 13:18, Acts 23:9); tempt with evil (1Corinthians 7:5); and, pose as objects of pagan worship (Deuteronomy 32:17, 1 Corinthians 10:20, Colossians 2:18).[1]

Per the tetrapartite-soul hypothesis of personality, God unites four spirits to form a human soul. The soul forms the nucleus of a Born Again heart's-and-name's angelic retinue. According to this multiple-intelligences metatheory (i.e., tetrapartite psychology), a person is strictly identical with the private inward spirit of his heart, and is identified with his lifelong, verbalized transcript. A man's name is identified with his cognitive processes and cardiac rhythms, much more so than with his peristaltic motion.

Western science has focused, so far, upon relational and chemical correlates of the psyche. Tetrapartite psychology studies the composition, characteristics, and processes of the soul, in light of angelology, which is a branch of systematic theology.

According to tetrapartite psychology, the human soul is a dynamic, tri-modal psychospiritual unity, created from four spirits. Optimism for eternal personality with God the Father is imparted to the soul's trans-natal integrity by the New Birth. Traumatic separation of the parts of one's soul, of their

259

undergoing scattering, may be the "sift you as wheat" described in Luke 22:31. "The LORD said, Simon, Simon, behold Satan hath desired to have you, that he may sift you as wheat." The Koine Greek word for 'sift' is *siniazo*, meaning 'riddle, sift.' It implies chaotic rearrangement of parts, scattering of integrity, destruction of order. A human being undergoing such a sift would suffer dysfunction, intense misery and sickness, and demonic oppression.

Within a human soul, one's conscious mind is distinct from one's lower soul. One's angelic (or demonic) retinue is distinct from one's human soul.

One's body, heart, soul, natal angelic gifting, acquired angelic [or demonic] retinue, and the star of one's name comprise the human being. God the Holy Ghost is more-or-less consciously relational, but he prefers cardiac to ruminative centrality.

The Biblical Hebrew word translated "soul" is *nefesh*. *Nefesh* (Strong's number 5315) means "a breathing creature, vitality, breath, creature, heart, lust, man, mind, one, person, pleasure." *Nefesh* is a Hebrew feminine noun meaning "the inner being with its thoughts and emotions." It implies "breath, the inner being, and the whole person."[2] Wholeness of person implies an ono-unified (i.e., a name-unified) multipart integrity of body, soul and spirit.

Post-mortem, God inspects a man's harmonized soul-fields, to assign due reward or punishment for what the human said and did during biological life. "Meats for the belly, and the belly for meats: but God shall destroy both it and them." (I Corinthians 6:13) And, "For he is not a God of the dead, but of the living: for all live unto him." (Luke 29:38)

Let's look at a few competing psychological models, by way of background.

Competing Psychological Models

During the inter-testamental period between the Babylonian captivity and the Advent, ancient Greeks correctly thought the human soul consisted of three modes: reason, spirit and appetite[3], similar to the mind, will and emotions. The soul was thought to sustain biological life in a body, but also to impart varied personality traits, as though by its unique components. *Reason, spirit and appetite correlate to mind, will and emotions; also, to heraldic, seraphic and cherubic psychoangelic influences.*

Diagram 11.1: Overview, Multiple-Intelligences Metatheory.

God the Father			
Heralds	Tetrapartite human soul	Jesus' atonement and discernment-synergizing Holy Spirit	Man's heart and body
Seraphim			
Cherubim			

"The way in which the human soul accounts for the life of a human organism is by accounting for the distinctively human life that the individual in question leads. But to account for such a life, it must also account for the cognitive and intellectual functions which guide and shape such a life. Moreover, the dramatic differences in how good people are at leading lives, and relatedly the dramatic differences in how well they exercise their cognitive and intellectual functions, are due to differences in the conditions of their souls, namely the presence or absence of the virtues of justice, wisdom, courage and temperance. This answer significantly clarifies . . . the ordinary Greek notion of soul."[4]

Intertestamental Greeks such as Socrates, Aristotle, the Stoics, the Epicureans and the Hellenists advanced theories of the soul that influenced early Christian writers such as Clement of Alexandria and Gregory of Nyssa.[5]

In contrast to Christianity, objectivism is a philosophy developed by Ayn Rand and Nathaniel Branden. Ayn Rand was born Alice Rosenbaum, to Franz and Anna Rosenbaum, in St. Petersburg, Russia, on February 2, 1905. Her parents were Jewish, and her father was a self-employed chemist. A longtime cigarette smoker, Rand died of lung cancer on March 6, 1982, in New York City. In the intervening years, her literary efforts attracted an enthusiastic coterie of readers, who were energized by her characterization of materials science, structure and reason. More about Ayn Rand, farther on in this chapter.

Multiple Intelligences: A Metatheory

By this multiple-intelligences metatheory (tetrapartite psychology), each of the four angelic components of the human soul adds unique gifts to the personality and name they comprise, such as intelligence, ardor, values, reason, perception, warmth, strength, and capability. Each spiritual soul-influence demonstrates thematic consistency with its angelic order: heraldic, seraphic, or cherubic. Each soul-component is capable of independent thought. Let's look at characteristics of the three angelic orders.

According to this multiple-intelligences metatheory, the living soul interacts with the human heart through the body's neuroelectrical, circulatory, muscular, pulmonary and endocrine systems. Also, through synaptic patterning, beginning from conception, and through dreams, feelings, visions, and thoughts. The living soul initiates and sustains cardiopulmonary and peristaltic rhythms, and brain waves, in its biological body. A person's soul is the engine of his metabolism, the wings of his heart, and the eye of his intellect.

In common usage, the words "intellect" and "cognition" refer to brain activity, while "mind" can refer to both brain and enteric nervous system activity. Crowning cognition and intellect are quicker and more scientific, but the holistic mind (rooted in orthoradicality) is a fact of human nature. Lofty intellect amounts to more than radical holistic mind.

A multipart soul is implied in "Let the LORD, *the God of the spirits of all flesh*, set a man over the congregation." (Numbers 27:16, emphasis added) This verse implies the truth that a plurality of spirits sustain each biologically living body. The wording "spirits of all flesh" implies the multiplicity of spirits per each discrete biological body. This is the implication of the saying, "Being in good spirits."

A tetrapartite soul is also implied in Matthew 18:10, which reads "Take heed that ye despise not one of these little ones: for I say unto you, that in heaven *their angels* do always behold the face of my Father which is in heaven." (Emphasis added) The plural 'angels [of children] that look constantly upon the face of the Father in heaven,' in psychological realtime, are the tetrapartite components of each child's soul. Invited cognitive meditation dynamically implores God for deliverance, in adults, too.

C.S. Lewis wrote, in his *Space Trilogy*, that angels are like thinking minerals, implying comparability to a transparent energetic crystal. If this is true, perhaps soul-comprising angels admit of a few apocryphal, albeit theologically consistent, principles, conceding a minimum of mere speculation.

The three orders of angels are the heralds (or "thrones"), the seraphim, and the cherubim.[6]

Gabriel is a herald. Michael is a seraph. Satan is a cherub. This three archangels doctrine is the concept that Gabriel, Michael and Satan were created by God to be the archangels over the heraldic, seraphic and cherubic orders of angels. This theology is attributed to Pastor David T. Moore of Palm Desert, California, in a *Moore on Life* radio broadcast from autumn, 2001. Michael is the archangel over the seraphic order, and is called 'the great prince which standeth for the youths of the Hebrews' in Daniel 12:1.

Levitical Colors, Angels, and the Human Soul

The three orders of angels (heraldry, seraphy, and cheruby) correlate to the three priestly colors (purple, blue, and scarlet), and to the three temple metals (gold, silver, and bronze). These three Levitical pigments and three Tabernacle metals symbolize the three angelic orders. God combines four spirits from the three orders to form one living soul. In the interest of right-brained *eurekas*, Tables 11.3 through 11.16 relate aspects of these three angelic orders to human personality.

Levitical priests' woven ceremonial garments illustrate God's intention that man's trimodal tetrapartite soul synergize into holistic integrity. *Priestly garments were sewn by twining together blue, purple and scarlet linen threads into cloth.* "From the blue, purple and scarlet yarn they made woven garments for ministering in the sanctuary . . . They hammered out thin sheets of gold and cut strands to be worked into the blue, purple and scarlet yarn and fine linen . . ." (Leviticus 39:1,3 NIV) The three colors of threads, typifying the three angelic orders comprising the soul, were integrally woven together into minimally-sweaty linen garments, to be worn by Y'howah Elohim's priests.

Even as Levitical priests' clothing was woven from linen threads of the three tabernacle colors (of purple, blue and scarlet), so does God harmoniously weave the trimodal influences of a soul's herald, seraphim and cherub into a holism greater than the sum of its parts. Yeshua of Nazareth's coat was gambled for, in entirety, at Golgotha, not torn apart. Similarly, God wills grace through His Holy Spirit for seamless soul-integrity, for Believers' minds, wills and emotions to work harmoniously together as more than the sum of their parts. He wills for dynamic integrity of man's mental, physical and emotional fields. *The Levitical weaving of blue, purple and scarlet flaxen threads into priests' garments symbolizes Triune Yahweh's holistic intentions for human beings and our souls.*

By interpretation of Louis Berkhof's theology, within the three orders of angels, elect heralds have a special relationship with God the Father! They transmit His enlightening glory downward to elect seraphim. Elect seraphim transmit God's glory downward to elect cherubim.[7]

This idea is extremely important to psychology: that book-"throned" heraldry is a higher (i.e., nearer to Elohim and His *shekinah* glory) order than the seraphic order, which is in turn higher than the cherubic order. It means that within natural revelation God intends there to be an inter-order angelic transmission of His knowledge and glory, from heraldry down to seraphy and then to cheruby. And, it means that heraldic principles within human personality are nearer to God's heart and mind than are earthy cherubic principles.

Meditation

"The light of the body is the eye: *if therefore thine eye be single, thy whole body shall be full of light.*" (Matthew 6:22, emphasis added) 'Singleness of eye' occurs in a harmoniously integrated trimodal four-part soul, like a Levitical linen garment woven of blue, purple and scarlet threads. "And when these things begin to come to pass, then *look up and lift up your heads*; for your redemption draweth nigh." (Luke 21:28, emphasis added) 'Looking skyward' unites the mind's eye of the heart in singleness, much more so if one's conscience is in good standing with Triune Yahweh. Many meditative disciplines involve looking up, focusing the eyes upon the nose, or rolling the eyes up toward the brow, but without a Christian conscience such meditation is brief and tenuous, at best! *Raja yoga* to the contrary, neither meditation nor tinnitus absorption can remove sins. Only faith in "Christ Jesus, resurrected!" persuades God to forgive men's sins.

Cognitive meditation involves dynamic cognitive relationship, according to the *Logos*, between one's heart (and soul-angels) and God the Father. Upward-looking cognitive meditation should dynamically seek God's holiness, not wallow in entranced perplexity.

During conscientious skyward-looking meditation, God weaves, as it were, the blue, purple and scarlet threads of souls' seraphim, heralds and cherubim. Sanctified cognitive meditation results when one "looks up" (Luke 21:28) so that "thine eye be single." (Matthew 6:22, Luke 11:34). Christian cognitive objectivity invites a man's soul's angels to look upon the face of God, who looks back. By contrast, yogic meditative trance invites a curse, if psychic powers are sought.

Upward-looking conscientious cognitive meditation receives invitation for one's soul's angels to exchange looks with God. Cognitive meditation without a heart relationship with Christ Jesus can be dangerous.

Heraldry, Cognition, and the Inner Man

Elect heralds have a special relationship with God the Father. By this means, cognition-intensive teachers, writers and intellectuals find grace. Cleanliness, literacy and clinical intellectual astringency are next to godliness. Self-absorbed emotionality or narcissism, sin and stench are closer to the radical cherubically diabolic.

God the Father and His *Logos* adjust society toward heraldic themes of languages, erudition, publications, law, and communications, as compensation against cherubic themes propagated by Satan, the created fallen archcherub. But, what are heraldic, seraphic and cherubic themes?

Outside of living souls, elect heralds, which "throne" in books, descend to the biosphere to obey God or to refresh their minds from printed texts. When the NAZIs burned Torah scrolls, the pagan spirituality energizing them intended to alienate the German people from Adonai the Christ and His influence. Thus distanced from God the Son, the German middle class further submitted to Adolph Hitler, and wrought his butchery.

Heralds recognize scripted text, and pertain to the upper, face and head region of the human body and soul. "The man Gabriel" (Daniel 9:21) is thought by Pastor David T. Moore, of *Moore on Life Ministries*, to be the archangel Gabriel over the heraldic order.

Additional scriptural evidence for this aspect of tetrapartite-psych metatheory includes that Daniel the prophet understood by books (Daniel 9:2), and was approached by Gabriel (Daniel 9:21) the arch-herald. Heralds are thought to "throne" in books.

Other names in the literature for a herald are *throne* [8] and *man* (Daniel 9:21). Elect heralds have a special relationship with God the Father, and can impart clarion objectivity to the human heart.

What brightens one face compared to another? The word 'clarion' is derived from the Latin *clarus*, meaning 'clear.' It is used here to mean haloic Father-God-implying facial brightness: heart clarity. Brightness of brow. Light to the conscience and heart. To keep brightness for his brow and dangerous heart, a man should believe in Messiah Yeshua, and live like it.

Diagram 11.2: The Multiply-Intelligent Tetrapartite Human Soul, Depicted as Bioenergetic Fields Superposed upon Christ Jesus' Cross.

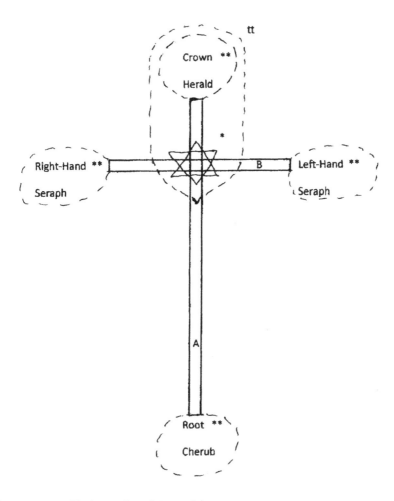

*	=	The heart, the quintessential name;
		[a star of David as a non-marist symbol for heart].
**	=	A soul-component spirit: a bioenergetic, psychoangelic "field."
tt	=	The inner man, the ego, the "I," the name's executive function.
A	=	Columnar Principle.
B	=	Lateral Principle.

Lofty, clinical cognitive processes structure man's contribution to civilization. Intellectually-astringent logical thought stands in contrast to sin's raunchy pungent radicality.

Ideas, research and publication matter a great deal to God the Father. Words and semantics, the domain of heralds, matter enormously to Him. Corporate salvation is a myth. The Hebrew word *ziyv*, meaning "brightness," is a roughly equivalent idea to the conscientious clarion light of mental-math-cued visuocognition.

The word clarion is defined as "a small high-pitched trumpet. [Now chiefly poetical]." [9] Haloic light of conscience, recognized during fleeting cognitive eye contacts, unites lovers of truth like shared hearing of a high, awakening, clarion trumpet music. In the realm of cognition, a clarion thought of God the Father elucidates mental torpor like a treble trumpet blast from a medieval king's court herald would alert a sentry. Soul heraldry's clarion light relates to the bioenergetic field of "the helmet of salvation" (Ephesians 6:17) and "the spirit of your mind" (Ephesians 4:23).

Lyrical octave-upshifts, baroque violin-and-trumpet tunes, and baritone *shofar* blasts symbolize angelic clarion's stirring calls to the inner man, and to his cognition and hopeful heart. The haloes shown in some Medieval religious art imply the idea of a clarion crown. A barely-perceptible halo of clarion light to the conscience corresponds to brightness of face and brow, and quick surety of mathematical mind. Clarion as used here refers to conscientious cognitive light, and comes from heraldic angels.

Conscientious clarion light gives height to the human heart, for cognition, for one's face and for language acquisition and communication. Spiritual clarion relates to research and development. The phrase "I watched the wheels turn in his head" describes the light of clarion (Heb., *ziyv*) penetrating to the man's understanding heart.

Heraldic clarion light invites each observing conscience, 'Look up, learn of God the Father!' A human soul's herald may act like a lens of spiritual transparency between a human conscience in the first heaven and God the Father in the third heaven.

Without at least a modicum of conscientious clarion light in each person's face within a relationship, there can be very little interpersonal love of goodness. There may be lust, animus, hate or passion but, without clarion

Table 11.3: Psychoangelic Attributes:

	Archangel:	Symbolic Tabernacle Metal:	Symbolic Levitical Color:	Role in Heavenly Praise:	Related Academic Competency:
Heralds:	Gabriel	Gold	Purple	Lyrics	Language, Mental Mathematics
Seraphim:	Michael	Silver	Blue	Melody	Art, Music
Cherubim:	Satan (A Hebrew word meaning "Enemy")	Bronze	Scarlet	Rhythm	Materials Science

conscientious light, there can be very little kindness, love of goodness, or true friendship. The word *philagathon* is New Testament Koine Greek for 'love of good (men).' God meters clarion carefully. Clarion objectivity is essential for rational intellect, for credible righteous indignation, for forcefulness of conscience, and for awarding of respect.

Respect, honor and worship from a rebellious or filthy conscience amounts to an insult. Language's hope content, crucial to human endeavors, is immediately under God's control via His authority over elect heralds, both psychical and extrapsychical.

The neocortices- and clarion-cognition-crowned inner man is to conscience, invitation, relationship, and obedience, as the cherub-rooted lower soul is to emulation, compulsion, experience, and submission.

The human tradition of submission to authority diverges from holy chivalry, because some truths are loftier, nobler and more-cherishable than are mere organizational business relations. Clarion-alight conscience is the intersection between God's permissive will and man's volition. How well man listens to his conscience influences the length and purity of his lines. Conditional clarion exceptionalism is the basis for both personal excellence and efficient nerve conduction.

Heraldic conscientious clarion's "freeing upward cognitive hope" winsomely invites one's heart upward, forward and outward, toward authenticity, brightness of face, mental accuracy, quickness of the inner man, and the mind and personality of God the Father. This is one blessing of education. The soul-herald is to neocortices and foveae, as the soul-cherub is to feet and gonads.

Biblical evidence of the cruciality of the inner man produced by God-related heraldry includes, "And be renewed in the spirit of your mind." (Ephesians 4:23) The spirit of your mind is the grace-sanctified, crowning herald of your soul.

Cognition should structure intuition, not *vice versa*. Cognition is to calculation, as intuition is to estimation. Cognition is to intellect as intuition is to instinct.

Clarion cognitive objectivity is the treasure of the holy and of the academically gifted, while tactile intuition is a sanctity-conditional

Table 11.4: Psychoangelic Attributes:

	Traditional Soul Function:	Neurological Activity:	Recognizable Logic:	Psychic-Membrane Factors:
Soul-Heraldic Traits: Gabriel is this order's archangel.	Mind	Cerebrocortical Cognition, Mental Calculation	All Valid Logic	Mathematical Conscience
Soul-Seraphic Traits: Michael is this order's archangel.	Will	Respiration, Volition, Affection	Cause-and-Effect	Spatial Integrity Energized by Heartsongs
Soul-Cherubic Traits: Satan was created to be this order's archangel, but he Fell.	Emotions	Enteric-Nervous Systemic Intuition, Estimation, Rumination, Orgasm, Procreation	Binary and Algorithmic Logic	Fundamental Chastity

contribution of elders. Narrowly-true canon scripture reinforces cognition, but Torah observance develops stable intuition. Mere human tradition falls short of building cognition patterned toward the mind of God the Father.

Technology is researched and developed by cognitive intellect, but popularizes to become intuitive and reflexive. Psychomotor routines, once learned, require more intuition than sustained cognition. Cognition is to *upward*, as intuition is to *lateral* and *deep*. Cognition is to pre-existent truth, as intuition is to optimistic thinking. Cognition should shape intuition, not intuition, cognition.

Conscientious clarion cognition invites God's intervention, entreating Him for forgiveness, protection and deliverance. Holy Yahweh attends to cognitive persons, to meet their minds and cleanse their hearts, because elect heralds have a special relationship with Him.

Conscientious visuocognitive clarion light to the heart implies that one has a viable psychic membrane, such as is envied and hated by diabolophiles, for almost any excuse. Depressives seek radical joviality from cognitive men, for they are uncomfortable communing with justice. Cognition and a dirty mind, obsessed with illicit eroticism, are opposing trends. The fruit of the Spirit tends toward highly-conditional conscientious clarion cognition, while the works of the flesh tend toward depression and dementia.

Mathematics-cued visuocognition tends toward personal authenticity, but intuition's authenticity varies greatly between persons, within environments, across time, and by subject. Severe sin diminishes cognition, so sinners compensate with emotion, intuition, rumination, or estimation. Conscientious clarion cognition has its own tones of voice, tempo, math-like quickness and accuracy of expression, not to mention vocabulary, by which cognitively bright people identify each other. Scholastics develop cognition; temperate, godly living retains it; cognitive nutrients enhance it. Conscientious clarion cognition (Gr., *ginosko*) relates to brotherly love (Gr., *phileo*), but politics-intensive social power relates to radical mental processes (Gr., *gnosis*).

Students learn cognition and cognitive habits for most of elementary, secondary, college and post-graduate education, so cognition is affirmed as authentic by society, in addition to God the Father's general delight in it, through elect heralds. Cognition cannot be attained by emulation of a creature, but must come from God. Cognition-structured prophecy is called a spiritual gift, but psychic-powers-structured intuition may be called mental illness.

Human debaucheries increase root-influences at the expense of clarion cognition, since extremes of either diminish the other. Aging, such as from biological oxidative stress, tends to decrease the ratio of cognition to intuition, in living personalities.

Aging exacerbates root influences at expense to clarion cognition, as some positive function of sin. The tendency from aging is more intuition, less cognition. Caloric restriction, vigorous exercise and a holistic lifestyle postpone some aging, but do nothing for sin.

Hypothetically, a child receives his souls' herald and cherub through his father, and his souls' seraphim through his mother. This may have some bearing on Israel's law of return. Michael the arch-seraph stands for the youths of the Hebrews.

Souls store emotions in their cherubic roots and bowels. "Lest any root of bitterness springing up trouble you, and thereby many be defiled." (Hebrews 12:15)

Jesus said, "The light of the body is the eye: if therefore thine eye be single, thy whole body shall be full of light. But if thine eye be evil, thy whole body shall be full of darkness." (Matt. 6:22, 23a) If God banishes a man's crown herald from His presence, that darkens the man's spiritual eye and heart. Such excommunication of a man's crown herald may be of brief or long duration, and may convey acute or chronic spiritual depression or dementia upon that piteous name. " . . . When they [as youth] knew God, they glorified Him not as God, neither were they thankful: but became vain in their imaginations, and their foolish heart was darkened." (Romans 1:21, KJV)

Darkened panicky human hearts crave heraldic clarion cognitive light, which God the Father measures down to consciences, hearts and faces, during preachings of the everlasting Gospel. Clarion, like oxygenation and digestion, is capacitable. That is, it is somewhat storable, dispensable, and rechargeable within one's being, if not one's body. Oxygenated blood amplifies clarion cognitive light shown in a bright face. Oxygenation intensifies facial clarion.

To a frustrated darkened heart, only heraldic clarion hints about God the Father seem safely trustworthy, making Biblical preaching the comfort that it is. Illicit sex or any serious sin can obscure clarion cognitive light to the heart and mind of man, briefly or for many years.

Posers (i.e., fakers, phonies), whose hearts have gone dark of clarion light to the conscience and who compensate with chronic comfort-eating, often resent and seductively envy cognitive intellectuals and bright youths.

Haloic clarion of a clean conscience hints at the mind of God the Father, comparably to natural revelation. How to enjoy more clarion light? Believe in Jesus! Publish! That is, publish relevant evangelical, exegetical, scientific or other helpful literature! Charismatic evangelical anointing (i.e., spiritual tingling of the scalp) implies holy heraldic action upon a haloic clarion conscience.

Did Nebuchadnezzar's insanity (in Daniel 4) involve God removing his soul's heraldic clarion cognition and brightness (Heb., *ziyv*)? Then did his recovery involve its re-instatement?

"At that same time my reason returned unto me; and for the glory of my kingdom, my honor and brightness (Heb., *ziyv*) returned unto me; and my counselors and my lords sought unto me; and I was established in my kingdom, and excellent majesty was added unto me. Now I Nebuchadnezzar praise and extol and honour the King of heaven, all whose works are truth and his ways judgment: and those that walk in pride he is able to abase." (Daniel 4:36, 37) Conscientious clarion cognition and *ziyv* correspond to educated brightness of face and objectivity of heart.

By discernment, twelve identical copies in existence, of a hardcopy paper document, constitute factual published status for it to God and His third heaven. For deeper study, God may "throne" a herald into a text (i.e., a hardcopy book) that He has interest in. At least twelve such identical "thrones" in material existence yield to God keen ongoing factual insight into the inner man of the author. Heralds, which "throne" in books, have a special relationship with God the Father and enlighten spirits of the two lower orders. God can use heralds to brighten the faces and hearts of men.

The effects of e-books on elect heralds' ministry to mankind remain to be seen. Natural revelation testifies of the orderly logical pre-existent brilliance of God the Father's mind, but cyberspace testifies of the minds of men.

Table 11.5: Psychoangelic Attributes:

	Contributions to the Ego:	Socializations:	Laterality:	Filiality:
Soul-Heraldic Traits:	Truth, Authority, Quickness	Personality	Relationship	Obedience (in truth)
Soul-Seraphic Traits:	Power	Nature	Experience	Submission (to authority)
Soul-Cherubic Traits:				

The apostle Paul wrote about conscientious haloic clarion in Romans 12:2, "And be ye not conformed to this world: but be ye transformed *by the renewing of your mind . . ."* (Emphasis added) This scriptural injunction implies the need to seek conditional clarion light instead of satiating earthiness.

"Her Nazarites were purer than snow, they were whiter than milk, they were more ruddy in body than rubies, *their polishing was of sapphire . . ."* (Lamentations 4:7, emphasis added) This "polish" may be a reference to haloic heraldic clarion light, to facial brightness and soul clarity. "And all they that sat in the council looking steadfastly upon him, saw his face as it had been the face of an angel." (Acts 6:15) God visibly intensified Stephen's conscientious clarion cognitive objectivity for his incipient sermon. According to J.A. Wylie quoting Theodore Beza, Reformer John Calvin's eye "retained its brightness to the last," throughout his final illness.[10]

Spiritual oppression may be macrocosmic (to a society, through economic, political, or military conquest) or microcosmic (to a man, via removal of clarion light or occlusion by a cherub).

Elements of the three orders of angels may cooperate as a *tria* (Gr., three). Good books attract elect spirits starting with heralds. Occult books attract fallen demons, heralds first. This is the spiritual principle behind book burnings as an instrument of social engineering. Fallen heralds frequent occult books. Fallen seraphim frequent profane speakers. Fallen cherubim frequent pagans and gross sexual sinners. To incite diabolophobia, demons try to sicken proximal humans they can't deceive or seduce.

If a person graduates from "throne"-intensive schooling to work in industry, but stumbles into severe sin, heraldic clarion cognitive light departs from his brow, darkening his heart. The neologism *scotocardia* (Gr., *skotos-*, dark, + *kardia*, heart) describes the effects of sin and ingratitude to God the Father. A word to the wise is sufficient. The penalty for sin is worse sin, and worse difficulty obeying the LORD Jesus.

Ministry and academia impart heraldic clarion cognitive light, and anabolize the mind. Academia occupies a niche between ministry and industry. If heinous sin obliterates clarion light, it may at great trouble be restored by Christ Jesus and retained via costly grace and wise, obedient, conscientious comportment. Pertaining to the humans, elect heralds ("thrones") are to man, as seraphim and cherubim are to nature.

The Torah is to root radicality, as the Gospel is to clarion objectivity. Communicating the Gospel is both simpler and more complex than behaviorally trying to keep the Torah's 613 laws. Strive for clarion Christianity, instead of hierarchic psychocherubic radicalism. To paraphrase John 1:5, 'And the clarion shineth in depravity; and the depravity comprehended it not.'

Heraldic clarion light of conscience is most recognizable in lofty clinical environments, encompassing the bright-faced brows of sanctified occupants of church buildings, schools, libraries, law and counseling offices, and silver and gold storage sites.

Crown-heraldic clarion instances of cognition and conscience promote Christlikeness, and should be encouraged whether or not they affirm Jewishness or any other ethnicity.

Seraphim, Heartsongs, and Child Psychology

Seraphim pertain to the median reaches of the soul and body. Hypothetically, seraphim may harmonically amplify or interfere with cardiac rhythms to stimulate or depress selected human organs. The English word 'hormone' derives from the Greek *hormonos*, "to set in motion". The word 'enzyme,' from Greek *enzumos*, "to boil." Material reality proceeds from spiritual reality, *raja yoga* notwithstanding. Seraphim store their tears in songs, and exult in precision and quickness. The word 'aristocrat' derives from Greek *aristos* (best) + *cratos* (strength), as in '(genetic and moral) best strength'.

Regarding heavenly praise and natural revelation, heralds are to lyrical logic, as seraphim are to melody, and as cherubim are to rhythm. Rock and roll music's emphasis upon pounding rhythm and corrupting lyrics reflects fallen cherubic influences and their earthiness. A major theme of 1960's sex, drugs and rock 'n roll spirituality was to exacerbate cherubic radicalism within the Baby Boomers. Street drugs open one's mind to spiritual bondage, making a drug abuser more radical by default. Cognitive persons study under book—"throned" heralds, youths imagine playfully with elect seraphim, and laborers toil before materials-oriented cherubim.

Heartsongs (i.e., inward songs, tunes, melodies and/or rhythms) help the soul's seraphim authentically adjust and shift cardiac rhythms into exceptional psychological wellness and physical strength. Ephesians 5:19 says, "Speaking to yourselves in psalms and hymns and spiritual songs, singing and *making melody in your heart* to the LORD." (Emphasis added) Clearly, inward melodies have positive spiritual significance, as well as positive effects upon mood and optimism. This explains the value of music to a person being "in good spirits." Music and song occupy the intersection between language and worship. As someone once noted, 'When music changes, so does society.'

The soul's seraphim translate and amplify heartsongs into healthy biorhythms, psychospatial-membrane integrity, and personal fearlessness. Table 11.6 relates heartsongs to the human soul and personality. Hypothetically, seraphim can en-luster any given lady or gentleman, to heighten good looks and encourage romantic desire.

Antitheses of heartsongs are profanity and tinnitus (yogic *nadam*, the occult-supposed substrate of manifested structure). Tinnitus can result from either nerve damage or magnetic resonance in the head or central nervous system.

Hypothetically, avid seraphim can repel electrons, even from biological molecules, ionizing and aging tissues. But, seraphic ardor can stir human sentiment, such as through heartsongs, to melt brittleness and anabolize hormonal activity. Hypothetically, cherubim can attract neutrons and invite projectiles. Any implied connection between obesity and emotionalism is not to deny that stout people can be extremely cognitive.

Compression of energetic space results in thrall (like repelling of lines of Gauss). Upper atmospheric churning, by seraphim, permits clarion-cognitive energy and respiratory movement to reach any given human intellect and pumping heart, which comprise the inner man.

A soul's seraphim act as vital parts of its psychic membrane, but occultists claim that all subconscious minds are connected. Perhaps sinners' subconscious minds are. (The subconscious mind consists of the carnate lower soul plus augmenting discarnate spirits, assigned to help or hinder.) This phenomenon reflects the idea of pantheistic universal infusion. Satan's lie of universal diffusion of spirituality and energy reveals his antagonism to man's heart's spatial integrity. Within man's conscientious psychic membrane, heartsongs and warrior-like dynamic imagination help his soul prevail with spatial integrity. The lie of universal diffusion suggests a consequent lie, that 'Resistance to pagan spirituality is futile, since you and the entire cosmos are already pervaded and controlled by a ruthless Impersonal Being.'

Personal space yielded to pagan spiritual infusion impinges upon rulership of nature by man's dangerous heart. Defaulting on spiritual reality, by relinquishing essential spatial integrity, would be suicidal, whether such default resulted from consequences of one's sins or from one's broken submission to The All. Don't give up!

Cherubim, Earthiness, and Radical Roots

Secular motivator Seth Godin said, "Our lizard brain, the prehistoric brain, deals with anger and fear . . . Every successful person I know—and I've studied a lot— has come up with a way to quiet the lizard brain, to soothe it or steer it or ignore it . . . [The lizard brain is] the voice that says, 'Maybe I should run this by Legal one more time.'"[11] Godin's idea of man's "lizard brain" relates to the influence of the soul's root cherub upon human personality. The cherubic domain, of the three orders' domains, lends itself most readily to empirical analysis.

Multiple-intelligences metatheory's tetrapartite hypothesis of psychology is supported by recent psychobiological research. The enteric nervous system (ENS) in the lower body functions as a semi-autonomous secondary brain,[12] implying the bioenergetic field called the soul's root cherub. The enteric nervous system originates from the gut, which contains 100 million neurons and produces more than 30 neurotransmitters.[13] Per the tetrapartite hypothesis of human personality, the subdiaphragmic abdominal region of the human body holds a bioenergetic field identified as the root cherub. This spirit is hypothetically capable of some independent thought and emotional memory, with special appreciation of materials science (such as that of gold), fact-based Aristotelian logic, and moral Saturday-sabbath rests. Pure chemical elements symbolize ideal, nonconfused radicality. Set-apart holiness of the human root-cherub, distinct from fornication unto righteousness and personal chastity, is critically important to healthy personality.

The enteric nervous system's 100 million neurons exceed in number those found in the spinal cord, but are much much fewer than the neurons comprising the brain in the head.[14] The human gut contains approximately 100 trillion bacteria, the gut biome, contained within a surface area one-hundred times that of the skin.[15] Helpful symbiotic bacteria, called probiotics, may be introduced into the human metabolism via designer dietary supplements. Jane Foster, a Canadian neuroscientist, says "The gut biome is actually an interface between your diet and your genetics." And, "The crosstalk between the gut biome and the brain is continual."[16]

Researcher Michael Gershon, M.D., doubts that the ENS's abdominal brain is conscious or capable of complex emotions or reasoning, while opining that religion, philosophy and poetry comprise the domain of the head's brain.[17] Tetrapartite psychology asserts that the root cherub is of a divided angelic order, that its neurological domain is far less complex than the head brain, and that cognitive ego and executive functions reside in the human head and heart, only tertiarily in the ruminative bowels.

"Decision-making may be firmly monopolized by the executive center of the brain located above the neck. But that doesn't minimize the contributions to our mental life now being discovered in our gut. Unfortunately, the gut's reputation fails to rise to the occasion. 'The gut is a reptilian, disgusting organ, and we're told to forget about it,' Gershon says. 'The head is a serious organ; the heart is a serious organ.'"[18] Tetrapartite psychology asserts that the abdominal-root bioenergetic field is cherubic, and that it is refinable via orthodox Toraic morality and Christian relationships. Further, that it is capable of some independent reasoning and of storage and processing of emotional memories, and that it should yield to the inner man of the heart and head, not usually *vice versa*. Then, that cherubic psychoradicality should be rationally structured, not customarily dominant, in support of a healthy personality. This said, purity of the human root cherub has fundamental importance, both in this life and in the life to come, to one's person and progeny. Root lineage conveys blessings, curses and radical influences, from puberty onward.

If enteric-nervous systemic ruminative thought overwhelms neural afference and efference between the cererbral cortex and voluntary muscles, then such rumination acts as a cognitive component of the metabolic syndrome.

Don't let Toraic righteousness's orthoradicality make you arrogant: heraldry is the highest order. Bright-faced heraldic Christian conscience wields more authority, for winsome interpersonal communication and evangelism, than do cherubic storehouses of one's earned Toraic righteousness, and the two themes tend to diverge in any given psyche. Toraic earned righteousness induces psychoradical authority, but other peoples' inner man trusts clarion-conscientious brightness of faces, from Christian conscience. Psychoradical authoritarianism from Toraic earned righteousness can

Table 11.6: Psychoangelic Attributes:

	Semantic Tendency:	Psychical Effect:	Bioelectric Patterning:	Respiratory Metabolism:
Soul-Heraldic Traits:	Denotation	Logic, Math, Languages, Creativity, Imagination	Low-Wattage, High-Velocity Brain Waves	Aerobic
Soul-Seraphic Traits:	Cogent Idiom		Respirative Heartsongs and Instant In-Phase Biorhythm Shifts	
Soul-Cherubic Traits:	Physical Science, Orthodoxy and Allegory, OR Self-Serving Connotation and Outright Lies	Olfaction, Memory, Confections, Massive—Object Intuition, Procreation, Repetition, Monotony	Higher-Wattage, Sluggish Brain Waves	Anaerobic

bring to bear un-Christlike, even arrogant, cherubic influences upon one's emotional center and inner man. Clarion cognitive hygiene and rampant psychoradicality, as in the case of sexual or pride addiction, annihilate each other, as genius heraldic and earthy cherubic themes tend to thematically oppose each other within a sinful human personality.

The human root needs righteousness, refinement, spontaneity and clarion light, which are not identical with formulaic quieting, soothing, steering or ignoring. Extremely habitual, formulaic behaviors, typical of radical earthy roots, quench God the Father's Holy Spirit. The soul's root develops binarily, toward either truth or lies, toward either science or myth, toward either straightness or perversion, toward either chastity or lewdness.

Advanced in truth (by evangelism and relationships), or retarded in earthiness (by tradition and sensuality): these two exist in inverse ratio. The former is closer to the Father in heaven and His mind.

The neologism 'psychoradicalism' describes a human personality dominated by earthy radical cherubic spirituality. Such an individual tends toward sensual or aggressive dominant traits, or (if sin is his problem) toward true evil. Psychoradicality is to emotional memories, as cognition is to keeping one's mind on the problem. Psychoradicality's domain is raw physical power, but mental-math-cued visuocognition is closer to the mind of God the Father. Condonable psychoradicality is one correlate of youth. An involuntary frown indicates psychoengagement: one's fleetingly aiming his soul to actively discern some aspect of reality.

Earthiness trends toward vulgar diction and 'stinking thinking,' and those, toward sin. Stinking thinking implies cherubic themes upon a man's head, while cherubic themes belong below his diaphragm, toward his feet. Stinking thinking often begins with a dirty mind. Sexual sin is the root cause of much, if not most, mental illness.

At the very least, since Satan is a cherub (Ezekiel 28:14-19), it seems important to recognize characteristics of his order, the cherubic order. Such comprehension may assist Believers in resisting his temptations and avoiding the stinking thinking implicit to sin.

Although many equate spirituality with minimal earthiness, earthiness itself should not be totally rejected (as gnosticism attempted), since each and every living soul is rooted by its cherub into some radicalism and earthiness. Grace through faith in Elohim's *Logos* attempts symbolic refinement of conscience and civility, and chemical refinement of biosomatic metalloenzymes. If souls' roots are of the same spiritual order as Satan (i.e., the cherubic order), then keeping our roots pure is essential to resisting him and his deceptions.

The two demonic 'beasts' of Revelation 13 may be 'compound cherubic.' That is, a unitary hierarchy of fallen cherubim, unified in cunning and volition, capable of possession of a multitude of humans over long periods of time, and of subtly nudging their decisions and careers toward Satan's strategic societal goal of global governance. The ten-horned compound-cherubic beast is thought to be associated with weapons, violence, money, promiscuity and sodomy. By discerning of spirits it was given authority over the Diaspora on or around April 6, 2000, which was the lunar-observed Biblical-calendar Nisan 1 of that year. This date, and April 8, 2000 (its subsequent sabbath), of the first Biblical new year in the 3rd millennium may have concluded the church age and begun Christ Jesus' millennial kingdom.

The inner man of the heart and mind prospers in an inverse relationship to earthiness and root dominance, due to Satan's fall. Personal ideals risk nullification from sin, which imprints extremely earthy influences upon the soul's root and cognitive processes. The inner man develops either conscientious absolutes or conscientious syncretism, in mutually-exclusive fashion. The human root stores emotional memories, but extreme habituation stifles creativity and instant obedience to God the Holy Ghost and to conscience. By this system, orgasm involves a root-cherubic-induced neuroelectrical discharge.

The apostle Paul wrote, "That ye put off concerning the former conversation the old man, which is corrupt according to the deceitful lusts, and *be renewed in the spirit of your mind.*" (Ephesians 4:22, emphasis added) The "old man" may be a fallen cherubic impression of an autocratic masculine authority figure in one's history or circle of acquaintances; "the spirit of your mind . . ." is heraldic. "Lie not one to another, seeing that ye *have put off the old man with his deeds.*" (Colossians 3:9, emphasis added) "The old man" may be a fallen cherubic similitude of an intimidating paunchy older man.

At least two Biblical reference indicate this idea of the cherubic root of the soul. Firstly, Abraham instructed his eldest servant to swear an oath with his hand placed *under his thigh* [part of his lower body] to find Isaac a bride of his own people (Genesis 24:2-4, emphasis added). Secondly, the reference to "the *root* of Jesse" (Isaiah 11:10, emphasis added) alludes to the Davidic line. The ideas in both cases may refer to psychospiritual continuity and independent thought life of the cherubic roots of those two men's souls.

Psalm 18:10 describes the LORD God of Israel (later incarnate as Jesus of Nazareth) in relation to a cherub. "And he rode upon a cherub, and did fly: yea, he did fly upon the wings of the wind." Is Christ's riding upon a cherub a reference to a cherub comprising the mobile root of His soul?

Elect cherubim, related to the subdiaphragmic roots of living souls and bodies, are of a divided order and are the last class of spirits to know God's instant will. God the Father intends that man's literary heraldic crown be his glory, and ideas of his cherubic root (such as materials science, scents or sex) should be preserved strictly orthodox. As the former archcherub, Satan can guess purposes and localities held by elect cherubim. Hence, tentmaking support of controversial ministry via blue-collar manual trades is intrinsically difficult, due to the earthiness of trade work. Pastor Steve Reynolds said, "The water of life is free, but the plumbing is very expensive."

A soul's elect cherub pertains to the lower, root region of each created soul and body. A soul cherub influences the human being's relation to scents, memory, earthiness, emotionality, sex, materials science and sixth-sensing of massive objects. 'Intuition of mass' refers to the experience many persons have sensing proximal tonnages of rock, while exploring a cave, hiking a canyon, or climbing a mountain.

Root intuition, distinct from cerebral cognition, can confirm generalizations of chemistry, materials science, and *eros*. *Root intuition may be highly refined by Biblical righteousness of the Torah, but it cannot totally replace a healthy brain's and educated mind's executive cognition within a sanctified, productive human personality.*

Elect cherubim pertain to God's righteousness and justice upon empirical reality. The Hebrew language ideas of *laybab* (Heb., center) and *ahavah* (affection) connote a lower-soul root-cherubic emphasis. This contrasts with the New Covenant ideas for love, of *agape* (Gr., charity), *phileo* (friendship), and *storgey* (cherishing), which imply the face and upper body.

Convivial sinners can feel considerable *ahavah* (Heb., visceral affection) for each other, but intelligent youths trust translucency of clarion logic-cued visuocognitive intensity from bright faces, such as evokes teachable

284

moments. The King James Bible describes Hebrews as "children of Israel," not "persons of Israel." Bright-faced children feel frustration at adults who sycophantically mitigate to each other's conceited torpor. "May their table become a snare . . ." (Psalm 69:22) Persons may contentedly satisfice ideals with oral fixations and traditions, but bright children tell it like it's written. "The light of the body is the eye . . ." (Matthew 6:22)

By discerning of spirits, cherubim rapidly process binary-logic facts, such as: yes/no, true/false, A/A', right/wrong, front/back, x/y, anode/cathode, friend/enemy, boy/girl, learning/application, and boundary/incursion. Satan (Heb., *ha satan*, "The Enemy") is a created spirit, a cherub. He is called that great red dragon, in Revelation 12:3, consistent with symbolic Levitical scarlet. Earthiness describes the root-cherubic theme in human personalities. Root spirituality is of a divided order: "This wisdom descendeth *not from above, but is earthly, sensual, devilish.*" (James 3:15, emphasis added) Common sense dictates that extremes of radical earthiness are prone to confusion and opposition. A prime example of cherubic binary thought is the nature of biological genetic root-functionality: either maleness or femaleness, either XY or XX. Binary, algorithmic, and psychomotor logic exemplify the soul's root-cherubic thought processes.

If Satan truly is cherubic and radical in orientation, then human radicality should be per knowledge and according to specification, rarely reactively rebellious.

Strong odors pertain to the cherubic domain. The Israelites told Moses, "We remember the fish, which we did eat in Egypt freely; the cucumbers, and the melons, *and the leeks, and the onions, and the garlic. . .*" (Numbers 11:5, emphasis added) The ancient Israelites' torpid satiety with odiferous earthiness (of the cherubic theme) made the LORD God of Israel (normatively identical with the preincarnate God the Son) quite impatient with them.

In athletics, the team that sets the tempo often wins the game. In human organizations, the tempo of business relations is often set by psychoradicality (e.g., sympathy gluttony, self-serving connotation, emotionalism or cherubic diabolophilia). Fools deny that they can be judged for their use of their souls, but that is a lie.

Hypothetically, regarding cherubim, the color scarlet is to verbal expressivity, as antiphasic yellow-with-black patterns are to algorithmic physical activity.

Even *ortho*radicality amounts to a tenuous basis for optimism, because man's observation of Toraic earned righteousness tends to affirm what he optimistically feels to be true about himself.

"Out of your belly [abdomen, lower body] shall flow rivers of living water." (John 7:38) I.e., Shall flow mankind-positive, cherubic-domain psychomotor energy: promotive of intellectual orthodoxy, scientific chemistry, and personal establishment.

As the words are commonly used, "intellect" and "cognition" occur in the brain, while "mind" can occur in both the brain and the enteric nervous system. Crowning cognition and intellect are quicker and more scientific, but the holistic mind (rooted in orthoradicality) comprises an asset in psychomotor activity and interpersonal relationships.

Related Concepts

God the Father's orderly, logical, brilliant mind primarily encompasses theology, logic, mathematics, cognitive psychology, languages, law, athletics, pedagogy, leadership, and parenthood. It deals with "who." Secondarily (but most representative of empirical reality), His mind encompasses chemistry, biology, medicine, engineering, physics, and technology. This secondary tier of knowledge of empirical reality deals with natural properties. It deals with "what."

Psychologically, a response of '1' signifies monosyllabic 'No!', as in *curt refusal*. A response of '2' signifies 'Yes!', as in *insistent will*. Somatically, the right hand means 'yes' and the left, 'no'. This latter derives from Middle Eastern cultural history, where the left hand was used for post-defecatory cleansing.

Despite Satan's fall as the created archcherub, the LORD God of Israel (the preincarnate God the Son) commanded that the mercy seat in the tabernacle of the congregation be framed by two cherubim of pure beaten gold (Exodus 25:19). *Satan was created to be the archcherub (the archangel over the cherubic order) but Jesus Christ's soul's root cherub will replace him in that office, when He returns.* Perhaps elect heraldry reminds us of God the Father's intellect, as the *Paraclete* reminds us of His heart, and as Christ Jesus reminds us of His radicality.

Table 11.7: Psychoangelic Attributes:

	Bioenergetic Fields:	Ontological Factor:	Predominant Sentiment:	Contributions to Music and Worship:
Soul-Heraldic Traits:	Mental Field	Haloic Clarion, Mathematical Conscience	Freeing Upward Cognitive Hope	Lyrical Semantics
Soul-Seraphic Traits:	Physical Field	Energy, Upper-Body Strength (Might)	Joy	Melody, Treble
Soul-Cherubic Traits:	Emotional Field	Stability, Lower-Body Strength (Main)	Loyalty, Radical Earthiness	Rhythm, Bass, Percussion

Approaches by man to YHWH and Jesus Christ clarify our cognition of empirical reality, and invite the justice that inexorably pursues material nature. Sensual luxuriation in false gods of petty infatuations (on Toraic or Christian high days), of public lewdness or profanity, or of sin of any sort, endrosses orthodoxy of material nature with earthiness, torpor, vulgarity and obtuseness. Toraic earned righteousness invites God to refine roots and metalloenzymes.

It is not accidental that the relatively-godly Victorian era saw exponentially dramatic advancements of research into the pre-existent truths and logic of Yahweh the Father's mind, as incorporated within nature. "Where the Spirit of the LORD is, there is liberty." (2 Corinthians 3:17) *Where Jesus' Father's Spirit is, there is more cognition; where there is cognition, there are more wise decisions made; where there is wisdom, there tends to result more freedom.*

Intellectual cognition is the realm of heralds, which stand nearest to God the Father. Rumination (e.g., intuition) is the domain of soul-cherubim, which yearn for men of orthodox intellect of Triune Yahweh's version of reality. God's version of empirical reality includes Toraic law, sound doctrine, and orthodox science, versus Satan's version of reality, which descends to tradition, self-serving connotation, lies, debauchery and occultism.

By contrast, the cherubic domain orients to empirical reality, which implies inexorable justice upon itself, as a function of God's judgment. Of the three orders, the cherubic domain lends itself most easily to empirical analysis. Empirical reality is the will of Adonai the *Logos*, and is implied by God the Father's mind regarding the logic, precision and rigor of mathematics, chemistry, and engineering. Hard-heavy expressivity in oratory attracts listeners' emotions. But, ruminative emotions do not creatively 'do' (or 'gest'-ure), they *di*gest (L., *di-*, apart from, + *gerare*, to carry). *Emotional oratory essentially commands its hearers to eat well and emulate.*

The New World Order (the so-called new order of the ages) seeks for satanic inversion of God's hierarchy of angelic-orders. For example, by it living souls' elect crown heralds would be made to submit to fallen seraphim; and living souls' elect seraphim, to fallen cherubim. New Age heresies are not new, they are an intensified re-hash of ancient occultic mystery religion.

Perversions, such as oral sex, invite psychospiritual inversion. 'Inversion,' in the sense of a soul's cherub positionally superior to another's herald and seraphim. The effect of attempted orderic inversion of the angelic hierarchy

Table 11.8: Psychoangelic Attributes:

	Freudian Analog:	Punctuations:	Human Objectivity:	Leadership Development:
Soul-Heraldic Traits:	Superego	Instants (as in, Optical)	Spatial Depth Perception	Invention
Soul-Seraphic Traits:	Ego		Linearity Discernment	Adaptation, Exploitation
Soul-cherubic Traits:	Id	Moments (as in, Magnetic)	Density- and Assay-Intuition	Formulation, Habituation, Emulation

upon the souls of men is spiritual depression, with demonic deception to mold their inner man, to satisfy wrath through suffering. In a nutshell, the varied meta-Left's ideas of progress derive from fallen cherubim. A New World Order's orderic inversion, as implied by the red-at-top visible spectrum on the homosexual flag (taken from rainbows, which naturally are red at the top), would position fallen cherubim (such as Satan) at the top of Elohim's creation.Blue symbolizes seraphim; purple, heralds; and, scarlet, cherubim. This is one meaning of the Levitical colors.

For punishment or to command attention to His voice, God can attenuate a man's crown herald's access to His presence, darkening his heart. Or, for similar reasons, He can allow a cherub to be interposed against a human's head, occluding his intellect and exacerbating rumination. Cherubic occlusion of a human brow from its crown herald implies stinking thinking. Innocent children have minimal awareness of 'scary' radical earthiness, since the soul's root cherub and its earthiness begin to become part of outward personality at puberty. This truth gives additional meaning to "Except ye be converted, and become as little children, ye shall not enter into the kingdom of heaven." (Matthew 18:3) Don't be ruled by cherubic themes, if you value your inner man.

Angel and *spirit* are alternate phases of the same entity. An angel is a God-serving spirit with personality and a message. Footwashings? They diminish strong lower-body odors, easily identifiable and trackable by cherubim, out upon the elements. "Jesus saith to him, He that is washed needeth not save to wash his feet, but is clean every whit . . ." (John 13:10) Were these words of Yeshua haNotzri (Jesus of Nazareth) a clue in spiritual warfare, to minimize susceptibility to pro-satanic earthiness? By discerning of spirits, fallen cherubim may be driven out of a metal base, but scent must be washed off with soap and water, to break cherubic hold on a scent base.

Energy (Gr., *en-*, inward + *ergos*, work) is to human biological metabolism, as the neologism 'ekergy' (Gr., *ek-*, outward + *ergos*, work) is to angelic retinue. Energy and ekergy intersect at one's face, lit either from above by a respectable clear conscience (a heraldic crown) or from below by satiated bowels' secretive glowing (a cherubic root). Faith, holiness, published works, good deeds and fasting (read, *grace*) increase holy ekergy. Sin contaminates ekergy and energy both, with Yahweh-hating demons. This newly-coined idea illustrates a main point of Christian living. Ekergy relates to either spatial clarion cognitive light or occluded depression.

Table 11.9: Psychoangelic Attributes:

	Healing Influences [Rev.4:7]:	Psychological Structure:	Vehicular Analogy:	Information Technological Analogy:
Soul-Heraldic Traits:	Man	Conscious Mind	Visibility, Instrumentation	Information
Soul-Seraphic Traits:	Eagle	The Subconscious Mind: A Psychic Membrane Partitioning Out The Collective Unconscious	Horsepower, Handling	Software
Soul-Cherubic Traits:	Lion, Calf (not, Bull Lusting for Heifers)		Torque	Hardware

Osmotic psychospatiality, between Believers and sinners, is why to "Come out of her, my people." (Revelation 18:4) As a trend, good ekergy relates to efficient nerve conduction. To be "in good spirits" means to have gracious elect ekergy. Man is more-or-less an open system, not a closed system.

Jesus said, "Which of you by taking thought can add one cubit unto his stature?" (Matthew 6:27) Why would He have specified "one cubit," when a cubit is the distance from elbow to little-fingertip, around eighteen inches? Eighteen inches is a very large unit for measuring the height of men's biological bodies. Possibly, the stature He referred to is the height of a man's spiritual heart, or angel. That is, the height, breadth and depth of a man's body and proximal atmosphere, that is filled with his soul, and sanctified from evil spirits, by God. 'Being in good spirits' alludes to highly-conditional sanctity, resulting in harmony with elect-or-fallen, morally-binary spiritual election. Such harmony occurs ultimately only by grace through professed faith in Christ Jesus and His atoning death. Other virtues fall short.

Theme songs that accompanied movie characters in early motion pictures were intended to remind viewers of the actor's soul and angelic retinue, and of his or her heartsong and personal ambience. The good or evil spirits that light any given personality comprise his or her *parousia* (Gr., brightness of coming). Your (any) good spirits light your face and heart, and preserve your personal space within your elastic psychic membrane. *Being 'in good spirits' requires, in ultimate reduction, being in orthodox relationship with Triune Yahweh, which begins only through a personal relationship with the LORD Jesus Christ.*

The neologism *cardiospatiality* refers to the spatial volume occupied by a man, his heart, and his soul; a volume of space analogous to an elastic, transparent electronic crystal, bounded by his psychic membrane. Cardiospatiality that is innocent or sanctified efficiently transmits cardiac rhythms. Occlusion of cardiac rhythms (by unclean, evil or wicked spirits, especially radical cherubim) interferes with the man's personality, facilitating Satan's attempts to kill off his spirit. Godliness tends to result in cleaner cardiospatiality and better nerve conduction. Psychoradicaliism and cardiospatiality relate inversely to each other. Excesses of earthiness inhibit cardiospatiality, while exacerbating pschoradicalism. New Age writers have referred to psychosocial trends using the term 'the hundredth monkey principle,' implying that if enough people do or say an idea, it catches on rapidly. It 'goes viral', in Internet parlance.

Elect angels constitute part of the "true riches" Jesus spoke of in Luke 16:11. "If therefore ye have not been faithful in the unrighteous mammon, who will commit to your trust the true riches?" Jesus Christ, the King of the angels, awards elect "thrones" for worthy scholastics, seraphim for courageous deeds or soul-winning, and cherubim for observances of Toraic righteousness. Or, simply according to His divine holy fiat.

Idealism walks a fine line between radical earthiness and antimaterialistic gnosticism, with Protestant Christian faith by sound doctrine and due righteousness yielding grace to thrive. God and nature tend to resist human earthiness. Some react willfully against this tendency by overindulgent comfort eating or sexual acting-out. Obey your conscience, not your gut, should the two support divergent courses. If you are frustrated that your speaking voice matters little in society, teach or go back to school; don't yield to oral addictions.

Total removal of a soul results in biological death. " . . . Thou fool, this night thy soul shall be required of thee" (Luke 12:20) means that God was taking away that wealthy farmer's soul in preparation to judge his spirit, the spiritual "I" and essence who was at the core of his four-part soul. An unclean spirit is an elect angel (in spirit mode), that has become offended at a human by witnessing his or her sin.

Conscience and Mental Health

Conscience is one's soul-herald urging and imploring one to think and act with moral fastidiousness. The Koine Greek term for feeble-mindedness *oligopsuchos* (loosely, 'partitioned soul'), the opposite of tetrapartite integrity. Resurrection of a deceased Believer's spirit and original soul reveals God the Father's inquiring acceptance of him as His angelic son, the fulfillment of Christ Jesus' troth to him during his biological life on earth. In childhood and in holistic health, the soul's components mesh seamlessly.

Good habits sustain efficiency and ease stress, but habits of behavior alone cannot refresh from earthiness or lift one's head! Habitual, formulaic problem-solving utilizes earthy radicalism, but may stultify creativity. No one should love their root formulas more than clarion prophetic Gospel.

The apostle Paul called emulation (of others) 'the flesh' (Galatians 5:20). John Eldredge called emulators "posers," and wrote that "The world of posers is shaken by real men."[19] If so, this is because fallen cherubim and heart-darkened humans hate and envy those with clarion cognitive light to the heart and mind, imparted there by God as grace for conscience and for words of the Gospel.

George Sheehan, M.D., the runner, wrote of "The Lie" that can occur in human personalities. In tetrapartite-psych terms, The Lie occurs in a human being if his inner man is 'denied' by God the Holy Ghost, or if the man is un-saved and occluded. The Holy Spirit's silence about a man, to spiritual election, would permit domination of him by fallen spirituality. The Lie in the heart of a man involves the satiating contents of his abdomen, a slumped deflated posture, a tongue's tactile thrust, and a stiff-necked visual field, gravitating into unified sensation suggestive to him of a false persona. Worse, suggestive to him of a false persona connotatively validating his own radicalized self-will. "May their table become a snare . . ." (Psalm 69:22) The reverse of The Lie is sanctified uprightness, inward straightness, holistic health and forcefulness of conscience supported by the Paraclete's testifying to election of the man's faith. He doesn't have to, and no creature can coerce him. Honor, worth and respect can be imparted only by a heart with a clear conscience. A rebelliously-filthy conscience's proffered respect amounts to an insult. Sexual sin is the root cause of much, if not most, mental illness. Even if a contemplated decision would be only ambiguously wicked, the penalty for sin is worse sin.

Staying "in the Spirit" (Galatians 5:19-23) brings respect; descending into "the flesh" brings shame. This is the heraldry-and-cognition intensive means which God has ordained to build character and integrity, using people to sharpen each other's countenances. Acting according to "the flesh" subjects one to the ceremonial Torah, the oral law, romish spirituality, and/or the cruel vengeful occult.

The neologism *ono-occlusion* results from ". . . the beam [an oppressing spirit, for sin] that is in thine own eye." (Matthew 7:3) The term ono-occlusion derives from Greek and Latin, *ono-* (Gr., name) + *occlusion* (L., oc- (before) + *claudere* (shut, close)). It denotes obscuration of one's heart's brightness from one's face and mind, via the mechanism of spiritual depression.

Table 11.10: Psychoangelic Attributes:

	Ministry Styles:	Timing:	Typic Fiber:	Baseline Habit:
Soul-Heraldic Traits:	Theologians, Preachers, Evangelists, Prophets	*Chronos* (Gr., "Interval Progression"; Columnar Principle)	Linen	Creative and Orthodox Uses of Language
Soul-Seraphic Traits:	Musicians, Youth Leaders	*Kairos* (Gr., "Boundless Instants"; Lateral Principle)	Wool	Effective Use of Hands
Soul-Cherubic Traits:	*Minchaw* Priests, Righteous Men	*Chronos* (Columnar Principle)		Keeping Oneself

Virgins Deliver From Evil Spirits

A virgin's face can deliver himself and others from possession by evil spirits, by virtue of Christian grace or of Toraic attainment. God the Father can reinstate a human male's virginity, by His angelic riches in Christ Jesus. Virgins who become monogamists never lose their spiritual virginity, and enjoy enhanced fundamental truth, authority, and power their entire lives—a huge competitive advantage. Spiritual warfare, involving sluts as honeypots or mata-hari's, acquires entirely new meaning in this high-stakes diplomatic battle of lifelong monogamous virginity. Satan and his slaves hatefully deride virgins as prudes, nerds, wimps, or wallflowers. He tries to intimidate, shame or entice us into promiscuity. He pressures virgins to mitigate to the promiscuous or otherwise foolish, as a plea for acceptance by their generation. Judge them consciously, or join them subconsciously. That the sights of virgins authentic faces can sometimes deliver from spirit possession, is the tertiary apostolic concept I acknowledge.

Human Spirit and The WORD of God

By the multiple-intelligences metatheory, animals are thought to have a soul but not a spirit. That is, an animal has a three-part soul, but lacks a crown herald and thus has no inner man or spirit. Hypothetically, a large fish has only a root cherub. Animals love Christ Jesus as the WORD, the Designer of all Creation, but it requires crowning human neocortices, family-nurtured ego, and a Born Again heart to love Adonai the Christ as the LORD Jesus Christ, God the Father's firstborn Son! Animals love the WORD of Yahweh, their Designer, but it takes a son or daughter to love Jesus Christ, God's Son, who obeyed His heavenly Father to the death.

The LORD Jesus Christ is to the conscientious inner man of the heart and mind, as The WORD is to heartbeats. Both are faces of God the Son. Adonai the WORD, the *Logos* of Yahweh who became Jesus of Nazareth, is the poetic eternal Soul of the Hebrew nation and of objective Western rationality.

The Angel of Yah, who was the preincarnate God the Son, is poetically the eternal Soul of the Jewish nation. From the Exodus plagues to the immaculate conception, He reigned as the LORD God of Israel over the Jews and Hebrews, then was born in the First Century as Jesus of Nazareth to reveal His Father to those who believe on Him.

MULTIPLE-INTELLIGENCES METATHEORY

Table 11.11: Psychoangelic Attributes:

	Contribution to Personality:	Ergonomic Substance:	Objective Qualities:	Symbolic Levitical Primary Color:
Heraldic-Orderic Traits:	Reason	Lights (Clarion)	Truth	Purple
Seraphic-Orderic Traits:	Zeal	Gasses, Liquids (as Flux)	Ardor, Affect	Blue
Cherubic-Orderic Traits:	Steadiness	Solids, Liquids (as Static)	Mathlike Internally-Consistent Reality	Scarlet [Antiphase: Yellow/Black]

Intelligent design is a theory explaining the existence of human beings. Intelligent design theorizes that God personally designed and created the world and started biological life using vast expanses of time. If intelligent design is a valid theory, perhaps the addition of a crown herald to biological creatures' heretofore three-part souls may possibly have been God's instrument of bestowing the light of conscience, of moral intellect, upon *man*. "For thou hast made him a little lower than the angels, and hast *crowned him with glory and honor.*" (Psalm 8:5, emphasis added)

If intelligent design may be true, as a theory of the universe's existence, it is remotely possible that Adam was the first created hominid bestowed by God with a crown herald. That Adam was thereby the first corporeal creature crowned with a conscience, a moral intellect, and an intelligent face. If the space-time continuum can be compressed, as Albert Einstein theorized, then geological processes may be of variable, not constant, rates, and the age of the earth may be unpredictable according to physical science.

Where children are, God looks, and where God looks, evil shrinks. The Bible belt in the southeastern United States is at the same latitude as the land of Israel. Possibly, God's elect angels access this planet above Israel, then follow the latitude westwardly against the rotation of the earth to the coasts of South Carolina, North Carolina and Georgia, then to points northward, southward and westward.

Balaam's donkey spoke to warn him, in Numbers 22:28. Did Adonai Elohim, the preincarnate Christ, suddenly apply a herald to the donkey's nervous system, to approximate intelligible speech? Animals are said to have a soul, but not a spirit. Tetrapartite psychology would say, Animals have neither a spirit nor a crown herald. The spirit of man, the dangerous-hearted inner man, depends upon a heart, mind and will in right relation to God the Father through cognitively-precise truths of Christ Jesus.

Adonai (God the Son) truly is one. Jesus of Nazareth's soul was whole and indivisible on the cross. His soul is symbolically portrayed by His seamless coat, for which the Roman soldiers cast lots rather than rip up. He is our ideal, as Christians (meaning 'little Christs'). In a sense, a psyche has integrity according to one's control of his tongue and attentiveness to conscience.

Table 11.12: Psychoangelic Attributes:

	Religious Focus:	*Aliyah-*Semblance:	Ecclessiology:	Psychological Orientation:
Heraldic-Orderic Traits:	Scripture and Speech about "YHWH" on Saturday Sabbaths, "Jesus Christ" on Sundays	Ascent	Reformation	Inner-Man Integrity
Seraphic-Orderic Traits:	Notable Sights, Purity of Zeal		Revival	Outer-Man Character
Cherubic-Orderic Traits:	Righteous Feet, Specie Metals, Lands, Biosphere	Descent		

Christ Jesus' psycho-unity, just as His coat was gambled for but not ripped into parts at the cross, is the meaning of *The Shema*: "The LORD our God is one LORD . . ." (Deut. 6:4) The body, soul, and personality of Adonai the Christ, God the Son, was, is, and will be indivisible.

Adonai the *Logos* was the preincarnate God the Son. "For there are three that bear record in heaven: the Father, the WORD, and the Holy Ghost, and these three are one." (I John 5:7, KJV) The LORD God of Israel, of the Old Testament, was the preincarnate God the Son, not all three persons of the Godhead. Knowledge of these was first widely dispensed to man's understanding during the First Century! (Matthew 3:13-17; Luke 3:21-22; John 1:32-34)

Human Factors

Kosher meats aren't sinful to eat, but meat inflames appetites. With inflamed appetites come exacerbated subdiaphragmic, earthy, lower-soul, root-cherubic traits— such as touch, group persona, loquacity, gluttony and survivalism. Men with a paunch should probably not eat much meat, especially not much red meat. Commercially-raised cattle are often fed estrogens to fatten them up, but xenoestrogens feminize men's hormones, contributing to many chronic diseases.

Ascetic self-control of suggestible root cherubic influences epitomize spirituality to many. We human beings tend to comfort ourselves either in clarion cognitive objectivity, or else in sensual contact with others or with food. Either in vision or in touch. Either in upright cognitive manhood or in engrossing cherubic themes. Either in orderly space or in satiated tactility. True manhood does not bow to reverence fallen cherubim, neither in petition, in idolatry or in fear, according to grace.

True manhood in Christ Jesus enjoys strength to transcend satanic idolatry, but the point is to serve the Father in heaven, not dissipatingly flail away at Satan's works! *"Vertus tentamine gaudet"* is Latin for "Strength rejoices in the challenge" (the motto of Hillsdale College). The word *college* is from the same root as 'colleague,' while *university* derives from the Latin *universitas*, meaning 'community.'

These two themes of personality (heraldic or cherubic) are inversely related, and typify the extreme somatypes of either ectomorphy or endomorphy.

Table 11.13: Psychoangelic Attributes:

	Opponent Management:	Quantitative Orientation:	Working Tongue:	Symbolic Tabernacle Metal:
Heraldic Orderic Traits:	Diplomacy	Base-Ten (10), Approaching Mathematical Infinity	Vernacular Denotation	Gold
Seraphic Orderic Traits:	Maneuver Warfare, Projectile Warfare	Two's (2), Fours (4; e.g, 4/4 Count Musical Tempo), Eights (8)	Koine Greek	Silver
Cherubic Orderic Traits:	Siege Warfare	Threes (3), Fives (5), Sevens (7), Twelves (12)	Hebrew	Bronze

Advice? In your imagination, don't let your mind take orders from the food you're digesting (L., *dis-*, apart from + *gerere*, to carry). Conform diet primarily to science and secondarily to naturalism. Cherubic roots shouldn't command the inner man, even as materials science did not invent logic.

Man is more than the sum of his parts. This holistic adage fits nicely with the tetrapartite-soul hypothesis of personality. Man-the-spirit is the inner man identified with his verbal transcript, sustained by his soul, as it breathes him and pumps his heartbeats. His four-part soul would sum his being to *five* (pentapartite). God the Holy Ghost in Believers would impart to the human being a synergizing *sixth* component spirit. The star of David is six-pointed. *Six is the number of man.* (Genesis 1:26-31, Revelation 13:18) A Born Again's grace thus embodies *holistic hexapartite integrity.* His grace-quickened, conscience-unified hexapartite *identity in Christ* is *more than the sum of his parts.* Regarding intelligence quotient (I.Q.), *nature* is to genes, spirituality and biosomatic mineral composition, as *nurture* is to education, environment and diet.

Born Again identity, the synergistic sum of his parts, is also his *personality,* his *sonship* to our Heavenly Father, and his potential someday *angel.* Such identity in Christ tends toward the gift of life, health, and freedom of soul. Hexapartite integrity moves toward true grace and holistic health of body, mind and spirit. If sustained by grace and unmarred by gross sin, hexapartite integrity may, by grace, endure all of one's biological life and be resumed in eternity. True Christians' biorhythms and hormones better balance, synergistically, because of Jesus' costly grace. Soul quickening in Twice Borns is a gift of God to a clean conscience, and imparts grace to become great, teach fluently, and do exploits, as long as one controls his tongue, obeys God and keeps the vessel of his body.

Sometimes society refers to a person with hexapartite integrity as 'a true individual,' but that would be optimistic. While man's sum is greater than his parts, created human personality can suffer division, if God wills him to endure trial. The word 'individual' may refer either (admiringly) to a pro-angelic, integrated, erstwhile son of God, or (sardonically) to a human personality reduced by divine judgment to the ego of only his beating, pumping heart. That is, to a personality reduced to essentials, to account for his inner man, naked before Y'howah Elohim's severe holy justice.

Table 11.14: Psychoangelic Attributes:

	Ontological Category:	Typic Vice:	Thematic Temptation:	Opposing Themes (Uplifting Heraldic versus Bruising Serapho-Cherubic):
Heraldic:	Civilization's True Essence	Perfidy	False Doctrine	Education
Seraphic:	Natural Kingdom	Appeals to Ecospirituality	Altered States of Consciousness (ASC's)	The Politics of Experience (R.D. Laing's term)
Cherubic:		Lechery for Lewdness	Pornonoia, Kunonoia	

Algebraically, *works* = f (power (authority (truth))). Leaders' coercing emulation from followers risks what C.I. Schofield identified as Nicolaitanism (Gr., *nikao-* (conquest) + *laos* (laity)). Forgiveness of sin, deliverance and sanctification result from true leadership. This truth points to our urgent need for Christ Jesus. From now until Christ's return, Believers will primarily either be ideally *exceptional* (via consistent faith, as for the Father) or habitually *submissive* (via identification with sin, as to The All). Both exceptionality and submission have their place, but Satan wants Twice Born leaders ashamed and submitted to him and his second heaven.

Most occult meditation, such as the emergent church's centering prayer, involves submission of a living soul's heart and crown herald to earthy fallen cherubim. Heraldry is the highest of the three created spiritual orders, and has a special relationship with God the Father. Submission of the mind (of the inner man) to fallen cherubim results in earthy personality traits, stinking thinking, perverse radicalism, disastrous decisions, and worse temptations. The inner man of the mind and heart ought not unconditionally submit to any but Christ Jesus and His truth. Limited authority merits limited submission.[20]

By the tetrapartite system of psychology, lower-soul correlated seraphic and cherubic spirituality administer authority by pressing human hearts' electrocardial rhythms to motivate or to evoke compliance. By contrast, nearest-to-God-the-Father, highest-order heralds administer authority by drawing students' attention to truth via semantics of bright-faced haloic clarion. Heralds intangibly, painlessly invite curiosity and evoke cooperation (L., *co-*, together + *operari*, work) from bright students. For lying or rebellion, removal of clarion darkens hearts. "For even though they knew God [in their youth], they did not honor him as God or give thanks, but they became futile in their speculations, and their foolish heart was darkened." (Romans 1:21, NASB) In heraldic administration of eager truth as precursor to authority, there is virtually no submission pressure, no 'pressing upon,' no 'sending below.' It's just 'Lift your brow and figure-it-out quickly, else have less clarion facial brightness.' Just 'Math it, or lose!' The results, from education, are conscience-lit personalities.

Upper-soul crown-heraldic obedience to truth says 'I will [or will not] allow you to teach me.' Mesopsychical seraphic submission says, 'I will [or will not] look where you look.' Lower-soul cherubic submission to authority says, 'I will [or will not] wait upon your purpose.' "And ye shall know the

Table 11.15: Psychoangelic Attributes:

	Character Component:	Approx. % Elect, per Order [2/3 of Angels Didn't Fall]:	Associated Somatype:	Conscientious Orientation:
Heralds: archangel Gabriel	Clinical	70%	Ectomorph	Relational Conscience, per the Spirit of the Law
Seraphim: archangel Michael	Vital	90%	Mesomorph	Ritual Conscience, per the letter of the Law
Cherubim: fallen-archangel Satan	Radical	40% (This invites siege for most radical-versus-radical spiritual warfare.)	Endomorph	

truth, and the truth shall make you free." (John 8:32) God created light [clarion] on the first day, and the stars on the fourth — Genesis 1:3, 14-18. Clarion cognitive light may have pre-existed starlight.

Elect heraldry's clarion clues about the Father in heaven elicit *freeing upward cognitive hope* and urge obedience to truth, in human personality. By contrast, submission to authority experiences organismic nature. Natural submission must allow for distinctions of erudite truth and ideals, or it ceases to represent the Father in heaven to the children of men.

Learning is of upper-soul personality, touched upon by the divine, while submission is a principle of lower-soul nature, easily temptable by The Liar (Satan). Clarion psychospatiality can fill man's space at the facial, the room, the domocilic and/or the regional scale.

Clinical, intellectually-astringent cognition constructs lofty thought processes within man's domain. Sinful, pungently-raunchy radicalism descends from clarion-conscientious loftiness. Psychological radicalism taken to extremes ceases to be orthodox. Psychoradicalism, in excess, falters from orthoradicality, because heraldry is a higher order than cheruby, and is more intrinsic to the inner man. Re philosophies of religion: any who vaunt psychoradicalism as a feature, not a flaw, in so doing descend from orthoradicality. The Lie in human hearts arises from extremes of visuo-emotional psychoradicalism.

Authority: Canon versus Tradition

The human tradition of submission to authority is to the hands and feet, as obedience is to the face and mind; the former pacifies, the latter invites. The two are not totally interchangeable. Submission to authority does not necessarily create the teachable moments and curiosity that are essential to learning. Urgent demands for submission may not be predicated upon mutual assent to topical truth. The only man to whom you owe unconditional submission is Christ Jesus.

In the LORD Jesus, nobody need suffer having his religion (his relationship with God) micromanaged by a third party, be it pope, rabbi, *imam*, or *guru*. Some submission to authority remains inevitable, because God the Father will not allow any creature to be His equal, nor any man to be the full coequal of Messiah Yeshua. Being submitted to authority is not

Table 11.16: Psychoangelic Attributes:

	Bloom's Taxonomy:	Luminosity:	Interpersonal Focal Objects:	Biophysics:
Heralds: archangel Gabriel	Cognitive Domain	Light	Facial Brightness (Clarion Light)	Cobalamin Metabolism
Seraphim: archangel Michael	Affective Domain		Glances	Electron Motility
Cherubim: fallen-archangel Satan	Psychomotor Domain	Heat	Stares, Frowns	Neutron Motility (Projectile-Invitation)

the same as "Submitting yourselves *one to another*, in the fear of God." (Ephesians 5:21, emphasis added) Marital submission is not military submission. Psychological submission is not political submission. There are distinctions.

One's face set in hope to go to Jerusalem (Luke 9:51) involves very different breathing patterns from one resignedly submitted to human authority. The former is more thoracic, the latter, more abdominal.

Messianic pastor Scott Brown said, "That which is not ministry is manipulation." And, that which is not conviction is compulsion. Charismatic power to depress another, to submit him against his understanding and will, does not necessarily impart truth to convict him.

Submission to authority is a tradition of men, an oral-law-generated human tradition. In terms of human psychology, it is an especially lower-soul principle: a particularly radical, lower-soul, outer-man seraphocherubic principle. Submission to authority is not always wrong, it is just something to be cautious about. Submission to Born Again religious authority should reflect a flatter organizational pyramid comprised of brethren, rather than a steeper pyramid consisting of numerous layers of officious functionaries.

Oliver Wendell Holmes stated, "A good catch phrase can stop thinking for fifty years." Rabbinic 'submission to authority' has stopped most fresh reasoning about the Messiahship of Jesus of Nazareth for centuries. Submission to good judgment offers much more promise than submission to authority. Why should anyone tolerate being conditioned to submit to archetypes or dogmas? To yield good judgment to hidebound prejudices?

Seen in its best light, submission to religious authority (e.g., rabbinic submission to authority) may emphasize spirituality and God's calling, over banality and confusion. As a principle of administration, submission to authority can preserve order. Religious authorities may care more for one's relationship with God than do one's familiars, than does one's nexus. However, submission to religious authority comprises a major stumbling block to the evangelism of orthodox Jews, who tend to reject even internally-consistent theological truths that lack specific authorization by some respected rabbi. Truths are to your heart, as facts are to your mind. Within civilization, line authority must be more clinical than radical.

Submission to religious demagoguery is not a pinnacle of virtue or true morality, but is a Pharisaic and Talmudic tradition of men. Submission to authority has a definite dark side, and can sometimes be a satanic principle. Many adults resign themselves to 'My inner man need not innovate beyond the leader I submit to,' and so perpetuate un-Christlike apathy, torpor and passivity, while spitefully suppressing genius and instant evangelism within their peers and juniors.

"But Jesus called them unto him and said, Ye know that the princes of the Gentiles exercise dominion over them, and *they that are great exercise authority upon them. But it shall not be so among you:* but whosoever will be great among you, let him be your minister; and whosoever will be chief among you, let him be your servant: even as the Son of man came not to be ministered unto, but to minister, and to give his life a ransom for many." (Matthew 20:25, emphasis added)

For example, the word *Islam* means "submission." Untold millions of people count themselves safe in eternity from their earthly submission to Allah, a moon god (probably a fallen cherub). For billions of people around the world, religious submission to creature authority is misperceived as blamelessness. But, Triune Yahweh requires a higher standard, beginnable only by a personal relationship with Christ Jesus and involving good stewardship of gifts. God the Father wants to know us via God the Son, not for our relationship with Him to be micromanaged by a third party, be it pope, *imam*, rabbi, or *guru*, or transacted by prideful works. Submission to a religious demagogue must not habitually quench the Holy Spirit. (I Thessalonians 5:19) A leader succeeds when his students exceed him.

Mystification of religion via an oral tradition amounts to job security for ambitious, blameworthy leaders. The antidote to obfuscative tradition? Evangelism, which is the spirit of prophecy! (Revelation 19:10)

As another example of coercion of the inner man, the Hindu caste system also insists upon submission to the religious authority generated by Hindus' belief in reincarnation. Souls incarned as Brahmins (supposedly for soul work in prior incarnations) are to be deferred to (even worshiped) by lower castes. Religious submission according to the Hindu caste system is one of the biggest problems facing modern Indian society. Who dares to lift his head above the caste of his birth, against the authority of Hinduism and its Brahmin priests? Rabindranath (Rabi) Maharaj, a Brahmin himself, found salvation in Jesus Christ and proceeded to show the way of soul freedom to thousands of seekers, including both students and Hindus.[21]

The human tradition of submission to authority points a psyche down, away from the celestial conscience it cedes to authorities, toward its abdomen, feet and root. Submission implies the lower soul as the trustworthy focus of the heart. But, the living soul's root cherub is of the lowest, most divided and least trustworthy of the three angelic orders. Gluttonous comfort eating would turn unwise theological and spiritual submission into character structure. Judaizing gravitates is adherents to radicalism, the remedy for which is clarion cognitive light. Canonic cognition, not submission, is the remedy for radicalism.

Submitting another Believing Born-Again adult should be done extremely deferentially (diplomatically), irrelevant of disparate giftings, as to a fully-coequal brother in Christ, else with temptation for one's soul and others to shame and despise him, perceiving him as contemptible. *Those who will not obey the truths of the Father in heaven will be made by Him to submit to authority*, despite that conscience is a higher principle than such submission to officials.

Cognitively-objective relationships comprise a different theme and mood than coercive lower-soul experiences. Heraldic administrations of authority affect the human soul differently from seraphocherubic administrations of authority. Learning and cognitive-relationships are fun.

Submissionism means, 'Whatever the problem, submission is the answer.' As effected in many adult organizations, submissionism is not fun, but is designed to weed out the weaklings, and to produce and run a tight ship. To illustrate this distinction: cadre's of earthy salarymen regard loyalty to the official [loosely, to the office-occupier] in charge as a higher virtue than the advancement of truth, than pure or applied research. Submission involves 'Deference to the judgment of another.' Submissionism (to the All) involves deferring one's conscientious intellect to crowd mentality and its representatives. Some adults grumble at one, if one fixes them with conscientious mind's-eye contact: face to face, head to head, man to man. Submissionism relates to chronic social-defeat stress.

Love of truth, by ultimate implication, relates to a love of Jesus and of His testimony, which conflicts with the world system. Authority is administered differently, between heraldic and seraphocherubic themes. Both types are

Diagram 11.17: Venn-Diagrammatic Model of the Human Intellect

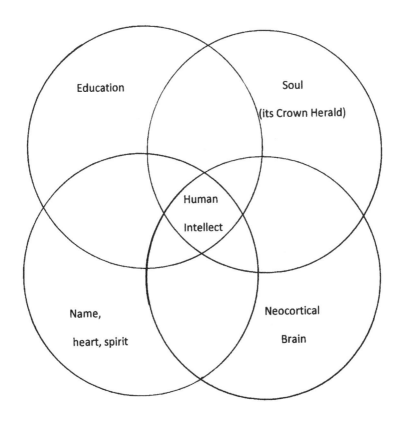

sometimes necessary, according to situation, but the heraldic theme is closer to God the Father's preference. Submissionism results in an earthy, rigid bellicosity bearing little in common with charitable, meek-hearted, inner-man-oriented evangelical Christianity. As Jewish missionary Lynn McCoy stated, "Some of those Messianic congregations don't care much for the inner man." Sad, but true. They emphasize seraphic and cherubic over heraldic themes of authority, via seraphic ardor.

God quickens teaching ministries more than He does submission agendas. Teaching reasons, *eureka's* and gestures apace with crown-heraldic clarion cognitive light; submission ponders at the momentum of the abdomen and radical emotions. Ministry versus manipulation. Evangelism versus empty pageantry. *Education by teachable moments is a higher outcome than submission to authority, should the two conflict.*

God the Father harbors some love for boys who cultivate games of heraldic-style diplomacy (e.g., homiletics and debate) and seraphic-style maneuver-projectile warfare (e.g., chess, football, tennis, archery, riflery), to demonstrate resilience against the siege-warfare principle latent in radical, cherubic-intensive, occasionally-pederastic adult society.

In stressful romish regions, thayraic beast spirituality tempts leaderless boys and childless adults to dwell in thought more upon columnar than lateral properties. Examples of personalities' columnar themes bordering on the pathological include materialism, profane banter, and one's table becoming a snare. (Psalms 69:22)

In Revelation 17:4, the woman that rides the red-colored beast is herself arrayed in purple and scarlet. The Biblical omission of the color blue symbolizes the minimal involvement of Michael's seraphim in support of the Vaticanic harlot church and her propagation of Babylonian mystery religion, ecumenically devoting her body to strange suitors of occult spirituality, instead of to the church's true Husband, who will return to earth as Yeshua haMashiach. The woman riding the beast symbolizes Ashtoreth, queen of heaven, masquerading as the Virgin 'Mary' while the Vatican interacts with the satanic spirituality of the United Nations and its looming one-world government.

Columnar-Lateral Distinctions

Binary allegiance, either to Triune Yahweh or to Satan, synergizes local, regional, national and continental psychospatiality, vitality and strength, from faith associated with real estate owners. This is through reaching seraphim motivated by lofty heralds ("thrones"), cooperating high above material-reality-based cherubim. A herald vertically aligned in the atmosphere above a cherub, resembles a column. (See Diagram 11.2) Hence the term 'columnar principle', in effect melding thronocherubic themes. Macrocosmic columnar pneumo-atmospherics is the principle behind both the expansion of civilization and spread of urban squalor, depending upon residents' literacy, publication content, zeal for Christ, and holiness.

Elect heralds "throne" in reality-cognizant books. Elect seraphim thrill at holy speech and stirring song, resulting in wholesome heartsongs, healing sentiments, and anabolic hormones. Elect cherubim rest upon godly-administered land, within gold, and at righteous feet. Lofty ectomorphs depend upon metalloenzymatic refinement more than do radical jovial endomorphs. Ectomorphs resemble priestly flax more than soldierly wool, in this regard.

Per the multiple-intelligences metatheory, with comparisons to Christ Jesus' *Tau* cross, *columnar theme* alludes, to a stake-like crown-throne superposition above a root–cherubic base. Tetrapartite psych's *lateral theme*, relative to the Cross, alludes to crosspiece-like seraphic-related horizontal psychospiritual influences (e.g., reaching, heartsong-rich aerobic and melodious properties).

Radical Materiality

"The silver is mine, and the gold is mine, saith the LORD of hosts." (Haggai 2:8) Silver and gold are intrinsically valuable as tangible earthy reminders of the narrowly-true, set-apart holiness of Y'howah, within a society arrogantly straying theologically, economically and politically farther and farther from His conditional favor. Gold, stewarded, is like land owned; silver stewarded is like springs of water on that land. Physical silver and gold in one's possession objectify ground-level first-aid to human-sin-wounded elect seraphim and cherubim. To reassure His Babylon-submitted people, the LORD God of Israel (en route to becoming the glorified Christ Jesus) said, "For brass I will bring gold, and for iron I will bring silver . . ." (Isaiah 60:17)

313

Protestant exceptionalism resulted from Triune Yahweh's highly-conditional narrowly-true love for men's consciences, and made the United States great. Elect cherubim flock to physical gold on sabbaths, for heraldic reminders of the intellect of God the Father, who listens through them and dispenses grace to humans in proximal space. Seraphim, to silver. A mass of silver is to a spring of water, as a mass of gold is to ownership of the land surrounding that water source, and as Bible knowledge, applied and taught, is to a mansion built upon that land.

Interestingly, Yah, the preincarnate Jesus, didn't claim copper in Haggai 2:8. With silver and gold, copper would fill the periodic table's chemical column and imply a natural completion, if it yet applied to the cherubic order and its fallen created archangel, Satan.

Copper is in the same column of chemistry's periodic table as silver and gold, the two metals which are claimed by Adonai the Christ in Haggai 2:8. But, Satan can occasionally produce strange psychical effects in and upon copper. Did God, knowing that, deviate from the naturally expectable by making bronze the third Mosaic tabernacle metal? The LORD God of Israel not claiming copper as His in Haggai 2:8, may be symbolic of His rejecting fallen Satan! The New King James Version Bible lists bronze as the third temple metal, and the Authorized King James Version lists brass, but the Jewish Publication Society's TaNaK (Old Testament) translates that word as copper. Only one metal of the three can be true in this context.

The Hebrew word used here is *nechosheth*, Strong's number 5178, translated "brazen, brass, copper." Copper, with Haggai 2:8's silver and gold, would complete the column of chemistry's periodic table, and would superficially seem to fit the logic of creation better than would bronze or brass. Unless *El Shaddai*, the preincarnate Jesus, preferred bronze to copper for use in the tabernacle of the congregation, perhaps due to copper's natural utility for Satan in effecting aberrant psychical phenomena or occult miracles. Copper would have been easier to standardize than bronze (copper alloyed with tin) or brass (copper alloyed with zinc), and for ancient Hebrews to smelt from raw ore. Brass silences magnetic resonance in carrier fields passing through it, while copper does not. Pure copper adds its own frequency to the carrier field.

Theoretically, bronze was indeed the third temple metal, as the NKJV declares, and neither pure copper nor brass was it. Ancient civilizations used bronze more widely than they did brass, which was not invented until much later in history. Bronze is a nobler metal than brass or copper. Bronze is a heavier, harder, more corrosion-resistant metal, and has a higher melting point, than copper or brass.

Corroboratively, in the Smithsonian Institution's Natural History Museum in Washington, DC, there is a huge native copper boulder, from the Great Lakes region of the United States, which was believed by ancient Native-American Indians to be imbued with shamanistic powers. This fact implies the theoretical connection between copper, psychical effects or occult miracles, and fallen cherubim.

University towns are to heraldry, as coastal or riverine settlements are to seraphim, and as lands atop limestone bedrock are to elect cherubim: these terrain favor them. Silver and gold specie metals represent the intersection between theology and economics. Tithing constitutes a second such intersection.

Jesus of Nazareth's feet are described as like "fine brass," in Revelation 1:15 and 2:18. The Greek word used there for "brass" is *chalkolibanon.* Why brass?

Hypothetically, elect cherubim (such as a soul's cherub) need not penetrate down (or look) lower than bedded limestone or sheet brass placed horizontal to the earth's surface, thus parrying discouragement from subterranean spiritual darkness.

Tetrapartite-Psych Metatheory and Bloom's Taxonomy

Pedagogy instructs using Bloom's taxonomy, which is comprised of the cognitive domain, the affective domain, and the psychomotor domain. Multiple-intelligences metatheory (tetrapartite psychology) meshes with Benjamin Bloom's pedagogical taxonomy as follows. Clarion-conscientious intellect, from heraldic spirituality, is *de rigeur* in cognitive-domain heuristics (i.e., decision making). Forehandedness in music, art, and sports, from seraphic spirituality, can boost affective-domain heuristics. And, Toraic orthoradicality assures soul-cherubic power to assist psychomotor-domain behavioral algorithms and intuitive assay of materials walked upon. Most relationships should usually emphasize the cognitive domain more than the affective, and the affective domain more than the psychomotor.

Competing Models, Recapitulated

Ayn Rand, whom we mentioned at the beginning of this chapter, was a twentieth-century secular novelist. She wrote descriptively of human spirit in the context of structural steel, tooled granite, electrical copper, monetary gold, professional engineering, iconoclastic architecture and Aristotelian logic, and thereby won vast credibility with her readers. Ayn Rand's idealistic cerebral protagonists appeal to bright-faced readers' instinctual *noblesse oblige* (Fr., nobility obligates). Heralds have a special relationship with God the Father. True *noblesse oblige* propagates, in civilization, from the love of God the Father toward innocence.

Ayn Rand sensed the cruciality to mankind of clarion objectivity. But, Rand failed to grasp that clarion objectivity is imparted to Western man, via elect heraldry, by the *Logos* of Yahweh: the LORD Jesus Christ.

Rand's materials- and ego-oriented characterizations revealed her refined Jewish sensitivity to principles of human souls' radicality, implying her extensive ancestral Toraic righteousness. Her plots involved tensions between heroic individuality and toxic-group codependency.

Ayn Rand's appeal as a novelist and philosopher stemmed from her intriguing tenet that clarion intellect can, with authority born of native intelligence, analyze and dominate physical and human nature. Intellect does analyze, synthesize and evaluate universal reality, but occult spirituality within nature scoffs at (and tempts) human hearts and intellect, outside of passionate orthodox faith in the LORD Jesus Christ. Rand derided occultism through Ivy Starnes, an antagonist to heroine Dagny Taggart in *Atlas Shrugged*, her longest novel.

Novelist-philosopher Ayn Rand made copper telephone wire, not silver objects such as coins or finery, the focal literary device beginning her longest novel, *Atlas Shrugged*. Copper has special significance to fallen cherubim. Rand's fascination with metals and intellectual purity may have been a reaction to widespread low-grade lead toxicity from leaded gasoline, during the twentieth century.

Philosopher Ayn Rand was a talented writer, but a morally-corrupt pedagogue[22] and an influential rebel against the *Logos* of Yahweh. Rand's un-Belief and immorality cut her off from the noble Vine and sap of the *Logos*.

Ayn Rand lauded facial purity in her powerful protagonists. She half understood the problem: *virgins' faces* can deliver from evil-spirit possession. Rand unfortunately opposed this eternal truth by extolling the philosophy of fornication and adultery.

During most of her prominent years, Ayn Rand participated in an adulterous affair with her primary and most prolific disciple, twenty-five-year-younger Nathaniel Branden, despite that she and he were each simultaneously married to another person (to Frank O'Connor and Barbara Branden, respectively).[23]

However, on the trail of something, Ayn Rand identified *social metaphysics* as the spirit of toxic-group codependency. By social metaphysics, Rand meant a soul and mindset seeking personal meaning and worth from complacent earthiness-exalting groups. That is, from radical anti-idealistic conclaves.

Submission to narcissistic self-servingly connotative groups has pressured bright youth from time immemorial. Youth ask, 'Certainly there is more to life than toil, eating and sleep?' A nexus would retort, 'Don't disturb our connotative self-absorbed *status quo.*'

Scottish psychiatrist R.D. Laing, a medical doctor of psychiatry and anti-establishment poet[24] in the 1960's and 1970's, paralleled Ayn Rand's thinking regarding codependent social groups. He identified them with the term *nexus* (L., knot). Laing defined a nexus as "characterized by enduring and intensive face-to-face reciprocal influence on each other's experience and behavior."[25] In essence, a nexus consists of a group gravitating together for sensuality, for radicality, for "the flesh," or for lawlessness.

Classically, a nexus is a family group that commences to carbohydrate-binge (or booze, or smoke, or change the subject, or stare its juniors and zealots down), to stoke torpid psychocherubic radicality. Stereotypically, toxic relationships resort to that if their members become angry at each others' lawlessness, or compromises of conscience or grace. That, instead of charitably, courageously calling one another to face up and repent. In-denial adult nexi can be especially cruel to bright children. Nexus abusiveness roughly equates to enabling of codependence. Stoking psychocherubic radicality aggravates earthy tendencies that impinge on the human heart, to edge Christ Jesus out and Satan in.

Nexus metaphysics, to combine the two related ideas, is a real, enormous spiritual, psychological and theological problem, that tends toward mostly-fallen cherubic radicalism. However, it is insoluble by atheistic philosophy or psychiatry. Factors in nexus metaphysics include the cherubic nature of souls' roots, the Fall of creation, human weaknesses, stress of guilt, habitual ruts, earthy formulism, sympathy-gluttony, submission to corrupt authority, theological sin, and the vanities of groupthink.

Nexus formation can be called 'nexation.' 'To nexate' is to gravitate toward groupthink. Defaultive nexation means to submit to the herd and its implosive radicalism, via apathy or perplexity. Nexation proliferates from desire for a Mr. Big to supply cradle-to-grave satiation. A heart seduced by root desires tends to submit to narcissistic sensuality and to groupthink.

Nexus diabolophilia and social metaphysics represent a far vaster problem than secular philosophy and atheistic psychiatry can admit. Social metaphysics affects humanity directly from The Fall of creation, when created-archcherub Satan rebelled against Jesus Christ's Triune Y'howah Elohim.

In athletics, the team that sets the tempo usually wins the game. Tempo of nexation intensifies with lies, carbohydrate-binging, drunkenness, profanity, fornication, occultism, altered states of consciousness, kunonoia, and the Mass. Tempo of nexation abates with true religion, straight personality, distance running, fasting, chelating, personal freedom (such as wise gun ownership), travelling, interaction with children, and lofty habitations (such as in upper stories or atop limestone bedrock). Postural nexation means character structure, muscle tension, and breathing patterns that emphasize reassuring emotionality over cognitive intelligence. Postural nexation can result from occluded cardiospatiality, spirit possession, gluttony, or an elevated toxic metal tare.

Subsequently, the controlling, torpid, self-servingly connotative earthiness Ayn Rand vilified as social metaphysics results from radical or even satanic influences against human psyches. Such influences are exponentially compounded by sexual immorality, oral addictions, and excess sensuality. The permanent antidote to the spiritual root of nexus metaphysics can only be found in Yahweh's *Logos*, who is Yeshua haNotzri (Heb., Jesus of Nazareth).

Laing's nexus psychiatry and Rand's objectivist philosophy strove to understand the larger more-dreadful subject of diabolophilic (demon loving) human personalities, but in merely atheistically scientific terms. *Objectivism's analysis of social metaphysics is extremely naive, compared to the enormity of the true evil addressed by systematic theology.*

Stable, formulaic, left-brained orthodox intellect often characterizes establishment, at expense to the spirit of truth and to creativity. Adults often resent youths' precocious intelligence which destabilizes their groups' self-serving connotations, and in retaliation demand creative youths submit to the adults' self-serving prideful connotative *status quo*. How to explain this facet of reality?

The athletic team that sets a game's tempo usually wins the contest. In human organizations, tempos are often set by gluttonous emotional satiety and sedentary stasis. Per Diagram 11.2, such a throno-cherubic "columnar" psychological theme, if out of synch with the mind of Yahweh the Father, diminishes soul-seraphic ardor of the "lateral" psychological theme, possibly causing electrocardial rhythm problems. Disgruntled psychoradicality, stifling intellectualism and phlegmatic character structure tend to result.

Social metaphysics intersects with theological evil at fallen cherubic influences upon the soul. Satan is the created archcherub whose rebellion against Elohim constituted the Fall of creation. He is wicked and diabolical, a murderer and a liar. He probably has a numerical advantage of fallen cherubim. The word *Satan* comes from the Hebrew *ha satan*, meaning 'the Enemy.'

The unspoken creed of Satan-influenced nexus metaphysics, of its component human spirits and their bitter, panicky souls, is often 'You *will* rebel with us against the *Logos* of Yahweh, or else forcibly submit to our agenda!' Codependency, child neglect, diabolophilia and all sorts of lies flourish by such illogic. Man's submission to or fear of Satan does not appease him. Only men's worse and worse sin appeases Satan, but that results in men's destruction.

Yeshua of Nazareth likened the satiated envious religious hypocrites of His day to a brood of vipers (Matthew 12:34 and 23:33, NIV). He discerned them coiled around each other, narcissistically sycophantically flattering each other's radicalism, earthiness, mitigation and arrogance. He deplored the scribes' and Pharisees' self-oppositional denying of the logical truths He presented to them, as they denied the reality of His Messiah-hood and led the people astray.

Yeshua of Nazareth, the Fountainhead of hope and the eternal poetic Soul of Jewish and Western rationality, offered Jewish leaders victory over Satan, the Tempter of their souls, but they were rapt upon political autonomy from Rome and refused His offer, ungratefully crucifying Him in the process.

Without Messiah Yeshua's grace and truth, submission to the connotation-intensive old-boy paradigm characterizing social metaphysics is fairly common. Very bright young people can plummet to nexus metaphysics, if they stain their souls with the Vile 3 (fornication, occultism, or drug abuse). Adults descend toward it, too, merely for verbally denying the identity of the true Messiah.

Satan, a cherub, is called the god of this world for a reason. He probably thinks most-easily in binary logic, and in terms of material substances: the chemical atoms, ions and molecules composing massive physical reality and the roots holding onto it. According to God's grace, Satan has no authority over the biological body, spiritual heart, or living soul of a sanctified Believer in Jesus Christ. Within the realm of empirical reality, silver, gold and Twice Borns' bodies uniquely belong to Adonai Yeshua. (Haggai 2:8, I Corinthians 6:19) Our bodies are not United Nations' property, to be covenanted via a VeriChip to one-world government or its god, or Vatican-endorsed New Age religion.

Social metaphysics is endemic and will proliferate upon earth under the occultism, politics and sexual ethics condoned by the United Nations. Outdistancing social metaphysics is ultimately impossible without grace and truth in the LORD Jesus. The only vaccination against nexus metaphysics comes from the grace and truth found in Triune Yahweh. The younger one meets Jesus, the better.

Seeking to avoid cabal-like radical dominance, Ayn Rand's objectivism strayed into meritocratic gnosticism. *Meritocratic* as in earned by lofty atheistic ideals, *gnostic* as in condemnation of earthiness as intrinsically sinful except for remediation by secret knowledge and mental discipline. Categoric rejection of soul-cherubic roots falls into gnostic futility, since each living soul is positively rooted into some earthiness by its cherub!

A chaste root innocent of radical fornication may be earthy without being evil, and indeed may become commendable in establishment. *Refined metals and chemical elements represent purified earthiness, symbolically devoid of incursion or confusion.* In Haggai 2:8, Adonai Elohim (the preincarnate Jesus of Nazareth) chose silver and gold out of all the dust of the earth as His, to radically symbolize His refined majesty.

A better hope for the soul and root is sanctification (through faith in Yeshua's atonement, borne out by Toraic earned righteousness) and metalloenzymatic refinement of one's fleshly body (through chelation and orthomolecular nutrition). These help *Eloheynu ha Shiloosh haKodesh* (idiomatic Heb., 'our God the Holy Trio') separate us from undue earthiness and spiritual confusion.

Materials purity, such as described by Ayn Rand, is of special significance to cherubim, which are the lowest, earthiest, most-divided, and most mnemonic-, gold-, and Toraic-righteousness-oriented of the three orders of angels. Cognition of materials purity invites Yeshua the *Logos'* justice and empiricism upon reality. This is especially true with heirloom silver and gold, but not with copper.

Ayn Rand confused the fruit of virtuous noble appearances with the seeds of righteousness and rectitude which cause it. Such righteousness may be Christian (via faith in Jesus of Nazareth), or Toraic (via punctilious human righteousness). *Overwhelmingly, God can be satisfied by faith in Jesus and His perfect righteousness, although we creatures continue to reap what we sow.*

Rand's confusion of cause-and-effect was evidenced throughout her several novels. Her protagonists excelled in ideals, intelligence, strength and egoism, but woefully lacked even basic sexual morality. *A formidable intellect that is not nobly rooted in chastity is a futile hope against nexus metaphysics and its spirituality. Integral psychic membranes and chastity relate positively to each other.*

Ayn Rand erroneously believed that morality must be first to oneself. The eternal truth, however, is that *one may be ethical to oneself, if one is first moral to Triune Yahweh.* Objectivism failed theologically by its atheism. It failed at its root by Rand's and Branden's sexual immorality, which filtered into her philosophy and writing. Objectivism is interesting for its encouragement to transcend nexus metaphysics, to apply creativity to real life, and to mature beyond honor-oblivious group cohesion sustained by self-serving connotation and spiteful mediocrity. Nevertheless, objectivism is a theologically and psychologically false system.

How do nexus theory and social metaphysics fit with the Bible and systematic theology? The primary tension in the Bible is between Y'howah Elohim and sinners. The secondary tension is between Jesus of Nazareth and the scribes and Pharisees, with their pre-Talmudic oral tradition. The tertiary tension is between the apostle Paul and Judaizers. And, the quartenary tension is between children of God and root-cherub-dominated, narcissistically-proud, tradition-submitted radicals. Radical traditionalists are most susceptible to nexus metaphysics via root-cherubic principles influenced by Satan, and make veneration of group identity into the price for respectability. While not a major Biblical theme, narcissistic earthiness, gluttony and groupthink predispose a person to group complacency, intellectual connotation and un-leaderlike strategic decisions. David imprecated his enemies with, "Let their table become a snare . . ." (Psalm 69:22) The LORD God of Israel said of group ethics, "Do not join a crowd that intends to do evil. When you are on the witness stand, do not be swayed in your testimony by the opinion of the majority." (Exodus 23:2, NLT) *Ad populum* does not justify anyone, although it may temporarily authorize demagogues.

If there is a grain of truth to objectivist philosophy's and nexus psychiatry's objections to back-biting mediocrity-enforcing group personalities, it is that earthiness' larger cherubic content makes earthy traditionalists prone to error, diabolophilia, and bitter envy. Nexus psychology is notoriously procrastinative, while the LORD God of Israel expects instant obedience to the truth of His Father. Nexi are often defensively left-brained, money-oriented, and normative within un-Saved society. Submission to a nexus can hinder authentic conscientious answers to God's calling. Nexus identification invokes the politics of experience, whereby the world, the flesh and the devil encroach upon the domain of the inner man, mostly via his fellows. All paths other than clarion Christianity ultimately gravitate to hierarchic psychocherubic radicalism and its nexus metaphysics.

Summary

How to prevent falling into the clutches of nexus metaphysicians? Listen to and obey your conscience. How to get out, if you're trapped in a nexus?

Hear the Gospel preached, and seek the face of Jesus in assemblies naming Him. Pray. Evangelize. Confess. Diet. Chelate. Work out. What's on the other side of the thin edge? Triune Yahweh is, if you truly believe on Jesus. If you don't believe and live in sin, Satan is on the other side of the thin edge. If you ignore your conscience for truth, you'll sooner or later find yourself submitting to more-or-less-corrupt authority. Don't become indignant at consequences of sins: meekly repent and seek forgiveness, as many times as necessary. Give God at least as many years to heal you as you took to ruin your life.

Defeatism does not accomplish God the Father's will for Christians and Believing Jews. If we despair at the increase of Satan's global governance, we will be tempted to waver in confrontations with sinners. And, in wavering, fail to speak the truth with charity or even seem to condone their sin. " . . . Every idle word that men shall speak, they shall give account thereof in the day of judgment." (Matthew 12:36)

Chapter 11 notes:

[1] John Ankerberg and John Wheldon. *Encyclopedia of New Age Beliefs*. Eugene, OR: Harvest House, 1996, 35-37.

[2] Spiro Zodhiates. *The Hebrew-Greek Key Word Study Bible*. Chattanooga, TN: AMG Publishers, 2008, 1923.

[3] Henrik Lorenz. *Ancient Theories of Soul*. *www.plato.stanford.edu/entries/ancient-soul*. August 28, 2010.

[4] *Ibid*.

[5] *Ibid*.

[6] Millard J. Erickson. *Christian Theology, 2nd Ed*. Grand Rapids: Baker, 1998, 459-467.

[7] Louis Berkhof. *Systematic Theology*. Grand Rapids: Eerdman's, 1996, 141.

[8] *Ibid*.

[9] William Dwight Whitney and Benjamin E. Smith. *The Century Dictionary: An Encyclopedic Lexicon of the English Language, Revised and Enlarged*. New York: The Century Co., 1914, 1028.

[10] J.A. Wylie. *The History of Protestantism, Vol. II: Calvin's Death and Burial*. New York: Cassel, Potter and Galpin, 1878, 369.

[11] Hara Estroff Marano. "Personality Q/A: Maverick Messenger." *Psychology Today*, August 2010, 30.

[12] Dan Hurley. "Your Backup Brain." *Psychology Today*. December 2011, 44, 6, 83.

[13] *Ibid*.

14 *Ibid*, 85.

15 *Ibid*, 83.

16 *Ibid*.

17 *Ibid*, 86.

18 *Ibid*.

19 John Eldredge. *Wild at Heart*. Nashville: Thomas Nelson, 2001, 151.

20 Tim Baldwin and Chuck Baldwin. *Romans 13: The True Meaning of Submission, 2nd Ed*. Kalispell, MT: Liberty Defense League, 2011, 56.

21 Rabindranath Maharaj. *Death of a Guru*. Eugene: Harvest House, 1984.

22 Barbara Branden. *The Passion of Ayn Rand*. Garden City: Doubleday, 1986, 256-265.

23 *Ibid*, 272-280.

24 R.D. Laing. *Knots*. New York: Vintage, 1970.

25 R.D. Laing and A. Esterson. *Sanity, Madness and the Family*. Baltimore, MD: Penguin, 1970, 21.

Chapter 12

Invocation of Faith

For more facts on the global governance movement, as of winter, 2013, surf the 'Net to:

- *www.garykah.org*. High-level Christian reporting on, and analysis of, globocratic pantheism and New Age religion and politics.
- *www.redmoonrising.com*. Re: theosophy, globalism.
- *www.discerningtoday.org*. Re: radical environmentalism, deep ecology, pantheism.
- *www.PositiveIDCorp.com*. Implantable subcutaneous RFID microchips, identical with or similar to the VeriChip, can anchor a one-world government's computerized population management system.
- *www.AE911Truth.org*. Architects and Engineers for 9/11 Truth. "And ye shall know the truth, and the truth shall make you free." (John 8:32) Truth heals.

For more about Messianic congregationalists, their testimonies, their beliefs, their practices, and related issues and items of interest, click on:

- *www.Jews-for-Jesus.org*. Jewish evangelists
- *www.Messianicmusic.com*. Hub for Messianic music.
- *www.sidroth.org*. Messianic Vision.

To shop online for Messianic worship music, Judaica, literature, click on:

- *www.store.Jews-for-Jesus.org*
- *www.messiah.net*

By believing in your heart and professing with your mouth, you can resume life free as an eagle!

"All that the Father giveth me shall come to me; and him that cometh to me I will in no wise cast out," John 6:37.

"If the Son therefore shall make you free, ye shall be free indeed," John 8:36.

Holy Y'howah is to Krishna, Buddha, Shiva, 'Mary' and Allah, as Creator is to creature. Christ Jesus' YHWH Elohim is the Creator. Those others are rebellious creature spirits.

Yeshua of Nazareth is *Elohim haBeyn*, Adonai the Christ, and preincarnately the holy LORD God of Israel. He is a virgin, Hebrew male with a distinct personality and a temper. Jesus is the only true Messiah. He is capable of savage righteous indignation and may reply to fools in their folly, but His Father in heaven is very, very earnest: in Him is neither darkness nor confusion.

Normatively, between the Exodus plagues and the immaculate conception, the LORD God of Israel was the preincarnate God the Son, who became the resurrected glorified Christ Jesus. The LORD God of Israel as the resurrected Jesus Christ reigns with His Father and Holy Ghost over each who believes.

Seeker, if you want forgiveness of your errors, a transformed life and salvation from eternity in Hell, then:

1. *Research*, to see if you may believe in your heart that Jesus of Nazareth is the true Christ or Messiah, Yahweh born flesh, and that God raised him from the dead.

2. Address our heavenly Father, in the name of Yeshua of Nazareth, just as you would talk to a person in the same room with you.

3. If you can be sincere, tell Him you are sorry for your sins, and why, and what you were thinking about when you made your decisions to sin.

4. *Ask* Him to forgive you your sins on the basis of Jesus' atoning blood.

5. Tell him that you accept His unspeakable gift of salvation, of Messiah Yeshua.

6. Ask God the Father to place His Holy Spirit (Heb., *Ruakh haKodesh*) in your heart, while you resolve to let Him speak through you—He is better than you can imagine!

7. *Thank Him in advance* that you are newly justified, by grace through faith, and are now resurrectable.

8. Get hold of a Bible, read it, memorize from it, believe it. The Bible contains the most trustworthy intellectual truth about God. Control you tongue.

9. Express your faith by observing the Moral Law while loving Yeshua God's Son, and your neighbor as yourself.

10. Unburden your conscience (confess your sins) to God before a trustworthy pastor, then undergo water baptism (a once-in-an-eternity embarkation) in the name of the Father, the Son, and the Holy Ghost (Heb., *B'Shem ha Av, ha Beyn, v'ha Ruakh haKodesh*).

11. Destroy all occult books and objects, and pornographic photographs, videos and writings, in your possession, and resolutely desist from all occult practices, drug abuse and illicit lust.

12. Fellowship with fellow Born Again Believers, call unto them for intercessory prayer as needed: "The effectual, fervent prayer of a righteous man availeth much." (James 5:16)

13. Now that you are justified and resurrectable, give God at least as many years to heal your life as you took to mess it up. He will faithfully transform you, then glorify Himself through you, through the new wine of His Holy Spirit.

14. Rejoice to say with us, "Blessed is Jesus of Nazareth, who comes in the name of Y'howah!"

Maybe you say to me, "How do you know that if I lovingly believe in my heart that Jesus is Elohim the Son, that I'll be eternally saved?" There is a sequence of Bible verses known as "the Romans Road" that clearly spell out the Biblical plan of salvation:

1. Romans 3:23—"For all have sinned and come short of the glory of God."

2. Romans 5:8—"But God commendeth his love toward us, in that, while we were yet sinners, Christ died for us."

3. Romans 6:23—"For the wages of sin is death; but the gift of God is eternal life through Jesus Christ our LORD."

4. Romans 10:9,10—"That if thou shalt confess with thy mouth the LORD Jesus, and shalt believe in thine heart that God hath raised him from the dead, thou shalt be saved. For with the heart man believeth unto righteousness; and with the mouth confession is made unto salvation."

5. Romans 10:13—"For whosoever shall call upon the name of the LORD [Jesus-YHWH] shall be saved."

Baruch ata Adonai-i-i, Eloheynu Melech haOlam, ki Elohim haBeyn va Yeshua haNotzri-i. A-a-men! (Heb., "Blessed art Thou, LORD our God, King of the Universe, who art God the Son and Jesus of Nazareth. *A-a-men!*")

Baruch ha Shem Yehoshuah Moshieynu, baruch ha Shem Adonai! (Heb., "Bless the name of JESUS our Messiah, bless the name of Y'howah the Son!")

Baruch ha Shiloosh ha Kodesh, ayn melech aval Yehoshuah Moshieynu! ("Bless the Holy Trinity, none king but JESUS our Messiah!")

When we can say "Christ Jesus has returned! Messiah Yeshua has come back in the name of Y'howah!", it will be like all of the Christian and Jewish holidays, all of the snow days, all of the high days, and all of the summer vacations that students worldwide throughout history have ever exulted in, combined into a holy Today, week upon authentic week, for one-thousand glorious years!

Appendix

Cogent Diagrams

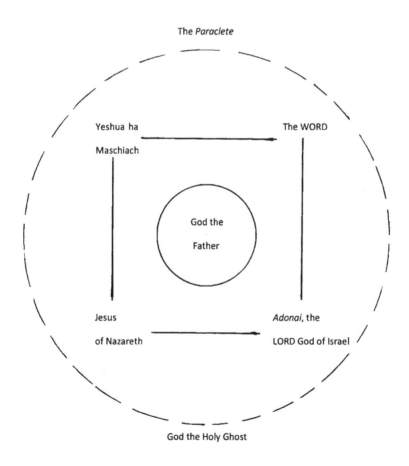

The *Paraclete*

Yeshua ha Maschiach

The WORD

God the Father

Jesus of Nazareth

Adonai, the LORD God of Israel

God the Holy Ghost

"I am the way, the truth and the life: no man cometh unto the Father, but by me." (John 14:6)

Schematic A.1: Triune YHWH and Four Personas of the WORD.

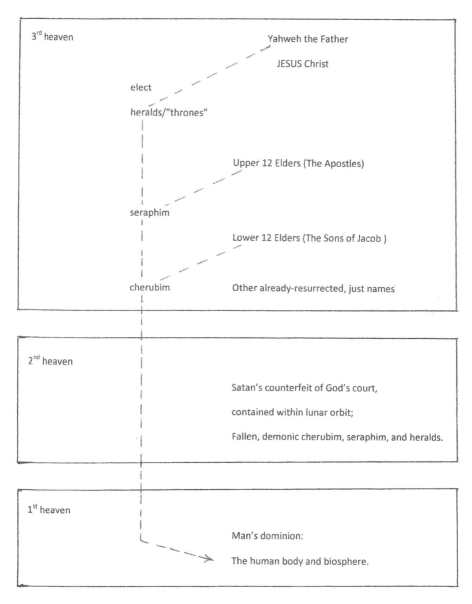

Schematic A.2: Model Diagram of the 3 Heavens.

Glossary of Neologisms

androcardia (n.)   (Gr., *andro-* (man) + *kardia* (heart))

cardiorizoic (adj.)   (Gr., *kardia-* (man's four-chambered heart) + *rizo* (root))

cardiospatiality (n)   (Gr., *kardia-* (heart) + L., *spatium* (space))

cardiostephanic (adj.)   (Gr., *kardia-* (man's four-chambered heart) + *stephanos* (crown))

chirovitality (n.)   (Gr., *chiro-* (hand) + *vital* (power to survive))

diabolophilia (n.)   (Gr., *diabolo-* (demon) + *philia* (friendship))

diabolophobia (n.)   (Gr., *diabolo-* (demon) + *phobos* (fear))

doulonoia (n.)   (Gr., *doulo-* (slave) + *noia* (mind))

ekergy (n.)   (Gr., *ek-* (outward) + *ergos* (work))

ethnopraxy (n.)   (Gr., *ethno-* (race or nation) + *praxis* (actions))

kunophile (n.)   (Gr., *kuno-* (sodomite) + *phile* (lover))

kunonoia (n.)   (Gr., *kuno-* (homosexual) + *nous* (mind))

(to) nexate (v.)   (L. *nexus* (knot))

ono-occlusion (n.)   (Gr., *ono-* (name) + *occlusion* (L., oc- (before) + *claudere* (shut, close)))

orthoradical (adj.)   (Gr., *ortho-* (straight, right) + L., *radix* (root))

pornonoia (n.)   (Gr., *porno-* (prostitute) + *noia* (mind))

psychoradicality (n.)   (Gr., *psycho-* (soul) + *radix* (root))

skotocardia (n.)   (Gr., *skoto-* (dark) + *kardia* (heart))

theophile (n.)   (Gr., *Theo-* (Creator (Yahweh)) + *philia* (friendship))

theophobia (n.)   (Gr., *Theo-* (Creator (Yahweh)) + *phobos* (fear))

zoocardia (n.)   (Gr., *zoo-* (animal) + *kardia* (heart))

Bibliography

Katherine Albrecht and Liz McIntyre. *The Spychip Threat: Why Christians Should Resist RFID and Electronic Surveillance*. Nashville: Nelson Current, 2006.

Daniel G. Amen. *Making A Good Brain Great*. New York: Crown, 2005.

Neil T. Anderson. *Victory Over the Darkness*. Ventura: Regal Books, 1990.

John Ankerberg and John Wheldon. *Encyclopedia of New Age Beliefs*. Eugene: Harvest House, 1996.

Tim Baldwin and Chuck Baldwin. *Romans 13: The True Meaning of Submission, 2nd Ed*. Kalispell, MT: Liberty Defense League, 2011.

Louis Berkhof. *Systematic Theology*. Grand Rapids: Eerdman's, 1932, 1938, 1996.

George Ricker Berry. *Interlinear Greek-English New Testament*. Grand Rapids: Baker Books, 2005.

Dietrich Bonhoeffer. *The Cost of Discipleship*. New York: Touchstone, 1959.

Shawn Boonstra. *The Appearing*. Ontario: Pacific, 2005.

Barbara Branden. *The Passion of Ayn Rand*. Garden City: Doubleday, 1986.

Paul C. Bragg. *The Miracle of Fasting: Proven Throughout History for Physical, Mental and Spiritual Rejuvenation*. Health Science, Box 7, Santa Barbara, CA 93102. 2009.

Joseph J. Carr. *The Twisted Cross*. Lafayette: Huntington House, 1985.

Oswald Chambers. *My Utmost for His Highest*. Grand Rapids: Discovery House, 1963.

Mahesh Chavda. *Only Love Can Make a Miracle*. Charlotte, NC: Mahesh Chavda, 1990.

Michael Coffman. *Saviors of the Earth?* Chicago: Northfield Publishing, 1994.

Darrel Cole. *When God Says War is Right*. Colorado Springs: Waterbrook, 2002.

Peter Collier and David Horowitz. *Destructive Generation: Second Thoughts about the '60's*. New York: Simon and Schuster, 1996.

Irving M. Copi. *Introduction to Logic, 4ᵗʰ Edition*. New York: MacMillan, 1972.

Constance Cumbey. *The Hidden Dangers of the Rainbow*. Lafayette: Huntington House, 1983.

Ed Decker. *The Dark Side of Freemasonry*. Lafayette: Huntington House, 1994.

John Eldredge. *Wild at Heart*. Nashville: Thomas Nelson, 2001.

Mircea Eliade. *Occultism, Witchcraft and Cultural Fashion*. Chicago: University of Chicago Press, 1976.

David H. Freedman. *Corps Business: The 30 Management Principles of the U.S. Marines*. New York: HarperCollins, 2000.

Janet Glenn Gray. *The French Huguenots: Anatomy of Courage*. Grand Rapids: Baker Book House, 1981.

Henry H. Halley. *Halley's Bible Handbook*. Grand Rapids: Zondervan, 1965.

Michael A. Hoffman II. *Judaism's Strange Gods*. The Independent History and Research Co., PO Box 849, Couer d'Alene, ID 83816. 2000.

Dave Hunt. *A Woman Rides the Beast.* Eugene: Harvest House, 1994.

Dave Hunt. *Peace, Prosperity and the Coming Holocaust.* Eugene: Harvest House, 1983.

John Paul Jackson. *Needless Casualties of War.* Sutton, NH: Streams Publications, 2002.

David Jeremiah. *Signs of Life: Back to the Basics of Authentic Christianity.* Nashville: Thomas Nelson, 2007.

Gary H. Kah. *En Route to Global Occupation.* Lafayette: Huntington House, 1992.

Gary H. Kah. *Hope for the World Update.* Noblesville, IN. Fall, 2002.

Gary H. Kah. *Hope for the World Update.* Noblesville, IN. Summer, 2008.

Gary H. Kah. *Hope for the World Update.* Noblesville, IN. Winter, 2010.

Gary H. Kah. *The New World Religion: En Route to Spiritual Deception.* Lafayette: Huntington House, 1998.

Buzzy Killeen. *Cajuns of the Louisiana Bayous.* Metarie, LA: Authentic American Art, 1985.

Berit Kjos. *A Twist of Faith.* Green Forest: New Leaf Press, 1997.

Berit Kjos. "Homeland Security and the Transformation of America." *Hope for the World Update,* summer 2003.

Arthur Koestler. *The Thirteenth Tribe.* New York: Random House, 1976.

Alfred J. Kolatch. *The Jewish Book of Why?* Middle Village, NY: Jonathon David Publishers, 1981.

R.D. Laing. *Knots.* New York: Vintage, 1970.

R.D. Laing and A. Esterson. *Sanity, Madness and the Family.* Baltimore, MD: Penguin, 1970.

Lee Lanning. *The Military 100: A Ranking of the Most Influential Military Leaders of All Time.* Secaucus, NJ: Citadel, 1996.

Bruce J. Lieske. "Something Old, Something New: The Messianic Congregational Movement." *Christian Research Journal,* 22, 1, 1999.

Scott Lively and Kevin Abrams. *The Pink Swastika: Homosexuality in the NAZI Party (3rd Ed.).* Keiser, OR: Founders Publishing, 1997.

John F. MacArthur, Jr. *Hebrews.* Nashville: Thomas Nelson, 2007.

Rabi Maharaj. *Death of a Guru.* Eugene: Harvest House, 1984.

Felix Morley, ed. *Essays on Individuality.* Indianapolis: Liberty, 1977.

Swami Narayanananda. *The Primal Power in Man or the Kundalini Shakti.* Rishikesh: Narayanananda Universal Yoga Trust, 1970.

Adam Nicholson. *God's Secretaries: The Making of the King James Bible.* New York: HarperCollins, 2003.

Gary North. *Unholy Spirits: Occultism and New Age Humanism.* Tyler, TX: Institute for Christian Economics, 1994.

John Pakkanen. "Why Is Lead Still Poisoning Our Children?" *Washingtonian Magazine,* August 2006.

Edmond Paris. *The Secret History of the Jesuits.* Chino, CA: Chick, 1975.

Jessie Penn-Lewis and Robert Evans. *War on the Saints (Unabridged).* Thomas E. Lowe, Ltd., (PO Box 1049, Cathedral Station, NYC, NY 10025), 1913.

McCandlish Phillips. *The Bible, the Supernatural, and the Jews.* Camp Hill, PA: Horizon Books, 1970.

Rich Robinson and Naomi Rose Rothstein. *The Messianic Movement: A Field Guide for Evangelical Christians.* San Francisco: Purple Pomegranate Productions, 2005.

Bob Rosio. *Hitler and the New Age.* Lafayette: Huntington House, 1993.

Agnes Savill. *Alexander the Great and His Times.* New York: Barnes and Noble, 1993.

S. Fred Singer and Dennis T. Avery. *Unstoppable Global Warming: Every 1,500 Years.* Blue Ridge Summit, PA: Rowman and Littlefield, 2008.

Samantha Smith. *Goddess Earth.* Lafayette: Huntington House, 1994.

Daniel Sitarz, Ed. *AGENDA 21: The Earth Summit Strategy to Save Our Planet.* Earthpress, 1993.

Stan Telchin. *Messianic Judaism Is Not Christianity.* Grand Rapids: Chosen Books, 2004.

Merrill F. Unger, PhD, ThD. *Unger's Bible Handbook.* Chicago: Moody Press, 1967.

Cornelius Vanderbreggen, Jr. *The Promise of His Coming.* Toccoa, GA: Currahee Printing Co., 1983.

Marvin R. Wilson. *Our Father Abraham: Jewish Roots of the Christian Faith.* Grand Rapids: Eerdmans, 1989.

Richard Wurmbrand. *Christ on the Jewish Road.* Bartlesville, OK: Living Sacrifice Book Co., 2002.

Spiro Zodhiates. *The Hebrew-Greek Key Word Study Bible.* Chattanooga, TN: AMG Publishers, 2008.

Index

glorification, 72, 156
gnosticism, 121, 282
God the Son, 64, 70, 89, 108
gold, 51, 162
Gorbachev, Mikhail, 221-22
GPS circuitry, 210, 225
grace and peace, 92
grain offering, 23, 25-27, 34-35, 38-39,
    42, 50-52, 56, 58
Great Reformation, 89, 110, 180
Great Tribulation, 85, 91, 211-12, 228,
    234, 236, 238-39, 241, 247
greenhouse gasses, 129
groupthink, 65, 147, 151-53, 183, 318
guns, 227, 230, 245

H

hands, work with own, 70
heartsongs, 159
Hitler, Adolph, 122-23, 126, 129, 131,
    187, 224, 253, 255, 266, 336
holy, 38-40, 42, 47-48, 55
holy matrimony, 136, 192-93, 197
Holy Trinity, 9, 87, 90, 93, 99-100, 111,
    133, 135-36, 152, 229, 243, 328
homosexuality, 111, 176, 185, 190, 336
honey, 31, 50-52

I

ICC (International Criminal Court), 218
identity, 26, 28, 52, 66, 105, 116, 135,
    144, 149, 168, 187, 210, 254, 302,
    320
Illuminati, 122, 124
incubus, 137, 178
inductive reasoning, 146
instant *minchaw*, 37
intelligent design, 298
interfaithism, 14, 109, 118, 202, 204

Islam, 26, 28, 199-200, 202, 205-6, 208
Islamism, 199, 205, 207
Israel, 106, 177, 181, 238, 240-41,
    244-45, 253

J

Jesuits, 113, 126, 336
Jesus of Nazareth, 70, 108, 152-53, 241
Jewish Book of Why? 23, 59, 335
Jews for Jesus, 146, 245
Judaizing, 17, 61, 76, 93, 95-96, 98,
    136, 310
justification, 71
justifies, 72, 152, 156

K

Kabalism, 121
Kah, Gary H., 16, 120, 126, 182, 198,
    234, 255, 335
kilotons, 205
Knights Templar, 121-22, 189

L

Laing, R.D., 151
lead (metal), 164
leader, 14, 101, 110, 122, 222, 227, 236,
    309
leadership, 64, 153, 163, 170, 172, 183,
    199, 228, 232, 286, 289, 304
leaven, 31, 38-39, 50-52, 149
Lewis, C.S., 263
logic, 143, 146, 149, 152-53
logical fallacies, 71, 146, 150, 211
LORD God of Israel, 10-11, 19, 32, 35,
    37, 44, 50, 58, 65-68, 70, 75-76, 78,
    80, 111-12, 132-33
Luciferians, 209
Lucis Trust, 216

M

MacArthur, John, 72
Macedon, 116, 141, 152
magnetism, 117-18
marism, 111, 120
market nexus, 153, 213, 239, 251
mark of the beast, 212, 216, 228, 230, 232
mathematical outcome, 227
meat offering, 23, 34, 38, 50
Melchisedec, 24, 43-44
Mensa, 14
metal chelation, 164-66
metals, 51, 120, 161-66, 180, 264, 269, 301, 314, 316
mezzuzah, 87
minchaw, 9-12, 15, 19-20, 22-24, 26-27, 30-31, 34-40, 42-44, 46-52, 54-56, 58-60, 82
minchaw of fire, 23-24, 30-31, 38-39, 44, 46-47, 49, 55
minchaw of firstfruits, 23, 49, 51, 54-56, 58
minchawth bikkuwrim, 26-27, 34, 48, 51-56, 83
Mohammed, 199, 204
monism, 14, 116-17, 123
Montenegro, Marcia, 116
moon, new, 80, 82
moral law, 19, 24, 60, 64, 90-91, 327
Moses, 47-48, 66, 85, 121, 152
mosques, 202
mother, 13, 69, 111-13, 136, 273
mullahs, 202, 204
murder, do not, 69, 202
Muslim women, 205

N

name, your, 65
National Rifle Association (NRA), 249

NAU (North American Union), 131, 207, 210, 227, 244
NAZI Germany, 209
NAZIsm, 122, 252
neighbor, 62, 66, 70, 327
neologism, 96, 183, 189, 192, 276, 282, 290, 292
New Age, 14, 16-17, 108-10, 122-23, 125, 221-22
New Age physics, 157-58, 160
New Agers, 14, 123, 158, 193, 197, 209
Nicolaitanes, 116
North, Gary, 104, 336
nuclear weapons, 206
nutrients, cognitive, 166-67, 272
nystatin, 83, 167

O

Obama, Barack, 193
occult, 109, 116, 124, 160, 221
occultism, 104-5, 107, 109-11, 120-22, 124, 190, 219
offering made by fire, 9, 11, 20, 23, 30-31, 34-36, 48-50
orderic inversion, 288

P

pagan religions, 118, 120
Paleo-Hebrew, 98
pantheism, 109, 116, 119, 183, 214
parthenovindicator, 194
Passover, 27, 34-35, 49, 55-56, 78-79, 83-84, 167
Paul (apostle), 30, 61, 70, 72, 89-90, 93, 115, 141, 152-53, 177, 186, 240
pederasty, 181, 189-90
penalty for sin, 71-72, 124, 185, 245, 276, 294
Pharisees, 71-72, 99, 101, 134, 320, 322

systematic theology, 24, 30, 75, 108,
137, 142, 150-51, 157, 161, 195,
198, 211, 257, 259, 322-23

T

tallitim, burlap, 85, 243
Talmud, 23, 58, 62, 76, 83, 93, 95, 98,
101
Talmudism, 62, 67-68, 73, 96, 98, 134,
147, 229, 240, 242, 251-52
Temenos Books, 221
tetraethyl lead, 163-64
Teutonic occultism, 219
theology, 10-12, 15, 17, 22, 27, 30, 93,
108-9, 119, 130, 142, 150-51, 257,
263-64, 322-23
theosophy, 108, 122-23, 217, 219, 325
tinnitus, 109, 117-18, 159, 168, 278
Torah, 19, 24, 60-62, 64, 68
transmute, 161
Tribulation revival, 181, 241, 244
Triune Yahweh, 70, 112, 118, 142, 204,
217
tzit-tzit, 16, 85-86

U

United Nations, 130-31, 208, 216-18,
222

V

Vatican, 68-69, 76-77, 110, 113, 116,
182, 199, 210, 227, 229, 234, 239,
242-44, 312
VeriChip, 4, 92, 153, 181, 208-13, 215,
217, 219, 223-28, 230-33, 238-40,
242, 247-48, 252, 254-55
Vile 3, 105, 179, 194-95, 197, 242, 320
virginity, 113, 170-71, 183, 194-96

virtue, 47, 86, 193, 209
vitamin B_{12}, 88, 168

W

warrior homosexuality, 190
Wilson, Marvin R., 98, 337
witch, 106, 108
witchcraft, 106-7, 109, 112, 116, 160
worship, 15, 28, 66, 69, 76-77, 91, 114,
127-28, 153, 176, 178, 212-14, 232,
247-48, 254
Wurmbrand, Richard, 252-53, 256, 337

Y

Yahweh, 32, 116, 326
Yeshua haMashiach, 56
Yeshua haNotzri, 97, 132, 212, 240,
290, 318
yoga, 14, 109, 115, 117, 121, 123, 125,
159, 265, 277, 336
Yom Kippur, 27, 31, 36, 56, 58
Yom Teruah, 23, 27, 31, 36, 48-49

Z

Zaccharius, Ravi, 127, 149, 222

Printed in the USA
CPSIA information can be obtained
at www.ICGtesting.com
JSHW020902011124
72725JS00001B/2